The Dilemma of
Amazonian Development

Also of Interest

Involuntary Migration and Resettlement: The Problems and Responses of Dislocated People, edited by Art Hansen and Anthony Oliver-Smith

*Authoritarian Capitalism: Brazil's Contemporary Economic and Political Development, edited by Thomas C. Bruneau and Philippe Faucher

Rethinking Human Adaptation: Biological and Cultural Models, Rada Dyson-Hudson and Michael A. Little

*Human Adaptability: An Introduction to Ecological Anthropology, Emilio F. Moran

*Brazil: A Political Analysis, Peter Flynn

Brazil: An Industrial Geography, John P. Dickenson

The Future of Brazil, edited by William H. Overholt

*Managing Development in the Third World, Coralie Bryant and Louise G. White

*From Dependency to Development: Strategies to Overcome Underdevelopment and Inequality, edited by Heraldo Muñoz

Development Strategies and Basic Needs in Latin America, edited by Claes Brundenius and Mats Lundahl, with a Foreword by Jon Sigurdson

*Farming Systems Research and Development: Guidelines for Developing Countries, W. W. Shaner, P. F. Philipp, and W. R. Schmehl

Agroclimate Information for Development: Reviving the Green Revolution, edited by David F. Cusack

*An Introduction to the Sociology of Rural Development, Norman Long

Managing Development Programs: The Lessons of Success, Samuel Paul

Multiple Cropping and Tropical Farming Systems, Willem C. Beets

Small Farm Development: Understanding and Improving Farming Systems in the Humid Tropics, Richard R. Harwood, with a Foreword by A. Colin McClung

*Available in hardcover and paperback.

Westview Special Studies on Latin America and the Caribbean

The Dilemma of Amazonian Development
edited by Emilio F. Moran

This book--the first to apply the combined approaches of anthropology, geography, ecology, economics, and sociology to the analysis of the Amazon River region and its imminent development--explores the impact of development on Amazonian populations and the results of rural and urban growth strategies. The authors use the methodologies of environmental and social impact assessment in a variety of Amazonian settings to derive realistic evaluations of the dangers and potential of current development approaches. In the final section of the book, they focus on those methodologies that promise to provide future researchers with improved tools for the management of the Amazon region's human and natural resources.

A central theme of the book is the need for the government planners and local populations making these necessarily complex decisions to consider the realities of the local environment, existing environmental management practices, and the culture and demographic structure of the region, as well as how these factors are affected by external social, economic, and political factors.

Dr. Moran is associate professor in the School for Public and Environmental Affairs and in the Department of Anthropology, Indiana University, and chairman of the Department of Anthropology. Among his many publications are Agricultural Development Along the Transamazon Highway (1976) and Human Adaptability: An Introduction to Ecological Anthropology (Westview, 1982). Between 1973 and 1976 he held two Fulbright-Hays fellowships, a Social Science Research Council Fellowship, and two National Institute of Mental Health fellowships for research in the Brazilian Amazon.

The Dilemma of Amazonian Development

edited by Emilio F. Moran

Westview Press / Boulder, Colorado

AO POVO DA AMAZÔNIA

AL PUEBLO DE LA AMAZONÍA

Westview Special Studies on Latin America and the Caribbean

Published in 1983 in the United States of America by
    Westview Press, Inc.
    5500 Central Avenue
    Boulder, Colorado 80301
    Frederick A. Praeger, President and Publisher

Library of Congress Cataloging in Publication Data
Main entry under title:
The Dilemma of Amazonian development.
    (Westview special studies on Latin America and the Caribbean)
    Includes bibliographical references and index.
    1. Man--Influence on nature--Brazil--Addresses, essays, lectures. 2. Man--
Influence on nature--Amazon Valley--Addresses, essays, lectures. 3. Environ-
mental policy--Brazil--Addresses, essays, lectures. 4. Environmental policy--
Amazon Valley--Addresses, essays, lectures. 5. Brazil--Economic conditions--
Addresses, essays, lectures. 6. Amazon Valley--Economic conditions--
Addresses, essays, lectures. 7. Agriculture--Brazil--Addresses, essays,
lectures. 8. Agriculture--Amazon Valley--Addresses, essays, lectures. I.
Moran, Emilio F. II. Series.
GF532.B7D54 1983   333.75'09811   82-23693
ISBN 0-86531-373-3

Contents

Figures and Tables

TABLES

Preface

The rapid pace of deforestation in the Amazon Basin has attracted popular and scientific attention. This interest is not unwarranted: The Amazon Basin is the largest remaining tract of tropical moist forest and generally believed to be the most complex biome in the biosphere. Rapid extinction of floral and faunal species, disruption of the hydrologic cycle, soil compaction, unimpressive agricultural yields, and violence between native and colonist populations are but a few of the host of urgent problems in need of policy-relevant recommendations. This volume brings together a number of researchers whose findings bear upon the current processes of social and ecological change in the basin.

Unlike other recent collections of Amazonian research, this one is not the result of a conference. Rather, the editor invited the authors to address problems that have emerged in their areas of expertise during the process of Amazonian development. Agronomists, anthropologists, ecologists, economists, geographers, and sociologists have contributed to this effort. Each author shows considerable knowledge of the interactions between environmental, institutional, cultural, and technical aspects of development, rather than being limited to any single factor.

Given the rapid pace at which current research efforts are taking place, I felt that it would be useful to have a volume that dealt with the policy dilemmas of development. The authors of these papers are guided by an awareness of the immediacy of the problems faced by people in Amazonia and of the need, when addressing policy issues, to keep a solid base in empirical findings. Too much development planning and implementation has been undertaken in the absence of even elementary data. It is my hope that this volume will be one step toward correcting these past deficiencies.

The authors of the papers in this volume were selected because of their active research programs in the Amazon and their expertise in evaluating various forms of production strategies that have been undertaken in the Amazon. A number of colleagues who were invited to contribute to this volume had to decline due to competing professional obligations. Among them were Robert Goodland (staff ecologist, World Bank), Nigel Smith (Department of Geography, University of Florida), Nils Tcheyan (staff economist, World Bank), and Eugene Parker (Department of Geography, University of

Massachusetts). I miss their potential contributions to this volume and take comfort only in seeing their work frequently cited throughout.

No volume is ever complete and I regret a number of omissions, such as a detailed assessment of the impact of mining operations. Mining and other forms of resource development remain poorly studied in the Amazon Basin, but changes in this situation are forthcoming. It is my hope that volumes in the near future will give adequate attention to this and other aspects of development. On the positive side, this volume addresses the major foci of development activities: pastures, cropping, fisheries, and forestry. In turn, these production systems are connected to social processes that bring native, colonist, and multinational enterprises into conflicts that are all too often addressed by policy in a simplistic fashion. The authors of the papers in this volume present modes of analysis and evidence for the economic and environmental rationality of bringing together human resources, rather than pitting them against each other. Economic growth and the preservation of forests need not be mutually exclusive. It is toward resolving this dilemma that the authors have worked.

I want to begin by thanking the authors of the papers in the volume for their cooperation in meeting deadlines and for staying within the policy thrust of this volume. I had heard many stories about the lack of cooperation often encountered in tasks such as this one, but these scholars have proven such stories partly wrong. As a result, readers will be able to read these papers about two years earlier than the average edited volume. In a topic on which so much pioneering research is taking place, timeliness is particularly valuable.

I also thank Lynne Rienner of Westview Press for her encouragement with, and, indeed, excitement about, this project. To the many colleagues in Amazonian research who have over the years provided a constant flow of stimulating and new ideas that make Amazonian studies substantially rewarding at this time, I am grateful--in particular, to Luis Aragón, Stephen Bunker, William Denevan, Italo Claudio Falesi, Joe Foweraker, Samuel Sá, Donald Sawyer, Marianne Schmink, Anthony Seeger, Nigel Smith, Anthony Stocks, Otavio Ghilherme Velho, and Charles Wagley. I hope they find the volume of interest. I thank Rita Harper for retyping portions of the manuscript and for processing a massive correspondence with the authors that came to be comparable in extent to the book manuscript itself.

This volume is dedicated to the peoples of Amazonia, in the hope that future development policy can assure both the conservation of the Amazonian environment and the increased participation of the Amazonian peoples in the management and rewards of Amazonian development.

E.F.M.

Part 1

The Human Dimension
of Amazonian Development

Introduction to Part I

This volume begins with four papers that focus on the human factors of development. The paper by Moran introduces the volume's concern with the persistence of growth without development in the Amazon. Like the other papers, Moran's analysis shows that implementational capability must be explicitly provided for in development planning. Without the management capacity to guarantee the protection of the environment and access to the natural resources by all people, aggregate increases in economic output will be unsustainable and regional development will remain a distant dream. Moran advocates a policy shift to bring land prices more in line with the scarcity of management capacity as a way to reduce the current incentive to abuse land resources. Such a tax policy would also buy time to train more managers and generate more accurate knowledge about the use of Amazonian resources.

The paper by Vickers provides a comparative view of the impact of development policies on native Amazonians. The experience of the Aguarico Indians in Ecuador can be extrapolated to almost any other ethnic group in Amazonia: decimation through diseases brought to the area by outsiders, rapacious exploitation and destruction of the natural resources on which native peoples depend, and increasing levels of conflict between native peoples and colonists. These processes have increasingly pushed native peoples from their territories until they have become increasingly dependent on outsiders--rather than capable of supporting themselves as in the past. The process of Amazonian development has not benefited native Amazonians--either materially or culturally. Native Amazonians have remained excluded from any significant role or benefit in the processes of economic development. Vickers correctly points out that developmentalists often create a false dichotomy between the traditional sector and the modernized sector. If the goal is to transform society so that it has greater productive capacity and provides greater participation by the population in this

1

process, then the development planners should seek explicit ways to help the goal be realized. This point is further elaborated in the paper by Posey in Part 3 of this volume.

The paper by Stearman is a tightly written synthesis of the colonization process in the Bolivian Amazon. This process in Bolivia is representative of the dominant transformation of the Amazonian landscape: from forest to pasture (see also the paper by Hecht in this volume). The transformation evokes a fundamental dilemma of Amazonian development: On the one hand, ecologists remind us that pasture is the most destructive use to which the tropical forest can be put (see paper by Lovejoy and Salati in this volume); on the other hand, the colonists and national financial institutions view it as the most economically rational way to convert a free good into one that yields capital. This fundamental dilemma of short-term economic forest-to-pasture conversion vis-à-vis the irreversible loss of biological species and loss of agronomic productivity requires a great deal more re-search than has so far been undertaken.

The paper by Miller focuses upon the private and public entrepreneurs in Amazonia. Miller demonstrates that the flow of inputs into Amazonian rural development has benefited urban entrepreneurs and the bureaucratic administrators of development more than it has benefited the farmers for whom the inputs were allegedly intended. His close examination of this process in the city of Itaituba, on the Tapajós River in Brazil, is tied to theoretical considerations that would have allowed one to predict just such an outcome. His paper is an excellent reminder that the development process worldwide seems to have an incapacity to benefit from theoretical formulations and even from experiences in the recent past.

E.F.M.

1
Growth Without Development: Past and Present Development Efforts in Amazonia

Emilio F. Moran

The history of Amazonian development to date can best be characterized as one of growth without development. The causes for the underdevelopment of the Amazon have remained relatively constant through time: an export-oriented, extractive economic system imposed by forces outside the region and susceptible to wide fluctuations in prices. The systems of production do not represent ecologically appropriate and research-based strategies. Rather, they reflect the imposition of production strategies that limit internal development.

Amazonian development efforts serve to highlight the dilemmas presented by development everywhere: how to achieve equity and growth; how to work for conservation and development; how to modernize the agricultural sector when improved agronomic practices for the humid tropics have yet to be developed; whether to favor extensive (pastures) or intensive (crops) forms of land use; whether to guarantee native rights to land or the claims of peasants and corporations that invade those areas. None of these dilemmas can be easily resolved. Each dilemma is the product of structural and functional relations within nation-states and between nations. The choice to give priority to one aspect of a dilemma over another reflects local, national, and international demands.

The Amazonian development experience serves to remind us that human resource development and structural transformations must be explicitly planned for and their implementation assured rather than simply be allowed to "trickle down" as a result of policies aimed at increasing economic output. "Real" regional development enhances the access by all sectors of society to goods and services and seeks a balance between equity and growth.

Growth-oriented development strategies reflect the tendency of political systems to engage in a state-building process. Such strategies tend to be

3

operationalized through centralization of functions.
Centralized states are presumably capable of effectively
mobilizing people and resources and of bringing about
significant change in aggregate output. The process of
state-building tends to ignore local social and environmental consequences, inequities in distribution, and
capital costs. Centralization is also a response to the
insufficient administrative capacity of modernizing
states to undertake the complex tasks of development
planning, implementation, and evaluation (Waterston 1965).
In short, states engaged in political and economic integration tend to place higher value upon strategies that
assure them of greater control over political and
administrative functions, rather than on strategies for
developing the learning capabilities of bureaucratic
organizations to bring about a balance between local
control over some functions and central control over
others, which might also contribute to a larger sense of
nationhood (Bryant and White 1982).

None of the Amazon countries can be said to be
Amazonian in functional orientation (see Figure 1.1).
Brazil and Peru, with the highest proportions of their
territory in the Amazon Basin, have only recently paid
attention to these vast areas (see Table 1.1). The
Amazonian territories in all these countries have lagged
behind in the development of educational, infrastructural,
and other services. Research geared toward improved
management of food crops, wild fruits, and wild game have
been miniscule. All that has begun to change.

PAST DEVELOPMENT EFFORTS

For most of its history the Amazon Basin has been
inhabited by linguistically varied native populations and
an ethnically diverse peasantry. These populations have
typically lived in small settlements along riverbanks and
practiced swidden agriculture supplemented by hunting/
fishing/collecting. The strategies of resource use are
distinctly aboriginal and represent responses to the
environmental variation present (Meggers 1971; Wagley 1953
and 1974; Furley 1980; Moran 1982).

Although it is possible to see antecedents for
Amazonian development in the colonial and national
periods, it was not until the 1950s that anything re-
sembling current development thrusts began. Before the
1950s, Spain and Portugal, in efforts to exploit their
colonies, obviously did not consider internal development
important (Anderson 1976; Sweet 1974) nor did their
extractive use of resources end with independence (see
Goulding, Chapter 7 in this volume). Colonial use of
Amazonian resources was characterized by the simultaneous
presence of an extractive sector oriented to the gathering of forest products and an agricultural sector favoring cash crops, with staple food production a weak

Table 1.1. Major development zones in the Amazon

Country	Amazon Area (km^2)	% National Territory	Major Development Regions
Brazil	3,560,000	54%	Paragominas Araguaia Upper Xingú Western Maranhão Rondônia Carajás
Peru	785,000	61%	Tingo-Maria Apurimac Caballoche Jenaro Herrera Alto Marañón San Ignacio Pucallpa
Bolivia	510,000	47%	Alto Beni Yapacaní Chimoré
Colombia	309,000	27%	Caquetá Putumayo Vaupés Guainía
Ecuador	138,760	48%	Shushufindi Payamino San Miguel Palora-Pastaza Morona
Venezuela	100,000	9%	Minimal and mainly in the Caura and Caroní drainages

Adapted from Hecht (1981)

Figure 1.1. Current development areas in the Amazon

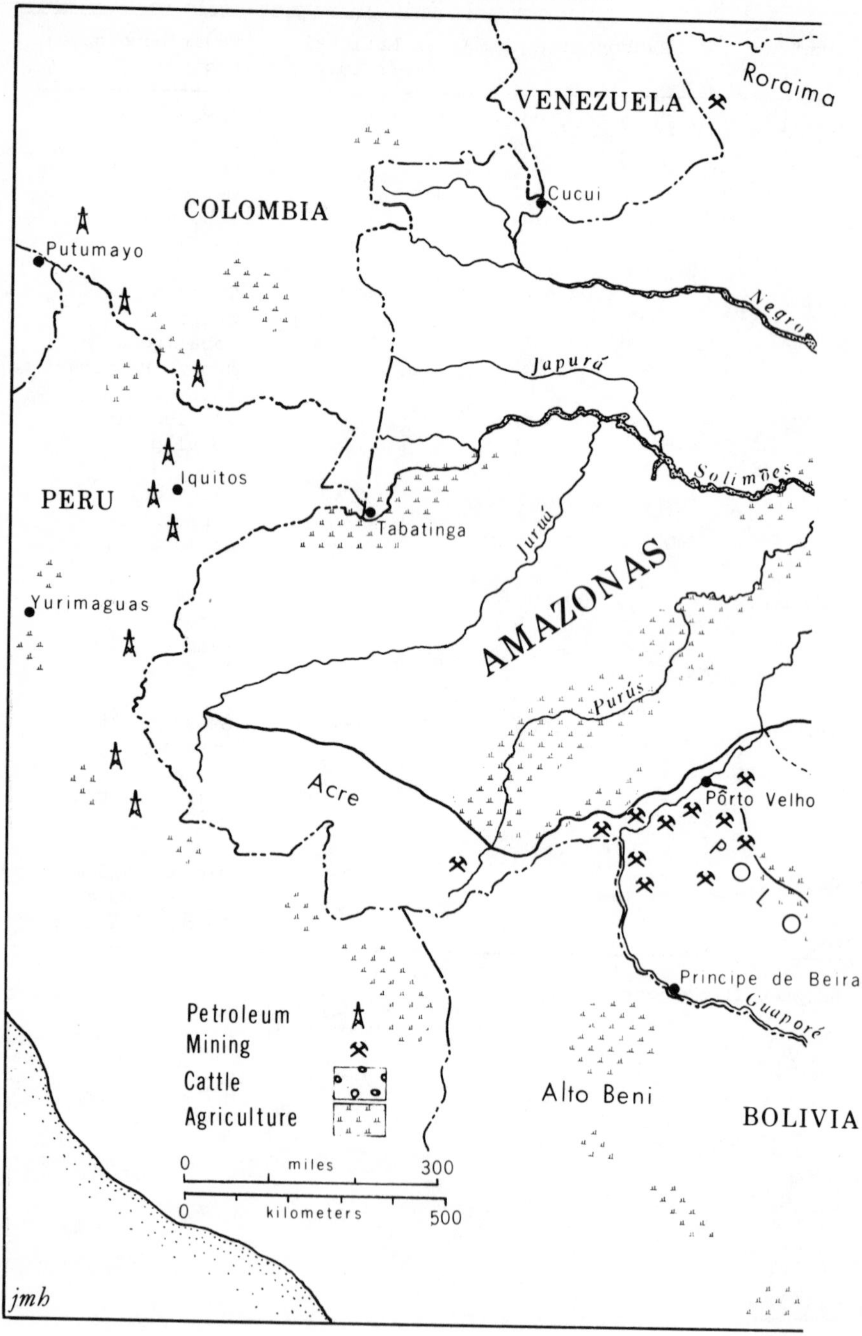

VENEZUELA   Roraima

COLOMBIA

Cucui

Putumayo

Negro

Japurá

Solimões

Iquitos

PERU   Tabatinga

Juruá

AMAZONAS

Yurimaguas

Purús

Acre

Pôrto Velho

P O L O

Principe de Beira

Guaporé

Alto Beni

BOLIVIA

Petroleum
Mining
Cattle
Agriculture

| 0 | miles | 300 |
| 0 | kilometers | 500 |

jmh

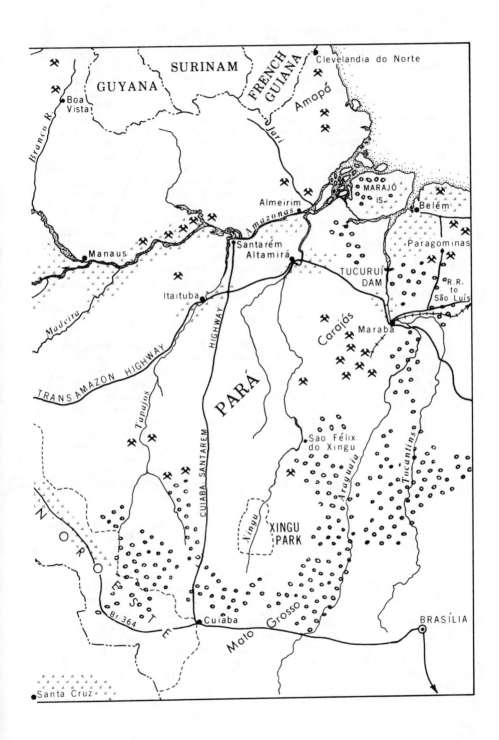

appendage. This structure continued into the national
period. During most of the colonial period, and into the
national period, the Amazon Basin did not offer favorable
conditions for economic development, due to endemic
disease, vast distances, and availability of preferred
resources on the coast and highlands. Economic exploitation of the region's resources was sporadic, resulting
from short-lived increases in the prices of a few products
in world markets. The most significant of these price
fluctuations resulted from the demand for rubber in the
late nineteenth century and led to the one economic boom
experienced by the Amazon region. Even this boom was of
short duration (1870-1920) as a result of competition
from plantations in Malaysia that began to produce natural
rubber in 1911, at lower cost than for rubber from the
natural stands of Hevea in Amazonia (Collier 1968;
Anderson 1976). Unlike the agriculturally based society
dominant elsewhere in Latin America, the Amazon region
had little to fall back on during the bust periods. Its
entrepreneurs left, few services remained, and there was
little communication between isolated towns. In other
words, there was little to spur internal development.
Isolation, not only from the rest of the country, but even
within the region, made growth and/or development a
distant dream.

The construction of Brasília in the 1950s heralded
an era wherein the Amazon frontier became a focus of
attention in the political integration and economic
growth strategies of the Brazilian state (see Figure 1.1).
Frontier military colonies were built at Príncipe de
Beira, Tabatinga, Cucui, and Clevelandia do Norte (Tambs
1974). In turn, the Peruvians strengthened their
garrison at Iquitos, pushed forward an ambitious roadbuilding program, and sent settlers into the Ecuadorian
and Brazilian territories. Bolivia and Ecuador, on their
part, pushed similar road and colonization projects but
with less success than Brazil or Peru. Of all the countries,
Venezuela has been least involved in Amazonian development.

Since 1964 Brazil has had the most coherent strategy
for planning and implementation of Amazonian development.
The military intelligentsia nurtured at the Escola Superior
de Guerra are guided by a grand plan formulated in the 1950s
by Goldberry do Couto e Silva (1957). Since 1964 the Brazilian authorities have announced a series of interventions:
(a) Operação Amazônia (Mahar 1979); (b) replaced the bureau-
cratically bottlenecked and understaffed SPVEA (Superintendência do Plano de Valorização Econômica da Amazônia) with
SUDAM (Superintendência do Desenvolvimento da Amazônia)
(SPVEA 1960; Cavalcanti 1967); (c) transformed the old Rubber Bank into the Banco da Amazônia (BASA), a supportive
financial institution to the Amazon Development Agency
(SUDAM); and (d) the Program of National Integration (1971)
within which a second Plan for Amazonian Development was
spelled out in surprising detail (cf. Mahar 1979; Moran 1981).

The Brazilian strategy has clearly emphasized growth and put aside matters of equity. For a brief time, critics of the regime were thrown into confusion by the apparent priority given to social goals, which promoted colonization by small farmers along the new roads of national integration so designated in the second Amazon development plan (1972-1974). Within three years, however, the regime reversed itself in the third Amazon development plan (1975-1979) and returned to the pre-1964 strategy of alliance with local and foreign capital for encouragement of large-scale projects and high rates of growth (Schmink 1982).

The incentives offered to investors include subsidization of their capital for highly speculative projects. Between 1971 and 1976 SUDAM approved 335 ranching projects, 171 industrial projects (mostly to cut and process wood), and only 22 service and infrastructure projects (Kleinpenning 1978). One result has been that vast areas of forest have been deforested, transforming the landscape from that of a free good to one that has risen in price at rapid rates while its productive potential declined (see Hecht, Chapter 6 in this volume). The creation of a free port at Manaus led to capital-intensive urban development, but few of the benefits of the zone have extended into the region as envisioned in the planning documents (Mahar 1979). In short, growth-oriented regional development planning policies of the late 1960s and early 1970s did not bring about structural change in Amazonian development. Rather, the same pattern of export-oriented, capital-intensive land exploitation of earlier days continued--providing increases in output without initiating regional development.

DEVELOPMENT POLICY AND NATURAL RESOURCES

Current development policy has responded to the underdevelopment of the Amazon chiefly by the provision of subsidies to encourage investment in large projects, especially cattle ranches and mining. The general effect of this subsidization has been to reduce the cost of land-- already the least expensive factor in Amazonian development--while at the same time increasing the cost of qualified managers, due to the historic scarcity in their numbers and the inability of institutions to train managers at the rate demanded by the development schemes (Norgaard 1979).

A cheap-land policy encouraged by subsidization of capital as well as the absence of a tax policy to bring the cost of land use closer to the cost of other, more expensive, production factors, has brought about severe environmental and social consequences (Norgaard 1979). Native peoples throughout the Amazon are being pushed off their lands, and serious conflicts have emerged between aborigines and colonists (Davis 1977; Wagley

1977). In this process, the extensive knowledge that
native Amazonians possess about their physical environment
is being rapidly lost and invariably is being replaced by
ignorance leading to inappropriate management.

The greater constraint in Amazonian development is
not the lack of land, the lack of labor, or even the lack
of capital. Rather, the lack of management capacity at
all levels of institutional functioning and the structural
inability to use expertise at lower levels in adjusting
the production process to specific environmental and
social conditions is the most severe of these constraints.
Indeed, Amazonian development planning has been characterized by the same classic biases that have been shown
by analysts to intensify the constraints and resistance
to development: a bias toward macro-models in plan
formulation to the neglect of micro-planning; a bias
toward the quantitative aspects of planning to the
neglect of crucial but unquantifiable aspects such as
human resource development; and a bias toward detailed
planning to the neglect of implementation (Meier 1976:
851). The consequences of these biases become evident
in the detailed plans to protect forest resources by the
Brazilian Forestry Development Institute (IBDF), but the
provision of only two foresters in the whole Altamira/
Transamazon colonization region to implement existing
policy in 1971. Despite the good will of these managers
it was impossible for them to monitor the implementation
of the planning documents. It can be argued that until
development planners can effectively implement their
well-meant conservation policies, development efforts
should not be undertaken.

In the process of incorporating expertise into the
management of natural resources, the native Amazonian
population can play an important role. Posey (Chapter 9
in this volume) demonstrates that native expertise can be
used to improve experimental research and to select rare
plants for economic uses. This type of endeavor makes
not only good economic sense but also reduces the rate
of species extinction and loss of forest cover, both of
which have potentially severe consequences (see chapters
by Lovejoy and Salati, Goulding, and Hecht in this
volume).

Not only do we need to learn from native Amazonians
about management of the rain forest, but also from close
observation of the behavior of other plant and animal
communities of the rain forest. Agronomists have long
noted soil/plant associations that indicate certain
constraints in, and opportunities presented by, micro-
habitats. Lovejoy and Salati (Chapter 8 in this volume)
focus attention on the behavior of leaf-cutting ants and
their role in identifying species of tropical forest
plants with natural fungicides--a finding that could lead
to improving our capacity to deal with the fungi that are
a constant problem in tropical agricultural and forestry

management. The lessons could be multiplied if sufficient attention could be devoted to such considerations.

The currently devastating rate of deforestation may lead not only to desiccation of adjacent forest and to disruptions in the world's hydrologic cycle, but also to a major drop in the productivity of Amazonian fisheries. Goulding (1980, 1981, and Chapter 7 in this volume) has demonstrated that many of the important food fishes in the Amazon migrate into the flooded forest where they feed on tree fruits and gain most of their weight. Dam construction that blocks these migrations, and destruction of flooded forest to convert the area to intensive agriculture, will very likely destroy the productive potential of this little-understood food chain that carries the burden of providing protein for Amazonian populations and that had begun to play a role in exports as well. Neither Goulding nor Lovejoy is insensitive to the need of Brazil and the other countries to develop their Amazonian natural resources. What is certain is that too little is known of the biotic and abiotic environment to permit accurate predictions of impacts. Research is currently being undertaken to understand the relative impact of different-sized forest clearings on climate and forest regeneration.

Eventually, the findings of these ongoing studies and many others can be incorporated into planning models. So far, planning for Amazonian development has been characterized by over-detailed centralized approaches that have been insensitive to the region's environmental variation. It is understandable that, given the lack of administrative capacity available, the government should avoid handing over decision making to inadequately trained managers. This incapacity, however, results not only from a historic lack of investment in human resource development, but also from a tendency to marginalize rather than incorporate rural populations into the process of development. Until such a time as appropriately trained managers are in place, native Amazonians and other regional populations who possess extensive knowledge of local resources can play a role in improving the quality of resource management (Hames and Vickers, n.d.).

There is growing support in some circles for the development of mining and minerals industries in the Amazon on the grounds that they destroy less forest than other forms of resource use such as pasture development and forestry (Goodland 1980). However, such an evaluation may overlook a number of significant externalities that in the long run, can be even more devastating to the region. The development of bauxite and iron deposits requires large energy inputs at low cost. Mining development has promoted the development of hydroelectric projects, such as the one at Tucurui, which are likely to disrupt fish migrations, the flow of silt down the floodplain, and consequently reduce the agricultural potential of what are believed to be the best soils of Amazonia (Denevan 1982). Although there is little doubt that the development of these mineral resources eventually will generate substantial returns (Mahar, Chapter 13 in this volume), these returns are not likely to improve the quality of human resources nor the distribution of income in the region. Moreover, minerals are nonrenewable resources, unlike fisheries and agriculture. Mineral exploitation without adequate monitoring of environmental impacts could undermine the potential for renewable resources to provide for human needs in the future (Santos 1981).

DEVELOPMENT POLICY AND HUMAN RESOURCES

The development of the Amazon has been hailed as a solution to the problem of inequitable land distribution and underemployment in other areas of the affected countries. Neither in Brazil nor in the other countries that possess Amazonian territories has there been any significant transformation of the structure of land tenure (Schmink and Wood, in preparation). The pattern of land concentration in large estates has thus far been reproduced in the Amazon after only a few years of settlement (Moran 1981; Wood and Wilson 1982; Hecht, Chapter 6 in this volume). Most of the land is underused and the major purpose of the development efforts appears to be to transform a free good into one that is capitalized through destruction of forest (Cardoso and Muller 1977).

This problem could very well be resolved by eliminating current subsidies that favor the process of speculative profit making and replace it with a tax structure that favors better use of human resources and more intensive use of cleared land. Evidence suggests that small farmers (on 100 ha or less) use 66 to 97% of the land they clear for crop production; larger estates (over 1000 ha) use only 0 to 26% of the land cleared (see Hecht, Chapter 6 in this volume). The switch in Brazilian development policy in 1974 away from small farm development and toward large-scale development reflects this tendency of development planning to favor GNP growth rather than sustainable development (Moran 1981).

Policymakers in Latin American countries usually mention that Amazon development is necessary to provide an escape valve for the numerous disenfranchised populations along the coast or on the highlands. There is very little evidence that the Amazonian frontier has provided much relief from these social and demographic pressures. Total immigration into the Amazon over the decade of the 1970s has represented only 0.5% of the value of rural to urban migration in a single year in Brazil (Wood and Wilson 1982). There is growing evidence that following the initial pioneering period, Brazilian frontiers have tended to lose population as land becomes increasingly concentrated in the hands of the more successful operators and the original pioneer population either moves on or returns to places of origin (Mougeot 1981; Mougeot and Aragón 1981).

The ineffectiveness in attracting labor to the Amazonian frontier and in developing this human resource, so that the skills required for sustainable development are in place, appears to be a result of the ineffective implementation of development. Farmers throughout Latin America are all too familiar with the incapacity of government institutions to deliver promised services. Their suspicions are confirmed in nearly every major land settlement project in Latin America (Nelson 1973) and the Amazon (Moran 1981; Shoemaker 1981; Bunker 1980). Promised roads remain either idle promises or become impassable with the arrival of the rains. Agricultural credit is tied to formal land titling, but insufficient human resources are provided to survey the land, resolve land conflicts, and cope with the unequal power between large and small operators. The result is that small farmers cannot get sufficient credit to adequately manage their land and are eventually dispossessed. Land settlement does not lead to the development of promised educational institutions geared to improving the quality of farm management in the Amazon; rather it fosters the education of urban-oriented civil servants. This urban orientation in the educational system, even in the Amazon frontier, leads to the perpetuation of a serious gap in communication between government personnel and farmers that reduces the effectiveness of management information even when it is appropriate. Production inputs such as fertilizers, pesticides, fencing, machinery, etc., are more costly in the Amazon not only because of the costs resulting from the great distances that must be traveled in the Amazon, but also because the providers of these technologies must be paid higher salaries to encourage them to leave their current locations, where the supply of such entrepreneurs is greater (Norgaard 1979).

The problem posed by the limited supply of trained managers becomes evident in the recent findings of the North Carolina State University Tropical Soils Research Program (see Nicholaides et al., Chapter 5 in this volume). The agronomists in the North Carolina program found that at Yurimaguas, Peru, they were able to facilitate multiple cropping and relatively high incomes on small farms by means of the controlled application of fertilizers and the use of selected varieties. However, the maintenance of this technology requires constant monitoring of soil fertility levels and the availability of management experts. For most of the Amazon these skills are precisely the ones in least supply and the ones that should be emphasized in the future.

There is considerable evidence from development

studies all over the world that project success requires
a favorable policy environment. Although there is no
doubt that countries with Amazonian territories favor
development, they favor growth-oriented development,
which suffers from the biases that repeatedly have been
shown worldwide to constrain rather than foster sustainable development. The benefits of Amazonian development appear to have been concentrated in the hands of
national and multinational corporations as well as urban
bureaucrats and entrepreneurs (Miller, Chapter 4 in this
volume). Although there has been some social mobility
by a few small farmers with previous management experience
(Moran 1979, 1981), their success in specific cases
merely reflects their skills and shows the heroic proportions of their courage. At the regional level, there has
been far more environmental destruction than conservation,
far more land concentration than equitable distribution,
far more speculation than sustainable improvement in the
structural capacity of Amazonian regions to support
development.

The contemporary thrust in the development of
Amazonia that began in the 1950s has changed our views
of the region. The Amazon is no longer an El Dorado or a
future breadbasket. Nor do we really see it as Green Hell
or totally wild. The development process has a way of
making researchers and developers confront a region not
as they would like to have it, but rather as infinitely
complex and full of surprises that challenge every one of
our assumptions. One might have expected the experience
of the 1950s and 1960s to have taught everyone that
development planning is hard--and that implementation
is even harder. The experience of the 1970s in Amazonian
development has reminded us once again that unless one
makes the major goals of development structural transformation and human resource development--difficult as
they may be--the achievement of sustainable development
will forever elude us.

During the decades of the 1950s and 1960s economists
dominated the literature on development. Their discussions equated development with growth--the latter
viewed primarily in terms of industrial output. Other
social scientists focused on how best to attain this
transformation from a traditional agricultural to an
urban/industrial sector, through overcoming resistance
to innovations, through development of elites, and
through creating a merit-based bureaucracy, to name but a
few of the topics that attracted the social scientists.

The aftermath of this period witnessed a critical
appraisal of these approaches. Scholars noted that
worldwide, and within countries, the income gap between
the rich and the poor has widened at alarming rates of 2
to 5% per year. During the late 1960s and the 1970s the
literature on development emphasized the differences between growth and development. In particular, scholars

began to note that the choice of a given type of production determined, to a significant degree, who benefits
from growth, and that such choices, in fact, target some
people to benefit and others to be deprived.

The current literature on development is representative of this dilemma. A small but growing number of
social scientists now believe that it is possible to have
equitable distribution without sacrificing economic growth.
The thrust of much of the current research is directed at
identifying what forms of structural change and what
modifications in the functional performance of sectors
and institutions can lead to improved benefits for that
large portion of the population heretofore overlooked in
development planning and implementation.

GROWTH WITH DEVELOPMENT: TOWARD SUSTAINED
YIELD AGROECOSYSTEMS

On what basis can we say that the Amazon's dilemma
of growth without development is resolvable? The papers
in this volume attest that under certain conditions local
development is possible. Likewise, and more often, they
show that growth without development is a consequence of
the persistence of a dualistic model of development, of
the persistence of extreme forms of social class differentiation and differential access to resource control,
of the persistence of administrative incapacities, and of
a tendency to ignore the significance for development of
the ecological differences between the resources of the
Amazon and those with which its managers are more familiar.

The dualistic model of economic development functions
as a constraint in that it pits the rural sector against
the urban sector, rather than incorporating the two in a
partnership to increase the share by both sectors in the
benefits of growth. Development planning tends to make
unwarranted assumptions about the Amazon, such as that
it is a "demographic void" or that "its vocation is
export production." If development planning is to be the
rational process that it often claims to be, it must
begin with resource surveys.

Most of the blueprints for Amazonian development have
been designed with an inadequate data base for making
detailed recommendations. The urban bias in Amazonian
development becomes evident in how the region is treated
as a non-resource until its forest is eliminated and it
is transformed into a recognized landscape into which to
introduce non-Amazonian forms of resource use. This
strategy of resource development errs on a number of
counts. The Amazon has the most complex biota on earth
and is consequently the least understood (Prance 1982).
The consequences of given forms of deforestation are unknown at this time, but rapid species extinction seems to
be one of them. Only a few of the wild animals of the
Amazon have been the subject of domestication experiments

and the results have been promising (Piccinini et al. 1971; Mondolfi 1973). Funding for such studies has been sporadic and has lacked continuity. The floral richness has been the subject of great admiration since the nineteenth century, but it has only rarely been the subject of sustained research programs. Rare medicinal plants are discovered regularly by botanists, as are plants of economic value (see Posey, Chapter 9, and Lovejoy and Salati, Chapter 8, in this volume). Nevertheless, there is very little salvage research undertaken before development projects are allowed to begin forest clearing.

Resource specialists have long argued that resources are a function of cultural perception (Sternberg 1973). Indeed, the myopia toward Amazonian resources is such that one wonders if there will be any forest left when this century is over. Not only does deforestation lead to species extinction, but it appears that it might also lead to desiccation of adjacent forest and to higher flood levels on the várzea (see Lovejoy and Salati, Chapter 8, and Goulding, Chapter 7 in this volume; see also Goodland and Irwin 1975). The former is serious because the Amazon contributes great volumes of water vapor to the atmosphere--far in excess of the amounts that are returned as rainfall. Desiccation of many areas outside of Amazonia is not beyond possibility in the near future. On the other hand, the flooding of the várzea also eliminates from reliable production many areas of alluvial soil that hold high potential for intensive cultivation. A scientific debate is already in progress over whether the rise in river levels is a function of deforestation or of secular climatic fluctuations (Gentry and López-Parodi 1980).

Earlier plans to develop the Amazon were informed by the mistaken notion that the soils of the Amazon were of excellent quality--a notion inferred from the lushness of the flora. This view has since been corrected, although in the 1960s and early 1970s overcorrection took place. Extremely negative views about the region's potential for anything other than shifting cultivation practiced by semi-nomadic villagers became popular (McNeil 1964; Meggers 1971; Goodland and Irwin 1975). Great attention in scientific circles was given to soils research in the 1970s; and it led to correction of past viewpoints (see Nicholaides et al., Chapter 5 in this volume). However, the findings from these studies have yet to be applied to development planning. One reason why they remain unapplied is that these studies repeatedly point out that cropping in the Amazon must be dealt with in a site-specific manner because of the complexity of the plant-soil interactions mediated by climate, locational characteristics, and management. This recommendation requires that development blueprints be limited to the broad sketches of design, allowing a considerable degree

of local flexibility. Such a structural requirement to
the appropriate management of Amazonian agriculture
contradicts the favored forms of public administration in
Latin America--characterized historically by centralization and bureaucratization (Veliz 1980; Uricoechea 1980).
     A dual perspective on development reflects the gap
between the rich and the poor and inequalities of access
to economically valued resources. The moving frontier
of Brazil has long been characterized by flows of population that have transformed a free resource, forested
land, into a capitalized one. However, access to the
speculative and productive value of this land is
regulated by access to land titles available from inadequately staffed and easily bribed officials in titling
bureaucracies. The result through time has been that
relatively few of those who transform the free good into
capital are able to get access to it but must, instead,
move on to profit only from the initial increase in value
rather than from the long-term increase that accompanies
the arrival of other forms of regional development.
     In short, the dual perspective is attractive to
elites who see in this model a reflection of their
perceptions of differences between the rural and the
urban. This difference in the value given to the two
sectors leads to an urban bias that demeans the contribution of the natural and human resources in the rural
sector. It also justifies differential access to control
over resources and misses the distinctiveness of the
resources of the Amazon and their inherent or potential
value. Instead, the urban bias leads to simplification
of the landscape, to reproduction of class differences,
to the destruction of natural resources, and to policies
that favor short-term economic growth rather than internal
development.
     The papers in this volume offer some hope. They are
diagnostic of the problems that have emerged in the last
decade of Amazonian development and they clarify the kinds
of policy changes that are likely to lead to the required
transformations. Lovejoy and Salati note the willingness
of President Figuereido to make a public commitment to
the protection of large areas of the rain forest. The
findings of Goulding that the flooded forest is an
absolute requirement for the sustainability of a commercial
Amazonian fisheries industry are likely to reverse the
ongoing process of deforestation in the affected areas,
thereby also helping to preserve floodplain areas.
The agronomic research of Nicholaides and his colleagues
is but the first stage of what must become a sustainable
pattern--the development of site-specific agricultural
practices guided by careful management of inputs and other
management procedures. Until such detailed resource
management studies are available for specific areas (the
"Yurimaguas technology" is the result of seven years of
intensive investigations by a large North American and

Peruvian staff), native and peasant Amazonians can play a
crucial role. The recognition of the value of these site-
specific practices will not only help guide future experimental work, but will also help develop a sense of worth
in the native cultures of the Amazon. Wagley once wrote
that the traditional cultures of the Amazon region contain much of great value that may be necessary in the
future. He hoped that a combination of modern technology
with the skills of Amazonian populations would be beneficial in regional development efforts (Wagley 1953:295).
His hope remains unfulfilled, but the investigators in
this volume have added further scientific support for the
environmental, economic, and social good sense of incorporating the folk cultures of the Amazon into the
effort required for a sustainable development.

The road to development seems to be paved more often
with good intentions than with a balanced interplay between expertise and common sense. A recent synthesis of
what we know about the management of Third World development points out that until one can structure learning
capability into development planning and implementation
bureaucracies, the process of development will always
encounter the same constraints (Bryant and White 1982).

Much more research into site-specific development is
needed before some of the problems we have identified can
be prevented. Folk knowledge is a start; the improved
quality of human resources along with bringing land prices
more in line with the limited supply of management will
help. Close study of the relationship between state
policies, access to land, and the availability of labor
is required before fine tuning in policymaking permits
appropriate project designs. The paper by Wood in this
volume provides a theoretical discussion of these relations. All these findings will need to be incorporated
at some point into simulation models so that it will not
be necessary to experiment with the Amazon and discover
that ill-laid plans destroy the ecosystem.

Stochastic modeling, a quantitative tool, holds
promise of assisting planners in the process of "what
if. . ." evaluation of alternative interventions that are
being considered in project planning. The paper by
Fearnside in this volume introduces readers to the value
of this modeling technique. The major difficulty with
stochastic modeling is that it assumes a data base
superior to that available for most areas. However, the
paper by Mahar in this volume provides some grounds for
optimism: Planners are more aware now than a decade ago
of the potential of the Amazon, and the pace of development has slowed from its hectic pace in the 1970s. The
slowdown has given more time for resource surveys to be
carried out on projected schemes, and experimental
advances can be made ahead of the growth-directed
development steamroller. International donors have
grown more sensitive to the needs of native peoples and

have begun to require resource surveys and guarantees
of land to native groups before approving loans for
development. These and other changes, together with the
worldwide economic slump, have served to provide the
scientists who have contributed to this volume, and the
host of others who carry out policy-relevant research,
with more time to generate new understandings of the
dilemmas posed by the complex social and environmental
processes currently taking place in the Amazon Basin.

ACKNOWLEDGMENTS

I thank Professors Dennis Conway and Phil Morgan of
Indiana University for their helpful comments on an
earlier version of this paper.

REFERENCES

Anderson, Robin
    1976   Following Curupira: Colonization and Migration
            in Pará (1758-1930). Ph.D. dissertation, Dept.
            of History, Univ. of California, Davis.

Bryant, Coralie and Louise White
    1982   Managing Development in the Third World.
            Boulder, Colo.: Westview Press.

Bunker, Stephen G.
    1980   Barreiras Burocráticas e Institucionais à
            Modernização: O Caso da Amazônia. Pesq. Plan.
            Econ. (Rio de Janeiro) 10(2):555-600.

Cardoso, Fernando H. and Geraldo Muller
    1977   Amazônia: Expansão do Capitalismo. São Paulo:
            Editôra Brasiliense.

Cavalcanti, M. de Barros
    1967   Da SPVEA à SUDAM. Belém: Univ. Federal do Pará.

Collier, Richard
    1968   The River that God Forgot. New York: Dutton.

Couto e Silva, Goldberry do
    1957   Aspectos Geopolíticos do Brasil. Rio de
            Janeiro: Biblioteca do Exército.

Davis, Shelton H.
    1977   Victims of the Miracle: Development and the
            Indians of Brazil. New York: Cambridge Univ.
            Press.

Denevan, William M.
    1982   Ecological Heterogeneity and Horizontal Zonation

of Agriculture in the Amazon Floodplain. Paper presented at the Conference on Frontier Expansion in Amazonia. Center for Latin American Studies, Univ. of Florida, Feb. 8-11.

Furley, Peter
1980   Development Planning in Rondônia Based upon Naturally Renewable Resource Surveys. In F. Barbira-Scazzocchio, ed., Land, People, and Planning in Contemporary Amazônia. Cambridge, UK: Cambridge Univ. Centre of Latin American Studies, Occasional Publ. 3.

Gentry, A. and J. López-Parodi
1980   Deforestation and Increased Flooding of the Upper Amazon. Science 210:1354-1356.

Goodland, Robert J.A.
1980   Environmental Ranking of Amazonian Development Projects in Brazil. Environmental Conservation 7(1):9-26.

Goodland, Robert J.A. and H. S. Irwin
1975   Amazon Jungle: Green Hell to Red Desert? Amsterdam: Elsevier.

Goulding, Michael
1980   The Fishes and the Forest. Berkeley: Univ. of California Press.

1981   Man and Fisheries on an Amazon Frontier. The Hague: Junk.

Hames, Raymond B. and William T. Vickers, eds.
n.d.   Adaptive Responses of Native Amazonians. New York: Academic Press. In preparation.

Hecht, Susanna B.
1981   Agroforestry in the Amazon Basin. In S. Hecht and G. Nores, eds., Land Use and Agricultural Research in the Amazon Basin. Cali: Centro Internacional de Agricultura Tropical (CIAT).

Kleinpenning, J.M.G.
1978   A Further Evaluation of the Policy for the Integration of the Amazon Region. Journal of Econ. and Soc. Geog. 69:78-85.

McNeil, M.
1964   Lateritic Soils. Scientific American 211(5): 86-102.

Mahar, Dennis J.
1979   Frontier Development Policy in Brazil: A Study
        of Amazonia. New York: Praeger.

Meggers, Betty J.
1971   Amazônia: Man and Culture in a Counterfeit
        Paradise. Chicago: Aldine.

Meier, Gerald M.
1976   Leading Issues in Economic Development.   3rd
        ed. New York: Oxford Univ. Press.

Mondolfi, Edgardo
1973   La Danta o Anta (Tapirus terrestris).   Su
        Importancia como Animal Silvícola y
        Posibilidades de su Cría en Cautividad.   Paper
        given at Simposio Internacional sobre Fauna
        Silvestre, Manaus, Nov. 26-Dec. 1.

Moran, Emilio F.
1979   Criteria for Choosing Successful Homesteaders
        in Brazil. Research in Economic Anthropology
        2:339-59.

1981   Developing the Amazon. Bloomington: Indiana
        Univ. Press.

1982   Ecological, Anthropological, and Agronomic
        Research in the Amazon Basin. Latin American
        Research Review 17(1):3-41.

Mougeot, Luc
1981   Alternate Migration Targets in Latin American
        Countries and Brazilian Amazonia's "Closing
        Frontier." Mimeo.

Mougeot, L. and L. Aragón, eds.
1981   O Despovoamento do Territorio Amazónico.
        Belém: Cadernos do Núcleo de Altos Estudos
        Amazónicos (NAEA), Univ. Fed. do Pará.

Nelson, Michael
1973   The Development of Tropical Lands: Policy Issues
        in Latin America. Baltimore: Johns Hopkins
        Univ. Press.

Norgaard, Richard
1979   The Economics of Agricultural Technology and
        Environmental Transformation in the Amazon.
        Paper prepared for a collaborative study between
        the Min. of Agric. and Center for Development and
        Regional Planning/Univ. of Minas Gerais
        (CEDEPLAR/UFMG), Brazil.

22

Piccinini, R., W. Vale, and F. W. Gomes
1971   Criadouros Artificiais de Animais Silvestres:
       I. Criadouros de Capivaras. Belém: Superin-
       tendência do Desenvolvimento da Amazônia
       (SUDAM).

Prance, Ghillean T.
1982   The Amazon: Earth's Most Dazzling Forest.
       Garden 6(1):2-10. Publ. of New York Botanical
       Garden.

Santos, B. A. dos
1981   Amazônia: Potencial Mineral e Perspectivas de
       Desenvolvimento. São Paulo: Editôra da Univ.
       de São Paulo.

Schmink, Marianne
1982   Land Conflicts in Amazonia. Forthcoming in
       American Ethnologist.

Schmink, Marianne and Charles H. Wood, eds.
n.d.   Frontier Expansion in Amazonia. Gainesville,
       Fla.: Univ. of Florida Press. In preparation.

Shoemaker, Robin
1981   Peasants of El Dorado. Ithaca: Cornell Univ.
       Press.

SPVEA
1960   Política de Desenvolvimento da Amazônia
       (1954-60). Belém: Superintendência do Plano
       de Valorização Econômica da Amazônia (SPVEA).

Sternberg, H.
1973   Development and Conservation. Erkunde 27:
       253-65.

Sweet, David
1974   A Realm of Nature Destroyed. Ph.D. dissertation,
       Dept. of History, Univ. of Wisconsin, Madison.

Tambs, Lewis
1974   Geopolitics of the Amazon. In C. Wagley, ed.,
       Man in the Amazon. Gainesville: Univ. of
       Florida Press.

Uricoechea, Fernando
1980   The Patrimonial Foundations of the Brazilian
       Bureaucratic State. Berkeley: Univ. of Califor-
       nia Press.

Veliz, Claudio
1980   The Centralist Tradition of Latin America.
       Princeton: Princeton Univ. Press.

Wagley, Charles
    1953   Amazon Town. New York: Macmillan.

    1977   Welcome of Tears. New York: Oxford Univ.
            Press.

Wagley, Charles, ed.
    1974   Man in the Amazon. Gainesville: Univ. of
            Florida Press.

Waterston, Albert
    1965   Development Planning: Lessons of Experience.
            Baltimore: Johns Hopkins Univ. Press.

Wood, Charles H. and J. Wilson
    1982   The Role of the Amazon in the Demography of
            Rural Brazil. Paper presented at the Conference
            on Frontier Expansion in Amazonia. Center for
            Latin American Studies, Univ. of Florida,
            Feb. 8-11.

2
Development and Amazonian Indians: The Aguarico Case and Some General Principles

William T. Vickers

INTRODUCTION

The purpose of this paper is to discuss the impact of development on the native peoples of Amazonia in general and on those of the Aguarico River of Ecuador in particular. The circumstances of the Aguarico provide a regional case for which the facts are fairly well documented and familiar to me and can serve as a microcosm of the major processes of change sweeping Amazonia.

In a very real sense, the native peoples of Amazonia have been experiencing "development" ever since Orellana's voyage through the basin in 1541-1542. Of course, this development has had little or nothing to do with indigenous well-being. European contact with the natives of the Amazon was characterized by enslavement and extermination occasioned by genocidal warfare and the transmission of epidemic diseases (cf. Hardenburg 1912; World Council of Churches 1972; Hemming 1978). The scope of this demographic disaster has been studied by Denevan (1976), who estimates that the population of greater Amazonia was reduced from 6.8 million at the time of contact to approximately 0.5 million in 1976. This is a decline of 92.6% over four centuries. So when we discuss current development and Indians, we are speaking of the survivors of this disaster. The present status of these survivors is variable; most groups are very small and extremely vulnerable to development pressures, while others such as the Jívaro, Campa, lowland Quichua, and Yanomamö have populations numbering in the thousands (Harner 1972; Bodley 1972; Whitten 1978; Ramos and Taylor 1979). Many groups have long histories of contact with their respective national societies and are to some extent "acculturated" (e.g., the jungle Quichua of Ecuador, the Cocamilla of Peru, and the Tenetehara of Brazil), whereas others have been contacted comparatively recently (e.g., the Yanomamö of Venezuela and Brazil, the Waorani of Ecuador, and the Kréen-Akaróre of Brazil). Therefore, it is not easy to make general statements about

25

the status of Amazonian Indians except to say that all
are, to one degree or another, threatened by the
expansion of the frontier.

The Amazon Basin does not form a unified geopolitical unit. Eight nations hold segments of Amazonian
territory (Brazil, Guyana, Surinam, Venezuela, Colombia,
Ecuador, Peru, and Bolivia). Yet, none of these nations
is primarily Amazonian in nature. They all are composed
of heterogeneous regions, and in all cases the Amazonian
portions of these national territories constitute
frontiers in that they have been the areas most remote
from national economic centers and least incorporated
into national political and economic infrastructures.
Each of the affected nations has, to one degree or
another, envisioned a "manifest destiny" that is to be
realized in terms of the economic development of the
Amazon and the extension of government controls and
services into the region.

In all of the Amazonian countries, mechanisms of
national integration are multiple and include military
and civil agencies, regional development banks, colonization programs, and fiscal incentives for investment
corporations (Mahar 1979). In Brazil no fewer than 51
agencies and institutions were involved in activities
associated with the construction of and colonization along
the Transamazon Highway in the early 1970s (Moran 1975:
280-282). The most glaring omission in this panoply of
government policies and institutions is the lack of
coherent planning vis-à-vis the native peoples of
Amazonia. The most comprehensive governmental organ
that deals with Indian affairs in Amazonia is the Fundação
Nacional do Indio (FUNAI) of Brazil. FUNAI was instituted
in 1967 as a reorganization of the Serviço de Proteção aos
Indios (S.P.I.) following a series of scandals indicating
that the older agency had become politically corrupt and
was implicated in activities such as the exploitation of
Indian labor, the sale of Indian lands, and collusion in
the killing of Indians (Wagley 1977:290; Davis 1977:56).
In several notable examples the agency has carried out
policies that have seemed progressive and might even have
served as models to be emulated in other nations. The
best known case of this type is the Xingú National Park,
which developed from the dedicated work of Orlando and
Claudio Villas Boas. The park was officially established
in 1961 and encompassed an area of 22,000 km^2 with an
initial population of 700 Indians belonging to ten ethnic
groups (Davis 1977). The problem with the Xingú Park is
that it represents a showcase for Brazilian Indian policy
rather than a typical example of a tribal situation resulting from comprehensive and coordinated government
programs.

The Xingú Park is not immune from the developmentalist
and political pressures that are common to other areas of
the frontier (see Figure 1.1). This point was made

emphatically in 1971 when the Brazilian government
arbitrarily announced plans to build highway BR-080
through the heart of the park over the protests of pro-
native groups in Brazil and from around the world. The
failure to establish a similar park for the Yanomami of
the states of Roraima and Amazonas despite considerable
national and international lobbying (cf. Ramos and Taylor
1979) supports the view that the recognition of Indian
land and civil rights has very low priority in official
Brazilian circles (Anthropology Resource Center 1981).
Yet other Amazonian nations have accomplished even less.
None of them has instituted agencies that are even
remotely comparable to FUNAI. In most cases their relations with lowland Indians have been poorly developed
or have simply occurred through contacts with missionaries
(often operating under contracts signed with government
ministries), the military, colonization institutes, and
petty officials. This failure to establish coherent and
integrated policies vis-à-vis native peoples has meant
that official contacts usually have a spontaneous, ad hoc,
or capricious nature and have few positive consequences
from the native perspective.

World history teaches that great natural areas inhabited by nonindustrialized native peoples have been and
will be developed (cf. Bodley 1975). Therefore, the
major questions for those concerned about indigenous
peoples are how the negative aspects of development can be
minimized and to what degree native peoples can exercise
their right to self-determination while having their
human rights respected by the nations in which they live.

Ultimately these questions devolve on the material
issues of land rights and the protection of natural resources, for no native culture can survive if its environmental underpinnings are denied or destroyed. The
decisions that must be made are economic and political.
Beyond the issues of policymaking lies the even more
difficult problem of implementation. One argument to be
made in this paper is that this perception of a polarity
of interests is fallacious. That is, if intelligent
integrated planning measures are adopted it is possible
to designate areas for environmental parks and reserves
and to recognize the legitimate land claims of native
Amazonians while at the same time allowing for the
rational and ecologically sound development of resources
in designated zones. The strategy for Amazonian development should emphasize the potential long-term benefits to
the involved nations and not the ephemeral profits of
rapacious exploitation so characteristic of the boom-bust
history of the Amazon Basin (cf. Wagley 1964; Moran 1981).

COMPETING SYSTEMS OF LAND USE

The process we refer to as "frontier development"
is a complex mixture of economic and environmental change.

One method of understanding this process is to identify
and analyze its component systems within a given geographical and historical context (cf. Vickers 1972).
An essential assumption of this approach is that each
identifiable system can be defined in terms of its goals,
rationale, strategies, and technological level. Towards
this end, the present section is divided into three parts
focusing on aboriginal adaptations, corporate enterprise,
and colonist settlement, with the primary context being
that of the Aguarico River Basin in eastern Ecuador.
Another assumption is that these systems come into conflict because they are based on the exploitation of finite
environmental resources and seek to establish and maintain
control over these resources. Government policy may be
viewed as a fourth and overriding system that attempts to
mediate the competing demands of the other systems while
at the same time representing the interests of the nation.

The Aboriginal Adaptation

The Aguarico River Basin lies to the east of the
Andes in the region where Ecuador meets with Colombia and
Peru. This area is the traditional homeland of Cofán and
Western Tucanoan-speaking peoples. The present settlement sites of the Cofán are Sinangöe, Dovino, and Dureno
(with populations of 42, 63, and 198 people, respectively)
in the western half of the basin, with the Siona-Secoya
(Western Tucanoan) at San Pablo, and Cuyabeno in the
eastern half (with 297 and 50 people, respectively). Like
most Amazonian Indians, the Siona-Secoya and Cofán base
their adaptation on shifting cultivation, hunting, fishing,
and collecting (Vickers 1976, 1979). This medley of
subsistence activities is fundamentally based on indigenous
cultigens and wild animals and plants, and this system of
environmental exploitation has proven its viability by
supporting native populations for thousands of years
(Lathrap 1970). Among the Siona-Secoya the principal
garden crops are manioc (Manihot esculenta), maize (Zea
mays), and plantains (Musa spp.; the one important food
plant of probable European introduction). In addition,
there is a wide variety of secondary cultigens including
the peach palm (Bactris gasipaes), sweet potato (Ipomoea
batatas), pepper (Capsicum spp.), papaya (Carica papaya),
avocado (Persea americana), inga (Inga spp.), achira
(Canna edulis), cacao (Theobroma cacao), and guayaba
(Psidium guajava). New gardens are cleared during each
dry season (November-January) in either primary or
secondary forest and are cultivated for two to three
years. Gardening is a relatively efficient and secure
activity (Vickers 1976, 1979) and provides about 85%
of the calories in the diet.
The most important game animals include white-lipped
and collared peccaries (Tayassu pecari and T. tajacu),
woolly monkeys (Lagothrix lagothricha), howler monkeys

(<u>Alouatta</u> <u>seniculus</u>), tapirs (<u>Tapirus</u> <u>terrestris</u>),
armadillos (<u>Dasypus</u> novemcinctus), curassows (<u>Mitu</u>
<u>salvini</u>), and guans (<u>Pipile</u> <u>pipile</u> and <u>Penelope</u> <u>jacquacu</u>).
Hunting is the male activity <u>par</u> <u>excellence</u> and is
extremely significant in that it provides about 81% of
the dietary protein (Vickers 1976, 1979; Hames and
Vickers 1982).   On the Aguarico, fishing is particularly important during the dry season, when it rivals
hunting as a supplier of proteins. At some locations,
such as on the Cuyabeno River (a northern tributary of
the Aguarico), fishing surpasses hunting as the primary
protein source throughout the year (this is due to
differences in the aquatic and terrestrial habitats of the
two areas).
        The collecting of wild food plants provides seasonal
fruits that add vitamins and variety to the diet, although
their total caloric contribution is rather small (less
than 5%).   The collected foods of significance include
<u>morete</u> (<u>Mauritia</u> sp.), <u>sapotes</u> (<u>Quararibea</u> sp.), <u>huito</u>
(<u>Tabernaemontana</u> sp.), <u>uvillas</u> (<u>Pourouma</u> <u>cecropiaefolia</u>),
pokeweed (<u>Phytolacca</u> sp.), <u>inchi</u> (<u>Caryodendron</u> <u>orinocense</u>),
and <u>Oenocarpus</u> <u>batawa</u>. Wild plants also have quintessential
importance as sources of medicinal and ritual plants and
as sources of craft and construction materials.
        It is no exaggeration to state that the very essence
of native material and spiritual culture is inextricably
intertwined with the native flora and fauna and that the
natives' knowledge of the tropical forest habitat is
immense. Botanists, zoologists, and other scientists
commonly recognize that when they study Amazonian ecology
they can do no better than to employ an Indian mentor to
guide them.
        Among the Siona-Secoya and Cofán peoples the relations
of humans and land have traditionally involved a pattern
of single or multi-family settlements dispersed along the
Aguarico and its tributaries. The annual round of
activities was and is marked by seasonal variations that
indicate the appropriate times for clearing and planting,
fishing, hunting monkeys, harvesting wild fruits, and
going on expeditions to hunt turtle eggs. This annual
cycle is based on the exploitation of widely scattered
resources throughout the Aguarico Basin and even carries
people into the adjacent areas of the Putumayo and Napo
Rivers. The pattern of movement also enhances the
cultural cohesion of the native settlements because it
provides valued opportunities for visitation among the
dispersed populace.
        In addition to the annual round of activities around
and beyond the home base, the Siona-Secoya and Cofán have
longer cycles in which to establish, inhabit, and then
abandon settlement sites. This pattern of semipermanent
villages is common among Amazonian peoples and is usually
interpreted as representing an adaptation to the
ecological constraints of the habitat at a given level

of technology (cf. Vickers 1976, 1979, 1981). That is, people practicing slash-and-burn cultivation, hunting, fishing, and collecting enhance the long-term viability of their adaptive system and the extant environmental resources when they relocate from time to time. Such movement can be viewed as a mechanism for "fallowing" the flora, fauna, and soils so that environmental degradation is minimized. The implicit goal of the native system described is to provide subsistence for the aboriginal population and is associated with a socially and symbolically coordinated cognitive system (cf. Reichel-Dolmatoff 1971).

In 1978 the Ecuadorian Institute of Agrarian Reform and Colonization (IERAC) gave land titles to the Cofán settlements of Dovino and Dureno, and to the Siona-Secoya of San Pablo-Eno (the Summer Institute of Linguistics was instrumental in lobbying for this allocation). These communal titles encompass areas of 3,863 ha, 9,571 ha, and 7,043 ha, respectively. In 1979 the Siona-Secoya settlement of Cuyabeno received title to 744 ha of land along the middle Cuyabeno River (as a consequence of contacts the community itself made with IERAC). Unfortunately, allocations of this scale reveal a near total lack of knowledge of and appreciation for the native subsistence system and equate it with the farming pattern of mestizos who are dependent on a market economy for both selling their production and purchasing their goods and who represent the lowest level of a hierarchical national class structure rather than a relatively autonomous and self-sufficient indigenous culture. The limitation of a native Amazonian people to a land base that averages 100 hectares per household, if enforced, could be a cultural death sentence because it ignores the larger land areas needed for hunting, fishing, the collection of wild plants, and the cyclical pattern of relocating settlements. The allocations also fail to provide for the population growth of future generations (the Siona-Secoya are increasing at a rate of 4% per year and will double their population within 20 years).

At the present time the Siona-Secoya continue to hunt, as they must, beyond the current boundaries of their communal lands, and they are requesting that the Ecuadorian government give them title to some of their traditional hunting areas on the north bank of the Aguarico. Based on my detailed study of the cultural ecology of the community of San Pablo (Vickers 1976, 1979; Hames and Vickers 1982), I estimate that the area presently used for all forms of subsistence activities and normal community movements covers approximately 2,000 square kilometers. But, it is extremely unlikely that the entire area could be titled to the community because significant portions have already been claimed by an African palm plantation (Palmeras del Ecuador), several colonist land groups

(precooperativas), a CEPCO oilfield (a subsidiary of First
National City Bank), and the Cuyabeno Fauna Preserve
(part of the Ecuadorian National Park system). The best
one can hope for is that the present Siona-Secoya holdings
can be quadrupled by extending into contiguous areas
primarily to the north and east. Such an expansion would
result in a holding of about 30,000 hectares (300 km^2),
which would be woefully insufficient for traditional hunting and collecting activities, but which would represent
a significant improvement over the present situation.
    The Cofán community of Dureno, located on the Rio
Aguarico about 50 km northwest of San Pablo, has already
been completely circumscribed by roads and colonist
settlement. Prior to the construction of the oil road in
the late 1960s the Cofán embarked on a "great circle"
route of seasonal hunting trips north to the Río San
Miguel, eastward along its course, south along the Río
Cuyabeno, and returning westward along the Aguarico. The
coming of the Lago Agrio oilfield and the concomitant
settlement of the land between the Aguarico and the San
Miguel have made this activity untenable, and now the
Cofán complain that they feel entrapped within the
perimeter of their small government-allocated holdings.
They still manage to fish and hunt small animals and
gain some income by manufacturing artifacts for tourists,
but a very significant part of their subsistence activity
and some of the vitality of Cofán culture have been lost.
Their situation is somewhat analogous to that of the
Shipibo of Peru, who now derive much of their economy
from the sale of artifacts to the tourists of Pucallpa.
The impact of such territorial circumscription has also
been described for the Xavante of Brazil (Flowers, in
press). The Cofán community of Sinangöe on the Upper
Aguarico has been forced from one traditional site on
the eastern side of the river by colonist expansion, and
to date the government has refused to title the Cofán
lands on the western bank because the area has been
designated as part of the Cayambe-Coca Ecological Reserve,
which is part of the national park system. Ironically,
several comunas of Quichua Indians who migrated into the
area from the Napo River within the last 20 years were
given land titles within the Reserve. This discrepancy
apparently relates to local politics and the ignorance
of the park planners in Quito.

Corporate Enterprise

    Large-scale capitalist enterprise is not new to the
Amazon Basin. What is new in recent times is the
diversity and degree of penetration of capitalist enterprise into both old centers such as Belém and Manaus, and
into formerly remote areas of the basin. In some instances such development has been stimulated by special
government incentives for corporate investors (e.g.,

electronic assembly plants in Manaus and corporate-
owned cattle ranches in Brazil, cf. Mahar 1979), but it
is also driven by the overall growth of the world's
population and economy and the continuing search for new
sources of essential raw materials and new sites for
agricultural production. Major capitalist activities in
the Amazon include mineral and oil exploitation (Robinson
1972; Vickers 1972; Davis and Mathews 1976; Davis 1977;
Ramos and Taylor 1979; Anthropology Resource Center 1981),
cattle ranching and other large-scale agribusiness
operations (Davis 1977; Mahar 1979; Fearnside and Rankin
1980), and outright land speculation (Lewis 1974:14-15;
Wood and Schmink 1979; Foweraker 1981; Lernoux 1981).

Ecuador has long favored the development of the
Oriente and its integration into the economic life of the
nation. However, throughout the Republican period there
was a notable lack of effective government initiatives
towards this goal; this was largely due to the difficulties of establishing transportation routes through the
extremely rugged terrain of the eastern Andean slopes and
the limited economic resources of the government. In
fact the first successful attempt to construct a highway
link with its Amazonian lowlands did not begin until the
1930s and was financed by the Royal Dutch Shell Petroleum
Company as part of its exploration program in the central
Oriente (which ended because of a reported lack of
success in locating deposits).

In the early 1960s a consortium of Texaco and Gulf
oil companies brought oil fields in eastern Colombia into
production and built a trans-Andean pipeline to the
Pacific coast. This consortium subsequently made
explorations in adjacent areas of Ecuador, and in 1968
discovered a major field at Lago Agrio on the northern
bank of the Aguarico. Ecuador's refusal to allow this
field to be linked to the Colombian pipeline forced
Texaco-Gulf to build a trans-Andean pipeline and
associated road within Ecuador. This road, which had
reached Lago Agrio by 1970, became the route of penetration and development in the Aguarico Basin. During the
1970s the road was extended east to Tarapoa to serve the
CEPCO oil concession and south to the town of Coca on the
Napo. At present the system is being constantly extended
with feeder routes that penetrate the interstitial areas
of the forest. The Quito-Lago Agrio section runs along
the northern bank of the Aguarico and bisects the traditional territory of the Cofán Indians. Dovino has lost
its lands on the northern side of the river to colonists,
and Dureno is now completely encircled by roads and feeder
routes. The Lago Agrio-Tarapoa section, which is now
being extended northward to the Putumayo River, is having
similar effects on the Siona-Secoya of Eno, San Pablo, and
Puerto Bolivar. Immediately to the south and west of Eno
and San Pablo, a 9,850 ha concession has been granted to
Palmeras del Ecuador (a multinational corporation) for an

African palm oil plantation. This area has been a primary
breeding ground for game hunted by the Indians. Now the
complex forest cover has been removed, the ground leveled
by tractors, and the area replanted with a simple associa-
tion of African oil palms and a leguminaceous ground cover.
Needless to say, the new man-managed system will not
support the complex fauna of the natural system, and the
Siona-Secoya have lost an area that was a traditional
source of animal and plant products.

The primary goal of the oil and other corporate
enterprises is, of course, to make profits for their
owners and stockholders. The "system" is to rationally
assess the cost-benefit factors of investment, production,
and marketing with the goal of maximizing earnings. These
corporations are highly capital-intensive, technologically
advanced, and politically influential. Unfortunately,
their concerns with long-term environmental quality and
their impact on indigenous or peasant populations are
peripheral to the profit or tax-incentive motives.

Colonist Activity

Despite the plans and efforts of governments and big
businesses to "develop" Amazonia, much of the activity in
the region stems from more individualized behavior.
Pioneer settlers (colonos), prospectors (e.g., the
garimpeiros of Brazil), job seekers, and small-scale
entrepreneurs (e.g., shopkeepers, pimps and prostitutes,
hotel and restaurant owners, traders, lumbermen) all form
part of the retinue attracted to the frontier (see
Stearman, Chapter 3, and Miller, Chapter 4, in this
volume). Such "spontaneous colonization" everywhere
outdistances cumbersome bureaucratic attempts at planned
colonization (Nelson 1973; Smith 1976, 1981; Mahar 1979:
164-167; Wood and Schmink 1979; Moran 1981). The multiple
service agencies incorporated into government-sponsored
colonization schemes often result in inflexible and inadequate bureaucracies that create as many problems as
they solve (Moran 1981). Although the type of behavior
that we label "spontaneous colonization" is likely to
entail disappointments and failures, it is enormously
flexible and dynamic. People search for a piece of unoccupied land and attempt to farm it, but may quickly
give up or move on in hope of better opportunities.
Disputes over titles and land ownership contribute significantly to the demographic flux. The existence of
colonist needs for food, tools, medicines, transportation,
and other goods and services, and the quest for enter-
tainment and communication, provide the basis for small-
scale entrepreneurial activity on the frontier. A house
with a crate of soft drinks and a few pounds of sugar
and noodles becomes a store. A man with a portable
Honda generator, a jukebox, and a refrigerator is the
proprietor of a restaurant and cantina. Someone with

an outboard motor runs a ferry service on a river. At
key points near crossroads, rivers, or construction sites,
clusters of corrugated tin and pole shacks emerge to form
towns.

In the Aguarico region the Cofán and Siona-Secoya
have witnessed colonist precooperativas springing up next
to their settlements and within their territories. Such
precooperatives consist of groups of socios or members who
elect officers and petition IERAC for titles to the lands
they have occupied.

These settlements pose serious problems for the
native community. Firstly, if these colonist claims are
legalized they will represent an immediate loss of native
territory and resources (attempts have already been made
by some of these colonists to chase the dispersed Siona-
Secoya households into the 7,043 ha area allocated by
IERAC). Secondly, many of the so-called "colonists" seem
to be primarily interested in putting chainsaws to work
to strip the region of its marketable hardwoods, and in
dynamiting the rivers to obtain fish to sell in Lago Agrio,
the frontier entrepôt. While conducting these "entrepreneurial" activities, the "colonists" frequently steal
from Indian gardens in order to feed themselves. Although
there are many legitimate colonists--the landless poor
seeking a viable livelihood for themselves and their
families--a significant number hold multiple claims that
they develop minimally and then sell to people who have
recently arrived at the frontier, in a speculative type
of exploitation. Daniel Vreugdenhil, a United Nations
consultant to the Ecuadorian Office of Forestry Development, estimates that if the current rate of spontaneous
colonization continues, the entire Ecuadorian Oriente
could be settled within 10 to 15 years (Vreugdenhil 1978:
41). He sees this as a potential crisis because such
unchecked colonization would preempt rational and
ecologically based planning for the region.

ASPECTS OF SOCIOECONOMIC CHANGE

To this point I have focused on the situation of
Amazon Indians vis-à-vis the broad and powerful forces
associated with frontier development (i.e., native land
questions, capitalist enterprise, colonization, and
government policies). But anyone who has spent time in
native communities realizes that the impact of development also consists of a plethora of problems and adjustments that affect the natives in significant ways. The
examples to be discussed are by no means exhaustive, but
illustrate the diversity of development-related issues
facing Amazonian Indians today.

Health and Environmental Issues

In historical terms, introduced diseases have

constituted the most serious environmental problem faced
by native Amazonians as a consequence of contact with outsiders. Epidemics of smallpox, measles, the common cold,
and other contagious diseases have contributed more to the
precipitous decline in native populations than any other
factor. The surviving Indians of Amazonia are still
vulnerable to health threats despite the fact that many
groups have a degree of access to modern medicines and
inoculation programs and some groups have apparently
"turned the corner" and are now experiencing a growth in
population.

The Siona-Secoya can serve as one example of a group
whose population is now on the increase after centuries
of decline. The earliest estimate of population in the
area was for the Aguarico-Napo "Encabellado" (the direct
ancestors of the Siona-Secoya), who were said to have
numbered 8,000 by Father Pedro Pecador and Captain Juan
de Palacios at the beginning of the seventeenth century
(Steward 1948:739). Julian Steward's demographic analysis
of Amazonian peoples in the Handbook of South American
Indians calculated a total Encabellado population of
16,000 (1949:663). Major missionary activity in the area
was begun by the Jesuits in the seventeenth and eighteenth
centuries and from that time through the early twentieth
century a series of major and minor epidemics reduced the
population to less than a thousand individuals (cf. Phelan
1967:23-42). One of the last major outbreaks consisted
of a measles epidemic during 1923, which wiped out whole
villages on the Putumayo River (Langdon 1974:40). During
the 1950s the surviving Indians in some of the communities began to receive vaccines, antibiotics, and other
medicines through mission stations established by the
Summer Institute of Linguistics. Since that time they
have also received some attention from the Ecuadorian
health service (e.g., vaccinations against yellow fever).
The area is periodically sprayed with DDT by the malaria
prevention service. In the period from 1973 to 1980
the population of the Siona-Secoya in Ecuador has
experienced an annual growth rate of 4%. Similar elevated
population growth rates have been reported for a number of
other Amazonian groups (Smole 1976:73; Wagley 1977:297;
Bodley and Benson 1979:78).

Although such recent growth is a positive sign, it
does not offset the fact that the groups represent
severely depleted populations whose small numbers render
them highly vulnerable from a demographic perspective.
Societies that are reduced to but a few hundred individuals
who must compete for resources with vastly larger numbers
of pioneers and multinational corporations cannot be said
to be in a strong situation. Disease continues to be
a major problem because the development of the Amazon is
leading to ever-increasing contacts between Indians and
non-Indians and because not all native individuals or
groups have access to medical treatment and facilities.

Groups that have remained relatively isolated are still subject to severe epidemics. When Brazil's Cuiabá-Santarém highway was built through the territory of the Kréen-Akaróre in 1972-1973 the Indians contracted colds and suffered a mortality rate of 55% (only 135 of 300 survived this episode; Davis 1977:66-73). Onchocerciasis, or African river blindness, has been reported as affecting 62% of the Aiwaterí Indians near the Brazil-Venezuela border, and also in the Serra de Surucucú area near Brazil's frontier with Colombia (Pinto 1973 and Viera 1973, cited by Goodland and Irwin 1975:52). The Yanomamö Indians along the route of the Perimetral Norte highway have also suffered disastrous outbreaks of influenza, pneumonia, measles, and malaria (Ramos and Taylor 1979). Reports such as these clearly indicate that Old World diseases continue to constitute a major threat to the health and survival of Amazonian Indians despite the increased accessibility of medicines among some groups.

Epidemic diseases are not the only development-related health risks for lowland Indians. The earlier discussion of declining natural resources and dietary patterns suggests the possibility and even probability of a declining nutritional status for Amazonian natives (cf. Bodley 1975; Flowers, in press). The consequences are likely to include both the direct effects of under-nutrition and malnutrition and the lowering of resistance mechanisms against other illnesses. The increasing overall human population and the use of domestic animals in Amazonia are causing increased health hazards due to parasites (cf. McDaniel, Harris, and Katz 1979).

Environmental pollution poses another health problem. Although this may seem unlikely in so large an area with so low a human population, the fact is that significant despoilation of the habitat is occurring in many areas of the basin, and with almost none of the controls required in the industrialized nations of the world. The Aguarico River Basin, for example, is now subjected to frequent oil spills as a consequence of the development of the Lago Agrio, Shushufindi, and Tarapoa fields. The oil comes from pipeline breaks and spills around well sites and is washed into streams and rivers during periods of heavy rain. The natives complain that this pollution renders fish inedible and the water undrinkable. Indians also complain of the garbage, trash, and sewage found downstream from frontier towns and settlements, and they claim that this pollution is responsible for illnesses within native communities.

The growing use of pesticides and herbicides in Amazonia is also causing concern among observers. Yost (1981) has documented the use of DDT as a fish poison by the Waorani Indians of eastern Ecuador, and a recent report by Cultural Survival (1981) suggests that the use of defoliants (Dow Chemical's Tordon 101 and 105) may be implicated in a variety of health problems among people

living there (including stillbirths, miscarriages, infant
deformations, and adult kidney ailments). The evidence
suggests that there is a pressing need for the Amazonian
nations to formulate effective environmental protection
controls. The quality of environmental resources should
also be an important consideration in the study of native
land needs.

Problems of Legal Identity

Indians are often beset by a variety of civil and
legal problems as they are drawn into increasing contact
with dominant national societies. One important
question is that of Indian legal identity and nationality.
Most Indians of Amazonia lack personal documents such as
birth certificates, military registration cards, tax
documents, official identification cards, and passports.
This, of course, should surprise no one, as it is the
natural consequence of being born into and living in a
preliterate culture whose political organization is at the
village or tribal-band level. The solution to these
problems can only come from enlightened government policies
that provide for Indian civil rights through the establishment of documentation procedures to establish the legal
status of indigenous peoples and guarantee them freedom
of movement within the nation as well as within their
traditional territories.

Tourism

Tourism has had a significant impact on a number of
Amazonian groups. The Yagua on the Amazon near Iquitos
are a key attraction for tourists and much of their
economy derives from this "human zoo" role (cf. Schreider
and Schreider 1970:117). Promoters have induced formerly
remote bands of the Ecuadorian Waorani (commonly referred
to as "Aucas") to build landing fields in their territory
to accommodate ever-increasing numbers of European and
American tourists. In one case a Waorani group was
promised large amounts of food and supplies for doing this
and cleared a field in an area where they had no gardens,
then waited futilely for the promised goods until near-
starvation forced them away (James Yost, personal
communication, 1980). In the late 1960s American and
Belgian promoters operating out of Iquitos had the Secoya
of the Río Santa María in Peru construct a hotel out of
native materials and paid them with shotguns. The Indians
were induced to have their children run around nude so
as to appear "more native," and when tourists began to
arrive informal parties were held in which the Indians
were plied with alcohol and drugs and attempts were made
to seduce young girls and boys (Jay Louthian, personal
communication, 1973).
Whereas such visits were initially received as

whimsical entertainments by the Indians, many of them
soon began to tire of the inconveniences and dislocations
as the tide of visitors increased. They also complained
of increased illness due to infections brought in by the
tourists and the fact that the tour organizers were making
large profits whereas they received little or nothing. By
August 1980 over 200 tourists per week were passing through
San Pablo (Eduardo Asanza, personal communication, 1980).

Although tourism is one modality for supplying
additional income to native communities, its impact can
be extremely disruptive to native life. Government
planners should be aware of this problem since tourism
is sometimes perceived as an economic plus for Indian
peoples who can no longer carry out traditional subsistence activities due to environmental circumscription.
The preferred alternative should be to recognize Indian
land rights so that their culture is not prostituted out
of economic necessity.

The Artifact Trade

The manufacture of artifacts for sale has become an
increasingly significant activity for many Amazonian
groups as they have become more involved in the economic
systems of the nations in which they find themselves.
The marketing of such artifacts occurs on an ad hoc basis
by Indians to tourists, by Indians selling to commercial
middlemen and shopkeepers, and through other agencies such
as FUNAI in Brazil and the Summer Institute of Linguistics
in various countries.

Some observers feel that the artifact trade is a
positive development because it is based on traditional
native crafts and provides needed income (cf. Aspelin
1975). The encircled Shipibo of Peru, for example, are
well known for their complex art designs and presently
derive much of their income from sales of their work.
Likewise, the marketing of tourist items has been
described in positive terms for peasants in Mexico (cf.
Foster 1979) and Eskimos (Emilio F. Moran, personal
communication, 1982).

Within the Aguarico Basin the Cofán of Dureno are
particularly active in selling tourist-quality (i.e.,
generally inferior) necklaces, spears, and other doodads
to visitors and middlemen in the frontier boomtown of
Lago Agrio. The Siona and Secoya are generally less
dependent on this trade, but occasionally sell such items
as hammocks, pottery, miniature paddles, and netted
string bags. These groups also sell materials such as
bird feathers to white middlemen who have learned to
manufacture their own "Indian" artifacts. A potential
danger of this type of trade is that it can lead to the
depletion of certain plants (e.g., the Astrocaryum
palm that provides fiber for hammocks, bags, and
cordage) and animals (e.g., ocelots for their prized,

but illegal, pelts, and assorted birds for their plumage).
When essential raw materials disappear the ultimate basis
for authentic native arts becomes threatened (the substitution of modern materials such as plastics is a
common response). Under the best of circumstances the
artifact trade can provide indigenous peoples with a
supplemental source of income. As with the tourist
trade, it should not be viewed as an economic substitute
for the proven subsistence adaptation.

Agricultural Innovation

Agricultural innovation is another example of how
development is altering the traditional economic structure
of Amazon Indians. Missionary groups and government
agencies often try to introduce to Indians "improved"
agricultural techniques, including domesticated animals
such as cattle, goats, chickens, and pigs, and new cash
crops such as cacao, hybrid corn, coffee, rice, and even
table vegetables such as pole beans, tomatoes, summer
squash, and cucumbers. One rationale that is often
expressed in support of these innovations is that frontier
development will force the Indians to "settle down" in
reduced territories and that under such conditions native
plant and animal resources will be severely depleted so
that the traditional hunting, collecting, and fishing
activities will lose their viability. According to this
view the Indians must adopt new agricultural patterns or
face starvation.

Of course no one doubts that the subsistence systems
of native peoples will be severely affected if the Indians
are forced to live on small reservations. A subsistence
system based on hunting, fishing, collecting, and shifting cultivation does require more land area per capita
than one based on intensive agriculture. The problem is
that in some cases the agricultural extension approach
has been used in lieu of the more fundamental need to
legalize Indian territories.

The missionary expectation that the Ecuadorian
Oriente would be filling up with colonists has come true,
but the Indians have not become settled farmers. For the
Siona-Secoya the plant varieties and domesticated animals
introduced by the missionaries have not yet proved to be
of significant economic value. Those Indians who have
attempted to raise cattle given to or purchased by them
under the Summer Institute of Linguistics (SIL) program
have invested much labor in attempting to establish
pastures, build fences, and otherwise care for the
animals. By and large it has been a losing proposition
(cf. Macdonald 1981). Some individuals have managed to
sell a few head (principally to the SIL base at Limoncocha),
but due to disease, accidents, and high calf mortality
most have seen no return for their considerable efforts.
As one Secoya who had labored with two head for ten years

put it, "El ganado es un patrón que no paga." ("The cow is a boss who doesn't pay.")

Some individuals have had somewhat better luck in raising pigs and chickens, but as yet these contribute almost nothing to the native diet because the few pigs, chickens, and eggs that are produced are sold to river traders or tourists for money to buy clothing, candy, cosmetics, alcohol, and other manufactured items. Some foods such as noodles, rice, and sugar (carbohydrates that are little needed given the preponderance of native root crops), and also coffee, are purchased; however, the bulk of the diet still consists of the traditional garden crops and wild animals and fruits.

Attempts have been made in Brazil (Piccinini et al. 1971) and Venezuela (Mondolfi 1973) to domesticate or manage indigenous animal species such as the tapir (Tapirus terrestris), the agouti (Dasyprocta spp.), the capybara (Hydrochoerus hydrochaeris), and various fishes. Such efforts may ultimately lead to economically viable strategies for managed protein production within Amazonia. In my view such approaches are unlikely to have significant benefits for most Amazonian Indians in the foreseeable future, although some observers have espoused them as the solution to anticipated protein deficiencies as development reduces faunal populations.

The idea that technocratic "fixes" can easily replace long-evolved and proven systems of adaptation are ethnocentric and potentially dangerous in that their imagined benefits may prove ephemeral. Indians can adapt to the changing conditions in Amazonia over time but should be allowed to do so on their own terms and without the expectation that the "solutions" offered by the dominant society are inherently superior.

MODALITIES FOR INFLUENCING POLICIES

The outlook for Amazonian Indians is not promising in that there is no easy solution to the complex problems that beset them. But the situation is not hopeless, and in this section I will discuss some of the potential areas for future action. Action may be private, corporate, or governmental. The level of such action may be indigenous, regional, national, or international, and the rationale may be conservationist, moral, legal, or economic. From this range of possibilities several modalities for dealing with the difficulties faced by native peoples have emerged. Private Indian rights movements have formed at all of the aforementioned levels (e.g., the Shuar Federation, the Indian Commissions of Brazil, and organizations such as Survival International, The International Work Group for Indigenous Affairs, and Cultural Survival) and have applied predominantly conservationist, moral, and legal arguments in favor of native causes. Governmental actions that have affected

Indians have been primarily in the legal and economic development areas. Additional international influences have derived from the foreign policies of powerful states (e.g., the United States' emphasis on human rights during President Carter's administration) and from agencies such as the United Nations, the International Labor Organization, and the Catholic Church.

It is obvious that no single approach can solve the problems of Indian lands, cultural self-determination, and civil rights. Rather, the existing modalities of indigenous organizations, national and international human rights movements, and national policy formation and implementation need to be extended and amplified. Scientific research and expertise can and should play a role in influencing such policy. There are many individuals in government service and in the corporate world who are increasingly receptive to scientific data concerning the environmental parameters of the Amazon, and who are attempting to use the information to influence the policy-making process (cf. Uquillas 1979).

With rational and integrated planning the Amazonian nations should be competent to guarantee native land rights. Since the surviving native populations are relatively small in most areas, the land requirements are not extreme and need not preclude the allocation of other lands for other development purposes. The involved countries have planning ministries and colonization and agrarian reform institutes which can implement policies or laws formulated at higher levels of government.

Native land requirements should be given a high priority because of the civil, ecological, and moral issues involved. The legalization of Indian territories should be based on an understanding of the dynamics of shifting cultivation, hunting, fishing, and collecting in the specific areas being considered. The future growth of the native populations should also be provided for; ideally, territories should accommodate populations two-to-three times larger than the extant populations (groups with growth rates like the Siona-Secoya can quadruple their populations in two generations or less). This is important because lands should be allocated on a communal basis to prevent unnecessary fragmentation of native societies. The land rights should also be inalienable. Because of variations in ecological conditions, the extent of frontier expansion, and the spatial dimensions of the involved nations it is difficult to specify a universal per-capita land requirement for Amazonian Indians. Denevan (1976:230) estimates that the mean aboriginal density for the Amazon was 0.7 people per km^2 (and ranged from 0.2 people/km^2 in the interior lowland forest to 14.6 people/km^2 in the interior floodplains). This figure can be taken as a rough estimate of typical land needs under the aboriginal subsistence system.

Of course, variations in habitat and the nature of the frontier conditions make it impossible to allocate lands for specific populations on the basis of a mechanically applied standard. Most importantly, it is necessary to know what lands are actually being used by specific Indian populations. (The concept of "use" as applied here refers to all subsistence activities including hunting, fishing, and collecting, and also to ceremonial and social activities). Ideally, these lands are the ones that should be allocated. In contact situations where territory has already been lost to the advancing frontier the strategy should become one of salvaging the maximum area possible. Relocations of native groups should be avoided unless exceptional circumstances threaten their survival.

Actual examples of land allocations in the Amazon reveal tremendous variations in areas per capita. When the Xingú Park was established in 1961 it had a population density of but 0.03 persons per km^2 (700 people in an area of 22,000 km^2)(Davis 1977). In contrast, the 475 Shipibo of San Francisco (on Lake Yarinacocha in eastern Peru) have title to but 1,400 ha of land (Bodley and Benson 1979:2) for a density of 33.9 people per km^2. In assessing the situation of these Shipibo, Bodley and Benson observe: "An insufficient land base condemns a native group to a vicious cycle of resource depletion and market involvement that can only end with their complete impoverishment and deculturation."

My analysis of the Siona-Secoya of the Aguarico indicates that they make use of an area of 2,000 km^2 in carrying out all of their subsistence activities (a density of 0.2 persons per km^2), but their current land titles provide a density of 4.5 persons per km^2. The titled lands for the Cofán at Dovino and Dureno provide densities of 1.6 and 2.1 persons per km^2, respectively. However, an allocation on the scale of the original Xingú Park (22,000 km^2) could never be a political reality in a country as small as Ecuador because it would cover 28% of its entire Amazon region!

The titled lands of the Siona-Secoya and Cofán in the Aguarico Basin must be considered inadequate under the conditions of the traditional subsistence system, and they can only be expanded with careful consideration of the existing frontier situation. An interagency government commission was established in 1980 to study the needs of the Cofán, Siona-Secoya, and Waorani Indians, and I served as a consultant for the Cofán and Siona-Secoya of the Aguarico (Cultural Survival, Inc. of Cambridge, Massachusetts was an important party to these developments). My report to this commission argued for an expansion of the Siona-Secoya lands north to the CEPCO oil concession and along both banks of the Aguarico to the east (Vickers 1980). If this recommendation is carried out it will allow for a current population density of about 1.2 persons per km^2. It was also recommended

that the Cofán comuna of Dovino be expanded to the south
and that the Sinangöe community be given title to significant lands within the Cayambe-Coca Ecological
Reserve. (The Cofán community of Dureno is bounded on
all sides, so that there is no avenue for expanding it.)
Whether or not this particular commission ultimately
succeeds in carrying out these recommendations, it is
evident that there are small but growing numbers of
government officials, scientists, and others who perceive
the worth of native cultures and of preserving some areas
as natural habitats. Of course, mere land allocations
mean little unless they are defended against encroachment.
If possible, boundaries should follow natural topographic
features (signs are likely to be destroyed). The defense
of lands is of necessity a continuous process and works
best when native communities and government agencies
collaborate in the effort.

Perhaps the most significant development is that
many Indian groups are themselves beginning to mobilize
for political action. The Shuar Federation of Ecuador
has attracted international attention (cf. Salazar 1977),
and many other indigenous organizations have sprung up
in that country in recent years (e.g., the Federación de
Organizaciones Indígenas del Napo, Unión de Nativos de la
Amazonía Ecuatoriana, and Asociación Independiente del
Pueblo Shuar del Ecuador). Brazilian Indians hold inter-
tribal conferences to discuss policies. They sent
delegations to meet with Pope John Paul II when he visited
Manaus in 1980. With increasing frequency intelligent
and politically aware Indian leaders are stepping foward
to articulate the needs and desires of their peoples (cf.
Cabixi 1979). Yet many smaller, more remote, or less
acculturated groups remain politically unorganized or
unrecognized. And even the best organized groups such as
the Shuar still have not resolved the land and resource
issues facing them as a consequence of "development."

CONCLUSIONS

Many native Amazonian societies have already disappeared, and the process of extinction continues. Darcy
Ribeiro (1967) estimates that of the 230 tribes existing
in Brazil in 1900, 87 (37.8%) had ceased to exist by
1957. Most of the surviving groups are so reduced in
population, or so overwhelmed by the dominant national
society, that their viability is questionable. The
situation is similar throughout Amazonia. If the
political and philosophical goal of the involved nations
is the "integration" of cultural groups into a national
"culture" that negates ethnic diversity, then the denial
of the material basis upon which native cultures depend
is a rational policy. Under such a policy, allocations
of 50 or 100 ha per household can be made and will assist
in the destruction of native cultures as cultures; the

native people may survive by adopting the strategies of other marginal, poor, lower-class, and politically weak peasants and frontier settlers with whom they will interact. In so doing they will adopt the national language, new religion, and other lower-class social and economic patterns. The end result will be assimilation, but not into "national culture" per se, but into a particularly disadvantaged segment of a class-stratified society.

If the political and philosophical goal is to recognize the legitimacy and worth of native cultures within a multicultural state, the rational policy should be to legalize native rights to the traditional lands that provide the material basis for their welfare. In a very real sense, policies that recognize the validity of Indian territorial rights and that allocate resources in a rational and fair-minded way will be beneficial to the Amazonian nations themselves.

In order to rationally allocate native lands, the Amazonian nations will have to conduct fine-grained studies of the Amazon Basin and give consideration to fairly long-term planning for land use for a variety of needs including agriculture, industry, colonization, and ecological reserves. The uncontrolled development of the frontier as seen in many areas of the Amazon today has led many scientists and even government officials to predict dire ecological and economic consequences that will benefit no one, least of all the involved nations. The arguments for more controlled and rational development policies are multiple and can be made from the cost-benefit perspective of economics and the desirability of long-term and stable growth, as opposed to the boom-bust cycles historically characteristic of the Amazon. The long-term benefits are ecological and genetic for flora and fauna as seen from both the biological and economic perspectives; there are scientific and economic advantages in maintaining viable native cultures with their consummate knowledge and understanding of the tropical forest environment and its resources which have contributed so much to our modern pharmacopoeia and our inventory of economic plants.

What is argued here is that the dichotomization of contending interests into anti-development/pro-Indian and development/anti-Indian factions is unfortunate; it represents an extreme distortion of the alternatives open to the Amazonian nations and obscures the paths that the interested governments ought to be pursuing. The Amazonian nations need to provide for their own economic growth and well-being, but must also consider the rights of their constituent peoples and the long-term maintenance of environmental resources and quality. The Amazon nations themselves will reap most of the benefits or disasters of their present and future policies, but the world as a whole will also be affected by what transpires in one of the last great frontiers of our planet.

ACKNOWLEDGMENTS

Research among the Siona-Secoya in 1973-1974 was supported by the Henry L. and Grace Doherty Foundation, and in 1974-1975 by the National Institute of Mental Health (Grant number 1 Fol MH 58552-01). Subsequent field trips in the summers of 1979 and 1980 were supported by the Florida International University Foundation, Inc., and Cultural Survival, Inc., respectively. Supplemental funding for the latter two trips was made by the Latin American and Caribbean Center and College of Arts and Sciences of Florida International University. The Instituto Nacional de Antropología e Historia under the directorship of Arq. Hernán Crespo Toral provided the Ecuadorian affiliation for the research during 1973-1975 and 1979. The Instituto Nacional de Colonización de la Región Amazónica Ecuatoriana provided the affiliations in 1980. William E. Carter, Charles Wagley, Theodore Macdonald, and Mark B. Rosenberg provided invaluable assistance during my various field trips. I would also like to thank Emilio F. Moran, the volume editor, for his critical comments on the original manuscript.

REFERENCES

Anthropology Resource Center (ARC)
    1981   The Yanomami Indian Park: A Call for Action.
            Cambridge, Mass.: Anthropology Resource Center.

Aspelin, Paul Leslie
    1975   External Articulation and Domestic Production:
            The Artifact Trade of the Maimainde of North-
            western Mato Grosso, Brazil. Latin American
            Studies Program Dissertation Series No. 58.
            Ithaca, N.Y.: Cornell Univ.

Bodley, John H.
    1972   Tribal Survival in the Amazon: The Campa Case.
            International Work Group for Indigenous Affairs
            Document No. 5. Copenhagen.

    1975   Victims of Progress. Menlo Park, California:
            Cummings.

Bodley, John H. and Foley C. Benson
    1979   Cultural Ecology of Amazonian Palms. Reports
            of Investigations No. 56. Laboratory of
            Anthropology. Pullman: Washington State Univ.

Cabixi, Daniel Mantenho
    1979   Reflections of a Brazilian Indian. In Brazil.
            Special Report No. 1, pp. 10-13. Cambridge,
            Mass.: Cultural Survival, Inc.

Cultural Survival, Inc.
  1979   Brazil. Special Report No. 1. Cambridge, Mass.

  1981   Poisons and Peripheral People: Hazardous Sub-
          stances in the Third World. Cultural Survival
          Newsletter 5(3):1-8.

Davis, Shelton H.
  1977   Victims of the Miracle: Development and the
          Indians of Brazil. New York: Cambridge Univ.
          Press.

Davis, Shelton H. and Robert O. Mathews
  1976   The Geological Imperative: Anthropology in the
          Amazon Basin of South America. Cambridge,
          Mass.: Anthropology Resource Center.

Denevan, William M.
  1976   The Aboriginal Population of Amazonia. In W.
          M. Denevan, ed., The Native Population of the
          Americas in 1492. Madison: Univ. of Wisconsin
          Press.

Fearnside, Philip M. and Judy M. Rankin
  1980   Jari and the Development of the Brazilian
          Amazon. Interciencia 5(3):146-156.

Flowers, Nancy M.
  In   Seasonal Factors in Subsistence, Nutrition and
  press   Child Growth in a Central Brazilian Indian
           Community. In R. B. Hames and W. T. Vickers, eds.,
           Adaptive Responses of Native Amazonians.
           New York: Academic Press.

Foster, George M.
  1979   Tzintzuntzan: Mexican Peasants in a Changing
          World, rev. ed. New York: Elsevier.

Foweraker, Joe
  1981   The Struggle for Land: A Political Economy of
          the Pioneer Frontier in Brazil, 1930 to the
          Present. Cambridge, UK: Cambridge Univ. Press.

Goodland, Robert J. A. and H. S. Irwin
  1975   Amazon Jungle: Green Hell to Red Desert?
          Amsterdam: Elsevier.

Hames, Raymond B. and William T. Vickers
  1982   Optimal Diet Breadth Theory as a Model to
          Explain Variability in Amazonian Hunting.
          American Ethnologist 9(2):358-378.

Hardenburg, Walter E.
    1912   The Putumayo, The Devil's Paradise: Travels in
           the Peruvian Amazon Region and an Account of
           the Atrocities Committed upon the Indians
           Therein. London: T. Fisher Unwin.

Harner, Michael J.
    1972   The Jívaro: People of the Sacred Waterfalls.
           Garden City, New York: Doubleday/Natural History
           Press.

Hemming, John
    1978   Red Gold: The Conquest of the Brazilian Indians.
           Cambridge, Mass.: Harvard Univ. Press.

Langdon, E. Jean
    1974   The Siona Medical System: Beliefs and Behavior.
           Ph.D. dissertation, Anthropology Department,
           Tulane Univ.

Lathrap, Donald W.
    1970   The Upper Amazon. New York: Praeger.

Lernoux, Penny
    1981   The Great Brazilian Land Grab. Inquiry,
           February 2, 1981:17-21.

Lewis, Norman
    1974   Genocide. In Supysáua: A Documentary Report on
           the Conditions of Indian Peoples in Brazil.
           Berkeley, Calif.: Indigena, Inc., and American
           Friends of Brazil.

Macdonald, Theodore Jr.
    1981   Indigenous Response to an Expanding Frontier:
           Jungle Quichua Economic Conversion to Cattle
           Ranching. In N. E. Whitten, Jr., ed., Cultural
           Transformations and Ethnicity in Modern Ecuador.
           Urbana: Univ. of Illinois Press.

Mahar, Dennis J.
    1979   Frontier Development Policy in Brazil: A Study
           of Amazonia. New York: Praeger.

McDaniel, John M., William Harris, Jr., and Solomon H. Katz
    1979   Effects of Behavioral and Ecological Variations
           upon the Incidence of Parasitic Disease Among
           la Gente de Concepción, Peru. In D. L. Browman
           and R. A. Schwartz, eds., Spirits, Shamans, and
           Stars: Perspectives from South America. The
           Hague: Mouton.

Mondolfi, Edgardo
  1973   La Danta o Anta (Tapirus terrestris). Su
         Importancia como Animal Silvícola y Posibilidades
         de su Cría en Cautividad. Paper given at
         Simposio Internacional Sobre Fauna Silvestre,
         Manaus, Nov. 26-Dec. 1.

Moran, Emilio F.
  1975   Pioneer Farmers of the Transamazon Highway:
         Adaptation and Agricultural Production in the
         Lowland Tropics. Ph.D. dissertation, Dept. of
         Anthropology, Univ. of Florida.

  1981   Developing the Amazon. Bloomington: Indiana
         Press.

Nelson, Michael
  1973   The Development of Tropical Lands: Policy Issues
         in Latin America. Baltimore: Johns Hopkins
         Univ. Press.

Phelan, John Leddy
  1967   The Kingdom of Quito in the Seventeenth
         Century: Bureaucratic Politics in the Spanish
         Empire. Madison: Univ. of Wisconsin Press.

Piccinini, R., W. Vale, and F. W. Gomes
  1971   Criadouros Artificiais de Animais Silvestres.
         I. Criadouro de Capivaras. Belém: Superinten-
         dência do Desenvolvimento da Amazônia (SUDAM).

Pinto, L. A.
  1973   As Doenças da Amazônia. Opinião (Rio de
         Janeiro), Dec. 17.

Ramos, Alcida R. and Kenneth I. Taylor
  1979   The Yanoama in Brazil. International Work Group
         for Indigenous Affairs Document No. 37.
         Copenhagen.

Reichel-Dolmatoff, Gerardo
  1971   Amazonian Cosmos: The Sexual and Religious
         Symbolism of the Tukano Indians. Chicago:
         Univ. of Chicago Press.

Ribeiro, Darcy
  1967   Indigenous Cultures and Languages of Brazil.
         In J. H. Hopper, ed., Indians of Brazil in the
         Twentieth Century. ICR Studies 2, Washington,
         D.C.: Institute for Cross-Cultural Research.

Robinson, Scott S.
  1972   El Etnocidio Ecuatoriano. Mexico, D.F.:
         Universidad Iberoamericana.

Salazar, Ernesto
 1977   An Indian Federation in Lowland Ecuador. Inter-
        national Work Group for Indigenous Affairs
        Document No. 28. Copenhagen.

Schreider, Helen and Frank Schreider
 1970   Exploring the Amazon. Washington, D.C.:
        National Geographic Society.

Smith, Nigel J.H.
 1976   Brazil's Transamazon Settlement Scheme:
        Agrovilas, Agropoli, and Ruropoli. Association
        of American Geographers Proceedings 8:129-132.

 1981   Colonization Lessons from a Tropical Forest.
        Science 214:755-761.

Smole, William J.
 1976   The Yanoama Indians. Austin: Univ. of Texas
        Press.

Steward, Julian H.
 1948   Western Tucanoan Tribes. In J. H. Steward, ed.,
        Handbook of South American Indians. Vol. 3.
        The Tropical Forest Tribes. Washington, D.C.:
        U.S. Govt. Printing Office.

 1949   The Native Population of South America. In
        J. H. Steward, ed., Handbook of South American
        Indians. Vol. 5. Anthropology of South American
        Indians. Washington, D.C.: U.S. Govt. Printing
        Office.

Uquillas, Jorge, ed.
 1979   La Problemática Socio-cultural de la Amazonía
        Ecuatoriana. Quito: Instituto Nacional de
        Colonización de la Región Amazónica Ecuatoriana
        (INCRAE), Ministerio de Agricultura y Ganadería.

Vickers, William T.
 1972   Indians, Oil, and Colonists: Contrasting Systems
        of Man-Land Relations in the Aguarico River
        Valley of Eastern Ecuador. Univ. of Florida
        Center for Latin American Studies. Latin-
        americanist 8(2):1-3.

 1976   Cultural Adaptation to Amazonian Habitats:
        The Siona-Secoya of Eastern Ecuador. Ph.D.
        dissertation, Dept. of Anthropology, Univ. of
        Florida.

 1979   Native Amazonian Subsistence in Diverse Habitats:
        The Siona-Secoya of Eastern Ecuador. Studies
        in Third World Societies 7:6-36.

1980   _Proyecto Limitación de Territorios Nativos_.
Quito: Instituto Nacional de Colonización de la
Región Amazónica Ecuatoriana (INCRAE), Instituto
Ecuatoriano de Reforma Agraria y Colonización
(IERAC), y Dirección de Desarrollo Forestal.
Unpublished report.

1981   Ideation as Adaptation: Traditional Belief and
Modern Intervention in Siona-Secoya Religion.
In N. E. Whitten, Jr., ed., _Cultural Transforma-
tions and Ethnicity in Modern Ecuador_. Urbana:
Univ. of Illinois Press.

Vreugdenhil, Daniel
1978   _Inventario de las Áreas Silvestres de la Cuenca
Amazónica Ecuatoriana_. Quito: Dirección General
de Desarrollo Forestal, Ministerio de
Agricultura y Ganadería.

Wagley, Charles
1964   _Amazon Town: A Study of Man in the Tropics_.
New York: Knopf.

1977   _Welcome of Tears: The Tapirapé Indians of Central
Brazil_. New York: Oxford Univ. Press.

Whitten, Norman E., Jr.
1978   _Amazonian Ecuador: An Ethnic Interface in
Ecological, Social, and Ideological Perspectives_.
International Work Group for Indigenous Affairs
Document No. 34. Copenhagen.

Wood, Charles H. and Marianne Schmink
1979   Blaming the Victim: Small Farmer Production in
an Amazon Colonization Project. _Studies in
Third World Societies_ 7:77-93.

World Council of Churches
1972   _The Present Situation of the South American
Indians_. Geneva: World Council of Churches.

Yost, James
1981   Twenty Years of Contact: The Mechanisms of
Change in Wao ("Auca") Culture. In N. E.
Whitten, Jr., ed., _Cultural Transformations and
Ethnicity in Modern Ecuador_. Urbana: Univ. of
Illinois Press.

3
Forest to Pasture: Frontier Settlement in the Bolivian Lowlands

Allyn MacLean Stearman

INTRODUCTION

For those Latin American countries that include portions of the Amazon Basin within their boundaries, development of this vast wilderness area has become a national imperative. The crowded coastal areas of Brazil, the demographic pressures of the Andean nations, a disenfranchised and poverty-stricken peasantry have all contributed to the prevalent belief that the Amazon represents a panacea for the socioeconomic ills of much of South America. The eagerness of governments and multinational corporations to exploit this territory has been met by a relatively ineffective counteroffensive to moderate, control, direct, or even halt the changes that are now taking place. Researchers such as Allan Holmberg (1950), Edwin Brooks (1973), Shelton Davis (1977), and others have documented the apparently inevitable cultural extinction of Amazonian aborigines. Betty Meggers (1971), William Denevan (1973), George Woodwell (1978), and Gómez-Pompa et al. (1972) are only a few of the scholars who have contributed knowledge and speculation on the agricultural potential of the Amazon Basin and the effects that massive clearing of the forest canopy may have on the world environment. It is unfortunate, however, that most efforts to present alternatives to the total destruction of this great wilderness have gone unheeded by those who have the power to halt the process. Part of the problem lies in the fact that most of the Third World has little else to exploit but its nonrenewable natural resources. To the unstable governments now in power in the regions encompassing the Amazon, short-term benefits look very good. Then too, the United States did precisely the same thing in its expansion into its western territories. It is rather chilling to reflect on the parallels between the two cases. Our perhaps overly romanticized history of "How the West Was Won" has in itself been a great incentive for others to try it again--this time throughout lowland South America.

Bolivia is among those many nations that have begun their push into the Amazon Basin. Although most of the country's 5 million people reside in the highlands, 70% of the national territory is located in the lowlands (Arze Cuadros 1979). In 1952, Bolivia underwent a major social revolution that was to radically alter the old social order and develop new national imperatives. Nationalization of tin mining operations and expropriation of hacienda lands were swiftly accomplished by the new revolutionary administration of Victor Paz Estenssoro. Nevertheless, elation over initial government public control of land and industry was soon dampened by some unexpected negative repercussions. Removal of private control of the mining industry resulted in administrative deficiencies and loss of technological expertise. Additionally, political patronage in the mining sector supported featherbedding, increasing the mining labor rolls from a pre-revolution figure of 24,000 to 36,558 in 1956. In spite of the increased labor pool, production from the three largest tin mines dropped from 34,660 tons in 1949 to 15,000 tons in 1961 (Zondag 1968). The mines were operating consistently in the red, draining the national economy rather than contributing to it.

The land situation in the Bolivian highlands was also worsening. With the expropriation of hacienda lands and their redistribution to the peasantry under the Agrarian Reform Law of 1953, minifundia (i.e., tiny land parcels) were developing in certain areas of the nation. In the Cochabamba Valley, for example, the average peasant was awarded less than 1.8 hectares of farmland. Early post-revolution economic reports indicated that agricultural production appeared to have dropped as well, although it was ascertained later that more food was now being con-sumed at the farmstead. The result was a reduction in the amount of marketed produce (Clark 1968).

In an effort to offset demographic pressures being experienced in the highlands, the Bolivian government secured international loans from the United States, West Germany, and the Interamerican Development Bank to begin colonization of its lowland territories. The plan was to resettle highland miners and landless peasants in the vast Amazon region east of the Andes in an attempt to resolve the problems of economic stress in the mines and scarcity of farmland. It was hoped that opening the lowlands for settlement would serve two additional functions: to increase agricultural production and to integrate the historically isolated and semiautonomous lowland popula-tion into the national sphere.

Three zones in the Bolivian Amazon were designated for settlement: the Alto Beni, east of the national capital, La Paz; the Chapare, east of Cochabamba; and the Yapacaní, northwest of the lowland city of Santa Cruz. The particular areas selected for government-sponsored settlement indicated other motives that contributed to the

surge of interest in colonization. The three zones did
not represent the prime arable land of the lowlands, and
all were relatively isolated from market centers. However,
they were situated in regions that held promise of
extensive hardwood tracts, oil, and mineral deposits.

STABILITY OF SETTLEMENTS

The early years of the new colonies were marked by
tremendous hardship. Many settlers chose to abandon their
parcels and return to the highlands. The most frequent
complaints by colonists included illness, isolation, lack
of schools, and lack of all-weather market access
(Stearman 1973; Zierten 1971; Wiggins 1976). As roads
and bridges eventually were completed, the quality of
life improved and other highlanders moved in to take up
the land left by their predecessors. In recent years,
government involvement in land settlement has slackened
primarily as a result of the poor cost-benefit ratio of
such programs. The original Interamerican Development
Bank proposal was to settle 8,000-10,000 families in the
lowlands over a ten-year period. By 1969 only 4,984
families had been settled, but 95% of the $9.1 million
loan had been expended (IDB 1970). Then, too, economic
expansion during the 1970s, particularly in the Santa
Cruz region, brought about a wave of spontaneous settlement by highlanders seeking escape from the stagnating
highland economy.
    At present, the National Colonization Institute is
involved in only one major colonization effort, San
Julián. This involvement is only peripheral, however,
since a multinational interdenominational church group has
been contracted to organize and implement the settlement
process. In an effort to avoid many of the problems
experienced in the older colonies, this group has initiated
several innovative programs including a three-month
orientation for each settler. (For a discussion of this
program see Stearman 1980.)
    One of the most serious problems reported in most of
the colonization projects is that of excessively high
abandonment rates, averaging over 40%, but going much
higher during the initial settlement period (Henkel 1978;
Wiggins 1976). The single exception is San Julián with
only a 20% rate during the first three years, perhaps a
testimonial to the efficacy of the orientation program
(AID-PES 1978). Nonetheless, much of the frustration
experienced by colonization agency personnel working in
new land settlements can be attributed to this traditional
emphasis on stable populations as measurements of success.
This frequent emphasis on stabilizing initial settlers
on the land can be attributed to a lack of understanding
by many observers of the true role colonization plays in
lowland frontier expansion. My research in lowland
Bolivia since 1964 indicates that colonization is only an

intermediate stage in Amazonian development, and to expect
the majority of settlers to remain permanently in these
areas is a contradiction of the expansion process itself.
Colonization in most instances is simply a catalyst; it
precipitates a series of events that are soon beyond the
control of the settler and ultimately even beyond control
of the colonization agency involved (Ortiz 1980; Barbira-
Scazzocchio 1980; Moran 1981).

In lowland Bolivia, land allotments to colonists have
ranged from 10 to 50 hectares. The smaller allotments
were increased after it was realized that small parcels
contributed to population instability (H. Peacock, personal
communication, 1975). Those settlers with only 10 to 20
hectares of land very quickly used up their virgin forest
and found themselves caught in what Simon Maxwell (1979)
aptly terms the "barbecho crisis." The Bolivian lowlands
are situated somewhat more fortunately for settlers than
much of the Amazon Basin, in that they encompass a large
alluvial plain between the Andes to the west and the
Brazilian shield to the east. Hence, the soils tend to
be heavier and more suited to agriculture than is typical
for much of the basin (Cochrane 1973). Even so, fertility
drops significantly after two to four years of cropping
because the high rainfall in many areas leaches and erodes
the soil (Henkel 1978; Nelson 1973). Lack of soil
fertility, however, is only one cause for abandonment
of farmland. Once the forest cover has been removed,
weeds and shrubs are quick to take advantage of the
open space. This second growth is what Bolivians call
"barbecho," and what they find themselves technologically
incapable of combating. Using traditional methods of
slash-and-burn horticulture, the peasant is soon overcome
by weed invasions that sap the strength from his crops
and require continual labor to control. Within a short
time, the cultivation of barbecho land simply does not
pay. Even worse, because there are large natural grasslands in some areas of eastern Bolivia, it is likely
that grass eventually will invade the colonists' cleared
land, rendering any subsequent traditional farming an
impossibility. There are effectively two options available: first, convert to mechanization, which, for a
time at least, makes farming second-growth land cost-
effective; or second, let natural grasses encroach or plant
improved pasture, and gradually convert to beef or dairy
cattle. Because there is little thought given to rotating
crops and thus conserving fertility, much of the land
presently under plow will eventually end up as pasture
in an effort to make the land commercially viable. It
should also be noted that either avenue requires substantial capitalization. Both machinery and livestock
represent significant financial investments for the
peasant who finds himself faced with the barbecho
crisis. If his parcel size is 50 ha, the crisis will be
postponed a bit but inevitably will come. Those few

colonists who have been successful in managing their
affairs find themselves able to make the necessary investments to move on to the next agricultural stage--
mechanization, cattle, or a combination of both. Those
who are not so fortunate must abandon their land to go
even farther in search of new wilderness. The "worthless"
land they leave behind is quickly acquired by their more
successful neighbors who consolidate it into their own
holdings. As both cattle ranching and large-implement
mechanized agriculture require land-extensive operations
to be cost-effective, the abandonment of farmland is
necessary for this expansion process.

For most colonists, then, their future as small
farmers is locked into shifting agriculture. Without
capital to meet the barbecho crisis, most settlers move
on to cut down more virgin forest, crop it for a few
years, and then sell out to those who can mechanize or
buy livestock.

The instability of market prices, which results
largely from ineffective government stabilization programs, has also contributed to the overwhelming desire
of all agriculturalists, small and large, to go into
cattle. Meat prices are continually on the rise and
there remains a shortage of milk and milk products. Many
farmers regard cattle as bank accounts, money on the hoof,
savings that will not disappear because of late rains,
insects, low prices, no transportation, no storage
facilities, or lack of harvest labor. Thus, even as
the colonist clears land for crops, he is likely to be
interested ultimately in ranching.

Because the lowlands still hold hundreds of thousands
of hectares of wilderness there is very little concern
about making the best use of the land that is under
cultivation or in pasture. As previously mentioned, crop
rotation is virtually unknown, partly because few
nitrogen-fixing crops have market value in Bolivia.
Soybeans show promise, but because they are not a crop
conducive to hand-harvesting they offer little hope for
the small farmer. A good example of typical land-use
practices in lowland Bolivia is the cotton boom of the
1970s, which created a wasteland of large areas in the
department of Santa Cruz. Monocropping cotton on extensive contiguous fields recreated the same ecological
disaster that occurred in the San Joaquin Valley near
Bakersfield, California, in the late 1960s (Rodale 1978).
New strains of pesticide-resistant insects developed
that could not be controlled. In the Bolivian situation,
however, the land was simply abandoned, unlike in
California where new technology came to the rescue.
In 1975, Bolivia was cropping cotton on 60,000 hectares
of land. As of 1978 this had dropped to less than
31,000 hectares (Cordecruz 1979). Much of this land
has now been devastated by severe wind erosion, a
continual and growing problem in the southern region of

the lowlands. Wind erosion is not normally associated
with humid tropical regions. The southern region of
Santa Cruz, however, is a transitional zone, bordering
on the flat, dry chaco of Argentina and Paraguay.
Strong winds continually blow into Santa Cruz, raising
dust storms that make life miserable for everyone for
days at a time. As more land is cleared, erosion increases and the winds begin to reach into areas formerly
safe from their scouring force. It is now a practice in
many areas to leave strips of forest as windbreaks, but
once the land is cleared, even these precautions do
little to protect the land from losing moisture. Inter-
views with older area residents have indicated that parts
of the chaco desert have encroached into areas previously
forested. Thus, it would appear that the deforestation
of certain regions of Bolivia not only may create grasslands but also may alter normal humidity patterns as well
(Goodland and Irwin 1975). The 1980 report to the U.S.
President on the world's tropical forest lends credence
to this observation:

> Consequences of large-scale tropical deforestation
> include changes in local climate. Once the forest
> canopy is removed, surface temperatures become
> more extreme, hotter by day and colder by night.
> Where widespread deforestation occurs, regional
> rainfall patterns also may be affected, although
> this possible effect is another of the many
> poorly understood features of deforestation
> (U.S. Department of State 1980:19).

DEFORESTATION AND COLONIZATION

In terms of its forest resources, Bolivia has
followed other nations in setting aside by legislative
decree certain portions of forest designated as reserves
(Cordecruz 1979). These national forests are subject to
exploitation, however, through the ceding of cutting
rights to individuals or corporations (Hinojosa and
Pedrazas 1974). The illegal extraction of wood from
forest reserves is also a problem due to the government's
inability to police these areas (Cordecruz 1979).
The cutting of hardwoods is a selective process that
does not have as a result the immediate ecological and
esthetic damage created by clear-cutting single-species
forests in temperate climates. Still, the long-term
damage may be just as devastating. Reforestation programs in Bolivia are poorly funded and remain in an
experimental stage. Sporadic attempts by extension
agents to replant hardwoods are insignificant compared to
extraction rates. Hardwoods such as mahogany do not grow
in stands, but are sparsely distributed with perhaps as
few as three mature trees per square kilometer. As a
result, natural reseeding occurs only on a limited basis.

In addition, most species of hardwoods are not adapted to disturbance conditions and their seeds do not possess qualities for long-range dispersal (Gómez-Pompa et al. 1972). As a result there is growing fear that many hardwoods may disappear.

Bolivian forestry statistics on hardwood cutting show better than a 100% increase in production between 1970 and 1978, from 22,726,516 square feet to 52,295,144 (Cordecruz 1979). Although the official figures are strong indicators of the rate at which logging is occurring, they tell only part of the story. Perhaps the most revealing "data" are those that remain conjectural: Many observers are convinced that as much wood is being exported illegally as reported legally each year. Current logging patterns also are good indicators of how quickly the Bolivian forests are being depleted of hardwoods, especially mahogany. In 1965, hardwoods were being cut at a radius of about 80 km from the lowland capital, Santa Cruz. As of 1980, logging crews were traveling distances of over 300 km to find mahogany. One government official estimated that by the year 2000 there would be no hardwoods of cutting size left in the entire lowland region of Bolivia.

The side effects of logging also ultimately spell doom for virgin forests. The cutting of valuable hardwoods will eventually deplete certain species, but the majority of the forest is left standing. Once a logging trail is cut, however, so that trucks or other means of transport are able to penetrate the wilderness, it is not long before spontaneous settlers take advantage of available land. In effect, these spontaneous colonists have no legal right to be on the land they are clearing for crops. To date, the Bolivian government has been unable, and to some degree unwilling, to prevent these invasions. The attitude of most officials is that the wilderness is there to convert to cropland and pasture. If colonists want to do this work on their own initiative, it simply saves cattle ranchers the time and expense of clearing the land at a later date. Royden and Wennergren (1973) have noted that the cost of preparing abandoned farmland for pasture is half that of clearing virgin forest.

Once a large tract of land has been colonized by numerous settlers, their population density precludes any further thought of trying to remove them. This type of land invasion and subsequent government inability to deal with de facto settlements has many precedents, both rural and urban. Probably the best known case in the United States was the illegal settlement of land in Oklahoma by pioneers who became known as "Sooners," people who in order to gain choice locations invaded government land before it was legally opened to settlers. In Lima, Peru, Mangin (1970), Turner (1970) and others have described the process whereby urban migrants move

onto government or private land on the outskirts of the
city and claim squatter's rights. For most governments
in these situations, the removal of illegal settlers becomes politically untenable and the squatters are usually
allowed to remain. In the case of spontaneous colonists
in the Amazon, the point of removing them to preserve
wilderness areas is moot. Once enough people are in an
area to arouse official concern, the likelihood is that
there is not much forest left to save.

   With regard to government-planned agricultural
colonies, the selection of suitable land for settlement
in eastern Bolivia has been influenced to some extent
by timber resources. The Bolivian government has
determined that it is difficult to negotiate development
loans for extractive purposes. Because it is less
difficult to receive funding for the resettlement of highland people, colonization becomes a means for securing
monies for building roads in areas that demonstrate
promise in terms of hardwoods. It is also significant
that to date colonists do not have legal rights to the
timber on their own land. These rights are ceded to
logging companies that pay fees to the government for
timber contracts. Settlers greatly resent this loss of
immediate income and have in turn begun to negotiate with
timber "pirates" who cut the colonists' hardwoods before
the contractors arrive. The result has been an outbreak
of violence in some colonization areas (H. Peacock, personal communication, 1978). Once again it is the peasant
who becomes the expendable factor in the development
process.

CONCLUSIONS

   The settlement process that has been outlined in the
preceding pages and the social, economic, and environmental factors that impact land use are found to some
degree in most of tropical Latin America. As yet, however, the Bolivian Amazon has not attracted the interest
of multinational corporations to the extent found in
Brazil. Bolivia's long history of political instability
and its lack of sufficient incentives for investment no
doubt have contributed to the relative lack of foreign
interest in land. Although Bolivia does not find its
forests threatened by projects such as Daniel Keith
Ludwig's 3.5 million acre Jari Forestry and Ranching
project, with its workers deforesting an average of
12,500 acres of land each year (Davis 1980), the ultimate
outcome may be the same. In 1979, Brazilian Congressman
Hélio Duque of the state of Paraná claimed that recent
INCRA (Instituto Nacional de Colonização e Reforma Agrária)
data indicated that foreigners may own perhaps as much as
10% of Brazil (Perkins 1979). Much of this land has been
purchased for speculation and remains uncleared at
present. Nonetheless, it cannot be overlooked that the

commercialization of agriculture by agribusiness has displaced thousands of small-scale agriculturalists who look to the frontier for hope. Although much of the blame for the clearing of large tracts of Brazilian forest and their conversion to pasture or interim crops has been justifiably placed on multinationals, the peasant will also contribute significantly to this threat. The conversion of forest to pasture, or the commercialization of land occupied by the slash-and-burn horticulturalist, inexorably pushes the subsistence agriculturalist farther into the wilderness. As the frontier reaches its ultimate limits in each nation, the peasantry will have no more wilderness to exploit. Governments will then be forced to deal with masses of unemployed persons without the convenient alternative of pioneering.

In Bolivia, there is mounting concern that the effects of the 1953 Agrarian Reform Law may be nullified as more land is consolidated into large holdings for commercial agriculture. The old patterns of elite patrons holding most of the available farmland, with an indentured peasant labor force, may come full cycle as mechanization and ranching begin to expand. In addition, natural population increase is likely to continue to stress available land resources. It is not the individual farmer in Bolivia, Brazil, or elsewhere who is the wrong-doer: Shifting horticulture under low-density populations has been shown to be an excellent means of allowing forest regeneration (Clark 1976; Nations and Nigh 1978). The problem is that low-density populations of indigenous peoples are giving way to thousands of peasants in search of land and opportunity. It is doubtful that government or international agencies will be willing or able to control the tide of humanity seeking its future on the Amazon frontier.

A recent article in Science News (Raloff and Silberner 1980:218-221) points out that 90% of world population growth in the next 20 years is expected to occur in the tropics, a prediction that if true can only lead to greater pressure to exploit the tropical forests. When development of the Amazon is considered as a regional process crosscutting national boundaries, and not as a problem inherent to any one country, the forecast for the future of the entire Amazon Basin is grim. Every nation that encompasses portions of the basin is contributing perhaps only a few hundred hectares a day to the demise of the forest, but the cumulative effect is staggering. It can only be hoped that the prediction of the U.S. National Research Council's 1980 report on tropical biology will not be fully realized: that the forests "will be reduced to scattered degraded remnants on steep slopes, to severely flooded delta areas, and to a few parks and reserves" (Raloff and Silberner 1980).

REFERENCES

AID-PES
1978   Project Evaluation Summary: San Julián.
        La Paz: Agency for International Development
        (AID)-Project Evaluation Summary. Mimeo.

Arze Cuadros, E.
1979   La Economía de Bolivia. La Paz: Los Amigos
        del Libro.

Barbira-Scazzocchio, François, ed.
1980   Land, People, and Planning in Contemporary
        Amazônia. Cambridge, UK: Cambridge Univ.
        Centre of Latin American Studies, Occasional
        Publ. 3.

Brooks, E.
1973   Twilight of Brazilian Tribes. Geographical
        Magazine 45(4):304-310.

Clark, R. J.
1968   Land Reform and Peasant Market Participation
        on the North Highlands of Bolivia. Land
        Economics 44:153-172.

Clark, W. C.
1976   Maintenance of Agriculture and Human Habitats
        within the Tropical Forest Ecosystem. Human
        Ecology 4(3):247-259.

Cochrane, T. T.
1973   El Potencial Agrícola del Uso de la Tierra en
        Bolivia. Misión Británica en Agricultura
        Tropical. La Paz: Ministerio de Agricultura.

Cordecruz (Corporación Regional de Desarrollo de Santa
Cruz)
1979   Diagnóstico Coyuntural: La Crisis Agropecuaria
        Regional y Sugerencias de una Nueva Política
        Económica Para el Sector. Santa Cruz, Bolivia:
        Unidad de Planificación Regional.

Davis, Shelton H.
1977   Victims of the Miracle: Development and the
        Indians of Brazil. New York: Cambridge Univ.
        Press.

1980   Ludwig's Castle: Built on Sand? Multinational
        Monitor 1(4):8-10, 21.

Denevan, William M.
1973   Development and the Imminent Demise of the
        Amazon Rain Forest. Professional Geographer

25(2):130-135.

Gómez-Pompa, A., C. Vázquez-Yañes, and S. Guevara
1972　The Tropical Rain Forest: A Nonrenewable Resource? Science 177:762-765.

Goodland, Robert J.A. and H. S. Irwin
1975　Amazon Jungle: Green Hell to Red Desert?
Amsterdam: Elsevier.

Henkel, R.
1978　The Move to the Oriente: Colonization and
Environmental Impact. In Proceedings, Conference
on Modern Day Bolivia, Mar. 15-17, pp. 1-46.
Tempe: Arizona State Univ.

Hinojosa, G. and H. A. Pedrazas
1974　Producción de Maderas en Bosques Naturales de
Santa Cruz. Ministerio de Asuntos Campesinos y
Agropecuarios. Dirección Deparmental.
Distrito de Recursos Naturales Renovables.

Holmberg, A.
1950　Nomads of the Longbow. New York: Natural
History Press.

IDB
1970　Tenth Annual Report, 1969. Washington, D.C.:
Interamerican Development Bank.

Mangin, W., ed.
1970　Peasants in Cities. Boston: Houghton Mifflin.

Maxwell, Simon
1979　Colonos Marginalizados al Norte de Santa Cruz:
Avenidas de Escape de la Crisis del Barbecho.
Doc. de Trabajo:4. Cali: Centro Internacional
de Agricultura Tropical (CIAT).

Meggers, Betty J.
1971　Amazônia: Man and Culture in a Counterfeit
Paradise. Chicago: Aldine.

Moran, Emilio F.
1981　Developing the Amazon. Bloomington: Indiana
Univ. Press.

Nations, J. D. and R. Nigh
1978　Cattle, Cash, Food and Forest: The Destruction
of the American Tropics and the Lacandon Maya
Alternative. Culture and Agriculture 6:1-5.

62

Nelson, Michael
    1973   The Development of Tropical Lands: Policy Issues
            in Latin America. Baltimore: Johns Hopkins Univ.
            Press.

Ortiz, S.
    1980   The Transformation of Guaviare in Colombia:
            Immigrating Peasants and Their Struggles. In
            F. Barbira-Scazzocchio, ed., Land, People, and
            Planning in Contemporary Amazônia. Cambridge,
            UK: Cambridge Univ. Centre of Latin American
            Studies, Occasional Publ. 3.

Perkins, P.
    1979   Multinationals in Brazilian Agricultural
            Production. Unpublished paper presented at a
            conference on Brazil, Latin American Studies
            Center, Univ. of California at Los Angeles
            (UCLA).

Raloff, J. and J. Silberner
    1980   Saving the Amazon. Science News 118(14):218-221.

Rodale, R.
    1978   The Chemicals Keep Coming. In Rodefeld et al.,
            eds., Change in Rural America, pp. 240-242.
            St. Louis: C. V. Mosby.

Royden, T. C. and E. B. Wennergren
    1973   The Impact of Access Roads on Spontaneous
            Colonization. La Paz: UTAH-Agency for
            International Development (AID).

Stearman, Allyn MacLean
    1973   Colonization in Eastern Bolivia: Problems and
            Prospects. Human Organization 32(3):285-293.

    1980   San Julián--Bolivia's Newest Experiment in
            Colonization. El Dorado 4(1):28-54.

Turner, J.
    1970   Barriers and Channels for Housing Development
            in Modernizing Countries. In E. Mangin, ed.,
            Peasants in Cities. Boston: Houghton Mifflin.

U.S. Department of State
    1980   Report to the President by a U.S. Interagency
            Task Force on Tropical Forests. Washington,
            D.C.: International Organization and Conference
            Series 145.

Wiggins, S.
    1976   Colonización en Bolivia. 2a ed. Sucre:
            Acción Cultural Loyola.

Woodwell, G.
   1978   The Carbon Dioxide Question. <u>Scientific</u>
           <u>American</u> 231(1):34-43.

Zierten, F.
   1971   <u>Colonización</u> <u>en</u> <u>Bolivia</u>. Montero, Bolivia.
           Mimeo.

Zondag, C.
   1968   <u>La</u> <u>Economía</u> <u>Boliviana</u>: <u>1952-1965</u>. <u>La</u> <u>Revolución</u>
           <u>y</u> <u>Sus</u> <u>Consequencias</u>. La Paz: Los Amigos del
           Libro.

4
Entrepreneurs and Bureaucrats: The Rise of an Urban Middle Class

Darrel Miller

INTRODUCTION

Significant changes have occurred following the construction of Brazil's Transamazon Highway. These changes have meant benefits for some but not for others. In large part, the goals set forth in the original development and colonization plan have not been met. The plan, called the National Plan of Integration, was initiated in 1970 and seemed to offer something for everyone--small farms for the poor, tax incentives for wealthy investors, and a nationalistic goal of bringing Brazil's least developed region into step with the "economic miracle." One group was little mentioned in the plan but has proven to be a major benefactor of the highway--the middle class. This article examines the urbanization of a small Amazon town and the concomitant growth of an urban middle class.[1]

The municipio (i.e., county) of Itaituba lies in the southwestern corner of the State of Pará. It is the county seat and largest urban center of the Upper Tapajós River Basin. From a sleepy Amazon village in the 1960s, Itaituba has grown rapidly and without the benefit of planning throughout the 1970s. Because the communities that lay in the path of the new highway were hardly mentioned in the original colonization plan, the rapid urbanization of Itaituba was almost totally unexpected.

Communities like Itaituba were to serve as staging areas for roadbuilding and colonization activities, and only later, with further "development," begin to serve as Ruropoli (Kleinpenning 1975:105). However, these communities proved to be population magnets from the very beginning. Itaituba has the appearance of a boom town, reminiscent of frontier towns in the North American West. The streets are as yet unpaved, but they have been graded and extended to accommodate the constant automobile and truck traffic that creates clouds of dust hanging over the city. New neighborhoods on the outskirts of the city expand daily. Water, sewer, and 24-hour electric service are available. A new hospital, post office, and several schools have been built. New businesses spring up each week. Government offices of all sorts dot the main streets. Air, land, and water transportation are available on a regular, daily, or weekly basis. All of this represents marked changes from 1970, before the Transamazon Highway.

The urban population of the município grew from 2,000 in 1970 to over 12,000 in 1977. A significant portion of this growth is due to the development of an urban middle class. In 1970, for example, the middle and upper-middle classes constituted 4.6% of the population, but in 1977, 20%. The focus of this article, then, will be on the impact of the Transamazon project on social class, especially the growth of an urban middle class, but also on the lack of benefits for the lower classes.

In many respects, lack of benefits for the poor is a common criticism of development projects in Brazil and elsewhere. Forman (1975:84) notes that the commercialization and industrialization of rural areas in Brazil in general have opened up new opportunities, but these new opportunities "have been taken by commercial elites and few real benefits have accrued to the rural peasantry." He goes on to suggest that the creation of a new national middle class in rural areas certainly represents a change, but it should not be construed as a restructuring of rural Brazilian society (see Moran, Chapter 1 in this volume).

The conclusions presented by Forman and those of this article are similar. The poor, indeed, benefit little from the massive federal investment in the Amazon. Invoking the Law of Cultural Dominance (Sahlins and Service 1960), one would have seen from the beginning that it could not have been otherwise. The upper and middle classes simply had too many resources at their disposal. Dominant cultures "exploit more different kinds of resources more effectively than lower; hence in most environments, they are more effective than lower; thus their greater range" (Sahlins and Service 1960:77). On the Transamazon, political, social, and economic pressures advanced the dominant type (i.e., the upper and middle classes). The remainder of this article will examine some of the causes and results of this process.

AMAZON ECONOMY AND HIGHWAY DEVELOPMENT

The Brazilian Amazon accounts for over 42% of Brazil's land area but less than 4% of its population, according to the 1970 census. As with other regions of Brazil, the economic history of the Amazon has been characterized by a series of booms and busts caused mainly by fluctuations of world price and demand for raw materials. The most important extractive product from the Amazon was formerly rubber, which fueled the Amazon's

economy from the last decades of the nineteenth century
until the bust of 1912 when the British began marketing
less expensive rubber from their Asian rubber plantations
(Burns 1970:245).

Except for a minor boom in rubber during World War
II, the Amazon remained Brazil's economic and social
backwater until the 1960s. A resurgence of interest
began in the Amazon with completion of a highway linking
the principal city at the mouth of the Amazon, Belém,
with the federal capital, Brasília, in 1960 (Kleinpenning
1975:42). Ten years later, in response to a disastrous
drought in the populous northeastern region of the
country, President Médici announced the National Plan of
Integration. One of the major components of the plan was
a vast highway network and colonization plan for the
Amazon. The keystone of the plan, the 5,400 km Transamazon Highway, would open up the vast Amazon tropical
rain forest to settlers from the drought-stricken northeast. The plan also included huge tax incentives for
investments in the Amazon and the formation of a new
federal agency, the Brazilian Institute of Colonization
and Agrarian Reform (INCRA), which would distribute land
and oversee the settlement of colonists.[2]

By 1976 it was evident that the plan had not
succeeded. The colonization, funded by large infusions
of public money, failed to relocate vast numbers of
northeasterners. Instead, many southern Brazilians
flocked to the region in addition to the northeasterners.
Their food crops proved impractical due to poor soils
and an underdeveloped transportation network (Katzman
1976). Other researchers feel that a lack of planning
for social services and institutional support was the
principal reason for problems that developed (Moran 1975;
Robock 1975). Eventually, the strategy of Amazonian
development changed from settlement of small farmers to
capital-intensive projects by large corporations in the
areas of livestock, mining, and extractive agriculture--
a familiar pattern for the Amazon (Katzman 1976; Wood and
Schmink 1979). Indeed, the Second National Plan of
Integration (1975-1979) fails to even mention the Transamazon project. Instead, it relies on the formation of
development poles that emphasize the aforementioned capital-
intensive projects.

These circumstances have been described in a number
of studies that focus on the agricultural sector and
colonization aspects of the Transamazon project (cf.
Moran 1975, 1981; Smith 1976; Wood and Schmink 1979). In
contrast, the subject of this article is an Amazonian
urban community. It should surprise no one that the
conclusions drawn from the data indicate that growth has
occurred, but with little or no development. What the
data reveal is not only remarkable urban population growth
associated with the Transamazon project but also a
concomitant expansion of the urban middle classes.

ITAITUBA: THE PRE-HIGHWAY PERIOD

Prior to the early 1970s when highway construction
began, Itaituba was no more than a small river village.
The major reason for its existence was its location below
the last set of rapids on the Tapajós River, which made
it an ideal entrepôt for trade in forest products. In
addition to its function as an entrepôt, Itaituba served
as a governmental and commercial center for the Upper
Tapajós Valley. The municipal dock and trading posts
that lined the first street parallel to the river were
the center of activity. The small upper class lived on
this street. The poor lived along two streets behind the
river front and paralleling the first street. Transportation in and out of the community was by riverboat or
private small plane. The state capital was a four- or
five-day journey by boat. Itaituba was an isolated backwater in the vastness of the Amazon rain forest.
    The town's population fluctuated with the rise and
fall of prices on the world market. In 1895, during the
peak rubber boom years, Itaituba had over 800 residents
(Coudreau 1897). By 1920, the population had dropped to
around 400. The census of 1956 reported a population of
653, reflecting a slight increase after the World War II
mini-boom in rubber. In 1968, the Handbook of Munici-
palities listed Itaituba's population as 2,000, a growth
resulting from the gold "rush" to the interior of the
município.
    From the time of the first European contact, the
primary mode of production in the Tapajós River Valley
was extractivism.[3] The first "product" extracted by the
early settlers was Indian slaves, who were used to work
in the fields in coastal and riverine areas (Hemming
1978). Concomitant with the need for slaves was the
abundance of marketable "jungle" products. These products
included: sasparilla, guaraná, Brazil nuts, rubber,
cloves, woods, vanilla, and cacao, among others (Ferreira
Reis 1974). The social and economic patterns of extractivism pervaded the Amazon during this period. Even after
the rubber boom ended, mini-booms centered around the
extraction of other products—lumber, gold, heart of
palm, and other raw materials and minerals—continued
earlier patterns up until the present (Velho 1972;
Cardoso and Muller 1977; Laraia and da Matta 1967;
Miller 1976).
    Forces in the international market controlled the
extraction of the above products during the first three
centuries of European contact. First it was the
Portuguese trading companies, later the European and
North American markets for raw materials (Ferreira Reis
1974). Still more recently, especially since the opening
of the highway system that connects the north of Brazil
with the south, economic dependency has become national
rather than international—with the notable exception of

the Free Trade Zone of Manaus--although international
factors certainly play an indirect role.

Periodic migrations to the region in response to the
various booms supplied necessary labor (the Indian
population died off, left as slaves, escaped, or inter-
married very soon after first European contact). During
"bust" periods some residents moved out of the region,
but there were always some who stayed behind subsisting
on slash-and-burn horticulture.[4] This system of cultivation is highly adaptive to the humid tropics and serves
as a fallback for the local population when other more
lucrative means of subsistence fail (Wagley 1976:50-51).

SOCIAL CLASSES: THE PRE-HIGHWAY PERIOD

Determining social class in Itaituba as in all other
communities is a relative and somewhat arbitrary means of
distinguishing the rich from the poor and of providing
a continuum on which a person may be ranked according to
his prestige. Owing to its underdevelopment, the Amazon
region has never been on a par with other regions of the
country for economic resources and the amenities of modern
life. Nor has rural Amazonia ever compared favorably
with the regional urban centers of Manaus and Belém.
Thus, a system for describing social class in Itaituba
should accurately reflect the social divisions within the
town and not necessarily rely on national or urban
standards.

Charles Wagley (1976) in describing Itá, a traditional Amazon River community, devised a system of assign-
ing social class that can also be used to accurately
describe the situation in Itaituba prior to the Transamazon Highway. The cognitive scale elicited by Wagley
includes: the First Class, the urban Second Class, and
a rural Second Class composed of subsistence farmers and
rubber collectors. Wagley states that the urban classes
would view all but a few government employees in the
interior towns as caboclos or "hicks" (1976:104). Social
class in such a system is determined primarily by economic
position based either on a salary from the government or
control over land and/or natural resources (such as
rubber trees, lumber, and the like). But other factors
such as education, family background, and achievement
within the community can affect an individual's ranking
within the class system (Wagley 1976:121).

The social class system as described by Wagley
was engendered by the extractive economy of the region.
Members of the First Class included ranking government
officials, local merchants or traders, and large landowners. Most traditional Amazon towns included only a
handful of such families. Older residents of Itaituba
identified only six families during the last twenty years
who could be considered members of the First Class (3-5%
of the population in 1960-1970). The self-appointed town

historian wrote in a local newspaper in April 1975 that
there were three classes in Itaituba during the rubber
boom. A first class (a primeira) was characterized by
men who wore frockcoats and women who dressed in Parisian
fashions. This group disappeared almost entirely after
the end of the rubber boom. The second class, who
corresponded to Wagley's First Class description, were
"middle class" who had employment within the community and
who were of good families. The local historian referred
to the third class as "plebians" who are racially mixed,
and he dismissed this large proportion of the population
as "masses of others." He himself is a descendent of the
first group.

Members of the Second Class are classified as such
by their lower economic status, which, more often than
not, is concomitant with a lack of education and lowly
family origin. The Second Class residents in town, by
virtue of their town/urban residence, regard themselves
as superior to the farmers and collectors who live in
the hinterlands. The perception of urban residence as
superior is common throughout Brazil (cf. Harris 1956;
Hutchinson 1957; Margolis 1973). Urban residents have
access to more goods at the local stores and can engage in
wage labor whenever there is an opportunity in town.
In summary, the extractive mode of production supplemented by slash-and-burn horticulture has produced a very
precarious existence for the majority of residents of
traditional Itaituba and other towns similar to it.
The social class system resulting from the extractive
mode of production makes a sharp distinction between the
"haves" and the "have-nots."

ITAITUBA: THE POST-HIGHWAY PERIOD

As previously noted, the original highway plan
mentioned the traditional river communities as temporary
staging centers. In point of fact, with the reduction
in the government's role in the colonization portion of
the Transamazon scheme, the emergence of these traditional riverine communities as urban centers has been
one of the most notable results of the highway project.
In the State of Pará, at the eastern end of the highway,
the cities of Marabá, Altamira, and Itaituba have experienced tremendous population growth (see Table 4.1).
In 1970, Altamira had a census of 1,800 but an estimated
population of 5,000; today it approaches 30,000.
Itaituba had approximately 2,000 residents in 1970 and
more than 12,000 in 1977.

The Itaituba sector of the highway has not had the
amount of colonization characteristic of the Altamira and
Marabá sectors. The colonization agency (INCRA) estimates
that through the end of 1976, 1,450 families had settled
in the Itaituba sector of the Transamazon Highway (INCRA
office in Itaituba), whereas more than 3,000 families had

Table 4.1. Census figures for selected Amazon cities: 1940-1980

City	1940	1950	Year 1970	1977#	1980@
Itaituba	381	624	2,000#	12,000	20,214
Altamira	1,202	1,809	6,625	20,000	25,379
Marabá	1,500	4,536	23,944	35,000	43,331
Belém	153,203	225,218	609,277	750,000	771,446
Santarém	6,315	14,061	*	100,000	104,866

Estimation of author

* Data not available

@ 1980 preliminary census figures

Source: IBGE (Instituto Brasileiro de Geografía e Estatística) Census: 1940, 1950, 1970, 1980.

settled in the Altamira area and 1,422 in the Marabá
sector by the end of 1974 (Moran 1981:83). The município
of Itaituba also includes the southern branch of the
Santarém-Cuiabá Highway, where by June 1977 there were
22 "communities" and approximately 345 families. This
lower level of colonization in the Itaituba sector (the
Santarém-Cuiabá colonization excluded) has been due in
large part to the poorer soils in that sector and problems
with colonization in the other two sectors, which halted
colonization along the more recently completed section
of the highway west of Itaituba (IPEAN 1974). Again,
because of poor soils, agricultural and livestock investments have trailed behind mineral exploration, the key
economic activity in the post-colonization period.

The most important mineral activities in Itaituba
center on gold. Deposits of salt and limestone have been
located, but remain unexploited. Gold deposits in the
region are fluvial deposits. Extraction is accomplished
by placer mining. Exact figures on the number of mines,
the number of miners, and the total production are difficult to compile. As yet, government agencies and law
enforcement personnel have not entered most of the mining
areas. The state tax collector (Coletor Estadual)
estimates that there are 186 gold mines (i.e., placer
locations) in the area and approximately 20,000 miners.
A local gold-buyer recently estimated that the number of
mines serviced by Itaituba was 84. There are eight
legalized buyers (registered with the Internal Revenue
Service--Receita Federal) and 33 pilots who fly supplies
and passengers to the mines and gold out. There is a 1%
tax on all gold flown out of the area. The tax is paid
to the Receita Federal. No portion of this money is
returned directly to the município. However, it is the
opinion of community business leaders that clandestine
smuggling of gold and contributions to the commercial
sector make gold mining the economic mainstay of the
community--more than off-setting the poor performance
of the agricultural sector.

The growth of the agricultural and mining sectors,
and the continuation (on a diminished scale) of collection
of traditional "jungle" products, have helped contribute
to a population boom in Itaituba. This has meant changes
in many sectors of the community. The completion of the
highway to Itaituba and the city's location on the
Tapajós River have increased the importance of Itaituba
as a transportation and communications hub for the Upper
Tapajós Valley. The importance of transportation and
communications infrastructure in development projects in
other parts of the world is well documented in the
literature. For instance, Belshaw notes:

> I have seen with my own eyes the way in which
> peasants enter management activity--commerce
> spreads, agricultural production can increase,

markets can be opened up, and ideas flow
faster, all as the result of the completion
of a 20 mile dirt road...(Belshaw 1976:175fn).

Prior to the highway opening, Itaituba's links to
the outside world were by riverboat, and in the post-
World War II period by small private aircraft that landed
at a short grassy field. A direct trucking link (lasting
one to two weeks depending on the weather) is now
possible between Itaituba and São Paulo, the industrial
and manufacturing hub of Brazil. Buses run daily to the
regional center of Santarém and three times a week to the
state capital. Air service is provided by a regional
carrier three times a week to Santarém, where there is a
major airport providing air connections to Belém, Manaus,
and Macapá. Riverboat service is much more frequent
(see Table 4.2). Regular mail service is three times a
week. Radiotelephone communication is possible to Santarém.
    Instead of just a few streets parallel to the river,
as before construction of the highway, today Itaituba has
a grid of streets spilling over from the central part of
town into four additional neighborhoods. Second Street
is the principal commercial street, lined with shops and
government offices. It carries more vehicle traffic
(there are 400 registered vehicles) than any other
street. Traffic makes crossing the street difficult at
times. Litter, dust, and mud attest to the street's
designation as Federal Route BR-230 (the Transamazon
Highway) passing through the middle of town.
    In general, there are more urban amenities in post-
highway Itaituba. A huge commercial expansion has
occurred; fostered, at least in part, by waves of
entrepreneurs drawn to an area experiencing rapid population growth. Even though activity in the agricultural
sector is slacking off, there are still some farm-related
businesses. These include hardware and farm implement
stores; agricultural storage, processing, and transportation firms; and the Bank of Brazil, which handles credit
for small- and large-scale agricultural operations.
Commercial warehouses that supply colonists, placer gold
mining operations, and other mineral exploration projects
have opened.[5] These are supplemented by stores of all
kinds selling foodstuffs, clothing, furniture and
appliances, and general merchandise. Entertainment-
related businesses include beauty salons, nightclubs,
a cinema, a magazine stand, and a record store. Even the
Avon Lady came calling at the researcher's door. The
1970 commercial census notes thirty-seven commercial
houses, eight warehouses, and eight businesses dealing
with agricultural and/or extractive products. Today
there are more than 300 businesses of all kinds. The
large number of commercial enterprises is physical evidence
of the town's transformation from a small riverine community

Table 4.2. Modes of transportation: Itaituba-Santarém

Mode of Transportation	Frequency of Service	Cost (U.S. Dollars)	Duration of Trip
Airplane	3 times/week	40	50 minutes
Bus	daily	8	7 hours
Car	Note[a]	Note[b]	5 hours
Boat	4 times/week	6	18 hours

[a]The National Road Department (DNER) estimates the average number of cars traveling in the direction of Altamira and Santarém at fifty per day (DNER 1977:37).

[b]The cost of gasoline in January 1977 was U.S. $0.62 per liter.

with a handful of trading houses to a city of 12,000. (Preliminary 1980 census figures now show 20,000.)

The importance of the presence of the Bank of Brazil cannot be overemphasized. Not only does the bank provide credit for colonists, but also for local businessmen and homeowners. In addition, a branch of the Federal Savings Bank (Caixa Econômica Federal) has opened in Itaituba. The savings bank provides small commercial loans and finances building construction and automobile purchases. For the first time in its history, the town has a steady supply of money. Credit is extended readily for the expansion of the local economy. In pre-highway Itaituba one had to travel to Belém to secure a loan or arrange credit through local patrons. The former was a time-consuming process--an option open only to members of the First Class--whereas the latter carried high interest rates and was available only as small loans. Finally, Itaituba is now tied into the national banking system, making it possible for national and regional firms to establish offices in a community with a branch of a major Brazilian bank.

In addition to the increased commercial activity, there has also been an increase in the number of state and federal agencies. As the county seat and only urban center for several hundred kilometers, Itaituba is the only location considered suitable for agencies, even those concerned exclusively with service along the highway. This follows a pattern of sending urban bureaucrats to rural areas, where they settle in the most urban area of their assigned region.

The sheer number of bureaucrats who have settled in Itaituba is remarkable--700 to 800 persons (including families), or 6.7% of the population, as opposed to 45, or 2.2% of the population, before the highway. The number of agencies since 1971 has increased from eight to thirty-one (see Table 4.3). The colonization agency itself (INCRA), once the largest bureaucracy, has been surpassed by the school system (SEDUC/MEC), the agricultural extension service (EMATER), and the army (53 BIS) following the deemphasis on colonization (Miller 1980).

The plethora of agencies and the massive bureaucracy found elsewhere in Brazil has finally reached the remote Amazon. The large number of agencies in Itaituba represents one of the most significant changes in that region following the opening of the Transamazon Highway. For Itaituba this means greater integration into the national culture, greater financial benefits from the state and federal governments, and perhaps most importantly, a profound change in the institutional structure of the community. Whereas prior to 1972, município government was the only significant administrative unit, now there are dozens of agencies providing services and jobs.

SOCIAL CLASSES: THE POST-HIGHWAY PERIOD

The influx of new agencies and new entrepreneurs from all regions of the country has altered the social order definitively. The most important change, as noted previously, has been the creation of a new urban middle class. The Brazilian middle class is not a cohesive class with a separate value system, but rather a variety of middle-income occupational groups who rely on the extended family, patronage relationships, and formal education to achieve upward social mobility (Miller, in press). In Itaituba, the middle class is comprised of two main groups--commercial entrepreneurs (10%) and bureaucrats (7%). With the inclusion of an additional 2% who are landowners from the pre-highway period, the middle class in Itaituba is approximately 20% of the population.

There are still no representatives of a national upper class, but there are representative families who are similar to what Wagley and Harris (1955:429) described as "metropolitan middle class..., an emerging group of big-city professional and white-collar workers and owners of medium-sized business" and what Ratinoff (1967) described as the "new urban groups." In addition to the creation of an urban middle class, population growth has resulted in considerably more gradations between the rich and the poor than in the former two-class system. Along with the increase in gradation, an increase in the gap has occurred between the richest and poorest families. The contrast between these two extremes is readily visible in the life-style and material goods of families of each group. The investigator's experience in Itaituba and the traditional Amazon River community of Itá allowed him to see and experience this change. In Itá no one had automobiles, everyone who had electricity had it for only

Table 4.3.   Bureaucratic agencies in Itaituba: 1970-1977

Type of Agency	1970	1977
Communications	ECT	ECT TELEPARA
Local Administration	PMI	PMI SMER CDI
Social Services	FAG	FAG[a] INPS MT
Health Services	Note[b]	FSESP SUCAM FUNRURAL
Public Utilities	CELPA COSANPA	CELPA COSANPA
Fiscal Agencies	SEFA Receita Federal	SEFA Receita Federal
Highway-Related Agencies		INCRA EMATER DNER COBAL
Educational Services	Note[c]	SEDUC MEC MOBRAL CNAE Project Rondon
Financial Services		Bank of Brazil CEF CFP
Military	FAB	FAB 53 BIS
Mineral and Resource Management		IBDF CPRM
Total Number of Agencies	8	31

[a] FAG is currently undergoing reorganization.

[b] FAG operated a hospital and SUCAM sprayed for malaria every six months.

[c] Although schools and teachers were present, agency personnel were located in Santarém.

ACRONYMS FOR TABLE 4.3

ACAR	Associação de Crédito e Assistência Rural
ACI	Associação Comercial de Itaituba
BIS	Batalhão de Infanteria da Selva
CDI	Conselho de Desenvolvimento de Itaituba
CDP	Companhia das Dócas do Pará
CEF	Caixa Econômica Federal
CELPA	Centrais Elétricas do Pará
CFP	Campanha de Financiamento de Produção
CIBRAZEM	Companhia Brasileira de Armazenagem
CNAE	Campanha Nacional de Alimentação Escolar
COBAL	Companhia Brasileira de Alimentos
COSANPA	Companhia de Saneamento do Pará
COTELPA	Companhia de Teléfones do Pará
CPRM	Companhia de Pesquisa de Recursos Minerais
DNER	Departamento Nacional de Estradas de Rodagem
DNPM	Departamento Nacional de Produção Mineral
EMATER	Emprêsa de Assistência Técnica e Extensão Rural
ECT	Emprêsa de Correios e Telégrafos
FAB	Força Aérea Brasileira
FAG	Fundação de Assistência dos Garimpeiros
FSESP	Fundação Serviço Especial de Saúde Pública
FUNRURAL	Fundo de Assistência ao Trabalhador Rural
IBDF	Instituto Brasileiro de Desenvolvimento Florestal
IBGE	Instituto Brasileiro de Geografia e Estatística
ICOMI	Indústria e Comércio de Minérios S.A.
IDESP	Instituto de Desenvolvimento Econômico-Social do Pará
INCRA	Instituto Brasileiro de Colonização e Reforma Agrária
INPS	Instituto Nacional de Previdência Social
MEC	Ministério de Educação e Cultura
MOBRAL	Movimento Brasileiro de Alfabetização
MT	Ministério de Trabalho
PIN	Programa de Integração Nacional
PMI	Prefeitura Municipal de Itaituba
RADAM	Radar da Amazônia
SEDUC	Secretaria de Estado de Educação e Cultura
SEFA	Secretaria de Estado da Fazenda
SEPLAN	Secretaria de Estado de Planejamento
SIMA	Sistema Nacional de Informação de Mercado Agrícola
SMER	Serviço Municipal de Estradas de Rodagem
SUCAM	Superintendência do Contrôle da Malária
UDESC	Universidade de Desenvolvimento do Estado de Santa Catarina

four hours a day, and the range of material goods was not
great. Of course, there were differences, but there was
a feeling of camaraderie in that all were suffering in a
backward community. In Itaituba the contrast is greater.
Private cars and taxi service are available. Most people
cannot afford U.S. $100 to buy a fan, but a number of homes
in Itaituba have at least one room air-conditioned. Most
people depend on a small transistor radio for music.
Others have stereo systems with cassette decks and AM/FM
radios. Most people cook on open fires or two-burner
hot plates, but 15% of the homes in Itaituba have a stove
with an oven. More than three-quarters of the homes (77%)
are furnished with rough-made benches, hammocks, and small
tables. Living room suites, beds, dinette sets, and the
like are available in at least three different stores.
None of these stores went out of business during the
investigator's stay in the area.

Perceptions of class by the residents themselves are
very inexact. Wagley's two-part class system was
elicited by him from the population itself. No clear-cut
consensus exists in Itaituba today. The situation can
best be described as being in a state of flux. The investigator's own attempts to elicit categories did yield
some broad equivalents to upper, middle, and lower classes.
In the poorer neighborhoods, however, there were several
gradations of what First Class informants simply called
the lower class (classe baixa). Using this information
along with income level (estimated) and ownership of
material goods, the investigator devised a system for
classifying residents. It is an objective stratification
and not a cognitive one.

The system is similar to Wagley's typology but with
greater differentiation within the classes (see Table 4.4).
The local upper class or urban middle class is composed
of two groups: the traditional upper class and the "outsider" upper class. The "outsider" group includes the
bureaucrats and entrepreneurs who have come to Itaituba
after the opening of the highway. The second or lower
class consists primarily of four groups: those town
residents who have steady jobs, those who work in town
but only do part-time or temporary tasks whenever work
is available, subsistence farmers who live in town, and
gold miners whose families live in Itaituba year-round.
The differentiation within each class is greater than in
Wagley's system largely due to the greater number of
economic niches available for exploitation. If the rural
population of the município were considered, there would
be even more gradations within the lower class.

THE ENTREPRENEURS

The expanded commercial sector has meant the emergence of many new entrepreneurs from the local population
and the migration of others to the Itaituba area.[6]

Table 4.4. Class system in Itá and Itaituba

Itá*	Itaituba
First Class	Local Upper or Urban Middle Class
Government officials	Government officials
Local merchants and traders	Entrepreneurs
Large landowners	Large landowners
	Pre-highway local elites (if not included in an above category)
Second Class	Lower Class (urban)
Town residents of lower socio-economic status	Town residents in steady, low-paying jobs
Rural farmers	Town residents who do part-time or temporary work
Rubber collectors	Subsistence farmers and families
	Gold miners and families
	Lower Class (rural)
	Small farmers
	Gold miners and other "collectors"

*Wagley (1976)

Initially the number of entrepreneurs was proportionally greater due to the influx of construction crews and the support personnel, all of whom supported many enterprises. Entrepreneurs, especially those of limited means, are attracted to frontier areas where they do not have to compete directly with larger and more capital-rich enterprises prevalent in the southern and coastal regions of Brazil. This initial group also included what Geertz termed "petty traders" (1963:17), small-scale entrepreneurs who open tiny stores in the front rooms of their homes, restaurants in their kitchens, barbershops in their bedrooms, and a dormitory hotel wherever there is room. After the construction boom ended, most local residents who engaged in this type of business returned to non-entrepreneurial activities or moved on to other frontiers. The number of such home businesses continues to decline except in the newest neighborhoods where new services are needed. Of the total population, the percentage of those involved in commercial entrepreneurial activities ranging from front-room stores to gold mining and sawmills is close to 10%.[7] Much of this group forms the nucleus of the expanded middle class.

The entrepreneurs rely on several occupational groups including colonists, gold miners and others connected with mineral exploration, and bureaucrats from government agencies. The spatial distribution of commercial enterprises within the town bears this out. Colonist-oriented businesses are concentrated near the north end of town, where the ferry carrying Transamazon Highway traffic across the Tapajós River docks. Businesses supplying mines and miners are located in the south-central area of the town near the airport, from which supplies and personnel are flown to the isolated mining communities. Stores for more affluent consumers, and businesses that supply paper goods and xeroxing and business machines for the agencies, are concentrated in the center of town.

As the new policy encouraging large-scale investments begins to take effect in Itaituba, new resources may appear and others may disappear (the colonist base is undoubtedly shrinking and the placer gold mines may begin producing less). To date, those entrepreneurs better able to adapt to changes in federal development policies have been the most successful. Excellent examples of failure and success in adaptation are provided by the two principal merchants in Itaituba. Merchant A, the most prominent in the pre-highway period, failed to alter his merchandising techniques when construction crews and new colonists crowded into town. His business has stagnated. Merchant B, a baker during the pre-highway period, expanded his stock to satisfy new customer needs, advertised, and modernized his business. Today he owns the largest and most successful store in town.

Merchant A is Tibiriça, who still owns a large
general goods store on the first street fronting the
river. He is a native of the State of Pará and began his
business thirty years ago. His store served as a major
trading post during the rubber boom of World War II, and
he still holds the rubber concession for the area.
Rubber yields are only a fraction of what they once were[8]
(but rubber has never been that profitable). The trade
goods that the rubber tapper bought from him on credit
were most important. His prices were high, but he sold
on credit during bad times. There was no national welfare
system--only the trader--to take care of tappers who had
a shortage of cash. Tibiriça not only received his portion of the rubber sent to Belém, the state capital, but
also a hefty proportion of the tapper's money. Tibiriça
had a reputation as a fair and honest trader. In this
way he built up a wide client network. Although he was
not the largest trader in Itaituba, he was a close second.

From his profits in the rubber trade, Tibiriça set
up a large cattle <u>fazenda</u> (plantation or farm) across the
river from Itaituba (it had been a small rubber trail or
<u>seringa</u>). There were no legal land titles during this
period, but no one argued with such an influential man.
On the other hand, there was no one who could use the
land for anything but subsistence farming. Along with
his cattle ranch, Tibiriça constructed a small slaughterhouse where cattle were butchered for local consumption.
He was the only supplier for the community. The income
from this enterprise allowed him to build a large house
on the first street and to travel frequently to Belém and
Rio de Janeiro.

Because of the gold boom Tibiriça had begun buying
gold and in a limited fashion had been supplying some of
the needs of the pilots who were flying to the gold fields.
Itaituba had not yet become a major supply point. By
1972, with the initiation of the Transamazon Highway construction and the first influx of colonists, business
expanded for Tibiriça. However, this period began on an
inauspicious note for him. When the first construction
crews arrived in Itaituba with several officials of the
colonization agency (INCRA), they set up camp across the
river from town. The camp was located on Tibiriça's
<u>fazenda</u>. Since he had no title to the land, the govern-
ment, through its agents, claimed a large parcel of
land fronting the river as the site of its new agropolis
and administrative center (Miiritituba). Tibiriça never
received any monetary compensation.

At this point in time, Tibiriça was the leading
merchant in the town of Itaituba, but with the advent of
the highway, another merchant opened a new store that
began to rival Tibiriça's supremacy. In the opinion of
many local informants, Tibiriça simply did not change
fast enough. Other merchants began to improve their

stock, especially with items that were in demand by the
construction crews and agency officials, who arrived in
greater and greater numbers. In short, Tibiriça had lost
his _fazenda_ and cattle operation, and although the
slaughterhouse was still his he had no cattle to slaughter.
At the same time, market demands were changing, supply
routes were being modified, and consumer tastes were
radically changing.

Three stores are operated by Tibiriça in Itaituba.
One of the stores is across the river in the community of
Miritituba, where he was granted permission to set up a
store as partial compensation for seizure of his land.
Since all other business takes place in Itaituba, people
in the agropolis do most of their buying at stores
there, where prices are lower. The remaining two stores
are on First Street. Tibiriça's original store stocks
foodstuffs, small appliances, yard goods, housewares, and
cosmetics. The shelves are dusty and poorly arranged.
The young female employees spend most of their day
sitting out in front of the store talking. Business is
slow, mostly because the store's prices are slightly
higher than those of the main competitor.

The third store is located near the second on First
Street. It is a successful enterprise. It is basically
a hardware store and sells bottled gas (the only place
bottled gas is sold in Itaituba). It is run by two older
men who are helpful and who try to keep the stock varied
and up-to-date. Almost all of the colonists from the
Transamazon buy their tools, lanterns, and other supplies
at this store.

Supplies are ordered from a warehouse in the southern
state of Minas Gerais and are delivered by truck. Because
they are bought from a wholesaler in the south, costs are
lower, but expensive overland transportation makes the
retail price about the same as for goods bought from
suppliers in Belém and shipped in by boat. The variety,
quality, and freshness (in the case of foodstuffs) is
superior, but because there is a slow stock turnover
in all but the hardware store, one must purchase soon
after a shipment of foodstuffs arrives.

Tibiriça's chief competitor, Samuca, has supplanted
him as the largest and most prominent merchant in town.[9]
Samuca is a native of the region. His older brother is
still involved in trading upriver from Itaituba. Samuca
worked for many years for his brother. In 1961, however,
he came to Itaituba in order to go into business for himself. He set himself up as a baker with the help of one
of the town's leading citizens. Samuca's brother had
fallen on hard times and was unable to give monetary help,
but he was able to leave his younger brother with a
legacy of knowledge about business in the region and
wrote an introduction for him to an influential friend
in town. By 1969, Samuca had progressed from baker to
owner of a small _barracão_ or front-room store in his

house on First Street. He tells of the rough time he had
in establishing this store. He and his wife worked long
hours and had a very small business.

In 1970, when the highway work began, it was Samuca
who decided to stock the goods the workers would need.
With a small amount of capital borrowed from relatives,
he bought an initial stock that included canned meats
and vegetables, a wide assortment of soaps, toothpastes,
colognes, cigarettes, ready-made clothes, soft drinks by
the case, beer by the case, and hardware items. The
construction workers and agency personnel began to
frequent his store and pay in cash. It was at this
point that Samuca decided he could offer credit to old
friends and relatives. With cash sales, he was able to
restock his shelves at regular intervals. In addition,
he was beginning to build a cash surplus.

As his business expanded, he hired new employees.
They were friends and kinsmen, all residents of Itaituba.
He hired the baker who had been his helper to bake bread
exclusively for his store. Another old friend was put
in charge of warehousing. His daughters and wife did the
clerking whenever they could. Finally, because of the
failure of a large business in the nearby town of São Luis
do Tapajós, Samuca was able to hire a skilled accountant
who was relocating to Itaituba.

With a good supporting staff, Samuca was able to
meet the needs of an expanding market. The advent of the
highway had an additional effect on the community. Since
more goods and support services were available, much more
of the gold began to move through Itaituba rather than
Santarém. Itaituba was much closer, after all, and had
only lacked a regular supply line. Now, Samuca was able
to meet the needs of the mine operators as well as the
highway-related market. He supplied the operators with
large quantities of staple goods that were shipped in
once a month along with the regular stock for his store.
These staple goods were warehoused until needed to fill
orders for the mines. More pilots were now located in
Itaituba, flying supplies for the mines and bringing the
gold out. Samuca often received payment in gold, and
this added to his profits.

With the increase in business, Samuca was able to
negotiate a loan in Belém for the construction of a
larger store. When the store was completed in 1972, it
was the largest of its kind on the Transamazon Highway.
It has not only a spacious first floor but a basement
where the property slopes downward to the river. The
building has approximately 7,500 square feet. It has its
own electric generator (the town at the time of the store's
construction did not have the capacity to supply all of
the power needed). The generator operates a meat freezer,
several coolers, overhead fans, lights, and assorted
other equipment. For a community that had received its
first refrigerator only several years before, this

building was a spectacular innovation.

At the front of the store are three check-out aisles with cash registers. The majority of the main floor contains shelves of foodstuffs (both canned and packaged), paper products, cosmetics, housewares, toys, small appliances, furniture, yard goods, a separate clothing counter with ready-made clothes, and a jewelry and perfume counter at the back. Above the main floor and at the back is a raised office for Samuca and his accountant. The office is air-conditioned and was the first unit of its kind in Itaituba.

In the basement, a meat counter and cooler have quantities of refrigerated beef. Alongside the meat counter is a delicatessen cooler with such rare items as bacon, cheese, sausages, lettuce, and other vegetables. As a complement to the meat and delicatessen sections, a lunch counter serves ice cream, cake, and other snack items. A large hardware corner rounds out the basement departments. All in all, the store can only be described as a small department store.

As the population of the town continued to increase, Samuca began to advertise his lower prices and his wide selection of foodstuffs and goods, using a succession of advertising gimmicks. On Christmas Day all children received a free toy from Samuca's department store. Pens, key chains, matches, and other such items were emblazoned with slogans and the name of the store. Samuca sponsored soccer games, festivals, parades, and a small newspaper. Modern advertising techniques had come to Itaituba.

With part of his profits Samuca invested in land, but most profits were reinvested in the store. He did little to develop his land. Whereas Tibiriça became involved in politics, land, and cattle, Samuca directed the majority of his attention toward his store. In the opinion of many local people, this is what allowed him to succeed in such a spectacular fashion.

The two case studies not only reveal the successes of two local entrepreneurs, but also demonstrate that the benefits accruing from entrepreneurs engaged in commerce have largely been aimed at the new urban middle class. The majority of goods and services offered are for their consumption. Other entrepreneurs, agency and military personnel, and the few local elite are a ready-made market. The poorer citizens of Itaituba participate only marginally in this new sphere of activity.

THE BUREAUCRATS

Bureaucrats arrived in Itaituba in almost the numbers of the entrepreneurs. The bureaucrats and their families make up about 7% of the city's population. The increased bureaucratic infrastructure benefits the bureaucrats themselves in several ways. In general, agency personnel come to Itaituba on a service contract

for two or three years. Itaituba is usually the first
step in one's administrative career or a chance for
administrative advancement. Since Itaituba is not a
sought-after post, an ambitious civil servant might accept
an assistant director's or director's position in
Itaituba, then after his or her tour of duty, seek a
transfer to a more urban area at this higher level. In
this way, one can achieve rapid advancement in the
bureaucratic hierarchy. Other administrators come to the
region to take advantage of investment and entrepreneurial
opportunities on the side, although this is expressly
forbidden by most agencies. The bureaucrats can do this
without much fear of discovery because their superiors
are unlikely to make visits to such a remote area. Examples of administrators who have profited from their
local business interests are numerous, particularly for
higher-level bureaucrats.

Other residents also find the new institutional
environment an excellent resource. The greatly expanded
school system, for example, provides teaching jobs for
those with the requisite education at the first level
(this means only completion of middle school). Although
the teaching jobs are low-paying, many teachers work only
four hours a day. Members of colonists' families have
taken teaching jobs to provide a steady cash income to
guard against crop failures and other calamities that be-
fall farm families along the Transamazon Highway. The
state has offered special courses in Itaituba during
vacations to help teachers upgrade their education. In
this way some teachers have moved up into better-paying
administrative positions. A local division of the state
education bureaucracy was created in Itaituba in 1972.
Expansion of the county education bureaucracy, then in the
planning stages, is taking place.

Lower-level positions in all agencies have been
opening up for the better-educated local residents. In
1977, for the first time, a local resident--the daughter
of a middle-class family--was accepted as a teller/
trainee with the Bank of Brazil. Another resident
returned from several years at the state university to
accept a position with the agricultural extension service.
Agencies are no longer relying solely on personnel from
outside the Tapajós region.

The plethora of agencies means greater integration
into the national administrative system, greater financial
benefits from state and federal governments, a significant
increase in services and job opportunities for the local
population, and a significant increase in the flow of
money (salaries) into the local economy.[10] Since most
agency personnel are from urban areas throughout Brazil,
they have brought new ideas and new customs. Itaitubans
have now been exposed to more aspects of the national
culture. Their salaries support restaurants, bars, and
the cinema.

For the local citizenry and new immigrants (many
from rural towns similar to Itaituba before 1970), coping
with the new institutional environment has been difficult.
The miners, subsistence farmers, and day laborers in
Itaituba often are totally unable to deal with administrators of the various agencies and therefore do not receive any benefits from them. The problem arises from
the different cultural and social backgrounds of each
group. On the one hand, administrators are well-
educated, urban residents, who are frequently natives of
a region other than Amazonia. On the other hand, the
residents of Itaituba who are served by these agencies
are poorly educated rural residents, most of whom are
natives of the north or northeast of Brazil--the two
least-developed regions of the country. These divergent
backgrounds lead to a lack of understanding between the
two groups. Moran notes similar problems between
colonists and administrators in his study of the Altamira
sector: "Each one plays his role well and fails to
communicate with the other" (1975:235). Rare is the
administrator who attempts to aid the illiterate or
backward client in his quest for help. As a result,
many townspeople see the administrators as unresponsive
newcomers who are in Itaituba only to get rich quick and
leave. All too often these suspicions are borne out.
Itaituba also includes some residents who have had
previous experience with agencies and administrative
personnel. One group with such experience is the local
entrepreneurial class. Among the reasons for the success
of one entrepreneur over another may be his past
experience in dealing with government agencies.

CONCLUSIONS

What has the Transamazon Highway project wrought in
terms of the original goals of the plan and the present
realities? As stated earlier, the principal objective
of resettling 100,000 families from the drought-stricken
northeast was not met. In fact, the entire small-farm
sector floundered under a number of constraints (see
Moran 1981 for an extended analysis of the Transamazon
project). The plan met more success in terms of the
second major objective--that of more fully integrating
the Amazon region into national Brazilian life. Improvements in transportation and communications certainly have
helped, but Itaituba's new position on Brazil's administrative map has meant much more national governmental
attention than the region had ever before achieved. In a
country with a centralized bureaucracy the size of
Brazil's, this is indeed an improvement.
Those who benefited most from the Transamazon Highway are the urban entrepreneurs and bureaucrats. In
terms of social class, these groups form a new middle
class where none had existed before. The influx of

outsiders to fill new economic niches has meant the displacement of the traditional First Class. There are still no representatives of the national upper class, but gradations between the rich and the poor have increased. The contrast between these two extremes is readily visible in the life-style and material well-being of the families of each group. The services and consumer goods provided to meet the needs of the new middle class are simply beyond the means of the vast majority of the population. A survey indicated that approximately 80% of the population allocated over 50% of their income to the purchase of foodstuffs such as meat, salt, bread, and other commodities not produced in the area. Often the remainder of the income was reserved for rent, leaving almost no money for discretionary purchases.

The financial positions of the majority can also be seen when comparing average increases in monthly income. For farmers, the price for rice (per sack) increased by only 14% between 1976 and 1977 (CFP office in Belém). The inflation rate for 1976 was 46%. Government employees received a 30% salary increase to compensate for inflation (O Liberal, Belém, 2/8/77). From very incomplete data on entrepreneurs (the 17 merchants who willingly revealed their incomes), incomes after adjustment for inflation increased 77%. It is apparent, then, that the groups who profited most from the Transamazon development project were not the small farmers and the other poor of the Amazon.[11] Even considering gross monthly income, the increase of 30% for an unskilled worker in a state agency is only U.S. $43.00 (based on an average monthly salary of U.S. $143.00), as compared to the increase for technicians and mid-level bureaucrats (all but directors and assistant directors), U.S. $215.00 (based on an average monthly salary of U.S. $715.00). One would expect to find a similar situation in other parts of the Amazon where development projects are underway. Benefits from federal development monies accrue more to the middle class than to the lower classes.

The rapid growth in Itaituba caused by the highway project created special opportunities for members of the middle class to fill a void on the frontier. The creation of a middle class in Itaituba from members of the traditional First Class plus immigrants is significant as an extension of what Florestan Fernandes calls the "middle class revolution" (a revolução burguesa). This class supported the military revolution in 1964 (cf. Fernandes 1975), and it is this class which fills the salaried positions of bureaucracies and comprises much of the entrepreneurial sector in Itaituba.

Because the middle class has more political influence with the government than does the lower class, it is quite possible that the government will be slower to dismantle the bureaucratic structures remaining in Itaituba than they were to end support of colonization

for small farmers. However, opportunities for entrepreneurs, in general, are much more transient than those
for bureaucrats because the entrepreneurs are more
dependent on national economic conditions and current
investment interests in the Amazon. Cuts in federal
subsidies for the Transamazon Highway, a weak agricultural
sector, and uncertainties about the size of current gold
deposits have already caused a retrenchment in commercial
activities.

For the community as a whole, predicting future
trends is difficult. Others who have done research in
the Amazon have described situations in other communities
indicating that a gradual replacement process is occurring
in the Amazon, as small farmers are being forced out by
large cattle interests (Wood and Schmink 1979; Lisansky
1980). Whether or not this will take place in Itaituba
is impossible to tell at this point. The city is certainly at an earlier stage of development than the
communities in the studies referred to above. Whether
or not cattle ranching or some other large-scale capital
venture such as mining will displace small farmers in
Itaituba, thus further altering the social class system,
is impossible to say. Researchers once thought of the
Amazon as a homogeneous region. Moran argues, in
reference to Amazonian ecosystems, that as more research
is done the heterogeneity of the Amazon will become more
apparent (1981:6-7). Hence it may be unsafe to predict
for Itaituba the same type of displacement noted for the
Marabá sector by Wood and Schmink (1979).

The only clear trend from all the research is that
big displaces small, and that the wealthy benefit more
from development programs than the poor. This is true
whether the large-scale investors are cattle ranchers or
mining firms. Change has taken place in the Amazon, but
it is more in the nature of bringing the region into line
with the national situation. With this in mind, one
could hardly expect the Transamazon project to have provided a panacea for the lower class.

ACKNOWLEDGMENTS

Research for this article was based on two field
trips, one in 1974 and the other in 1976-1977. The
former was sponsored by the Tropical South America
Program at the University of Florida and the latter by a
grant from the Organization of American States (#PRA-54903).

NOTES

1. The emergence of a middle class in Latin America
is usually associated with the process of urbanization
(Lipset and Solari 1967:62-67).

2. For an excellent description of the colonization plan, see Kleinpenning (1975).

3. Extractivism here refers to the collection of
natural products (raw materials) to market nationally
or internationally.

4. For descriptions of the slash-and-burn process,
see Wagley (1976) and Moran (1975, 1981).

5. Following completion of the highway and the
expansion of urban services (bars, stores, and restaurants),
Itaituba has replaced Santarém as the primary supply
center for mining operations. For a description of the
mining process and the patronage system that has grown up
around it, see Miller (1979).

6. Survey results show that 64.5% of the entrepreneurs were from the Northeast, 25.8% from Pará, and
9.7% from the South and Center-West regions. Only 15%
were local residents before 1970.

7. An accurate estimate of the number of individuals
involved in the commercial sector was impossible to
determine due to a number of factors including reluctance
on the part of some informants to reveal certain business
operations.

8. Rubber production for the município of Itaituba
in 1976 was 2,000 kg (Coletoria Estadual, Itaituba).
In 1875, at the beginning of the rubber boom, production
was in excess of 150,000 kg (Tocantins 1877:146-147).
During World War II, the figure fluctuated between
25,000 and 100,000 kg (Coletoria Estadual, Itaituba).

9. Tax information (ICM or Imposto do Comércio e
Mercadoria) on goods sold by each, one of the few
available and reliable estimates of a merchant's business,
for 1976 indicate Merchant B (Samuca) paid three times as
much ICM as Merchant A (Tibiriça).

10. Salary figures were unobtainable for more than
80% of the agencies (25 out of 31). Estimates of this
impact can only be generalized by the range and quantity
of goods and services available to that class of
individuals.

11. It should be noted that small farmers along the
Transamazon had varying degrees of success. Moran (1981)
estimates that 40% of the colonists in Vila Roxa could be
considered successful. Income levels vary extensively
among the small farmers so that not all should be considered "down and out."

REFERENCES

Belshaw, Cyril
  1976   The Sorcerer's Apprentice: An Anthropology of
         Public Policy. New York: Pergamon.

Brazil, Presidência da República
  1971   First National Plan of Development: 1972/74.
         Brasília: Office of the President of the
         Federative Republic of Brazil.

Burns, E. Bradford
  1970   A History of Brazil. New York: Columbia Univ.
         Press.

Camargo, José G. de Cunha
  1973   Urbanismo Rural. Brasília: Instituto Nacional
         de Colonização e Reforma Agrária (INCRA).

Cardoso, Fernando H. and Geraldo Muller
  1977   Amazônia: Expansão de Capitalismo. São Paulo:
         Editôra Brasiliense.

Coudreau, Henri
  1897   Viagem ao Tapajós. A. de Miranda Bastos,
         transl. São Paulo: Companhia Editôra Nacional.

DNER
  1977   A Transamazônica Faz uma Cidade. Rodovia
         II:36-39. Brasília: Departamento Nacional de
         Estradas de Rodagem (DNER).

Fernandes, Florestan
  1975   A Revolução Burguesa no Brasil: Uma
         Interpretação Sociológica. Rio de Janeiro:
         Editôra Zahar.

Ferreira Reis, Arthur Cesar
  1974   Economic History of the Brazilian Amazon.
         In C. Wagley, ed., Man in the Amazon.
         Gainesville: Univ. of Florida Press.

Forman, Shepard
  1975   The Brazilian Peasantry. New York: Columbia
         Univ. Press.

Gertz, Clifford
  1963   Peddlers and Princes: Social Change and
         Economic Modernization in Two Indonesian Towns.
         Chicago: Univ. of Chicago Press.

Harris, Marvin
  1956   Town and Country in Brazil. New York:
         Columbia Univ. Press.

Hemming, John
    1978   Red Gold: The Conquest of the Brazilian
            Indians. Cambridge, Mass.: Harvard Univ. Press.

Hutchinson, Harry W.
    1957   Village and Plantation Life in Northeastern
            Brazil. Seattle: Univ. of Washington Press.

IPEAN
    1974   Solos da Rodovía Transamazônica: Trecho
            Itaituba-Rio Branco. Belém, Pará: Instituto
            de Pesquisa Agropecuária do Norte (IPEAN).

Katzman, Martin T.
    1976   Paradoxes of Amazonian Development in a
            "Resource Starved" World. Journal of
            Developing Areas 10:445-459.

Kleinpenning, J.M.G.
    1975   The Integration and Colonization of the
            Brazilian Portion of the Amazon Basin.
            Nijmegen, Holland: Institute of Geography and
            Planning.

Laraia, R. de B. and Roberto da Matta
    1967   Indios e Castanheiros. Rio de Janiero:
            Difusão Européia do Livro.

Lipset, Seymour Martin and Aldo Solari, eds.
    1967   Elites in Latin America. New York: Oxford
            Univ. Press.

Lisansky, Judith M.
    1980   Santa Terezinha: Life in a Brazilian Frontier
            Town. Ph.D. dissertation, Dept. of Anthropology,
            Univ. of Florida.

Mahar, Dennis J.
    1979   Frontier Development Policy in Brazil: A Study
            of Amazonia. New York: Praeger.

Margolis, Maxine
    1973   The Moving Frontier: Social and Economic
            Change in a Southern Brazilian Community.
            Gainesville: Univ. of Florida Press.

Miller, Darrel
    1976   Itá in 1974. In C. Wagley, Amazon Town: A
            Study of Man in the Tropics. New York: Oxford
            Univ. Press.

    1979   Transamazon Town: Transformation of a Brazilian
            Riverine Community. Ph.D. dissertation, Dept.
            of Anthropology, Univ. of Florida.

Miller, Linda
  in   Patrons, Politics and Schools: An Arena for
  press   Brazilian Women. Studies in Third World
           Societies 15.

  1980   Schools, Community and Change: The Role of
          Educators in the Development of Itaituba.
          Unpublished ms.

Moran, Emilio F.
  1975   Pioneer Farmers of the Transamazon Highway:
          Adaptation and Agricultural Production in the
          Lowland Tropics. Ph.D. dissertation, Dept. of
          Anthropology, Univ. of Florida.

  1981   Developing the Amazon. Bloomington: Indiana
          Univ. Press.

Ratinoff, Luis
  1967   The New Urban Groups: The Middle Classes. In
          S. Lipset and A. Solari, eds., Elites in Latin
          America. New York: Oxford Univ. Press.

Robock, Stefan H.
  1975   Brazil: A Study of Development Progress.
          Lexington, Mass.: Lexington Books (D. C. Heath).

Sahlins, Marshall D. and Elman Service
  1960   Evolution and Culture. Ann Arbor: Univ. of
          Michigan Press.

Smith, Nigel J.H.
  1976   Transamazon Highway: A Cultural-Ecological
          Analysis of Colonization in the Humid Tropics.
          Ph.D. dissertation, Dept. of Geography, Univ.
          of California, Berkeley.

Tocantins, Antonio Manuel Goncalves
  1877   Estudos sobre a Tribu "Mundurucú." Revista
          Trimensal do Histórico, Geográfico, e
          Etnográfico do Brasil. Tomo XL:73-161.
          Rio de Janeiro: Garnier.

Velho, Otavio Guilherme
  1972   Frentes de Expansão e Estrutura Agraria:
          Estudo do Processo de Penetração numa Area da
          Transamazônica. Rio de Janeiro: Editôra Zahar.

Wagley, Charles
  1976   Amazon Town: A Study of Man in the Tropics.
          New York: Oxford Univ. Press. (Originally
          published, 1953.)

Wagley, Charles and Marvin Harris
    1955   A Typology of Latin American Subcultures.
            American Anthropologist 57:428-451.

Wood, Charles H. and Marianne Schmink
    1979   Blaming the Victim: Small Farmer Production in
            an Amazon Colonization Project. Studies in
            Third World Societies 7:77-94.

Part 2

Assessment of Current
Systems of Production

Introduction to Part 2

The second section of this volume provides assessments of current crop, pasture, fisheries, and forestry systems of production. These papers tear away at the blinders that seem to characterize project planning by pointing out the complexity of the environmental responses to management. Soils vary enormously from place to place, and after several years, they respond differently to standard fertilizer inputs than they do at first. Responses of pastures over the past decade have led to a reevaluation of their apparent potential. The apparently straightforward process of forest clearing may be implicated in the reduction of agricultural yields due to reductions in rainfall and to declines in the productivity of fisheries due to the feeding habits of many migratory species. This section is a state-of-the-art evaluation of systems of production with policy recommendations as to preferable research and development directions.

The paper by Nicholaides and colleagues is the product of the most intense research so far undertaken on the soils of the Amazon. Unlike the common wisdom, the authors' view of the potential of Amazonian soils is not negative. Although they admit that Amazonian soils are chemically poor, they find these soils structurally sound and more easily managed than other investigators report. In an area as vast as the Amazon, the 20% that has moderately fertile soils is a far from insignificant resource. The paper by Nicholaides et al. focuses upon assessing current estimates of soil potential and the response of various cropping experiments at the Yurimaguas experimental station in Peru. The authors' conclusion is that multiple cropping provides relief from the requirements of shifting fields, that yields from such cropping provide an income sufficient to purchase fertilizer inputs even at the inflated Amazonian prices, and that this transformation from shifting agriculture to permanent cultivation can slow down the rate of deforestation. This paper must be read and evaluated in

97

conjunction with several other papers in the volume. How likely is it that colonists will manage their farms with the care provided at the experimental station in the Yurimaguas project? Given that most of the land area of Amazonia is in the hands of large landholders, how much impact will a technology for the small farmer have? Despite the doubts raised by these questions, the research of Nicholaides et al. points to the potential that exists in Amazonia for a productive agricultural sector in selected regions when proper management can be provided. Without research of this kind, and a great deal more of it, the Amazon will remain an undeveloped region incapable of sustaining development and exploited solely for its wild resources.

Hecht, in another paper, provides an assessment of the productive capacity of pastures with particular attention to impact on soil fertility. She questions the fertility increase over time suggested by some investigators and tries to demonstrate that the increase, when it occurs, coexists with serious limiting factors that make the availability of the nutrients irrelevant to the productive potential of pastures. In addition, she points out that the favored species in current pasture development (Panicum maximum) may be ecologically inappropriate to the soils and climate of Amazonia. Correctly, she sees the alliance of capital with development bureaucracies as responsible for systems of land appropriation and fiscal management that favor pasture development despite its destruction of the biological resources and of the soil's future productive capacity.

The paper by Goulding is based upon the author's intensive research on Amazonian fisheries. He demonstrates the importance of the flooded forest to the productivity of many fish species and the variable impact of different fishing technologies. He explodes the myth that the Amazon River can serve as a protein factory for the world. Rather, what we have are delicately balanced species in still poorly understood micro-ecosystems and with yields that are already beginning to decline as a function of habitat destruction and overfishing.

The paper by Lovejoy and Salati explores the consequences of deforestation upon species extinction, climate, and the productivity of land and rivers. These authors advocate a cautious and flexible approach to development projects. Too little is known of the biotic and abiotic environment to permit accurate predictions of impacts. The authors' current research on the relative impact of different-sized clearings upon water vapor movement and forest viability needs to be carried out with an urgency that is impossible to overstate. Just as Posey demonstrates that we can learn a great deal from native peoples, Lovejoy and Salati show how observation of leaf-cutting ants can lead to identification of species that can be valuable in the development of fungus-resistant

varieties of cultivated plants--a development that could
have enormous value both economically and environmentally.

E.F.M.

5
Crop Production Systems in the Amazon Basin

J. J. Nicholaides III, P. A. Sanchez,
D. E. Bandy, J. H. Villachica,
A. J. Coutu, and C. S. Valverde

INTRODUCTION

This chapter centers on realistic agricultural alternatives to the traditional shifting cultivation practiced in the Amazon Basin. Shifting cultivation has been identified (Denevan 1977) as the primary cause for the clearing that some predict could result in the disappearance of the Amazon rain forest within less than 100 years (Denevan 1973). However, Myers (1980) and Hecht and Fearnside (personal communication, 1982) feel that the primary cause for clearing, at least in the Brazilian Amazon Basin, is the attempt at pasture development for cattle grazing. Shifting cultivation is certainly one of the major causes of the clearing of the Amazon Basin forest and has been decried by ecologists, geographers, and other concerned individuals who have recommended trying to establish, for both forest preservation and agricultural development, "permanent field cultivation without first going through a sequence of increasingly shorter fallowing and associated environmental deterioration" (Denevan 1977).

Since 1971, North Carolina State University's Tropical Soils Research Program, under U. S. Agency for International Development funding and in collaboration with the Peruvian Ministry of Agriculture, has been developing at Yurimaguas, Peru, continuous cropping systems for the acid, infertile soils of the upper Amazon Basin and other similar agro-ecological areas. The results of these research efforts, which offer attractive alternatives for shifting cultivators, are presented herein following summaries of the Amazon Basin's climate, soil resources, and current cropping systems. Also presented are the limitations and potential of these research results.

CLIMATE AND SOIL RESOURCES

Recent estimates of the geographical extent of the

Amazon Basin vary from 557 million hectares (Moran 1981)
to 484 million hectares (Cochrane and Sanchez 1982). The
Cochrane and Sanchez estimates, within the confines of
4°N to 12°S and 48°W to 78°W, eliminate small portions
of the Amazon Basin but will be used for the discussion in
this chapter, as most of the areal climatic and soils
data were derived from their study.

1. Climate

The Amazon Basin is found within the area known as
the humid tropics. For the purpose of this presentation,
the humid tropics encompass those areas with seven or
more humid months, with at least 1,500 mm of precipitation
annually (Nicholaides 1979), with no more than a four-
month period when potential evapotranspiration exceeds
precipitation, and with 5°C or less variation in mean
monthly air temperatures between the three warmest and
three coldest months (Dudal 1980).
Cochrane and Jones (1981) identified three major
climatic-vegetation subregions in the Amazon Basin:
tropical rain forest, 171 million hectares; seasonal
semi-evergreen forests, 274 million hectares; and well-
drained savannas, 39 million hectares (see Figure 5.1).
Thus, slightly more than one-third of the Amazon Basin
is in the tropical rain forest--mainly in the western
half or upper Amazon Basin. The seasonal semi-evergreen
forest occupies over half of the basin and is found
primarily east of Manaus, Brazil. The well-drained
savannas, which are natural grasslands surrounded by
forests, are interspersed within the other subregions
and include the savannas of Boa Vista, Rupununi, Amapá,
and Cachimbo. The Llanos of Colombia and Venezuela,
because of geographic limitations, and parts of the
Cerrado of Brazil, because of temperature limitations,
are not included.
The climatic differences within the Amazon Basin are
reflected by the meteorological data presented in
Table 5.1 for one site in each of the three climatic-
vegetation subregions. These subregions of the Amazon
Basin have only small temperature differences due to the
relatively small variation in elevation across the basin.
Mean annual temperature at the equator at sea level is
26°C and theoretically decreases by 0.6°C for each 100 m
increase in elevation. Soil temperatures at 5 cm depth
in the tropical rain forest subregion are fairly constant
during the year (see Table 5.1).
Precipitation in the Amazon Basin ranges from 1,500
mm to nearly 4,000 mm annually. Soil moisture regimes
of the Amazon Basin are primarily udic, though some ustic
regimes are also found (Cochrane and Sanchez 1982).
The udic soil moisture regimes are in those areas where
the rooting zone of the soil is dry for no more than 90
cumulative days during the year. The ustic environment

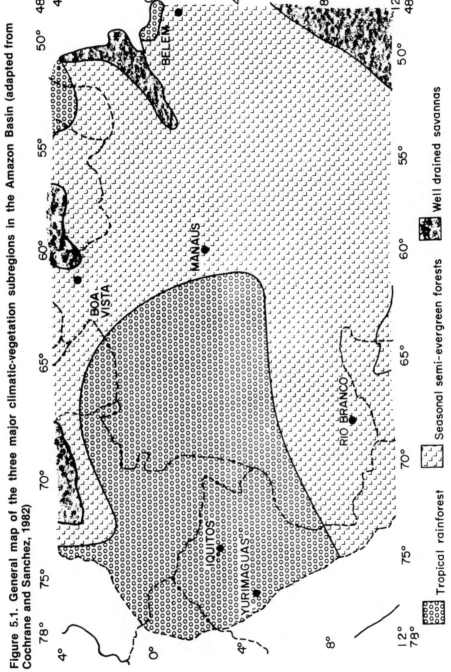

Figure 5.1. General map of the three major climatic-vegetation subregions in the Amazon Basin (adapted from Cochrane and Sanchez, 1982)

Tropical rainforest

Seasonal semi-evergreen forests

Well drained savannas

Table 5.1. Selected meteorological data from one site in each of the three climatic-vegetative subregions of the Amazon

A. Tropical Rain Forest: Yurimaguas, Loreto, Peru. 5°56'S, 76°5'W, 184 m.*

	Jan.	Feb.	Mar.	Apr.	May	Jun.	Jul.	Aug.	Sep.	Oct.	Nov.	Dec.	Annual
Air Temp. Mean, °C	26.6	26.7	26.5	26.2	26.3	25.2	24.8	25.2	26.0	26.4	26.3	25.9	26.2
Rainfall, mm	261	83	312	265	192	117	98	135	151	285	257	203	2218
Evaporation, mm	109	87	64	77	78	84	87	94	113	110	93	78	1061
Solar Rad., lang./day	357	331	309	317	322	314	335	376	411	392	351	346	347
Rel. Humid. Mean, %	85	81	83	90	87	87	77	77	78	81	81	83	82
Wind Vel., m/sec/day	6.0	4.9	5.0	5.7	4.8	5.4	4.8	5.5	5.9	6.6	6.1	6.4	5.6
Soil Temp, °C at 5 cm	33.5	32.5	30.5	31.5	32.0	31.5	32.0	33.0	33.5	33.0	33.0	31.0	32.3

B. Seasonal Semi-Evergreen Forest: Manaus, Amazonas, Brazil. 3°8'S, 60°1'W, 48 m.**

	Jan.	Feb.	Mar.	Apr.	May	Jun.	Jul.	Aug.	Sep.	Oct.	Nov.	Dec.	Annual
Air Temp. Mean, °C	25.9	25.8	25.8	25.8	26.4	26.6	26.9	27.5	27.9	27.7	27.3	26.7	26.6
Rainfall, mm	276	277	301	287	193	99	61	41	62	112	165	228	2102
Evaporation, mm	132	118	131	123	135	136	149	172	173	167	155	142	1732
Solar Rad., lang./day	420	415	418	404	426	441	462	525	541	509	491	443	458
Rel. Humid. Mean, %	88	89	89	88	81	74	71	63	67	76	78	85	79

C. Well-drained Savannas: Conceição de Araguaia, Pará, Brazil. 8°15'S, 49°12'W, 90 m.**

	Jan.	Feb.	Mar.	Apr.	May	Jun.	Jul.	Aug.	Sep.	Oct.	Nov.	Dec.	Annual
Air Temp. Mean, °C	25.1	24.9	25.2	25.6	25.6	25.1	24.9	26.0	26.7	25.8	25.6	25.2	25.5
Rainfall, mm	253	252	263	163	60	8	7	15	64	163	196	227	1671
Evaporation, mm	135	119	132	137	147	146	156	167	162	150	144	132	1727
Solar Rad., lang./day	437	431	428	453	470	448	510	530	521	479	477	427	471
Rel. Humid. Mean, %	88	89	88	79	65	48	44	54	70	83	83	89	73

*Yurimaguas data are derived from NCSU Tropical Soils Research Program Annual Reports for 1976-77, 1978-79. All data are averages of those from 1976, 1978, and 1979, except for evaporation and soil temperature, which are averages of 1978 and 1979 data, and relative humidity, which is from 1976 alone.

**Manaus and Conceição de Araguaia data are from Hancock et al. (1979) as presented by Cochrane and Sanchez (1982).

occurs where the soil's rooting zone is dry for more than 90 but fewer than 180 cumulative days, or 90 consecutive days, during the year (Soil Survey Staff 1975). One might suppose that crop production in the Amazon Basin generally would not suffer from moisture limitations, but during periods of erratic rainfall, moisture stress can restrict plant growth--even in the udic areas. Usually annual rainfall exceeds potential evapotranspiration in the Amazon Basin, though exceptions occur (Table 5.1). Thus, rainfall in the Amazon Basin can range from barely sufficient for crop production to excessive.

Solar radiation throughout the year is lower in the tropical rain forest subregion than in either of the other two subregions (Table 5.1). Theoretically, this lower solar radiation should have some dampening effect on crop yield potential in the tropical rain forest subregion compared to the other two, all other factors being equal.

Annual variation in daylight hours (day length) ranges from zero at the equator to 2 hours and 50 minutes at the tropical limits of 23.5° latitude (Sanchez 1976). As the Amazon Basin extends from 4°N to 12°S, day length variation in the basin ranges from 25 minutes to 1 hour and 10 minutes. Day length and solar radiation are not closely correlated in the Amazon Basin, or in any part of the tropics for that matter, as contrasted with temperate regions. This means that a wider range of illumination-radiation regimes occurs in the tropics (Sanchez 1976), and this has an obvious positive influence on the potential crops and their yields in the Amazon Basin.

2. Soils

The geology of, and consequent soil development in, the Amazon Basin was influenced primarily by the Guyana and Brazilian shields and the Andean uplifts (Sanchez 1976). The soils resulting from these geologic formations and actions belong to two main orders, Oxisols and Ultisols (see Figure 5.2), both of which are characterized as being weathered, acid, and infertile. According to the most recent and detailed study of the land resources of the Amazon (Cochrane and Sanchez 1982), almost 75% of the Amazon Basin is occupied by these two soil orders (see Table 5.2). It should be noted that the soil classification criteria (Soil Survey Staff 1975) are based largely on subsoil characteristics and may or may not reflect the surface soil characteristics. The Oxisols and Ultisols in other similarly based classification systems are known as Latosols, Red Yellow Podzols ("Podzolicos Vermelho Amarelo"), Ferralsols, Acrisols, and often incorrectly as "lateritic soils" (Sanchez and Buol 1975).

a. Resources. The Oxisols are estimated to occupy nearly 46% of the Amazon Basin (see Table 5.2), with the Haplorthox (29%) and Acrorthox (14%) great groups being the most dominant. These Oxisols, which originated from

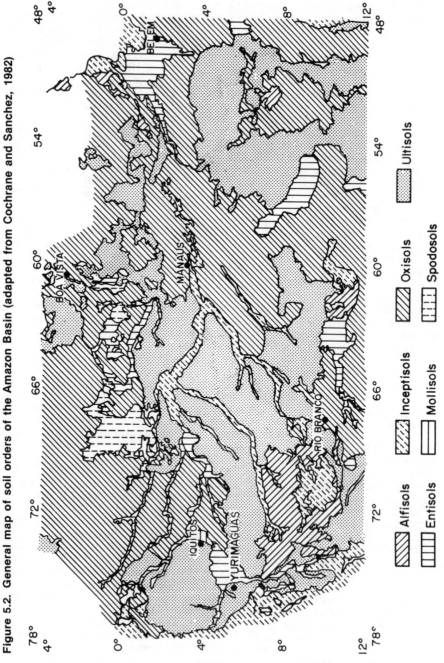

Figure 5.2. General map of soil orders of the Amazon Basin (adapted from Cochrane and Sanchez, 1982)

Table 5.2. General distribution of major soil types in the Amazon
Basin*

General soil grouping**	Million hectares	% of Amazon
1. Acid, infertile soils (Oxisols and Ultisols)	361.6	74.7
2. Poorly drained alluvial soils (Aquents, Aquepts)	66.0	13.6
3. Moderately fertile, well-drained soils (Alfisols, Mollisols, Vertisols, Tropepts, Orthents, Fluvents)	40.5	8.4
4. Very infertile, sandy soils (Spodosols, Psamments)	16.0	3.3
Total	484.1	100.0

*Adapted from Sanchez, Bandy, Villachica, and Nicholaides (1982)
and Cochrane and Sanchez (1982).

**Soil Survey Staff (1975) taxonomy in parenthesis.

materials from the Guyana and Brazilian shields, are
usually deep, well-drained, and have such uniform properties with depth as firm granular structure, low fertility,
acidity (see Table 5.3), and red or yellow color. The
Acrorthox differs from the Haplorthox only in the lower
cation exchange capacity of the clay. Their excellent
physical properties generally allow cultivation almost
immediately following rainfall, as the granular soil
structure permits rapid water infiltration. Consequently,
there is a relatively low erosion hazard except during
periods of intense rainfall. The Oxisols are found
primarily north of Iquitos, Peru, and eastward from
Manaus, Brazil (see Figure 5.2).
     Ultisols occupy 29% of the Amazon Basin (Table 5.2)
with the Tropudult (17%) and Paleudult (6%) great groups
predominating. Though both Tropudults and Paleudults
are well-drained, extensive areas of poorly drained
Ultisols are also found. The Ultisols of the Amazon
Basin were formed primarily from Tertiary deposits from
the shield areas and Andean uplifts. Generally these
soils are deep, have a clay increase with depth, are low
in weatherable mineral content and base saturation, resulting in low fertility and extreme acidity (see Table 5.3),
and are red or yellow. Ultisols in general have coarser-
textured surfaces and slower water permeability, hence
less desirable physical properties than do Oxisols.
The difference in depth of clay bulge in subsoil between
the Tropudult and Paleudult great groups is of little
agronomic management importance. The Ultisols are found

Table 5.3. Selected soil test data representative of general groups of the acid, infertile soils, the poorly drained alluvial soils, the moderately fertile, well-drained soils, and the very infertile, sandy soils of the Amazon Basin*

Horizon depth	Clay	Sand	Org. C	pH	Al	Exchangeable			Effective CEC	Al Sat'n
						Ca	Mg	K		
cm				(H$_2$O)						%
	----------- % -----------				----------- meq/100 g -----------					

1. ACID, INFERTILE SOILS (74.7% of Amazon Basin)

A. OXISOL: e.g., Haplic Acrorthox (Latosol Amarelo muito pesado); FCC: Caek, UEPAE-EMBRAPA Station, Manaus, Brazil.

Horizon depth	Clay	Sand	Org. C	pH	Al	Ca	Mg	K	Effective CEC	Al Sat'n
0-8	76	15	2.9	4.6	1.10	1.70	0.30	0.19	3.29	33
8-22	80	12	0.9	4.4	1.10	0.2		0.09	1.39	79
22-50	84	8	0.7	4.3	1.20	0.2		0.07	1.47	82
50-125	88	7	0.3	4.6	1.00	0.2		0.04	1.24	81
125-365	89	5	0.2	4.9	0.20	0.2		0.11	0.51	39

B. ULTISOL: e.g., Typic Paleudult (Yurimaguas series); FCC: SLeak. Yurimaguas Agr. Exp. Station, Peru.

Horizon depth	Clay	Sand	Org. C	pH	Al	Ca	Mg	K	Effective CEC	Al Sat'n
0-5	6	80	1.3	3.8	2.05	0.84	0.37	0.20	3.49	59
5-13	10	70	0.8	3.7	2.63	0.05	0.03	0.04	2.76	95
13-43	15	61	0.4	3.9	3.11	0.05	0.03	0.03	3.24	96
43-77	17	57	0.3	4.0	3.12	0.03	0.01	0.02	3.20	98
77-140	25	51	0.2	4.1	4.48	0.03	0.01	0.03	4.58	98
140-200	24	54	0.2	4.4	3.80	0.06	0.03	0.04	3.94	96

2. POORLY DRAINED ALLUVIAL SOILS (13.6% of Amazon Basin)

MOLLISOL: e.g., Fluventic Haplaquoll (Alluvial); FCC: Lg. Flood Plain (Restinga). Amazon River 30 km E of Iquitos, Peru.

Horizon depth	Clay	Sand	Org. C	pH	Al	Ca	Mg	K	Effective CEC	Al Sat'n
0-10	24	13	0.5	6.0	0.00	11.0	3.10	0.22	14.32	0
10-50	20	19	0.8	6.1	0.00	10.4	3.60	1.52	15.52	0
50-120+	10	36	0.4	6.3	0.00	6.80	2.30	0.20	4.78	0

Table 5.3 (continued)

Horizon depth	Clay	Sand	Org. C	pH	Exchangeable				Effective CEC	Al Sat'n
					Al	Ca	Mg	K		
cm	---------%---------				----------meq/100 g----------					%

3. MODERATELY FERTILE, WELL-DRAINED SOILS (8.4% of Amazon Basin)

ALFISOL: e.g., Orthoxic Rhodic Paleustalf (Terra Roxa Estruturada Eutrófica); FCC: Cd. Km 218 of Transamazonic Highway near Altamira, Brazil.

Horizon depth	Clay	Sand	Org. C	pH	Al	Ca	Mg	K	Effective CEC	Al Sat'n
0-20	48	34	1.5	5.9	0.0	5.59	1.20	0.16	6.95	0
20-40	57	24	1.1	5.8	0.0	4.40	0.62	0.06	5.00	0
40-60	69	19	0.6	6.0	0.0	2.62	0.58	0.04	3.24	0
60-80	62	16	0.5	5.9	0.0	2.30	0.82	0.04	3.16	0
80-100	71	15	0.4	6.1	0.0	2.18	1.06	0.04	3.28	0

4. VERY INFERTILE, SANDY SOILS (3.3% of Amazon Basin)

SPODOSOL: e.g., Arenic Tropaquod (Podzol Alico); FCC: Sgeak. Km 4.5 of BR-174 SUFRAMA, Brazil.

Horizon depth	Clay	Sand	Org. C	pH	Al	Ca	Mg	K	Effective CEC	Al Sat'n
0-3	2	89	6.3	3.8	5.4	0.30	0.10	0.16	5.86	92
3-25	2	95	0.5	4.4	0.7	0.10	0.10	0.04	0.84	83
25-50	2	94	0.1	5.0	0.1	0.10	0.10	0.02	0.12	83
50-90	1	98	0.0	5.1	-	0.10	0.10	0.01	-	-
90-105	5	93	1.1	3.7	3.0	0.10	0.10	0.04	3.14	96
105-125	9	91	2.2	4.7	2.9	0.10	0.10	0.03	3.03	96
125-165	16	76	0.8	5.6	0.4	0.10	0.10	0.03	0.53	75

*From Cochrane and Sanchez (1982) and Sanchez, Couto, and Buol (1982).

primarily south of Iquitos and eastward to Manaus, plus a few in a pocket southeast of Manaus (Figure 5.2).

Poorly drained alluvial soils account for 13% of the Amazon Basin soils (see Table 5.2) and include Aquents (11%) and Aquepts (2%). These soils, for the most part, are those with little or no profile development. Some are used for agricultural purposes but are subject to flooding. Most are found along the floodplain or the headwaters of the Amazon itself. Selected soil test data of Mollisol somewhat representative of these poorly drained alluvial soils are presented in Table 5.3. Other poorly drained alluvial soils are more acid and less fertile due to a lower percent base saturation (i.e., proportion of cation exchange capacity occupied by exchangeable bases).

Moderately fertile, well-drained soils comprise 8% of the Amazon Basin (see Table 5.2) and are extremely important, because it is on these soils that much of the Amazon Basin's food crops are currently produced. These soils include Alfisols ("Terra Roxa Estructurada"), Mollisols, Vertisols, and some Tropepts, Orthents and Fluvents. Soil test data from an Alfisol representative of these moderately fertile, well-drained soils are shown in Table 5.3.

Only 3% of the Amazon Basin (see Table 5.2) is covered by the extremely acid and infertile white sands (Spodosols, also known as Tropical Podzols, and Psamments). These soils have received more emphasis than warranted by the small percentage they make up of the total Amazon Basin landscape (Klinge 1975; Stark 1978). Soil test data from a Spodosol representative of these very infertile, sandy soils are given in Table 5.3.

Thus, the Amazon Basin is composed of the acid, infertile Oxisols and Ultisols (75%), poorly drained alluvial soils (13%), well-drained moderately fertile soils (8%), and very infertile, sandy soils (3%). Once the constraints to crop production on these soils are recognized, many can be made more productive through proper management.

b. Constraints. Realistic estimates of soil constraints to crop production in the Amazon Basin were made using the fertility capability classification (FCC) system (Buol et al. 1975; Buol and Coutu 1978; Buol and Nicholaides 1980; Sanchez, Coutu, and Buol 1982). Cochrane et al. (1979) also used this system in conjunction with the RADAM (1974-1978) soil maps, more detailed surveys, and on-site soil sampling. Major soil constraints to farming systems in tropical America and the Amazon Basin were identified by Sanchez and Cochrane (1980) and Cochrane and Sanchez (1982). Those data were further refined to develop estimates of the major soil constraints to crop production in the Amazon Basin (see Table 5.4). These estimates, though tentative and subject to revision with new information, are considered to give a realistic indication of soil constraints in that region.

Table 5.4. Gross estimates of major soil constraints to crop
            production in the Amazon Basin*

Soil constraint**	Million hectares	% of Amazon
Nitrogen deficiency	437	90
Phosphorus deficiency	436	90
Aluminum toxicity	383	79
Potassium deficiency	378	78
Calcium deficiency	302	62
Sulfur deficiency	280	58
Magnesium deficiency	279	58
Zinc deficiency	234	48
Poor drainage and flooding hazard	116	24
Copper deficiency	113	23
High phosphorus fixation	77	16
Low cation exchange capacity	71	15
High erosion hazard	39	8
Steep slopes (> 30%)	30	6
Laterite hazard if subsoil exposed	21	4
Shallow soils (< 50 cm deep)	3	<1

*Adapted from Sanchez and Cochrane (1980) and Cochrane and
Sanchez (1982).

**Nutritional deficiencies of manganese, boron, and molybdenum
also have been noted in some Amazon Basin soils, but are not
quantitatively estimable due to paucity of data.

    Computer-based maps of soil texture (to 50 cm) and
of fertility constraints (condition modifier combinations)
in the well-drained soils according to the FCC (Appendix
1 and 2) and as presented by Cochrane and Sanchez (1982)
are given in Figures 5.3 and 5.4. The most extensive
topsoil textural class is loamy (<35% clay, but not
sands or loamy sands), while in the subsoil loamy and
clayey textures (>35% clay) predominate. Thus, 72% of
the Amazon Basin soil textural classes are L and LC
(Cochrane and Sanchez 1982). The C class (>35% clay in
both topsoil and subsoil) makes up 21% of the Amazon
Basin. The CR and LR classes, which indicate physical
barriers to root development at 50 cm, are found in only
0.4% of the basin. Soils with sand or loamy sand topsoils represent only 4% of the soils of the Amazon Basin.

Figure 5.3. General map of soil textures in the Amazon Basin according to the fertility capability classification (FCC) system (adapted from Cochrane and Sanchez, 1982)

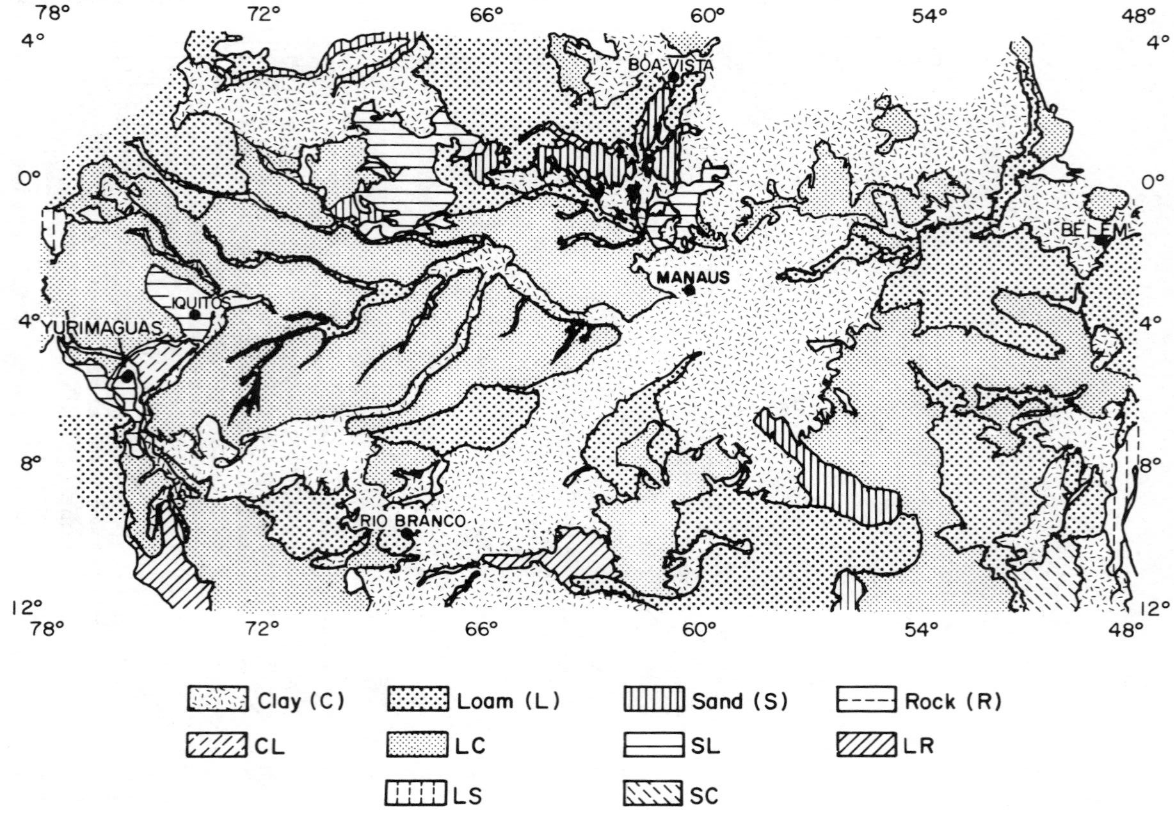

Figure 5.4. General map of the fertility of well-drained Amazon Basin soils according to the fertility capability classification (FCC) condition modifier combinations (adapted from Cochrane and Sanchez, 1982)

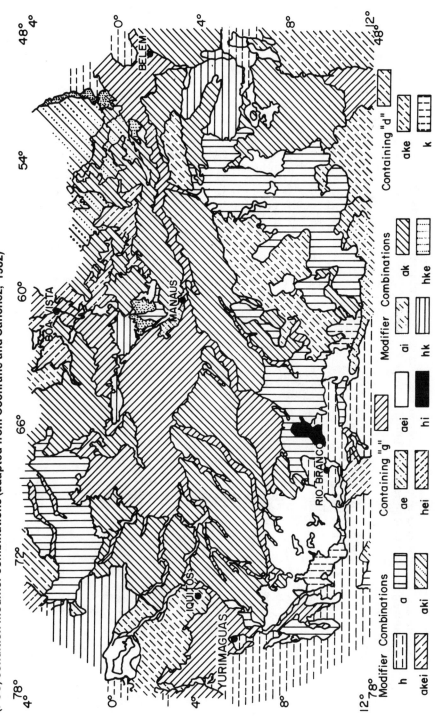

Soil nutrient constraints in the Amazon Basin are widespread (see Figure 5.4 and Table 5.4). Fully 90% of the soils of the Amazon Basin are projected to be deficient in nitrogen and phosphorus for crop production (see Table 5.4). The severity of these deficiencies depends on the crops grown. For instance, legumes such as peanuts, cowpeas, and soybeans need no nitrogen (N) amendments if the correct Rhizobia are present or added through inoculation. Some crop species and varieties are capable of producing reasonable yields on soils low in phosphorus (P), whereas others are not. It is fortunate that although 90% of the Amazon Basin soils are low in P, only 16% have the capacity to transform, or "fix," large quantities of P into relatively insoluble iron and aluminum phosphates. Thus, the required P amendments will not be as high on most Amazon Basin soils as on the higher P-fixing soils of the acid savannas such as in Brazil's Cerrado.

Over three-fourths of the Amazon Basin soils, or 79% and 78% respectively, are estimated to have aluminum (Al) toxicity and potassium (K) deficiency problems (see Table 5.4). Some varieties of certain crop species such as rice and cowpeas are more tolerant than others to high levels of Al. Given other desirable characteristics, these varieties could be used in cropping systems for the Amazon with less lime inputs than others require. Adequate K fertilization is a necessity for crop production on those K-deficient soils occupying three of every four hectares in the Amazon Basin.

The next most limiting soil constraints to crop production in the Amazon Basin are projected to be deficiencies of calcium (Ca, 62% of soils), sulfur (S, 58% of soils), and magnesium (Mg, 58% of soils), also as shown in Table 5.4. Use of dolomitic lime in areas as needed could help alleviate not only the Al-toxicity problems, but also the Ca and Mg deficiencies. The S deficiency could be addressed by simple superphosphate applications in areas deficient in both P and S. Very few soils of the Amazon Basin would be deficient in S without also being deficient in P.

Zinc and copper deficiencies are estimated to be problems in 48% and 23% of the Amazon Basin soils, respectively (see Table 5.4). Soil levels of these elements, as those of P, K, Ca, Mg, and S, must be monitored continually through soil testing during cropping to ascertain when, and in what quantity, amendments are necessary.

The major soil constraints to crop production in the Amazon Basin are chemical and not physical; 11 of the first 12 major constraints in Table 5.4 are chemical. The only physical limitation to crop production in these first 12 constraints is poor drainage and flooding hazard (24%), which occurs in many of the floodplains and inland swamps of the region. The low effective cation exchange capacity of 15% of the basin is a chemical limitation to crop production as it indicates low capability to retain nutrient cations such as K, Ca, and Mg. Thus, leaching of these elements from well-drained, low-cation-exchange-capacity soils can occur following their addition. Imbalances of these elements are easy to create by incorrect or overapplication of lime and/or fertilizers. Such lack of controlled application can also trigger deficiencies of K, Ca, or Mg (Villachica 1978).

Only 8% of the Amazon Basin soils are estimated to have a high erosion hazard (see Table 5.4). This is due in part to the fact that 73% of the Amazon has slopes from 0 to 8% (Cochrane and Sanchez 1982) and that the Oxisols and many Ultisols have favorable structures that permit rapid water infiltration, thereby reducing runoff. The key to erosion control is to avoid clearing the highly erodible soils that are on slopes greater than 30% and that have an abrupt increase of clay with depth (6% of Amazon Basin). If these soils are cleared they must be kept covered with protective vegetative canopies. The well-drained soils with less than 8% slope make up 50% of the Amazon Basin (Cochrane and Sanchez 1982). These gently sloping soils, which have no abrupt clay increase with depth, are not likely to have severe erosion problems if properly managed. However, improper management of these soils could result in erosion problems that could precipitate adverse consequences not only on-site, but downstream as well. The key to preventing erosion will be proper management.

The old laterization myth that the Amazon Basin soils will turn to brick when cleared (McNeil 1964; Goodland and Irwin 1975; Friedman 1977; Irion 1978; Posey 1982) is just that--a myth. Only 4% of the Amazon Basin soils possess a laterization hazard and this occurs only when the subsoil is exposed. The percentage of similar soils in the southeastern United States is 7% (Sanchez and Buol 1975) and many of these have been successfully farmed for the past 150 to 200 years. The key is to prevent the soft plinthite in the subsoil from being exposed by erosion of the topsoil. It is only then that the irreversible hardening takes place. As most of these plinthite soils (Plinthaquox, Plinthaquult, Plinthudult) occur only on flat, poorly drained land-scapes in the Amazon Basin, the erosion necessary for plinthite hardening is unlikely to occur (Cochrane and Sanchez 1982). Plinthite is an excellent, low-cost material for road beds, and many companies in the Amazon Basin would like to find more plinthite for such use.

Only 7% of the Amazon Basin soils are estimated to have no major constraints to crop production. These 32 million hectares are high in native fertility, well-drained, and are classed primarily as Mollisols, Alfisols, Vertisols, and some Inceptisols and Entisols. These soils are very important to crop production in the Amazon Basin. However, no soil can continually be "mined," no matter how fertile; therefore, nutrient amendments when needed and proper management are as necessary for continued productivity on these soils as on the less-fertile ones.

The soils of the upper Amazon Basin are very similar in chemical and physical properties to those of the southeastern United States--a fact realized by few people other than soil scientists and agronomists, but observed over 50 years ago (Marbut and Manifold 1926) and since confirmed by work reported herein. The tropical location of these soils results in an isotemperature regime that allows year-round cropping provided other crop production factors are nonlimiting.

Soil nutritional constraints to crop production and increased weed competition under depleted soil fertility conditions are the two primary underlying causes for shifting cultivation being the almost exclusive current crop production system in the Amazon Basin. If these constraints to crop production can be overcome by proper management practices, then shifting cultivation may be replaced by continuous cultivation, and one of the primary causes for the clearing of the Amazon forest will have been alleviated.

3. Crops

a. Resources. Although many crops are cultivated in the Amazon Basin, the most important economical annual food crops for small farmers in that area are rice (Oryza sativa), maize (Zea mays), cowpea (Vigna unguiculata), and cassava (Manihot esculenta). In addition, peanuts (Arachis hypogaea) and soybean (Glycine max) have considerable potential.

Quite obviously the acid, infertile conditions of the predominant Oxisols and Ultisols of the Amazon Basin are constraints to production of most of these species, except for some varieties of rice, cowpeas, and cassava, which are adapted to these conditions. However, there are also disease, insect, and some climatic constraints that require attention just as much as the soil constraints in order to produce sustainable crop yields (Bandy and Sanchez 1981).

b. Constraints. Rice: Blast (Pyricularia oryza) is the principal limiting factor to both upland and flooded rice production in Yurimaguas. Brown leaf spot (Helminthosporium oryza) also occurs, especially under potassium- and/or water-limiting conditions. Tall-statured varieties such as the Carolino of Peru are susceptible to lodging under high rainfall conditions and especially if fertilized with nitrogen.

Maize: Leaf blight (Helminthosporium sp.), kernel dry rot (Diplodia sp.) and European corn borer (Ostrinia nubilalis) are the main disease and insect problems in

the Yurimaguas area. Additionally, the relatively low
solar radiation (Table 5.1), relatively short day
length of 11.5 to 12.5 hours and high night temperatures
of >20°C contribute to low production efficiency and
distribution of photosynthate, thereby decreasing availability of carbohydrates for grain filling. Tall-
statured varieties are susceptible to lodging under high
rainfall conditions--especially if fertilized more than
adequately with nitrogen.

Peanut: Thrips, most likely Scirtothrips dorsalis
and Frankliniella schultzen, are carriers for virus that
can cause serious problems. Black spot (Cercospora sp.)
can be a major problem, especially for peanut varieties
introduced from the United States. Although the Peruvian
varieties appear to have some resistance to Cercospora,
problems can occur for them also. Cercospora incidence
is noted more on soils low in potassium. Peanut rust
(Puccinia erachidis) can cause problems, but not usually,
as many Peruvian cultivars are resistant.

Soybean: Frog eye spot (Cercospora sojina), pod
and stem blight (Diaporthe phaseolorum var. sojae) and
purple stain (Cercospora kikuchii) have been noted to
reduce yields and/or seed quality considerably when
cloudy, humid conditions occur during the pod-filling
stage. Seed viability in this humid climate is also a
problem.

Cowpea: Infestation of the pods by the fungus
Choanephora curcurbitaricum and others can be a major
problem if excessive rainfall occurs during the pod-
filling stage.

Cassava: Superelongation due to the disease
Sphaceloma manihoticola is the only potentially serious
problem of cassava in the upper Amazon Basin.

These disease, insect, and climatic constraints to
crop production on the predominant soils of the Amazon
Basin must be addressed and dealt with for that system
to become productive. Farmers of the region currently
are facing these problems. Some are doing so successfully, others less so.

CURRENT CROPPING SYSTEMS: SHIFTING CULTIVATION

The term "shifting cultivation" encompasses the many
variations practiced in the Amazon Basin, and, for that
matter, around the world. It includes any system under
which the soil remains fallow for a longer period of time
than it is cropped. Shifting cultivation has been discussed in numerous publications, among these Moran (1981),
Nicholaides (1979), Sanchez (1977a), Ruthenberg (1976),
Sanchez (1976), Grigg (1974), Manshard (1974), Sanchez
(1973), National Academy of Sciences (1972), and Nye and
Greenland (1960).

1. Clearing

Most shifting cultivators employ the slash-and-burn technique in which the larger trees and shrubs are cut by ax and machete or chainsaws during periods of low rainfall, allowed to dry at least 10 to 14 days, and burned either in place or in piles of smaller trees and shrubs. In the very high rainfall areas of the Ecuadorian Amazon Basin, farmers practice slash-and-mulch agriculture. After broadcasting crop seed in the forest, the farmers cut the undergrowth and use that vegetation as a mulch, instead of burning it. The Kayapó Indians in the Xingú River basin in the center of Brazil's Amazon Basin plant root crops in the cleared forest prior to burning (Posey 1982). The root crops lose their greenery with the burn, but not the vitality of their already established underground root systems, which absorb the nutrients from the ash when the rains begin. Obviously, there are many variations of slash-and-burn agriculture in the Amazon Basin.

However, not all land clearing in the Amazon Basin is by the shifting cultivators. Others may use heavy equipment such as bulldozers, tree crushers, tree pushers, and tractors with large chains between them. The amount of mechanical clearing was noted by Hecht (personal communication 1981) to be increasing, especially by the larger Brazilian farmers and ranchers who have access to capital. However, as we shall see, the increased popularity of this method is not necessarily equated with increased crop yields.

2. Cropping and Fallow

The most common cropping system practiced by shifting cultivators involves planting some combination of rice, beans, maize, cassava, sweet potatoes, and plantains among the ashes and debris using a "tacarpo," "espeque," "coa," or stick to make a hole into which seed or vegetative portions of the crop are placed. Moran (1981:34) states that cassava and bananas are sometimes planted at the same time as rice and that cassava may be planted to 90% of the cultivated fields in the Amazon. In the Yurimaguas region of the Peruvian Amazon, rice in monoculture is usually planted by small farmers following the slash-and-burn clearing. Then an intercrop of maize, cassava, plantains, and sometimes pineapple, is grown (Bandy and Sanchez 1981). The common intercropping practice reduces, but does not eliminate, the need for manually weeding the crops.

After only one or two harvests, especially on the acid, infertile soils, crop yields decline drastically due to soil fertility depletion and consequent greater weed competition. The land is subsequently abandoned to forest regrowth for a 17- to 20-year fallow period, during which time the fertility of the soil is rejuvenated by the nutrient cycling of the forest. Then the land is once again cleared, cropped, and returned to fallow.

This traditional form of shifting cultivation is ecologically sound (Nye and Greenland 1960; Moran 1981), but, though functional, guarantees perennial poverty for those who practice it (Alvim 1978). In several parts of the Amazon in recent years, however, due to the opening of the Transamazon Highway and other roads (Moran 1981), population pressure and a consequent increased need for food has shortened both the forest fallow period and the soil fertility regeneration process. This has converted an ecologically sound cropping system into an unstable, unproductive one that also is causing ecological damage (Smith 1981; Sanchez, Bandy, Villachica, and Nicholaides 1982). The effect of shortening the fallow period is especially pronounced on the less fertile soils, the Ultisols and Oxisols of the Amazon Basin. When one notes that these soils constitute 75% of the Amazon, the seriousness of the situation is realized. It becomes immediately evident that some alternate cropping systems must be made available to and accepted by the current shifting cultivators on both the more and less fertile soils of the Amazon Basin if there is to be any chance of producing more food for the people of the Amazon Basin while at the same time helping to preserve the ecological integrity of much of the yet undisturbed forests of that basin.

IMPROVED CROPPING SYSTEMS: CONTINUOUS CULTIVATION

Included among the alternate cropping systems for the Amazon Basin are the continuous cropping systems developed by North Carolina State University's (NCSU) Tropical Soils Research Program in cooperation with Peru's Instituto Nacional de Investigación y Promoción Agraria (INIPA) in Yurimaguas, Peru. Since 1971 these organizations have addressed the question whether continuous cropping of basic food crops would be agronomically possible and economically feasible on the acid and infertile Ultisols in the udic soil moisture regime of the upper Amazon Basin.

Yurimaguas was selected as the primary research site as it is representative in both climate and soil properties of much of the tropical rain forest of the upper Amazon Basin. Yurimaguas' mean annual temperature is 26°C and its well-distributed mean annual rainfall averages 2,100 mm with three months of about 100 mm each and the rest around 200 mm (Table 5.1). The flat, well-drained Ultisol at the Yurimaguas Agricultural Experiment Station (Table 5.3) has a sandy loam surface over a clay loam subsoil, both of which have high levels of Al, are deficient in P, K, and most other nutrients, and have a relatively low cation exchange capacity.

As Yurimaguas is the westernmost large fluvial port

of the Amazon headwaters, it is experiencing a large
population influx. About eight families arrive daily to
settle in the area. Its present population of 35,000 is
expected to triple by 1990. The population influx is
creating increased pressure on the land, shortening the
fallow duration and consequently breaking the soil
fertility regeneration process. Similar population and
land pressures are found in many other areas of the
Amazon Basin. (See chapters by Hecht, Moran, Stearman,
and Wood in this volume.)

1. Land Clearing

     The choice of land-clearing methods is the first
decision, and certainly one of the most important,
affecting crop productivity. Crop yields on soil cleared
by the traditional slash-and-burn methods at Yurimaguas
were found superior to those on the same soil cleared by
bulldozer (Seubert et al. 1977). The main reasons were:
(1) the fertilizer value of the ash, (2) less soil
compaction, or (3) no topsoil displacement as caused by
the bulldozer.
     The nutrient content of the ash and partially burned
material produced by slashing and burning a 17-year-old
forest fallow on an Ultisol of Yurimaguas contributed, in
kg/ha, 67 N, 6 P, 38 K, 75 Ca, 16 Mg, fairly large
quantities of iron and manganese, and some zinc and
copper (see Table 5.5). There is, of course, variability
in the nutrient content of the ash of various slash-and-
burn sites due to different clearing techniques, soils,
vegetation, and portion of biomass burned. Only 20% of
the forest biomass was estimated to have been ashed when
a virgin forest on an Ultisol in southern Bahia, Brazil,
was burned (Silva 1979). Extremely wide ranges in
nutrient content were found when the ashes of various
tree species were analyzed (Silva 1979), indicating that
certain species might be accumulators of certain nutrients.
In more fertile soils, the fertilizer value of the ash for
crop production may be of less importance. Cordero (1964)
found no concomitant increase in crop yield with increases
of P and K produced by burning vegetation on an Entisol
that was already high in those elements.
     Soil compaction produced by bulldozer clearing of
sandy loam Ultisols at Yurimaguas increased mechanical
impedance and decreased water infiltration rates substantially (North Carolina State University, 1978-1979).
Similar data have been noted for other locations in the
Amazon Basin (Table 5.6). The infiltration rates on the
bulldozer-cleared plots in Yurimaguas after six years of
cropping had only increased from 0.5 to 4.1 cm/hr, while
those of the slash-and-burn-cleared plots remained at
10 cm/hr, almost 250% better (see Table 5.6). The subsoil hardpan produced by bulldozer clearing has been
broken by chisel plowing or subsoiling with consequent

Table 5.5. Nutrient content of ash and partially burned material
produced by slashing and burning a 17-year-old forest
fallow on an Ultisol in Yurimaguas, Peru*

| Element | Content | |
	% or ppm	kg/ha
Nitrogen	1.72	67.0
Phosphorus	0.14	6.0
Potassium	0.97	38.0
Calcium	1.92	75.0
Magnesium	0.41	16.0
Iron	0.19	7.6
Manganese	0.19	7.3
Zinc	132	0.3
Copper	79	0.3

*Adapted from Seubert et al. (1977).

increase in crop yields (Alegre et al. 1981). Thus, it
is possible to reclaim land compacted by bulldozer clearing if high-energy equipment is available. Obviously,
it would be desirable to prevent the compaction problems
from occurring in the first place.

The topsoil displacement caused by bulldozers
dragging uprooted trees and logs across the topsoil has
not been quantitatively defined in the Amazon Basin.
However, even the most inexperienced observer notes
scraping in high spots and deposition in low spots following bulldozer clearing. The better jungle regrowth near
windrows of felled vegetation suggests yield reductions
due to topsoil removal in adjacent areas (Sanchez 1976).
Corn yields were found to decrease in Nigeria when 50%
of the top 2.5 cm of an Alfisol was removed (Lal et al.
1975).

Crop yields are very much affected by the land-
clearing method used. In no instance did rice, maize,
soybean, or cassava yields on bulldozed land at Yurimaguas
exceed those on land cleared by slash-and-burn methods
(see Table 5.7). Without fertilizer and lime the mean
relative yield of eight croppings on bulldozer-cleared
land was only 30% of that on land cleared by slash-and-
burn methods. Even with fertilization and lime, bulldozer-cleared land produced only 80% of the mean relative
yield produced on land cleared by slash-and-burn methods;
this is considered a combined effect of topsoil removal
and soil compaction.

The negative effects of bulldozer land clearing are
well recognized by many farmers and development

Table 5.6. Effects of land-clearing method on infiltration rates
in Ultisols in Yurimaguas, Peru, and in Manaus
(Amazonas) and Belmonte (Bahia), Brazil*

| Location | Infiltration rate at | | |
	Yurimaguas	Manaus	Belmonte
	--------------cm/hr--------------		
Virgin forest	117.0	15.0	24.0
15-year-old forest fallow	81.0	-	-
Path through virgin forest	5.2	-	-
Slashed-and-burned clearing (after 1 year of cropping)	10.0	-	20.0
Bulldozed clearing (after 1 year of cropping)	0.5	-	3.0
Slashed-and-burned clearing (after 6 years of cropping)	10.0	-	-
Bulldozed clearing (after 6 years of cropping)	4.1	-	-
Bulldozed clearing (after 5 years in pasture)	-	0.4	-

*Adapted from Seubert et al. (1977), Schubart (1977), Silva (1977),
and North Carolina State University (1978-1979).

organizations in the Amazon Basin.   In fact, since 1978
Brazilian government credits for large-scale mechanized
land-clearing operations have been sharply reduced
(Cochrane and Sanchez 1982).   Many farmers and development organizations are beginning to question the practice
of complete destruction of the forest versus its partial
harvest prior to burning. By removing the marketable
trees prior to cutting and burning the remainder, Silva
(1979) created an increase in income from the cleared
area as well as retaining the advantages of slash-and-
burn methods for soil fertility.   There were no fertility
differentials between Silva's method and the traditional
slash-and-burn clearing, probably due to the relatively
small portion of the biomass actually burned in both
clearing techniques.

The traditional slash-and-burn clearing system un-
questionably is the best for most farmers of the Amazon
Basin unless they can add additional fertilizer and use

Alternate methods of land clearing, such as using
two bulldozers dragging a heavy chain between them
(Toledo and Morales 1979), large tree crushers, or a
bulldozer with a KG shear blade with and without burn
(North Carolina State University, 1980-1981) offer both
advantages and disadvantages.

Table 5.7. Effect of land-clearing method on crop yield at
            Yurimaguas, Peru*

Crop (number of harvests)	Fertility Treatment**	Clearing Slash-and-Burn	Clearing Bull-dozer	Bulldozer÷ Slash-and-Burn
		--------t/ha----		-----%--------
Rice, upland (3)	0	1.33	0.70	53
	NPK	3.00	1.47	49
	NPK Lime	2.90	2.33	80
Maize (1)	0	0.10	0.00	0
	NPK	0.44	0.04	10
	NPK Lime	3.11	2.36	76
Soybeans (2)	0	0.70	0.15	24
	NPK	0.95	0.30	34
	NPK Lime	2.65	1.80	67
Cassava (2)	0	15.40	6.40	42
	NPK	18.90	14.90	78
	NPK Lime	25.60	24.80	97
Mean Relative Yields	0			30
	NPK			43
	NPK Lime			80

*Adapted from Seubert et al. (1977).

**N, P, K were applied at 50, 172, and 42 kg/ha, respectively, and
Ca(OH)$_2$ at 4 t CaCO$_2$-equivalent/ha.

tillage operations to compensate for the soil fertility
limitations and compaction disadvantages of bulldozer
clearing. The crucial question now revolves around how
to keep these slash-and-burn clearings continually productive in order to reduce migratory agriculture.

2. Continuous Cropping

Once the advantageous nature of the traditional
slash-and-burn clearing system had been established, the
NCSU/INIPA program turned its attention to developing
continuous crop production systems for these slashed-and-
burned areas of the acid, infertile soils of the Amazon
Basin. Components included determining the most important
crops, their best cropping sequences, their nutritional
needs, and changes in soil properties with time of cultivation (North Carolina State University, 1972-1981;
Bandy 1977; Bandy and Benites 1977; Sanchez 1977a, b, c,
d; Villachica 1978; Wade 1978; Valverde et al. 1979;
Nicholaides 1979). Crops grown and studied included rice,

Figure 5.5. Recommended planting dates for maize, soybeans, peanuts, rice, and cowpeas in the Yurimaguas, Peru, area of the Amazon Basin (source: North Carolina State University, 1978–1979)

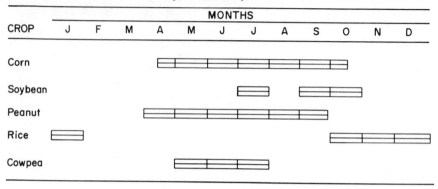

maize, cassava, peanuts, cowpeas, soybeans, sweet potatoes, and plantains in various rotations and combinations.

The production of three crops per year without any overlapping relay cropping is permitted by the climate and rainfall pattern of the Yurimaguas area. Recommended planting dates for the main annual crops in Yurimaguas are shown in Figure 5.5. Five crops per year were possible with intercropped combinations (Wade 1978); however, as intercropping has shown little or no advantage under these infinite seasonal conditions in Yurimaguas (McCollum 1982; Benites 1981) and as the farmers of the area are turning to rotational monocultures, only the most promising monoculture rotations obtained to date will be presented. These are the rotations of upland rice-maize-soybeans and upland rice-peanuts-soybeans, which keep the soil covered during most of the year. Monocultures without rotations did not produce sustained yields because of a build-up of many of the diseases and insects previously detailed.

Twenty-one consecutive crops of the upland rice-maize-soybean rotation have been harvested from the same field at Yurimaguas since it was cleared by a slash-and-burn procedure in October 1972. Without fertilization and lime, yields declined to zero with the third consecutive crop (Figure 5.6). The average long-term yield with "complete" fertilization treatment of this rice-maize-soybeans rotation was 7.8 tons grain/ha annually. Twenty-one consecutive crops of the upland rice-peanut-soybean rotation also have been harvested with equally high yields. In fact, peanuts, which have a higher yield potential than corn, may be more appropriate for the area due to the climatic constraints of corn. These

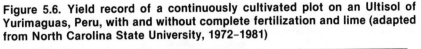

Figure 5.6. Yield record of a continuously cultivated plot on an Ultisol of Yurimaguas, Peru, with and without complete fertilization and lime (adapted from North Carolina State University, 1972–1981)

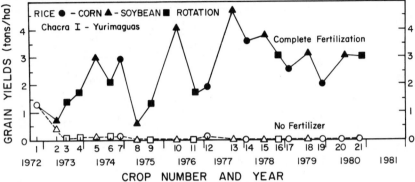

results indicate that with adequate fertilization (Table 5.8), sustainable moderately high yields of these annual crops can be achieved under continuous production on some of the most infertile soils of the Amazon Basin.

Not only are these systems agronomically feasible, but they are economically productive as well. A net return of U.S. $2.91 per U.S. $1.00 invested in fertilizer and lime at 1977 Yurimaguas prices, including transportation, was realized for the rice-peanuts-soybeans rotation (Bandy 1977). Coutu and Hernandez (personal communication 1980) used computers to project from experiment station trials in Yurimaguas the estimated incomes for small farmers using the improved "Yurimaguas technology" with inputs of U.S. $300 and only family labor. On farms of 1.5 to 2.0 hectares under these conditions, projected family net incomes ranged from U.S. $714 to $4,180 when rice, maize, peanuts, soybeans, and cassava were the crops grown.

3. <u>Soil Fertility Dynamics: The Key Factor</u>

The understanding of soil fertility dynamics was the key to the development of the successful "Yurimaguas technology." The nutritional needs of the crops in the Amazon Basin, as with crop production anywhere, can be determined only by continual monitoring of soil fertility dynamics through soil and plant sampling and testing. Only then can the most judicious use of lime and fertilizers for crop production be ascertained.

Soil fertility dynamics were monitored by sampling soils after each harvest and analyzing for pH; organic carbon; total nitrogen; exchangeable potassium, calcium, magnesium, and aluminum; effective cation exchange capacity (ECEC); and available phosphorus, zinc, copper,

Table 5.8. Lime and fertilizer requirements for continuous
           cropping of a three crop/year rotation of rice-
           maize-soybeans or rice-peanuts-soybeans on an
           Ultisol at Yurimaguas, Peru*

Input**	Rate	Frequency
Lime	3 tons $CaCo_3$-equivalent/ha	Once/3 years
Nitrogen	80-100 kg N/ha	Rice and maize only
Phosphorus	25 kg P/ha	Each crop
Potassium	100 kg K/ha	Each crop, split applied
Magnesium	25 kg Mg/ha	Each crop, unless dolomitic lime is used
Copper	1 kg Cu/ha	Once/year or two years
Zinc	1 kg Zn/ha	Once/year or two years
Boron	1 kg B/ha	Once/year or two years
Molybdenum	20 g Mo/ha	Mixed with legume seed during inoculation

*Adapted from Sanchez, Bandy, Villachica, and Nicholaides (1982).

**Calcium and sulfur requirements are satisfied by lime, simple
 superphosphate, and Mg, Cu, and Zn carriers.

iron, and manganese (Figure 5.7). Sulfur, boron, and
molybdenum were determined periodically by plant analysis.
Of special interest in Figure 5.7 is the "check", which
never received fertilizer or lime, and the "complete",
which received what was considered the best fertilization
and liming practices according to soil tests and accumulated experience.
     The appearance of fertility limitations and their
intensities varied among various clearings even though
they were near each other, on the same soil mapping unit,
landscape position, and had the same pre-clearing
vegetation. The intensity of the burn was considered a
factor contributing to this variability. A generalized
summary of nutrient dynamics follows.
     Ash from the burn produced a temporary increase in
soil fertility as reflected by increases in pH, total N,
available P, exchangeable K, Ca, Mg, and some micro-
nutrients, with a concomitant decrease in percentage of
Al saturation to below-toxic levels (North Carolina
State University 1972-1981; Sanchez et al. 1980). Similar
changes have been noted in other locations in the Amazon
(see Table 5.9). As a result, upland rice, the first

Figure 5.7. Soil fertility dynamics in Yurimaguas, Peru, following conversion of a forest fallow Ultisol into continuous crop production with and without complete fertilization and lime. Extractant used for determining available P, Zn, Cu, Mn, and Fe and exchangeable K was 0.5 m NaHCO$_3$ + 0.01 M EDTA; that for exchangeable Al, Ca, and Mg was I$\underline{N}$ KCl (source: Bandy and Sanchez 1981)

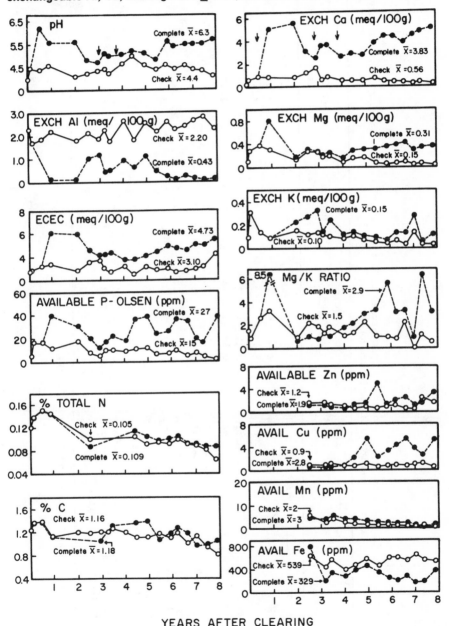

YEARS AFTER CLEARING

Table 5.9. Changes in topsoil-chemical properties before and shortly after burning tropical forests on Ultisols and Oxisols of the Amazon*

Soil property	Time in relation to burn	Yurimaguas (2 sites) I	II	Manaus (7 sites)	Belém (60 sites)	Barrolândia (1 site)
Months after burning:		1	3	1/2	12	1
pH	Before	4.0	4.0	3.8	4.8	4.6
	After	4.5	4.8	4.5	4.9	5.2
Exch. Ca+Mg (meq/100 g)	Before	0.41	1.46	0.35	1.03	1.40
	After	0.88	4.08	1.25	1.97	4.40
Exch. K (meq/100 g)	Before	0.10	0.33	0.07	0.12	0.07
	After	0.32	0.24	0.22	0.12	0.16
Exch. Al (meq/100 g)	Before	2.27	2.15	1.73	1.62	0.75
	After	1.70	0.65	0.70	0.90	0.28
Al sat'n. (%)	Before	81	52	80	58	34
	After	59	12	32	30	5
Avail. P (ppm) (mod. Olsen in Peru) ($HCl-H_2SO_4$ in Brazil)	Before	5	15	–	6.3	1.5
	After	16	23	–	7.5	8.5

*Adapted from Cochrane and Sanchez (1982).

crop planted in Yurimaguas, did not suffer from fertility limitations.

About eight months after clearing, however, the N and K levels were reduced such that deficiency symptoms appeared along with sporadic deficiencies of S, Cu, and B. Organic matter contents, as reflected by organic carbon (C) in the topsoil, decreased 25% during the first year, but reached a new equilibrium level starting with the second year. The rapid decomposition of organic matter released hydrogen and aluminum ions that acidified the soil and increased the percentage of Al saturation to toxic levels, nullifying the liming effect of the ash.

Phosphorus and Mg became deficient during the second year, Ca within the first 30 months, and zinc (Zn) during the fourth year; manganese (Mn) deficiency was suspected after the eighth year. Deficiencies of molybdenum (Mo) were detected occasionally in grain legumes, particularly when seeds produced in acid soils of the Amazon were used, but not when seeds came from more fertile soils of the Peruvian coast. After eight years of continuous cultivation, therefore, crops grown on this Ultisol have exhibited deficiencies of all essential soil nutrients but iron (Fe) and chlorine (Cl).

In the "complete" treatment, fertilizers and lime were added according to soil test recommendations. During the third year, however, yields declined rapidly in the "complete" treatment (Figure 5.6). Soil analysis identified two factors responsible for this decline: (1) a shorter than expected residual effect of the lime, and (2) the triggering of Mg deficiency induced by K applications and a consequent K/Mg imbalance (Villachica 1978). After these factors were corrected, crop yields stabilized (see Figure 5.6). Thus, a monitoring of the soil fertility dynamics during the period when the soil was undergoing a transition from forest to cropland provided the key for continuous cultivation.

Here it is relevant to emphasize the value of long-term field research. Second- and third-generation problems do not show early symptoms in the first years of continuous cultivation. Had the research been deemed successful and ended after one or two years, the answers to longer-term continuous cultivation of annual crops on these soils would not now be available for the farmers who need to know them.

The fertilizer needs for intensive continuous cultivation of these soils are no more than required, and are similar to those needed, for crop production in Ultisols in other parts of the world. The fertilizer rates for continuous production of corn, soybeans, and peanuts on Ultisols in the upper Amazon Basin do not differ substantially from the rates for these crops grown in Ultisols of the southeastern United States. On an annual basis, the total amounts are somewhat higher in the upper Amazon Basin because three crops a year are grown instead of one. After the first crop, which does not normally require fertilization, chemical inputs, whether inorganic or organic, are required to produce and sustain moderately high yields.

As with all sound fertilizer recommendations, these are site-specific and thus applicable only to the soil and cropping systems in question. In other soils, recommendations should be based on local soil analysis. Nevertheless, Table 5.8, developed after some eight years of cultivation, gives an indication of the inputs and their rates required for continuous crop production on an Ultisol typical of many soils in the upper Amazon Basin.

4. Effects of Soil Properties

The issue of soil degradation with cultivation in the humid tropics is a common concern in the literature (McNeil 1964). The results of NCSU's Tropical Soils Research Program, however, indicate just the contrary: i.e., soil properties improved with intensively managed, appropriately fertilized and limed continuous crop production systems (Table 5.10).

After seven years of properly liming and fertilizing 20 consecutive crops, the topsoil pH had increased from a very acid 4.0 before clearing to a favorable level of 5.7. Organic matter contents decreased by 27%, most of which occurred during the first year. Exchangeable Al was decreased by liming from very high levels to negligible amounts, decreasing Al saturation on the exchange sites from a toxic level of 82% to a negligible 1%. Exchangeable Ca levels increased nearly twenty-fold, a consequence of liming applications. Exchangeable Mg levels doubled, but this figure fluctuated with time. Exchangeable K levels did not increase in spite of large quantities of K fertilizer applied, suggesting rapid utilization by crops and perhaps leaching to the subsoil. Effective cation exchange capacity, a measure of the soil's capability to retain cations against leaching, doubled when the soil pH was raised from 4.0 to 5.7; this was probably a consequence of the pH-dependent charge characteristics of the kaolinite clay-iron oxide mixture. Fertilization also increased available P levels from below the critical level of 10 ppm to substantially above it. The same trend occurred with Zn and Cu, as both were applied as fertilizers. However, no Mn fertilizer was applied and the available Mn levels decreased to less than the critical level of 5 ppm, suggesting the possibility of Mn deficiency. Available Fe levels remained considerably above the critical range of 20-40 ppm. On the whole, these changes are indicative of a vast improvement in the topsoil's chemical properties and are reflected by the excellent cumulative grain production of about 8 t/ha annually.

No unfavorable changes in soil physical properties

Table 5.10. Changes in topsoil (0-15 cm) chemical properties after nearly eight years of continuous production of 20 crops of upland rice, corn, and soybeans with complete fertilization and liming at Yurimaguas, Peru*

Time	pH	Org. matter	Exchangeable				Eff. CEC	Al Sat'n.	Available				
			Al	Ca	Mg	K			P	Zn	Cu	Mn	Fe
		%	------meq/100 cc--------					%	------------ppm------------				
Before clearing	4.0	2.13	2.27	0.26	0.15	0.10	2.78	82	5	1.5**	0.9**	5.3**	650**
90 months after clearing	5.7	1.55	0.06	4.98	0.35	0.11	5.51	1	39	3.5	5.2	1.5	389

*Adapted from North Carolina State University (1978-1979).

**30 months after clearing.

have been detected thus far (North Carolina State University 1978-1979) because of the protection that three well-fertilized crops per year provides against the impact of rain on the soil. Although crop residues are left in the field until the experimental plots are tilled again in preparation for the next planting, the soil is exposed for a period of up to 30 days until the crop canopy is established. Occasional runoff losses on sloping land have been observed, but areas larger than one hectare have not been tested. Severe surface soil compaction, however, is rampant in the continuously cultivated plots that received no fertilization, because the very weak crops do not develop a complete canopy. In contrast, healthy fertilized crops do produce a good, complete canopy, thereby having less surface soil compaction and less potential runoff.

Figure 5.8. Corn root distribution (percent dry weight basis) as affected by shallow, deep, and normal lime placement in an Ultisol of Yurimaguas, Peru (source: North Carolina State University 1978-1979)

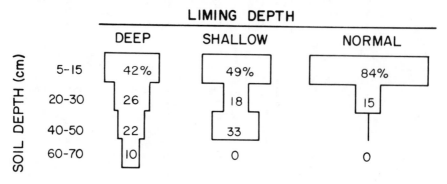

The acid, infertile subsoils of Oxisols and Ultisols frequently act as chemical barriers to root development. Crop roots are unable to enter a subsoil with high Al saturation and low exchangeable Ca (Bandy 1976; Gonzalez et al. 1979; Ritchey et al. 1980). This situation results in shallow root systems, causing the plants to suffer from drought stress during rainless periods while the subsoil has available water. Deep lime placement compared with normal or shallow lime placement results in corn roots being able to grow into the subsoil (Figure 5.8) and consequently use the subsoil moisture to reduce plant water stress. The deep liming treatment shows a more even distribution of soil water use by the corn plant throughout the 45 cm profile and results in at least 8.0 mm more soil water used by plants on deep lime plots (North Carolina State University 1978-1979). That amount equals 2 to 3 days of evapotranspiration from corn plants.

The subsoil chemical constraints have been somewhat alleviated with time following lime and fertilizer application. Significant increases in Ca, Mg, and effective cation exchange capacity (ECEC), and a decrease in Al saturation were found in subsoil layers of 15 to 45 cm depth after 92 months of continuous cultivation of the acid, infertile Ultisol at Yurimaguas (Figure 5.9). The lime and fertilization scheme promoted the downward movement of these basic cations, which resulted in a more favorable environment for root development than before clearing. Appropriate fertilization and continuous cultivation, after seven years, have improved rather than degraded this Ultisol of the upper Amazon Basin.

5. Farmer Acceptance

The true test of any improved technology for continuous cropping in the Amazon Basin is its acceptance and utilization by the target group--the small, shifting cultivators. Thus, in 1978, the NCSU and INIPA team felt that results from formal experiments appeared to have sufficient practical application to be tested at the farm level. A series of demonstration plots were established in shifting cultivators' slashed-and-burned fields within an 80 km radius of Yurimaguas.

The small farmers themselves, with NCSU/INIPA support, planted and managed several three-crop-per-year rotational systems (Mesia et al. 1979). The systems were (1) the farmers' traditional system, (2) improved agronomic practices without lime and fertilizer, and (3) improved agronomic practices with moderate rates of lime (1 ton $CaCO_3$-equivalent/ha annually) and fertilizer (60 kg N/ha for rice and corn only, 35 kg P/ha for each crop, 66 kg K/ha for each crop, and 22 kg Mg/ha for each crop). System 3 is improved "Yurimaguas technology" and was considered equivalent to the "complete" treatments developed at the Yurimaguas Agricultural Experiment Station. The year's rotational systems were planted on 1 to 10 year forest-fallow slashed-and-burned clearings, on soils (Typic and Aquic Paleudults and Tropudults) similar to and more fertile than those soils (Typic Tropudults and Vertic Eutropepts) of the Yurimaguas Agricultural Experiment Station.

The annual cumulative grain yields produced by the improved System 3 ranged from 7.5 to 11.4 tons/ha, while those from the traditional System 1 were 3.5 to 5.3 tons/ha (see Table 5.11). The System 3 yields are similar to those obtained at the experiment station. They are much better than the traditional yields of 1 to 1.5 tons grain/ha usually produced on the shifting cultivators' farms in the Amazon Basin (Moran 1981; Smith 1981).

After three consecutive crops in the traditional System 1, soil analysis revealed nutrient depletion due

134

Figure 5.9. Improvement in subsoil chemical properties after 7-1/2 years of continuous cultivation of a rice-corn-soybean rotation on an Ultisol of Yurimaguas, Peru (source: Sanchez, Bandy, Villachica, and Nicholaides 1982:826)

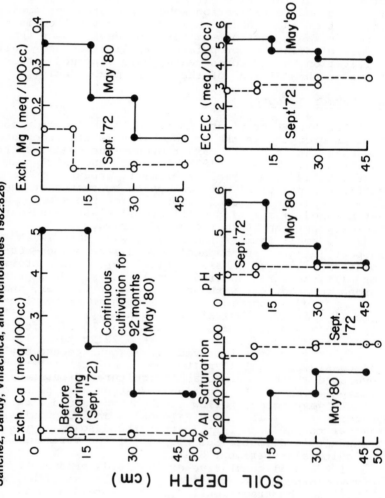

Table 5.11. Average grain yields of 11 small farmer-managed continuous-cropping demonstration trials from July 1978 through June 1979 within an 80-km radius of Yurimaguas, Peru*

Production system	Crop Rotation											
	Corn	Peanuts	Corn	Total	Peanuts	Rice**	Soybeans	Total	Soybeans	Rice+	Soybeans	Total
	----------------------------------Average grain yields, tons/ha----------------------------------											
I. Traditional	2.44	1.10	1.77	5.31	0.97	1.91	1.34	3.53	1.43	1.91	1.15	4.49
II. Improved, no lime or fertilizer	3.81	1.36	2.73	7.90	1.22	3.56	1.98	6.76	2.09	2.25	1.89	6.23
III. Improved, with lime and fertilizer	5.12	1.62	4.66	11.40	1.49	4.53	2.75	8.77	2.73	2.53	2.22	7.48

*Adapted from North Carolina State University (1978-1979).

**Rice in System I was the traditional Carolino variety, in Systems II and III the improved IR 4-2 variety.

+ Rice in all systems was the traditional Carolino variety.

to crop removal and loss of ash-liming effect. In all farm locations the soils had become deficient in P and more acidic--with exchangeable Al increasing and Ca, Mg, and organic C decreasing. This nutrient depletion was reflected in declining yields of corn and soybeans in the respective corn-peanuts-corn and soybeans-rice-soybeans rotation (see Table 5.11). As nutrient depletion became more severe in the second year of the trials, yields declined even further in the traditional System 1.

Economic analysis using no limits on the labor and capital resources revealed that the System 3 rotation of corn-peanuts-corn gave the highest net revenue per hectare with U.S. $1,661, at the current rate of exchange. Also, the marginal rate of return was consistently higher (exceeding 450% in all three systems) for the corn-peanuts-corn rotation than for the other two rotations (North Carolina State University 1978-1979).

The economic analysis using limited resources restricted the capital, labor, and output of work of the small farmer family to all possible levels and combinations. This analysis revealed that System 3 corn-peanuts-corn rotation on a 1.45 hectare farm using U.S. $90 as owned capital, another U.S. $90 as borrowed capital (at 68% annual interest rate), and a seven-member, small-farm family model as the sole labor pool could realize a net farm income of U.S. $2,797 (North Carolina State University 1978-1979) at the current rate of exchange. This net income is considerably greater than the current net farm income in the Yurimaguas area of U.S. $750, or the $1,500 annual net income of the top 25% of the families in Lima's slums (Hernandez and Coutu 1981).

In the 1980-1981 growing season, a pilot project with 27 rural schools in the Yurimaguas region was initiated in order to reach more small farmers and their families. This collaborative project among INIPA (under the Ministry of Agriculture), the Ministry of Education, and NCSU set up the same type of demonstration projects already described, but this time with the rural school students, their families, and teachers planting and managing the trials with the three systems. After only one year, over 50% of the 626 small-farm families involved in the project were interested enough to want to continue participating in the project (Benites, personal communication 1981). Given the favorable Peruvian government response to the "Yurimaguas technology," the local availability of fertilizer and credit has increased and marketing facilities have improved in Yurimaguas. Clearly, this is only a beginning, but it is a solid one and has the potential to be of benefit to small farmers throughout the upper Amazon Basin.

6. Continued and New Research

As important as the findings are that agronomically

and economically feasible continuous crop production
systems are available and acceptable to at least some
small farmers on the acid, infertile soils of the upper
Amazon Basin, not all the answers have been obtained for
changing the region's predominant agricultural practice
from shifting to permanent cultivation. Several comple-
mentary options for sustained agriculture in the Amazon
Basin are being investigated by the NCSU/INIPA team and
others. These include the following research thrusts.

   a. Alternate land-clearing methods. New research
in Yurimaguas is directed at determining whether any of
several combinations of the traditional slash-and-burn
clearing with some type of small- or large-scale mechanization might be advantageous in both clearing and subsequent crop yields for the small farmers of the region.
One of the most promising involves the use of a bulldozer
with a KG-shear blade to cut trees at the soil surface,
thereby minimizing topsoil removal, and removing the
larger trees prior to burning the vegetation for
fertilizer value of the ash (Cassel and Alegre, unpublished data 1981). Longer-term research is needed in
this area.

   b. Lower input systems. Emphasis is given to this
area of research in Yurimaguas in order to develop
alternate systems requiring lower inputs for the small
farmers of the region. One approach is evaluation of
varieties within species for their tolerance to Al in the
soil. As soil acidity is a main limiting factor to crop
production on the Ultisols and Oxisols of the Amazon
Basin, determining tolerant varieties would result in
lessening costly, though economical, lime inputs. Evaluation of varieties of rice, peanuts, cowpeas, soybeans, and
sweet potatoes has identified promising varieties of rice
and cowpeas (Piha and Nicholaides 1981). These efforts
are continuing.

   Increasing the efficiencies of N and K fertilizers on
these acid soils and evaluating, in collaboration with IFDC
(International Fertilizer Development Center) and CIAT
(Centro Internacional de Agricultura Tropical), the use of
rock phosphate compared with the more costly phosphate fertilizers are other components of the low-input approach.
The research in these areas, though promising, needs several more years before definitive answers can be given.

   The use of organic inputs to replace or supplement the
costly, though economical, inorganic inputs has included
mulching crops with residues from the previous crop or with
Panicum maximum and has produced inconclusive results after
over 20 experiments. Generally mulching has given detrimen-
tal results for upland rice, some positive yield increase
in corn, and has had little effect on soybeans and peanuts
(Valverde and Bandy 1982). The use of kudzu (Pueraria
phaseoloides) as a green manure has provided positive results, often attaining crop yields similar to complete fertilization (Wade 1978). However, the labor involved in hand-

harvesting, transporting, and incorporating kudzu into the soil has made this an unattractive alternative to the small farmers. Making compost out of crop residues appears to have some promise. For the first four consecutive crops, replacing complete fertilization with compost produced from crop residues resulted in only a 20% yield reduction (Bandy and Nicholaides 1979). In order to maintain this rate, it was found necessary to apply K fertilizer with the compost. The potential use of this practice, however, also is restricted by the high labor requirements of compost making.

c. Green manures. Research is also in progress on the use of managed kudzu fallows as an intermediate stage between shifting and continuous cultivation. Kudzu can establish itself on the acid, infertile soils and quickly develop a lush, green canopy underlain by an abundance of N-fixing nodules on its roots. After one or two years of fallow, kudzu can be killed by slashing with a machete and burning. Reasonable crop yields have been obtained by rotating three crops with one to two years of fallow (Bandy and Sanchez 1981). During the second rotation, K was again needed to obtain moderate crop yields. Additional research is needed.

d. Pastures and Agroforestry. Technology is also being developed for legume-based, low-input pasture production, primarily for the sloping Ultisols, using acid-tolerant grass and legume species selected by CIAT's Tropical Pastures Program (Toledo and Serrão 1982). Promising germplasm has been tested for adaptation in an Ultisol of pH 4.0 and 80% Al saturation with only 11 kg P/ha application as simple superphosphate. Results so far show that the grasses Andropogon gayanus, Brachiaria humidicola, and B. decumbens, and the legumes Desmodium ovalifolium, Pueraria phaseoloides, and Centrosema pubescens are well adapted to the soil, climate, pest, and disease constraints of the region. Grass-legume pastures are now being tested under grazing pressure (Ara et al. 1981), but it is too early for conclusive results.

Use of indigenous and imported tree species is also considered vital to development efforts in the Amazon Basin. Thus, agroforestry is an important new research component at Yurimaguas. Research is being initiated to combine crop production systems at various input levels with promising tree species that can produce food, oil, or pulpwood. These include the peach palm (Guiliema gasipaes), oil palm (Elaeis guinensis), and pulp-producing Gmelina arborea and Pinus caribea.

The Amazon Basin's relatively fertile alluvial soils not subject to flooding have great food-production potential. Application of research on improved rice varieties and spacing on these soils (Sanchez and Nureña 1972) resulted in doubling rice yields. The inherent native fertility of these soils and their proximity to natural transportation systems stress their importance. Current research at Yurimaguas is developing the most suitable paddy rice production technology with irrigation from the rivers and rotations of corn, soybeans, and cowpeas with paddy rice where these soils are moderately well drained by nature or improved by drainage systems. Similar innovative farming systems for similar soils are being developed by UEPAE/EMBRAPA (Unidade de Execução de Pesquisa de Ámbito Estadual)/(Emprêsa Brasileira de Pesquisa Agropecuária) near Manaus (UEPAE/EMBRAPA 1979-1981).

CONCLUSIONS

In spite of the objections of well-meaning individuals and organizations, the increasing demand for food within the countries sharing the common heritage of the Amazon Basin will continue, through both spontaneous and government-directed colonization, to increase the clearing of the Amazon Basin forests. The experience and data presented herein show clearly that the use of correct technology can result in increased food production on the acid, infertile soils of the upper Amazon Basin without ecological damage. The key to success is the development and extension of the correct agronomic technology of these soils so that sustained continuous cultivation can occur on the cleared lands, consequently preserving the ecological integrity of those yet uncleared portions of the Amazon Basin forests.

1. Limitations

It would be unwise to infer that the continuous production technologies described herein are directly applicable to all the Oxisols and Ultisols in the Amazon Basin. The work of NCSU/INIPA has concentrated on level Ultisols of the upper Amazon Basin, thereby avoiding the erosion hazards of cultivating the undulating lands. Adaptation of the "Yurimaguas technology" to undulating lands would be needed, perhaps including terracing as practiced in areas of humid tropical Asia. Other options for the undulating lands to be cleared could be legume-based pastures or agroforestry. Better yet would be to leave the undulating Amazon Basin forests in their pristine state and to concentrate food production efforts on the 205 million hectares of well-drained Oxisols and Ultisols with less than 8% slope (Sanchez, Bandy, Villachica, and Nicholaides 1982).

The socioeconomic conditions provide another limitation to the widespread adaptation of the "Yurimaguas technology." The Yurimaguas area, though not a privileged region of the Amazon, has an unpaved road to Lima and several rivers that link it with markets in the rest of the country and beyond. As discussed, present socioeconomic conditions indicate clear economic feasibility for the "Yurimaguas technology." Different

140

cost/price ratios, inelastic demand for products,
government policies, and many other time- and location-
specific factors could make the same technology economically unattractive elsewhere. Attempts at continuous
cultivation in isolated areas with little market
accessibility could be foolish. Site-specific economic
interpretations based on local and national factors are
in order for any region contemplating adopting the
"Yurimaguas technology."

Agronomic conditions could also be different from
region to region. Hence, the "Yurimaguas technology"
must be tested through adaptive research trials to local
situations prior to widespread implementation attempts.
Possible modification could include different fertilizer
rates, different crop species or varieties, and rotations.
Vital to these adaptive research trials for fertilizer
rates will be some type of soil fertility evaluation and
improvement service to assist farmers changing from
shifting to continuous cultivation.

2. <u>Potential</u>

Once the limitations are realized and addressed
successfully, the potential of the "Yurimaguas technology"
is that the indigenous people, settlers, and governments
in the Amazon Basin will have available the means to
increase food production while sparing many hectares of
forest. Farmers do not clear the Amazon forest because
they like to do so; it is excruciatingly hard work.
Farmers clear the rain forest because they need the
plant nutrients stored in the biomass, released upon
burning, to grow food. If they can produce more food
more economically with less work, as is being done by the
farmers involved with the NCSU/INIPA project, they will
do so without hesitation. If they cannot, then the
Amazon Basin forests will continue to fall from the
shifting cultivators' axes. The "Yurimaguas technology"
offers one agronomically, economically, and ecologically
sound alternative to that scenario.

ACKNOWLEDGMENTS

This work was supported in part by Contract AID
ta-C-1236 of the United States Agency for International
Development.

REFERENCES

Alegre, J. C., D. K. Cassel, and D. E. Bandy
1981   Effects of Tillage Practices on Reclaiming a
        Severely Compacted Ultisol in Yurimaguas, Peru.
        p. 38. In <u>Agron</u>. <u>Abstrs</u>., Amer. Soc. of Agron.
        1981 Ann. Mtgs. Madison, Wis.

Alvim, P. T.
1978   Perspectivas de Produção Agrícola na Regiâo
        Amazônica. Interciencia 3(4):243-249.

Ara, M., Pedro A. Sanchez, D. E. Bandy, and J. M. Toledo
1981   Adaptation of Acid-Tolerant Grass and Legume
        Pasture Ecotypes in the Upper Amazon Basin.
        p. 38. In Agron. Abstrs., Amer. Soc. of Agron.
        1981 Ann. Mtgs. Madison, Wis.

Bandy, D. E.
1976   Soil-Plant-Water Relationships as Influenced
        by Various Soil and Plant Management Practices
        on Camp Cerrado Soils in the Central Plateau
        of Brazil. Ph.D. dissertation, Cornell Univ.

1977   Manejo de Suelos y Cultivos en Sistemas de
        Agricultura Permanente en la Selva Amazónica
        del Peru. In P. Arens, ed., Reunión-Taller
        sobre Manejo y Conservación de Suelos. Lima:
        Food and Agricultural Organization (FAO) /
        Servicio Internacional de Desarrollo Agricola
        (SIDA).

Bandy, D. E. and J. Benites
1977   Proyecto Internacional de Suelos Tropicales,
        Yurimaguas. Lima: Ministerio de Alimentación.

Bandy, D. E. and J. J. Nicholaides, III
1979   Use of Composts for Crop Production on Ultisols
        of the Amazon Jungle. p. 42. In Agron.
        Abstrs., Amer. Soc. of Agron. 1979 Ann. Mtgs.
        Madison, Wis.

Bandy, D. E. and Pedro A. Sanchez
1981   Continuous Crop Cultivation on Acid Soils of
        the Amazon Basin of Peru. Paper presented at
        the Workshop on Management of Low Fertility
        Acid Soils of the American Humid Tropics held
        at the Univ. of Surinam, Faculty of Natural
        Resources, Panamaribo, Surinam, and sponsored
        by Instituto Interamericano de Ciencias
        Agrícolas (IICA): November 23-26.

Benites, J. R.
1981   Nitrogen Response and Cultural Practices for
        Corn-Based Cropping Systems in the Peruvian
        Amazon. Ph.D. dissertation, North Carolina
        State Univ.

Buol, S. W. and W. Couto
1978   Fertility Management Interpretations and Soil
        Surveys of the Tropics. In M. Drosdoff, R. B.

142

Daniels, and J. J. Nicholaides, III, eds.,
Diversity of Soils in the Tropics. Madison,
Wis.: Amer. Soc. of Agron. Spec. Publ. No. 34.

Buol, S. W. and J. J. Nicholaides, III
1980   Constraints to Soil Fertility Evaluation and
        Extrapolation of Research Results. In IRRI/
        Cornell, Priorities for Alleviating Soil-Related
        Constraints to Food Production in the Tropics.
        Los Baños, Laguna, Philippines: International
        Rice Research Institute (IRRI).

Buol, S. W., Pedro A. Sanchez, R. B. Cate, Jr., and
M. A. Granger
1975   Soil Fertility Capability Classification. In
        E. Bornemisza and A. Alvarado, eds., Soil
        Management in Tropical America. Raleigh:
        North Carolina State Univ.

Cassel, D. K. and J. C. Alegre
1981   Unpublished Report. Raleigh: North Carolina
        State Univ., Soil Science Dept.

Cochrane, T. T. and P. G. Jones
1981   Savannas, Forests and Wet Seasonal Potential
        Evapotranspiration in Tropical South America.
        Trop. Agric. 58(3):185-190.

Cochrane, T. T., J. A. Porras, L. Azevedo, P. G. Jones,
and L. F. Sanchez
1979   An Explanatory Manual for CIAT's Computerized
        Land Resource Study of Tropical America.
        Cali: Centro Internacional de Agricultura
        Tropical (CIAT).

Cochrane, T. T. and Pedro A. Sanchez
1982   Land Resources, Soil Properties and Their Manage-
        ment in the Amazon Region: A State of Knowledge
        Report. In S. B. Hecht, ed., Amazonia: Agricul-
        ture and Land Use Research. Cali: Centro Inter-
        nacional de Agricultura Tropical (CIAT).

Cordero, A.
1964   The Effect of Land Clearing on Soil Fertility
        in the Tropical Region of Santa Cruz, Bolivia.
        M.S. thesis, Univ. of Florida.

Denevan, William M.
1973   Development and the Imminent Demise of the
        Amazon Rainforest. The Professional Geographer
        25(2):130-135.

1977   The Causes and Consequences of Shifting Culti-
        vation in Relation to Tropical Forest Survival.

Paper presented at the Congreso Internacional de Geógrafos Latinoamericanistas, Paipa, Colombia, August 3-9.

Dudal, R.
1980   Soil-Related Constraints to Agricultural Development in the Tropics. pp. 23-53. In IRRI/Cornell Priorities for Alleviating Soil-Related Constraints to Food Production in the Tropics. Los Baños, Laguna, Philippines: International Rice Research Institute (IRRI).

FAO-UNESCO
1975   Soil Map of the World. Vol. IV, South America. Paris: United Nations Educational, Scientific, and Cultural Organization (UNESCO).

Friedman, I.
1977   The Amazon Basin, Another Sahel? Science 197:7.

Gonzalez, E., E. J. Kamprath, G. C. Naderman, and W. V. Soares
1979   Effect of Depth of Lime Incorporation on the Growth of Corn on an Oxisol of Central Brazil. Soil Sci. Soc. Amer. J. 43:1155-1158.

Goodland, Robert J.A. and H. S. Irwin
1975   Amazon Jungle: Green Hell to Red Desert? Amsterdam: Elsevier.

Grigg, D. B.
1974   The Agricultural Systems of the World: An Evolutionary Approach. London: Cambridge Univ. Press.

Hancock, J. R., R. W. Hill, and G. H. Hargreaves
1979   Potential Evapotranspiration and Precipitation Deficits for Tropical America. Cali: Centro Internacional de Agricultura Tropical (CIAT).

Hernandez, D. and A. J. Coutu
1981   Economic Evaluation of Slash/Burn Cultivation Options in Yurimaguas, Peru. p. 42. In Agron. Abstrs., Amer. Soc. of Agron. 1981 Ann. Mtgs. Madison, Wis.

Irion, G.
1978   Soil Infertility in the Amazon Rainforest. Naturwissenchaften 65:515-519.

Klinge, H.
1975   Root Mass Estimation in Lowland Tropical Rain-forests of Central Amazonia, Brazil. III. Nutrients in Five Roots from Giant Humus Podsols.

144

Trop. Ecol. 16:28-39.

Lal, R., B. T. Kang, F. R. Moormann, A.S.R. Juo,
and J. C. Moomaw
  1975   Soil Management Problems and Possible Solutions
         in Western Nigeria. pp. 372-408. In E.
         Bornemiza and A. Alvarado, eds., _Soil Management
         in Tropical America_. Raleigh: North Carolina
         State Univ.

Manshard, W.
  1974   _Tropical Agriculture: A Geographical
         Introduction and Appraisal_. London: Longman
         Group Ltd.

Marbut, C. F. and C. B. Manifold
  1926   The Soils of the Amazon Basin in Relation to
         Agricultural Possibilities. _Geogr. Rev._
         16:414-442.

McCollum, R. E.
  1982   Dynamics of Soil Nutrients in Multiple Cropping
         Systems in Relation to Efficient Use of
         Fertilizers. In _Proceedings, Fertilizer Use
         under Multiple Cropping Systems_. New Delhi,
         Feb. 1-6. Rome: Food and Agricultural
         Organization (FAO).

McNeil, M.
  1964   Lateritic Soils. _Scientific American_ 211:86-102.

Mesía, R., D. E. Bandy, and J. J. Nicholaides, III
  1979   Transfer of Agronomic Practices to the Small
         Farmer of the Amazon Jungle. p. 46. In _Agron.
         Abstrs._, Amer. Soc. of Agron. 1979 Ann. Mtgs.
         Madison, Wis.

Moran, Emilio F.
  1981   _Developing the Amazon_. Bloomington: Indiana
         Univ. Press.

Myers, N.
  1980   _Conversion of Tropical Moist Forests_. Washing-
         ton, D.C.: National Research Council/National
         Academy of Sciences.

National Academy of Sciences
  1972   _Soils of the Humid Tropics_. Washington, D.C.:
         National Academy of Sciences.

Nicholaides, J. J., III
  1979   Crop Production Systems on Acid Soils in Humid
         Tropical America. In D. W. Thorne and M. D.
         Thorne, eds., _Soil, Water and Crop Production_.

Westport, Conn.: AVI Publ. Co.

North Carolina State University
Tropical Soils Research Program Annual Reports.
1972, 1973, 1974, 1976-1977, 1978-1979, 1980-
1981. Raleigh: Soil Science Dept., North
Carolina State Univ.

Nye, P. H. and D. J. Greenland
1960   The Soil under Shifting Cultivation.
Harpenden, UK: Comm. Agr. Bur. Tech. Comm. 51.

Piha, M. and J. J. Nicholaides, III
1981   Field Evaluation of Legume, Sweet Potato and
Rice Varieties for Tolerance to Soil Acidity.
p. 45. In Agron. Abstrs., Amer. Soc. of Agron.
1981 Ann. Mtgs. Madison, Wis.

Posey, Darrell A.
1982   The Keepers of the Forests. Garden 6(1):18-24.
Publ. of New York Botanical Garden.

RADAM (Radar da Amazônia)
1974-   Levantamento de Recursos Naturais. Vols. 1-18.
1978   Rio de Janeiro: Ministério das Minas e Energia,
Depto. Nacional da Produção Mineral.

Richards, P. W.
1970   The Life of the Jungle. New York: McGraw-Hill.

Ritchey, K. D., M. G. Djalma, E. Lobato, and O. Correa
1980   Calcium Leaching to Increase Rooting Depth in
a Brazilian Savannah Oxisol. Agron. J.
72:40-44.

Ruthenberg, H.
1976   Farming Systems in the Tropics. Oxford:
Clarendon Press.

Sanchez, Pedro A.
1976   Properties and Management of Soils in the
Tropics. New York: Wiley-Interscience.

1977a   Alternativas al Sistema de Agricultura
Migratoria en América Latina. In P. Arens,
ed., Reunión-Taller sobre Manejo y Conservación
de Suelos. Lima: Food and Agricultural Organization (FAO)/ Swiss International Development
Agency (SIDA).

1977b   Advances in the Management of Oxisols and
Ultisols in Tropical South America. pp. 535-566.
In Proceedings of International Seminar on Soil
Environment and Fertility Management in

Intensive Agriculture. Tokyo: Soc. Soil Sci. and Manure.

1977c   Manejo de Suelos Tropicales en la Amazônia Suramericana. _Suelos Ecuatoriales_ 8:1-11.

1977d   Manejo de Solos de Amazoñia para Produción Agropecuária Intensiva. Bol. Inf. Soc. Bras. _Ciência Solo_ 2(3):60-63.

Sanchez, Pedro A., ed.
1973   _A Review of Soils Research in Tropical Latin America_. Bull. 219. Raleigh: Soil Science Dept., North Carolina State Univ.

Sanchez, Pedro A., D. E. Bandy, J. H. Villachica, and J. J. Nicholaides, III
1982   Soils of the Amazon Basin and Their Management for Continuous Crop Production. _Science_ 216: 821-827.

Sanchez, Pedro A. and S. W. Buol
1975   Soils of the Tropics and the World Food Crisis _Science_ 180:598-603.

Sanchez, Pedro A. and T. T. Cochrane
1980   Soil Constraints in Relation to Major Farming Systems of Tropical America. pp. 101-139. In IRRI/Cornell _Priorities for Alleviating Soil-Related Constraints to Food Production in the Tropics_. Los Baños, Laguna, Philippines: International Rice Research Institute (IRRI).

Sanchez, Pedro A., W. Couto, and S. W. Buol
1982   The Fertility Capability Classification System: Interpretation, applicability and modification. _Geoderma_ 27:283-309.

Sanchez, Pedro A. and M. A. Nureña
1972   _Upland Rice Improvement Under Shifting Cultivation in the Amazon Basin of Peru_. Raleigh: North Carolina Agr. Exp. Sta. Tech. Bull. 210.

Sanchez, Pedro A., J. H. Villachica, and D. E. Bandy
1980   Soil Fertility Dynamics After Converting a Tropical Rainforest to Continuous Cultivation in the Amazon of Peru. p. 43. In _Agron. Abstrs._, Amer. Soc. of Agron. 1980 Ann. Mtgs. Madison, Wis.

Schubart, H.O.R.
1977   Critérios Ecológicos para o Desenvolvimento Agrícola das Terras Firmes da Amazônia. _Acta_

Amazônica 7(4):559-567.

Seubert, C. E., P. A. Sanchez, and C. Valverde
1977   Effects of Land Clearing Methods on Soil
        Properties of an Ultisol and Crop Performance
        in the Amazon Jungle of Peru. Trop. Agric.
        54(4):307-321.

Silva, L. F. da
1977   Influéncia do Manejo de um Ecossistema nas
        Propiedades Edáficas dos Oxisols de "Tabuleiro,"
        Resúmenes de Ponencias,X Reunión ALCA, Acapulco,
        Mexico. Itabuna, Bahia: Centro de Pesquisas
        do Cacau (CEPLAC).

Smith, Nigel J.H.
1981   Colonization Lessons from a Tropical Forest.
        Science 214:755-761.

Soil Survey Staff
1975   Soil Taxonomy. Washington, D.C.: Soil
        Conservation Service/United States Dept. of
        Agriculture.

Stark, N.
1978   Man, Tropical Forests and the Biological Life
        of a Soil. Biotropica 10:1-10.

Toledo, J. M. and V. A. Morales
1979   Establishment and Management of Improved Pas-
        tures in the Peruvian Amazon. pp. 177-194.
        In P. A. Sanchez and L. E. Tergas, eds., Pasture
        Production in Acid Soils of the Tropics. Cali:
        Centro Internacional de Agricultura Tropical
        (CIAT).

Toledo, J. M. and E.A.S. Serrão
1982   Pastures and animal production in Amazonia.
        In S. B. Hecht, ed., Amazonia: Agriculture
        and Land Use Research. Cali: Centro Inter-
        nacional de Agricultura Tropical (CIAT).

UEPAE/EMBRAPA
1979-   Relatorio Técnico Anual 1978, 1979, 1980.
1981   Manaus: Unidade de Execução de Pesquisa de
        Âmbito Estadual (UEPAE)/Emprêsa Brasileira
        de Pesquisa Agropecuária (EMBRAPA).

Valverde, C. S. and D. E. Bandy
1982   Production of Annual Food Crops in the Amazon.
        In S. B. Hecht, ed., Amazonia: Agriculture
        and Land Use Research. Cali: Centro Inter-
        nacional de Agricultura Tropical (CIAT).

Valverde, C. S., D. E. Bandy, Pedro A. Sanchez, and
J. J. Nicholaides, III
    1979   Algunos Resultados del Proyecto Yurimaguas en
            la Zona Amazónica. Lima: Instituto Nacional
            de Investigaciones Agrarias (INIA).

Villachica, J. H.
    1978   Maintenance of Soil Fertility Under Continuous
            Cropping in an Ultisol of the Amazon Jungle
            of Peru. Ph.D. dissertation, North Carolina
            State Univ.

Wade, M. K.
    1978   Soil Management Practices for Increasing Crop
            Production for Small Farmers in the Amazon
            Jungle of Peru. Ph.D. dissertation, North
            Carolina State Univ.

APPENDIX 1:   THE SOIL FERTILITY CAPABILITY CLASSIFICATION
(FCC) SYSTEM (after Sanchez, Couto, and
Buol 1982)

This classification system consists of three levels:

Soil type is the texture of surface soil (to 20 cm
depth).
Substrata type is the texture of subsoil if within
50 cm of the surface.
Condition modifiers are specific properties noted
if a specific range of conditions is encountered.

Thus, every soil is named at the highest category by
the surface texture present, and further properties are
noted as needed in a systematic fashion.

Description of type, subtype, and modifier classes:

(A) Soil type: texture of plow layer or surface 20 cm
(8 inches), whichever is shallower.

S = sandy topsoils: loamy sands and sands (by
USDA definition).

L = loamy topsoils: <35% clay but not loamy sand
or sand.

C = clayey topsoils: >35% clay.

O = organic soils: >30% organic matter to a depth
of 50 cm (20 inches) or more.

(B) Substrata type: (texture of subsoil). Used only if
there is a textural change from the surface or if a
hard root-restricting layer is encountered within
50 cm (20 inches).

S = sandy subsoil: texture as in soil type.

L = loamy subsoil: texture as in soil type.

C = clayey subsoil: texture as in soil type.

R = rock or other hard root-restricting layer.

(C) Condition modifiers: Where more than one criterion
is listed for each modifier, only one needs to be met
to place the soil. The first criterion given is preferred, but additional criteria are selected to
facilitate semiquantitative use in the absence of
desired data.

g = (gley): Soil or mottles <2 chroma within 60 cm
(24 inches) of surface and below all A horizons,
or saturated with H_2O for >60 days in most
years.

d = (dry): Ustic or xeric environment (dry >90 cumulative days/year within 20-60 cm depth).

e = (low CEC): (applies only to plow layer or surface 20 cm, whichever is shallower).

<4 meq/100 g soil by Σ bases + KCl extractable Al, or
<7 meq/100 g soil by Σ cations at pH 7, or
<10 meq/100 g soil by Σ cations + Al + H at pH 8.2.

a = (Al toxic):
>60% Al saturation of CEC by Σ bases + KCl extractable Al within 50 cm (20 inches), or
>67% EA (exch. acidity) saturation of CEC by Σ cations at pH 7 within 50 cm (20 inches), or
>86% EA saturation of CEC by Σ cations at pH 8.2 within 50 cm (20 inches), or
pH <5.0 in 1:1 H_2O except in organic soils.

h = (acid):

10-60% Al saturation of CEC by Σ bases + KCl extractable Al within 50 cm (20 inches), or
pH in 1:1 H_2O between 5.0 and 6.0.

i = (Fe-P fixation): (used only in clay (C) types)
% Free Fe_2O_3/% clay >0.15, or
hues of 7.5 YR or redder and granular structure.

x = (X-ray amorphous): (applies only to plow layer or surface 20 cm (8 inches), whichever is shallower).

pH >10 in 1N NaF, or
positive to field NaF test, or
other indirect evidence of allophane dominance in clay fraction.

v = (Vertisols):
Very sticky plastic clay: >35% clay and >50% of 2:1 expanding clays; COLE >0.09. Severe topsoil shrinking and swelling.

k = (K-deficient):
<10% weatherable minerals in silt and sand fraction within 50 cm of soil surface, or
exchangeable K <0.20 meq/100, or
K <2% of Σ bases, if Σ bases <10 meq/100 g.

b = (basic reaction):
Free $CaCO_3$ within 50 cm of soil surface (fizzing with HCl) or pH >7.3.

s = (salinity):

    >4 mmho/cm of saturated extract at 25°C within 1 m depth.

c = (cat clay):

    pH in 1:1 H_2O is <3.5 after drying and jarosite mottles, with hues of 2.5 Y or yellower and chromas (6 or more are present within 60 cm).

APPENDIX 2:   SAMPLE MANAGEMENT INTERPRETATIONS OF FCC
              NOMENCLATURE

(A)   Interpretation of FCC types and substrata types:

L : Good water-holding capacity, medium infiltration
     capacity.
S : High rate of infiltration, lower water-holding
     capacity.
C : Low infiltration rates, potential high runoff
     if sloping, difficult to till except when "i"
     modifier is present.
O : Artificial drainage is needed and subsidence
     will take place. Possible micronutrient
     deficiency. High herbicide rates usually
     required.
SC, LC, LR, or SR:
     Susceptible to severe soil deterioration from
     erosion exposing undesirable subsoil. High
     priority should be given to erosion control.

(B)   Interpretation of FCC condition modifiers:

When only one condition modifier is included in the
FCC class nomenclature, the following limitations
or management requirements apply to the soil.
Interpretations may be slightly modified when two
or more modifiers are present simultaneously or when
textural classes are different.

Modifier	Main limitations and management requirements
g	Denitrification frequently occurs in anaerobic subsoil, and tillage operations and certain crops may be adversely affected by excess rain unless drainage is improved by tiles or other drainage procedures.
d	Soil moisture is limited during the growing season unless irrigated. Planting date should take into account the flush of N at onset of rain.
e	Low ability to retain nutrients--mainly Ca, K, Mg--for plants. Heavy applications of these nutrients should be split. Potential danger of overliming.
a	Plants sensitive to aluminum toxicity will be affected unless lime is deeply incorporated. Extraction of soil water below depth of lime incorporation will be restricted. Lime requirements are high unless an "e" modifier is also indicated.
h	Strong to medium soil acidity. Requires liming for most crops.

i   High P-fixation capacity. Requires high levels of P fertilizer. Sources and method of P fertilizer application should be considered carefully.

x   High P-fixation capacity. Amount and most convenient source of P to be determined.

v   Clayey-textured topsoil. Tillage is difficult when soils are too dry or too moist, but soils can be highly productive.

k   Low ability to supply K. Availability of K should be monitored and K fertilizers may be required frequently for plants requiring high levels of K.

b   Basic reaction. Rock phosphate and other non-water-soluble phosphate should be avoided. Potential deficiency of certain micronutrients, principally iron and zinc.

s   Presence of soluble salts. Requires special soil management practices for saline soils.

n   High levels of sodium. Requires special soil management practices for alkaline soils.

c   Potential acid sulfate soil. Drainage is not recommended without special practices. Should be managed with plants tolerant to flooding and high-level water table.

6
Cattle Ranching in the Eastern Amazon: Environmental and Social Implications

Susanna Hecht

INTRODUCTION

In Amazonia, the development decades of the 1960s
and 1970s were characterized primarily by the expansion
of cattle ranching. Through massive infrastructure
development and fiscal incentives, livestock production
eclipsed all other agricultural land uses both in area
and investment. Although colonization programs were
well publicized and served important ideological ends,
the conversion of tropical forest for pasture became the
hallmark of much Amazonian development, especially in
Brazil and Colombia.
The transformation of vast areas of forest to
grasslands has resulted in a great deal of controversy
in both the biological and the social sciences. Questions
pertaining to large-scale ecological changes such as
species extinction (Myers 1979), climatic change (Salati
et al. 1979), and hydrological effects are common in the
literature (Gentry and López-Parodi 1980). Further,
expansion of this form of land use has been associated
with bitter land conflicts, increasing peasant marginality,
expanded land concentration, and a dramatic rise in
migration from rural to urban areas (Aragón 1978;
Bunker 1979; Hébette and Acevedo 1979; Santos 1979).
This paper explores the magnitude of forest clearing
and emphasizes that ranching is the predominant use of
converted areas. General features of tropical forests
are briefly discussed, as well as the broad soil changes
that take place after conversion. The agronomy of ranching is discussed and the specific effects of conversion
of tropical rain forest to pasture are evaluated.
Finally, some of the social implications of this land
use are addressed.

MAGNITUDE OF DEFORESTATION

The extent of conversion has been a source of
contention in which various authors have suggested that

155

as much as 30% conversion has occurred (Myers 1979) while others argue that it is less than 1% (Lugo and Brown, in press). The unreliability of much of the data base, definitional differences, and the historical period in question have all contributed to conflicting assertions about the rate and area cleared. Until relatively recently, the inaccessibility of the region completely defied anything other than speculation about the magnitude of deforestation. The use of satellite imagery has improved the situation enormously, but LANDSAT data are not without their problems given the high frequency of cloud cover in the Amazon.

An important definitional question is whether secondary forested areas should be considered as forest or as cleared areas. Brown (1979) has indicated that about 8% of the basin is in secondary forests, presumably as a consequence of land abandonment following agriculture or ranching, yet the deforestation evaluations by Tardin et al. (1979) do not deal with this question. Finally, LANDSAT imagery has only been in use during the 1970s, and in many of the southern reaches of Amazonian forest, land clearing has been occurring for more than 20 years. Some Amazonian areas of Northern Goiás and Mato Grosso were converted from forest decades ago. Many kinds of questions still remain to be publicly resolved and are responsible for the diversity of clearing estimates.

The best data available for clearing in the Amazon are derived from LANDSAT photos, but only Brazil, at this time, has made the results easily available. This information and estimates for the other Amazon countries are presented in Table 6.1. It must be emphasized that these are "ballpark" numbers. As Table 6.1 suggests, the annual clearing rate in the Amazon at the close of the 1970s was over 1½ million hectares per year. Published data from Colombia (Alarcón et al. 1980) and Brazil (Tardin et al. 1979) indicate that at least 14 million ha have been cleared just in these two countries. The detailed data for the Brazilian Amazon are presented in Table 6.2 and show that between 1976 and 1978 more than one million ha/year were cleared in the Brazilian Amazon alone. Most of this area was converted to pasture. Rates of deforestation are erratic, however, reflecting credit policies, subsidies, interest rates, colonization projects, peasant situations in other parts of the country, national and global investment patterns, and land speculation.

Amazon forests are among the most ecologically complex and least understood vegetation formations on the planet. Amazonia encompasses the largest reserve of tropical moist forest as well as seasonal forest (UNESCO 1978). The number of plant species contained in the Amazon is thought to be, roughly, 250,000 (Lovejoy and Schubart 1980).

At the broadest level, Amazonian forests are

Table 6.1. Approximate area of forest, clearing rate, and dominant replacement land use in Amazonia

Country	Amazon Forest Area (million hectares)	Current Clearing (ha/year)	Dominant Land Use
Brazil	280	1,600,000[1]	cattle ranching (95%)
Peru	65	no data	Subsistence, cash crops cattle (15%)
Bolivia	51	3,000[2]	cattle, citrus, cacau, coffee
Colombia	31	150,000[3]	cattle, rice
Guyana	13	10,000[2]	subsistence
Surinam	13	3,000[2]	subsistence
Venezuela	13	no data	subsistence, cattle
Ecuador	10	no data	subsistence, cattle
French Guiana	8	no data	subsistence

Sources: 1) Tardin et al. 1979.

2) Myers 1980.

3) Alarcón et al. 1980.

Table 6.2. Deforestation in the Brazilian Amazon

State	Area Cleared by 1975 (ha)	Area Cleared 1976-1978 (ha)	% Increase 1975-1978 (%)	Total Cleared by 1978 (ha)	Total Cleared by 1980* (ha)
Mato Grosso	1,012,425	1,823,075	180	2,825,500	5,085,900
Pará	865,400	1,379,125	159	2,244,524	3,575,528
Maranhao	294,075	439,325	149	733,400	1,092,766
Rondônia	121,650	296,800	243	418,450	1,016,833
Acre	116,550	129,900	111	246,450	273,559
Amazonas	77,950	100,625	129	198,575	230,361
Roraima	5,500	8,875	161	14,375	23,000
Amapá	15,250	1,800	11	17,050	20,119
Total	2,859,525	4,857,650		7,717,175	11,318,060

Source: Tardin et al. 1979.

*This number is an estimate calculated by multiplying the % increase in clearing with the deforested totals of 1978.

generally classified into floodplain (<u>várzea</u>) and upland (<u>terra firme</u>) forests. However, Amazonian vegetation is far more complex than this typology suggests. Despite vegetation and forest surveys carried out in the Amazon by the Food and Agriculture Organization of the United Nations (FAO), the Brazilian Institute of Forestry Development (IBDF), and RADAM (Radar Imagery of the Amazon), detailed information on Amazonian forest dynamics remains spotty. Although 85% of the Amazon is covered by high-biomass and species-rich forests (Pires and Prance 1977), these forests are more usefully perceived as mosaics rather than as diverse in species but essentially uniform. Pest potential after conversion, resilience, and conservation values are also highly variable. The distribution of forest types in the Amazon is correlated with a complex of climatic, edaphic, and phyto-historical factors, the interrelationships of which are by no means clear. The extraordinary richness of Amazon forests has masked the low fertility of the soils on which they generally occur. The combination of biological exuberance and impoverished soils has made the development and occupation of these regions especially difficult.

The existence of high-biomass, ecologically complex forests on poor soils is possible due to complex nutrient cycling. Amazonian forest cycling pathways are reviewed elsewhere (Klinge 1973; Herrera <u>et al</u>. 1978; Stark and Jordan 1978) but consist of structural, physiological, and symbiont associations that recirculate and sequester nutrients in biomass and litter. Table 6.3 shows the relative amounts of nutrients stored in several different tropical forest systems. As is clear, most of the Ca, Mg, and K are held in the living plants rather than the soil.

When forest lands are converted to other uses, the nutrients held in the biomass are largely shifted into soil nutrient storage, crop and weed tissues, or are lost through leaching, erosion, and exports of the products away from the site. Since high-biomass forest systems (i.e., up to 500 tons/ha) are replaced by agroecosystems with biomass usually less than 20 tons/ha, one of the major questions in conversion concerns the fate of the nutrients when forests are cut and burned. First, as Silva (1978) has indicated, only about 20% of the forest is effectively burned, and even this value is variable. Leaves, small trunks, and branches combust, but the larger tree boles are usually left to rot. This means that it is possible to have a delayed release of nutrients as decomposition proceeds, and suggests that in many cases the soil nutrient increases, and later declines, may not necessarily be dramatic. In general, after cutting and burning, soil levels of organic carbon and nitrogen, and possibly sulphur, drop as a consequence of volatization. Soil pH increases due to the additions

Table 6.3. Above-ground biomass storage in ecosystem compartments; kg/ha and percent

Element		N	P	K	Ca	Mg	Site	Source
Total Reserve (Biomass)		741	27	277	431	133	Carare, Colombia[1]	De las Salas (1978)
Leaves	%	13.3	3.6	10.5	5.8	8.3		
	kg	101.4	9.7	28.0	25.0	11.0		
Wood	%	60.0	60.3	63.8	72.8	68.0		
	kg	447.6	16.2	176.7	313.7	90.4		
Total Reserve (Biomass)		---	144.2	2,982.3	3,576.5	382.3	Darien, Panama	Golley et al. (1975)
Leaves	%	---	11	4.5	6	6.5		
	kg	---	16	135.0	221	25.0		
Wood	%	---	88	95	93	90		
	kg	---	128	2,846	3,355	357		
Total Reserve (Biomass)		3,995	170	4,678	973	730	Gran Pajonal, Peru	Scott (1978)
Leaves	%	12	10	4	5	4		
	kg	478	17	229	57	32		
Wood	%	88	90	96	95	96		
	kg	3,517	153	4,449	916	689		
Mean percentages element storage								
Leaves	%	12.6	8.2	6.3	5.6	6.3		
Wood	%	74	79	84	86	84		

1) When totals are less than 100%, understory biomass storage has been excluded.

of Ca, K, Mg, and lesser amounts of P released from the forest with burning. The liming effect of the base-rich ash serves to reduce much of the aluminum saturation common in Amazonian soils. P levels initially increase from soil-heating ash additions, and when there are large pH increases, from "fixed" P in aluminum and iron sesquioxides. These changes reverse themselves with time. The rates and magnitude of nutrient change are affected by numerous factors including initial forest composition (Kang 1977; Silva 1978), clearing techniques (discussed elsewhere in this volume), and land use following conversion.

PROCESSES OF LAND OCCUPATION

The pressure for land acquisition in the Amazon comes from several quarters. Increased mechanization and the decline of a variety of tenancy relationships in other agricultural zones, the closing of older frontier areas, as well as demographic increase, have served to create a huge landless population who migrate to the Amazon to seek their fortune. These become the squatters on government and unoccupied (though often owned) lands, and the labor force for large-scale clearing.

At the same time, the increased importance of land in corporate portfolios, coupled with attractive credit lines for Amazonian investment, low capital gains taxes, and minimal control over, and monitoring of, land acquisition have created a speculative search for land unparalleled in recent Amazonian history (Mahar 1979; Pompermayer 1979; Schuurman 1979; Mueller 1980).

High potential profits to be made from land speculation (up to 100% per year according to Mahar 1979) produce an environment that favors the legal or illegal concentration of land into latifundia. While agronomic research oriented to enhancing small-scale production systems has made progress, the speculative nature of Amazonian land economics, plus infrastructure, input, and transport difficulties, favor larger holdings to the detriment of small farmers (Wood and Schmink 1979). Various fiscal incentives and credit lines, the ease of pasture implantation, and the possibility of discovering other valuable resources (gold, tourmalines, oil, diamonds), as well as capital gains on land, have fueled the transformation of agricultural and forest land into pasture.

When a cropping phase precedes pasture, several pathways for the transformation of land use are possible. One important way, widely employed by the less-capitalized ranchers, is troca pela forma (trade of one year's use for pasture formation). Land is lent to the small cultivator to clear and cultivate for one year, in exchange for which the farmer shares his crop with the owner and agrees to plant pasture. After the cropping cycle, the small farmer may relocate to another parcel on the ranch or move away. The rancher then introduces his cattle. Another technique is simple appropriation. This may be done through legal or semi-legal means (contested titles or surveys) or by running the farmer off the land through violence or threat of violence (Pompermayer 1979; Souza-Martins 1980; Almeida 1980). In lands that have been spontaneously settled by small farmers, who are then followed into the region by middle sized, mostly non-corporate ranches, this technique is not uncommon (Souza-Martins 1980; Almeida 1980). Land, of course, can also be bought.

PASTURES: AREAL EXTENT AND AGRONOMY OF THE
DOMINANT SPECIES

Pasture is the ultimate destiny of much of the land initially used for forestry or cleared for agriculture. Toledo and Serrão (1981) estimate that about 6 million ha of the Amazon forest have been converted to pasture, and of this about 1 million ha are degraded. I feel that these figures underestimate both the area cleared and the magnitude of degradation. Alarcón et al. (1980) indicate over 3 million ha have been converted to pasture in the Colombian Amazon. This information coupled with the Brazilian data in Table 6.2 argue for an area in pasture of at least 14 million hectares, particularly if we consider that much of the Bolivian, Peruvian, and Ecuadorian Amazon are also in pasture (Gazzo 1981; Torre 1981; Pereira and Salinas 1981). Tardin et al. (1977), in analyzing ranches in the Barra de Garças area of Mato Grosso, generally considered the most successful upland cattle region in the Brazilian Amazon, used LANDSAT imagery and ground testing to evaluate the level of pasture decline and weed invasion. They found that about half the pastures in the area they examined were degraded--i.e., heavily brush-invaded. The poor quality of pasture and extensive weed invasion in Paragominas, Pará, another major cattle development area, suggest a level of degradation exceeding 50%.

Only a few grass species are used in the Amazon for pasture formation. In the Brazilian Amazon, Panicum maximum, colonial guinea grass, is planted on about 85% of the area (Serrão and Simão-Neto 1975; Toledo and Serrão 1981). Brachiaria decumbens was also initially widely planted, but the attacks of a spittle bug (Deois incompleta) have limited the use of this grass. In the Paragominas area, more than one-third of the pastures planted to Brachiaria were destroyed by insect attack (Hecht 1982a). Kikuyu da Amazonia (Brachiaria humidicola), with its purported resistance to spittle bug and tolerance to low soil-nutrient levels, is increasingly important. In the western Amazon, Axonopus micay and A. scoparius

are the most important forage grasses. A grass of
interest due to its high productivity on poor soils is
Andropogon guyanus (Toledo and Serrão 1981). Most of the
research on ranching has occurred in areas planted to
Panicum, so a brief discussion of the major characteristics of this important forage is in order.

Panicum maximum is probably the most widely planted
forage grass in Brazil (Martins 1963). The cultivation
and the management of this grass are particularly well
developed in southern Brazil, where it is the basis of
the beef-fattening industry (Pardi and Caldas 1968;
Santiago 1970). Based on the success of Panicum-based
cattle production in temperate Brazil and the relative
success of the Commission for the Development of Cattle
Raising (CONDEPE) projects in southern Mato Grosso and
Goiás, Panicum production systems were transferred in toto
to the Amazon from the southern and central Brazilian
ranching areas.

The source areas for Panicum in Africa are the
savanna regions associated with volcanic, high-base
saturation soils in areas that are farther than 12 degrees south of the equator. These two factors, relatively
high nutrient requirements and adaptation to variable day
length, are essential to understanding the poor performance
of guinea grass in the Amazon. Panicum is relatively
nutrient demanding for P and N. In the impoverished soils
of the Amazon, except for the few years right after clearing, the grass becomes stressed and cannot compete well
with better adapted woody and weedy species. N, P, and
K deficiencies have all been documented for guinea grass
in the Amazon (Koster et al. 1976).

Panicum has low seed viability (about 27% according
to Agroceres, a major seed supplier) under the best
conditions. Two factors in the Amazon Basin reduce seed
viability even further. First, Panicum in optimal situations generally seeds twice a year, but in the Amazon,
continuous seeding occurs. This results in low quantities of seed at any given time, and lower germination,
because seed may fall during periods when the climate
may not be favorable. The high humidity in the region
also favors powdery mildew attack (Serrão and Simão-Neto
1975) that further reduces seed production and success.

Panicum plants become senescent within five years
(Vincente-Chandler et al. 1973); declines in productivity
in Amazon experimental plots corroborate this trend
(Simão-Neto et al. 1973). Without continuous vigorous
establishment of new plants, the yield reductions are
quite predictable and are compounded by the soil nutrient
declines that also occur--particularly for phosphorus.

The bunch-grass morphology of Panicum results in
relatively large areas of open ground between individual
plants when pastures are grazed. This can produce erosion
between plants as well as soil compaction due to rainfall
and trampling. Increased compaction further reduces the

capacity of <u>Panicum</u> seedlings to establish themselves.
The open area between the grass plants can also be
colonized by weeds that, for a variety of reasons (Hecht
1979), can outcompete grasses. Another characteristic
of <u>Panicum</u> in the Amazon is its relatively shallow
rooting depth. This may reflect increasing aluminum
levels in the soil subsurface. The roots rarely reach
below 30 cm, which limits plant ability to capture
nutrients below this depth and subjects the plants to
desiccation during the dry seasons.

There are serious problems associated with <u>Panicum</u>,
but local ranchers still consider it to be one of the
best fattening grasses. Seeds are readily available from
several suppliers, and the establishment of the pasture
is relatively simple: forests are cut, burned, and, at
the beginning of the rainy season, the <u>Panicum</u> is usually
aerially seeded.

THE EFFECTS OF CONVERSION OF FOREST TO PASTURE

Among workers in the Latin American tropics who have
investigated pasture performance and the soil effects of
conversion, one finds substantial differences of opinion.
In the eastern Amazon, the effects of forest conversion
to <u>Panicum</u> have been examined by Falesi (1976), Fearnside
(1978), Serrão <u>et al</u>. (1979), and Hecht (1982a).
Goodland (1980) has argued that ranching represents
the worst of all conceivable land-use alternatives for
Amazonian development due to high ecosystem losses relative to the short-term profits and to low employment
potential. Fearnside (1979) has also argued that ranching is a relatively unstable and unproductive land use
for the region. Central to the controversy about forest
to pasture conversion is the widely cited EMBRAPA study,
prepared by Falesi (1976). This study was expanded by
Serrão <u>et al</u>. (1979) and Toledo and Serrão (1981).
The EMBRAPA report argued that conversion of forest
to pasture actually improved soil properties, particularly
for pH, calcium, and magnesium. The report showed
dramatic increases in phosphorus in the first years after
clearing followed by a substantial decline. The very low
levels of P in the soil were presented as the most
critical parameter affecting pasture stability, but this
problem is quite responsive to fertilizer applications
although it may be economically questionable (Koster
<u>et al</u>. 1976; Serrão <u>et al</u>. 1979).
Based on these EMBRAPA results, a suggestion was
made that "formation of pastures on low fertility soils
is a rational and economic means by which to rationalize
and increase the value of these extensive areas" (Falesi
1976). Serrão <u>et al</u>. (1979) argued that "the subsequent
substitution of pasture with perennial crops would
require only a small amount of P fertilizer for development...due to the favorable conditions of the majority

of soil components after a long period under pasture."
Sanchez and Cochrane (1980) indicated that "the data
suggest a remarkable degree of nutrient cycling and maintenance of soil fertility under pasture....These data are
encouraging because they indicate a very high beef
production potential with minimum inputs."

The high percentage of degraded pasture areas and
the relative decline in the importance of the older upland ranching areas (such as Paragominas, Pará) over
the last decade (Hecht 1982a) suggest that the soil
effects of conversion may require further analysis.

In any study of soil changes where space is substituted for time, there is likely to be substantial
variation from site to site. As Fearnside has indicated
(1978), this is particularly true in Amazon conversion
studies due to soil micro-variability and the effects of
heterogeneous deposition of ash and unburned slash. The
EMBRAPA study used five composite samples from each
pasture of a given age. Fearnside's (1978) extensive
analysis of soil variability and sample size suggest that
this number may be too small. An evaluation of the
sample size necessary to estimate the mean at the 90%
confidence limit (Hecht 1982a) corroborates Fearnside's
assertion.

In the following section, my results on pasture conversion are compared with the EMBRAPA study. Methodologi-
cal differences can influence results, so it is necessary
to point out that for each 100 ha pasture of a given age,
80 random samples were collected on the clay-loam Oxisol
site.

Variation in the results of the different studies
may be affected by many factors, not the least of which is
the difference in sampling sites and the fact that my
"modal" soil, a yellow latosol (Haplorthox), differs in
certain parameters from those used in the EMBRAPA pasture
studies. However, when all the control sites in eastern
Amazonia are compared (see Table 6.4), there is no
statistically significant difference between the
Paragominas soils, although clearly the clay-loam Oxisol
is higher in P and lower in Ca than the other sites.

Other sources of variation may reflect the use of
different laboratories (even though the analytic
techniques were the same), pasture history, and site
management. With these caveats in mind, the soil effects
of conversion of forest to pasture follow.

When forests are felled and burned, an increase in
soil pH occurs as the bases held in the biomass are transferred to soils (Nye and Greenland 1960; Sanchez 1976),
regardless of the land use implemented. As Figure 6.1
shows, there are substantial increases in the soil pH
for the sites examined in the EMBRAPA study. By contrast,
the clay-loam Oxisol showed only moderate increases of
less than one pH unit. Although the ranges of pH in the
clay-loam Oxisol included some values as high as those of

Table 6.4. Comparison of forested control sites of pasture studies in the eastern Amazon

Location	Soil type	pH	C%	N%	P(ppm)	Ca	Mg	K
						----meq/100 gm----		
Paragominas[1]	Paleudult	4.2	.68	.05	3	.19	.11	.05
Paragominas[1]	Haplorthox	4.4	1.62	.16	.23	1.09	.33	.05
Paragominas[2]	Haplorthox	4.3	1.3	.09	5.5	.13	.13	.04
Altamira[3]	Haplustox	4.8	1.0	.12	1.2	--2.86--		n.a.
Suia Missu[1]	Haplorthox	4.3	1.13	.09	2	.31	.14	.14

1) Falesi (1976)

2) Hecht (1982a)

3) Fearnside (1978)

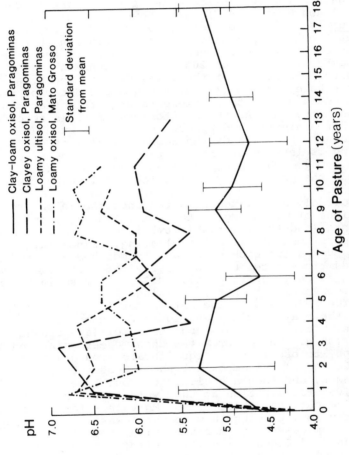

Figure 6.1. Changes in pH after conversion from forest to pasture

Clay–loam oxisol, Paragominas
Clayey oxisol, Paragominas
Loamy ultisol, Paragominas
Loamy oxisol, Mato Grosso

Standard deviation from mean

pH

7.0
6.5
6.0
5.5
5.0
4.5
4.0

0 1 2 3 4 5 6 7 8 9 10 11 12 13 14 15 16 17 18

Age of Pasture (years)

Sources: Clay–loam Oxisol compiled from Hecht (1982a)
Clayey Oxisol, loamy Ultisol, and loamy Oxisol compiled from Falesi (1976)

the other sites, with larger sample size the pH increases are not dramatic. This result is corroborated by another data set (presented in Sanchez 1979) that analyzed soil changes before and after deforestation on 60 sites. These samples were analyzed at the EMBRAPA laboratory.

One of the interesting aspects of the pH data is that the "liming" effect is maintained through time. Cochrane and Sanchez (1981) and Toledo and Serrão (1981) believe that the high cycling capacity of the grasses is responsible for the persistence of the pH improvement. Tietzel and Bruce (1972) have shown in Australia that Panicum is a reasonably effective cycler of Ca, Mg, and K, but there is an additional interpretation that also merits consideration. When forests are cut and burned for pasture, only about 20% of the biomass actually combusts. About 80% of the total Ca, Mg, and K is stored in tree boles on the ground; the gradual decay of the boles could supply these elements at a rate that could maintain the pH. As the maintenance of pH is recorded in other nonfertilized production systems such as Yurimaguas, Peru (Bandy and Sanchez 1981), it may be that cycling is less important for the maintenance of pH than slash decay. This hypothesis does not, of course, exclude the possibility of nutrient cycling by the grasses.

Closely associated with the increase in pH are additions of Ca and Mg to the soil. The rise in these elements (and their variability) is most pronounced in the years immediately after clearing. Since rain forests store over a ton each of Ca and Mg per hectare, and the ash additions after burning supply immediately at least 100 kg of Ca (Seubert et al. 1977), the rise in Ca and Mg after conversion is not surprising.

The EMBRAPA data indicate major increases in Ca and Mg in the clayey Oxisol as Figure 6.2 suggests, but these decline after five years and then oscillate around 2 meq/100 g. The other sites show modest gains and the tendency to oscillate or equilibrate around a fairly low value. The clay-loam Oxisol shows less substantial increases, and then a decline to about 1 meq/100 g and relative stabilization at this value. It is worth pointing out that these Ca and Mg values for all soils are very low, placing them in the lowest range for Ca and Mg of tropical South American soils, according to Cochrane and Sanchez (1981). While soils may be 'improved' in terms of Ca and Mg contents, in fact most of the values for these elements are below the critical level for pasture production (Coordenadoria de Assistencia Técnica Integral 1974).

Potassium is a monovalent cation that is stored mainly in the vegetation in tropical ecosystems, cycles quickly, and is quite vulnerable to leaching. In general more than 1 ton of K per hectare is stored in the vegetation. Because of the mobility of this element, K values

Figure 6.2. Changes in Ca + Mg after conversion from forest to pasture

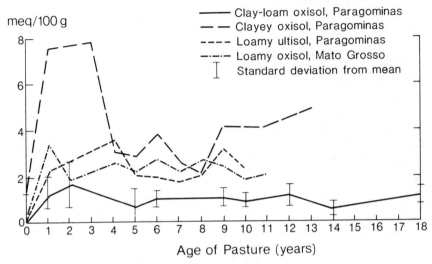

Sources: Clay-loam Oxisol compiled from Hecht (1982a)
Clayey Oxisol, loamy Ultisol, and loamy Oxisol compiled from Falesi (1976)

Figure 6.3. Changes in potassium after conversion from forest to pasture

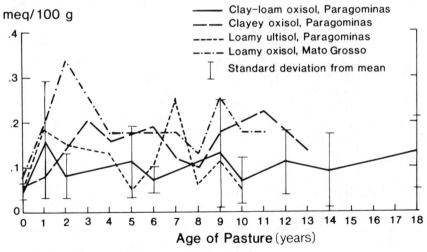

Sources: Clay-loam Oxisol compiled from Hecht (1982a)
Clayey Oxisol, loamy Ultisol, and loamy Oxisol compiled from Falesi (1976)

are erratic throughout the pasture sequence as Figure 6.3 indicates, reflecting periodic burning, weed invasion, and other management activities. The coefficients of variation for this element are so high (often up to 84), however, that there is no statistical significance between K values of forest and pasture (Hecht 1982a). Soil improvement in this element is thus open to question. K deficiencies have been documented for pastures in Paragominas (Koster et al. 1976).

The high value for K in the Mato Grosso Oxisol probably reflects a higher initial soil K level, as well as a higher frequency of palms, both in the native vegetation and in the pasture invaders. Both tend to be rich in palms (RADAM 1974; Hecht, field notes). As Silva (1978) and Salas (1978) have noted, palms have relatively high concentrations of K in their leaves.

Phosphorus is the most crucial element for pasture production in the Amazon (Koster et al. 1976; Serrão et al. 1979; Toledo and Serrão 1981), and 10 ppm is usually considered the minimum value for sustained production of pastures. After conversion, the P values increase dramatically, but by the fifth year they stabilize at about 5 ppm and steadily decline thereafter, as is indicated in Figure 6.4.

The decline in P has been identified as the major reason for pasture instability in the Amazon (Serrão et al. 1979). The high demand of Panicum for this element, coupled with losses due to erosion and animal export, and the competition the grass suffers from weeds adapted to low P, leads to drastic drops in pasture productivity, which often result in pasture abandonment. Serrão et al. (1979) and Koster et al. (1976) have shown Panicum's excellent response to P fertilization, but the high transport and application costs, coupled with erratic availability of P fertilizers in much of the Amazon, make widespread pasture fertilization uneconomical at this time.

Soil nitrogen values reflect N-accumulating processes like nitrogen fixation, atmospheric additions, and organic matter decay, as well as N-decreasing activities such as volatization, denitrification, leaching, erosion, and plant uptake. Many of these processes are mediated by the biota; rates of loss and addition also are affected by environmental factors (pH, temperature, soil moisture). N is an element that can vary strongly from site to site. The Paragominas Ultisol (see Figure 6.5) shows a slight initial increase and a subsequent equilibration, suggesting that the differences between forest and pasture N storage are insignificant. In the clay-loam Oxisol, soil N decreased, but when analyzed through multiple range tests, pasture soils were not significantly different from forest soils, except in the oldest pastures, and during the first year after clearing (Hecht 1982a).

The heavy clay Oxisol from Paragominas and the

Figure 6.4. Changes in phosphorus after conversion from forest to pasture

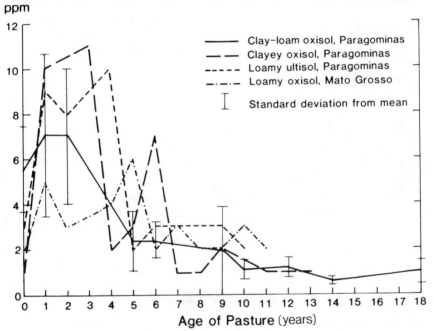

ppm

Sources: Clay-loam Oxisol compiled from Hecht (1982a)
Clayey Oxisol, loamy Ultisol, and loamy Oxisol compiled from Falesi (1976)

Figure 6.5. Changes in soil nitrogen after conversion from forest to pasture

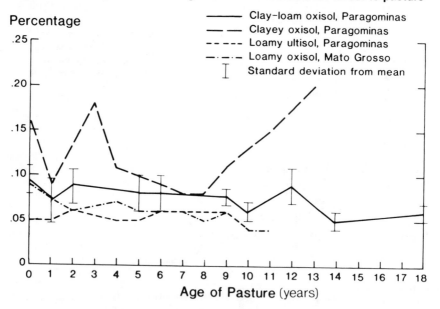

Sources: Clay-loam Oxisol compiled from Hecht (1982a)
Clayey Oxisol, loamy Ultisol, and loamy Oxisol compiled from Falesi (1976)

Oxisol from Mato Grosso both show N declines, although
the Paragominas clay is decidedly more erratic. The high
N values in year 13 in the Paragominas Oxisol may reflect
N-fixation by native weedy legumes and other N-fixing
organisms. The Mato Grosso site shows a decline in N of
50% after conversion.

N fertilizer is rarely used on Amazonian pastures,
and the introduction of legumes with forages is not widely
practiced (Serrão and Simão-Neto 1975). Management factors
that may have affected the variability in the sites include burning (volatization and possible erosion losses),
overgrazing, use of weed invasion as a temporary fallow
(N possibly increasing), and the use of legumes (N increasing).

The percentage of organic carbon in Amazonian soils
is quite variable, ranging in total storage from 0.92 to
over 124 kg/m^2 (Zinke 1976). Carbon levels in pastures
are affected by burning, grazing pressure, length of dry
season, soil moisture regime, soil texture, species
composition, and decomposition rates--in short, anything
that influences organic productivity or decomposition.
Not surprisingly, carbon levels are erratic over the time
sequence, between sites, and within sites.

Soil carbon levels often drop with burning, but they
can increase if there is addition of fine charcoal, which
probably occurred in the clay-loam Oxisol, loamy Oxisol,
and loamy Ultisol (see Figure 6.6). C levels can increase
after burning as a consequence of slash decomposition and
the organic matter additions of _Panicum_ before P becomes
seriously deficient. Heavy weed invasion can also increase soil C values. The high carbon values in the clay
Oxisol in year 11 and in the clay-loam Oxisol in years 11
and 13 reflect heavy weed infestation. Increases in soil
organic matter by secondary vegetation to levels almost
equal to those of virgin forest have been documented by
Turrenne (1977) and Zinke et al. (1978) for tropical
agricultural sites taken over by secondary vegetation.
The Mato Grosso Oxisol and Paragominas Ultisol both show
declines in soil carbon after clearing. The Mato Grosso
site shows an initial decline that oscillates around a
value less than 50% of the forest levels.

In short, the effect of conversion of forest to
pasture can be described as relatively neutral for N and
K, negative for P and C, and mildly positive for pH, Ca,
and Mg, particularly in the first years after clearing.
The widely cited "dramatic increases" in these elements
after conversion to pasture seem to be moderated when
larger sample sizes are used. In any case, the absolute
values of Ca and Mg are low-to-marginal for pasture
production. Soil nutrients during the first five years
after conversion are adequate for animal stocking rates
of about 1 animal unit per ha. These rates drop to about
0.25 after five or six years, reflecting not only soil
chemical changes, but compaction and weed invasion,

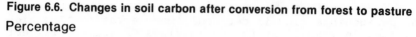

Figure 6.6. Changes in soil carbon after conversion from forest to pasture

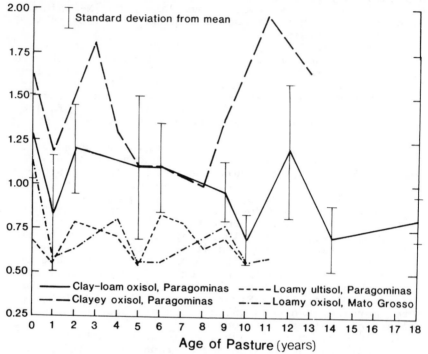

Sources: Clay-loam Oxisol compiled from Hecht (1982a)
Clayey Oxisol, loamy Ultisol, and loamy Oxisol compiled from Falesi (1976)

among other factors.

OTHER FACTORS THAT AFFECT PASTURE PRODUCTIVITY

While the soil changes after conversion are neither as catastrophic nor as beneficial as much of the literature suggests, there are other soil and vegetational effects that also influence pasture productivity. Figure 6.7 shows the increase in soil bulk densities that eventually double with increasing pasture age. High soil bulk density results in reduced infiltration that can affect the rate of sheet erosion (Schubart 1976). Erosion rates under young pastures have been studied by MacGregor (1980) in the Caquetá region of Colombia, where it was found that pastures have low erosion losses. The study did not include grazing animals or the influence of periodic soil exposure after burning, so the results must be extrapolated with caution.

Figure 6.7. Changes in bulk density after conversion from forest to pasture

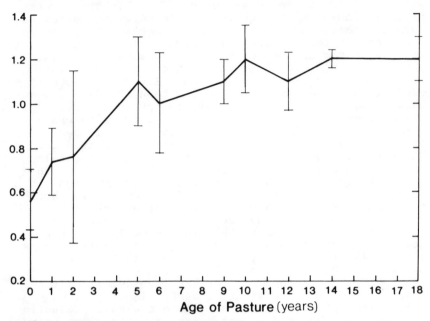

Sources: Clay-loam Oxisol compiled from Hecht (1982a)
Clayey Oxisol, loamy Ultisol, and loamy Oxisol compiled from Falesi (1976)

Amazonian pastures are rapidly invaded by weeds, and the latter also act to reduce pasture productivity by competing with forage grasses for nutrients and water. Although many weed species are in fact browsed by animals (Hecht 1979), weed control is expensive and absorbs about 20% of a ranch's operating costs. Ranches that do not receive fiscal incentives are squeezed between declining productivity and escalating weed and infrastructure-repair costs. Not surprisingly, when ranches pass the five-year mark, they are frequently sold or repossessed. By 1978, about 85% of the ranches in Paragominas had failed, according to the director of the Pará cattlemen's cooperative, Dr. Claudio Diaz.

The productivity declines that follow the first years after conversion, coupled with the enormous speculative gains in land value in the Amazon (Mahar 1979), result in a situation that further exacerbates the instability of existing pastures while favoring the expansion of this form of land use. Non-SUDAM ranches employ two basic strategies to maximize their returns over the short run: steer-fattening operations and overgrazing. These strategies involve buying young stock, fattening the animals, and selling them when the prices are good. Fat

steers are relatively liquid assets and can be sold or
withheld in response to market conditions. The process
of fattening animals requires little more than a few cow-
boys and can be handled in large paddocks. This reduces
labor and infrastructure costs such as fences and handling
corrals in comparison to the labor demands of smaller
pastures of higher quality, with high costs associated
with managing cow-calf operations. Steers are robust and
can tolerate weedy pastures better than breeding cows with
calves, without the risk of damaging expensive brood
stock and of excessive calf mortality. This tolerance
also means that pastures do not need to be cleaned as
often, which further reduces labor requirements. Credit
for fattening operations is relatively easy to obtain,
because the banker can expect to see his money returned
within three years. When inflation rates are high (in
Brazil they have been well over 40% since 1977), short-
term notes are favored by financial establishments.
Brood cow operations involve the initial purchase of
fairly expensive animals (heifers and bulls), with a
delayed return on the investment of at least five years
(SERETE 1972). In an attempt to break the fattening
cycle, CONDEPE (Conselho de Desenvolvimento da Pecuária)
and SUDAM (Superintendency for the Development of the
Amazon) developed preferential credit lines at low,
subsidized interest rates to promote cow-calf production
systems, but the credit, extension, and fiscalization
requirements are such that only the larger, well-
capitalized corporate entities can afford to take
advantage of them.

Given the high productivity of the first years,
ranchers try to maximize their returns as quickly as
possible, and they do this by overstocking. Pastures are
subjected to stocking rates four times the "optimal"
rate of 0.75 to 1.0 animal units per hectare. Overgrazing exacerbates the fertility decline (Toledo and
Serrão 1981) and favors weed invasion, but with this
practice the landowner is still likely to get fairly
reasonable returns on his initial animal and clearing
investment. Since land values increase by about 100% per
year in the active development areas, despite its
declining agronomic productivity, the rancher can pocket
a tidy profit on the land itself and begin a new cycle
elsewhere. Clearly not all ranchers are as predatory as
that, but the speculative nature of Amazonian land
economics makes this pattern a common one. As a consequence, the turnover in land titles in the cattle and
development areas of the Amazon has increased dramatically in the last 15 years (Santos 1979; Pompermayer
1979; Hébette and Acevedo 1979).

LAND TENURE IN AMAZONIA

Land values increase for pasture as well as for

virgin forest. Mahar (1979) points out that investors in
Amazonian rural property consider it as a store of value
rather than a factor in production. In the state of Pará,
for example, on farms of more than 1,000 ha only about
26% of the land is cultivated. These establishments
account for 84% of the land in the private domain, but
include only 8.4% of the farms. The area in use on farms
of greater than 10,000 ha drops to only 14%.

Small farmers, on the other hand, cultivate an
average of 66% of their claim, and this value can range
up to 97%. The small-scale farmer's acquisition of land,
legally or through squatting, is for its use value, since
the amount of land he owns and his labor expenditure
rarely add up to grand speculative gains. He must have
an annual rate of return on his production that is
sufficient to support himself and his family.

In spite of the low rates of use, large groups have
consistently captured land released from government
tenure and sold to the private sector. These lands,
known as terras devolutas, often have been colonized by
squatters. In areas where both large and small owners
have claims on land, either by title or simple occupation, the process of land acquisition has been accompanied
by bitter contention (Souza-Martins 1980). In the state
of Pará, well over 5,300 titles were contested in the
main colonizing and ranching areas of Paragominas,
Altamira, Marabá, and Conceição de Araguaia, and involved
well over a million hectares. Because small farmers can
neither afford the time nor the lawyers, they often lose
these conflicts. As a consequence, there is a tendency
toward land concentration. In the Paragominas area of
the Belém-Brasília highway, the Gini coefficients increased from 0.60 to 0.77 between 1960 and 1970 (Santos
1979), indicating an increasingly regressive land tenure
situation. Further, if land tenure patterns in predominantly livestock areas are compared with those of
Amazonia in general or with small farmer zones, an extreme
tendency toward land concentration is evident, as
Figure 6.8 shows. Land tenure systems in Amazonia in
general are by no means progressive; about 3.3% of the
farms control about 55% of the area in the private
domain. It is also notable that only about 0.1% of the
farms are larger than 10,000 ha, but these include about
30% of the land. Small farms of less than 100 ha occupy
about 11% of the land and constitute about 70% of all the
agricultural establishments in legal Amazonia.

In areas dominated by ranching, not only is the percentage of farms of more than 10,000 ha greater by a
factor of 10, but these establishments control some 56%
of the land. If all ranches over 1,000 ha are calculated, they occupy more than 85% of the privately
owned land. The small farms (less than 100 ha) account
for about the same percentage of establishments in livestock regions as they do in Amazonia as a whole, but in

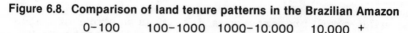

Figure 6.8. Comparison of land tenure patterns in the Brazilian Amazon

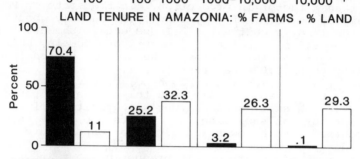

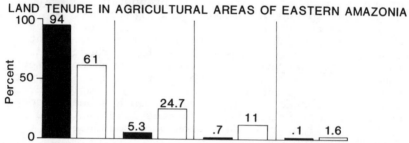

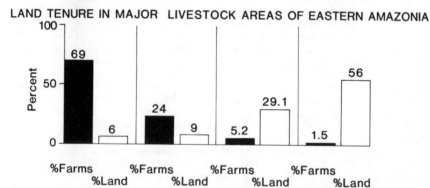

ranching areas they control only 6% as opposed to the
regional average of 11%.

By contrast, small farms in the predominantly
agricultural areas of eastern Amazonia represent 95% of
the holdings and control almost 62% of the land. If
farms of less than 1,000 ha are included, more than 86%
of the land is occupied by small- or medium-scale farmers.
These areas are essential to the food supply of Belém.
Not surprisingly, the disenfranchisement of small-scale
producers in cattle areas has resulted in serious problems
of basic commodity production in the Amazon (Sawyer 1979).

CONCLUSIONS

In the controversy over soil nutrient changes after conversion of forest to pasture the general results suggest that pasture is less beneficial and less catastrophic on soil properties than previously indicated. Conversion is neutral or negative for most soil fertility elements and results in modest gains for pH, Ca, and Mg. However, total ecosystem stocks of these elements are all reduced substantially.

Although soil nutrient status will affect productivity, factors such as weed invasion and increasing compaction also influence the decline in animal carrying capacity from 1 animal unit per ha (A.U./ha) to 0.25 A.U./ha. Maintenance of pasture at this time requires P fertilization and hand labor for weed control (Serrão et al. 1979).

In spite of the ephemeral productivity of areas cleared for pasture, the speculative context within which Brazilian Amazonian development occurred has spurred expansion of ranching because land increased in value even while its agronomic productivity declined. As I have argued elsewhere (Hecht 1982a), the high inflation rates, subsidized credit, and the role of ranching as a vehicle to capture enormous fiscal incentives meant that the primary value of Amazonian ranching land was not for production but exchange. In such a context there is little economic rationality in careful land management, but great advantages in controlling as much land as possible. Large-scale, rapid land accumulation has frequently brought ranching groups into sharp conflict with other elites, as well as with peasants and Indians. Ranching has marginalized peasantries and increased migration from rural to urban areas.

The high percentage of degraded pasture lands calls for more extensive agronomic and ecological analysis of this land use. However, the expansion and performance of Amazonian pastures is not just an agronomic but also an agrarian question. The effect of ranching on land tenure and social dynamics in the region has been extraordinarily regressive.

Policy Recommendations

The speculative land economics in Amazonia, initially spurred by road building and fiscal incentives, are now fueled by speculation linked to mineral and other resources. This context mitigates against wise land use and makes the implementation of careful management techniques especially difficult, since the production value of Amazonian ranching land is currently less important than its exchange value. Means of rationalizing livestock development will require both technical and fiscal approaches.

Technical Recommendations

1. The current research programs of EMBRAPA that test varieties of grasses and legumes, and various fertilization regimes, are important and should be expanded.

2. Amazonian pastures need to be planted with a greater diversity of species rather than the current method of pasture implantation with one or two species. Given the variety of microtopographies, soils, etc., this might well be a means of enhancing pasture stability.

3. We need increased research on native Amazonian legumes, particularly shrub legumes, both for forage and soil amelioration.

4. Agroforestry systems that include livestock have proved quite successful in many Amazonian situations and can be integrated into a variety of commodity production schemes (Bishop 1981; Hecht 1982b). This is an area of research that merits far more attention than it has so far received.

5. Emphasis on ruminants other than bovines, such as tropical sheep, goats, and especially buffalo for upland and degraded areas is a promising research area. While programs addressing these animals already exist, they should be expanded.

6. Small-scale livestock production systems exist in Amazonia and have been successful. Analysis of the factors that contributed to the performance of these systems needs to be developed.

7. Basic research on the dynamics of secondary vegetation in Amazonia is essential.

8. Recuperation of degraded sites through modified fallows, and analysis of secondary succession, is of primary importance.

9. Basic studies on leaching and erosion in pasture ecosystems need to be undertaken.

Fiscal Approaches

To adequately deal with the policy questions inherent in fiscal recommendations would require an expanded analysis that is beyond the purview of this article. The suggestions below are indicated only as a simplistic means of reducing the use of ranching as a vehicle for acquiring lands for speculation.

1. High taxation levels for capital gains on land holdings greater than 1,000 ha.

2. Removal of credit lines that subsidize land acquisition.

3. Enforced ceilings on size of holdings (ca. 100 ha).

ACKNOWLEDGMENTS

Field work for this study was supported by the Ford
Foundation. A National Science Foundation Doctoral
Improvement Grant and an AID grant funded the soil
analysis. This paper benefited from the comments of
Drs. John Nicholaides, III, Emilio Moran, Pedro Sanchez,
and Nigel Smith. Dr. Ilse Hecht provided valuable
editorial comments.

REFERENCES

Alarcón, E., M. Brochero, P. Buritica, T. Gomez Jurado,
T. Orozco, R. Parra, and L. Villamil
    1980   Sector Agropecuário Colombiano: Diagnóstico
            Tecnológico. Bogotá: Instituto Colombiano
            Agrario (ICA).

Almeida, A. W.
    1980   A Segurança Nacional e o Revigoramento do
            Poder Regional. Rio de Janeiro: Grupo Executivo
            de Terras do Araguaia-Tocantins (GETAT).

Aragón, L.
    1978   Migration to Northern Goias. Ph.D. disserta-
            tion, Michigan State Univ.

Bandy, D. and P. A. Sanchez
    1981   Continuous Crop Production on Acid Soils of the
            Amazon Basin of Peru. Paper presented at the
            Workshop on Management of Low Fertility Acid
            Soils of the American Humid Tropics. Univ.
            of Surinam, Paramaribo, Surinam, Nov. 23-26.

Bishop, J.
    1981   Integrated Farming Systems in the Ecuadorian
            Amazon. In S. B. Hecht and G. A. Nores, eds.,
            Land Use and Agricultural Research in the
            Amazon Basin. Cali: Centro Internacional de
            Agricultura Tropical (CIAT).

Brown, K. S.
    1979   Ecologia Geografica e Evolução nas Florestas
            Neotropicais. Ph.D. dissertation, Univ. of
            Campinas, Brazil.

Bunker, Stephen G.
    1979   Power Structures and Exchange Between Govern-
            ment Agencies in the Expansion of the Agri-
            cultural Sector in Pará. Studies in Comparative
            and International Development 14(1):56-76.

Cochrane, T. T. and P. A. Sanchez
  1981   Land Resources of the Amazon Basin. In S. B.
          Hecht and G. A. Nores, eds., Land Use and
          Agricultural Research in the Amazon Basin.
          Cali: Centro Internacional de Agricultura
          Tropical (CIAT).

Coordenadoria de Assistencia Técnica Integral
  1974   Normas Para Manejo de Pastagens. Boletim
          Técnico 81. Belém: Instituto de Pesquisas
          Agropecuárias do Norte (IPEAN).

Falesi, I.
  1976   Ecosistema de pastagem cultivada na Amazônia
          Brasileira. Boletim Técnico 1. do Centro de
          Pesquisa Agropecuária do Trópico Úmido (CPATU).
          Belém: Emprêsa Brasileira de Pesquisa
          Agropecuária (EMBRAPA).

Fearnside, Philip
  1978   Estimation of Carrying Capacity for Human
          Settlement of the Transamazon Highway
          Colonization Area of Brazil. Ph.D. disserta-
          tion, Univ. of Michigan.

  1979   Cattle Yield Prediction for the Transamazon
          Highway. Interciencia 4:220-225.

Gazzo, J.
  1981   Development Policies and Plans for Peru's
          Amazon Region. In S. B. Hecht and G. A. Nores,
          eds., Land Use and Agricultural Research in the
          Amazon Basin. Cali: Centro Internacional de
          Agricultura Tropical (CIAT).

Gentry, A. and J. López-Parodi
  1980   Deforestation and Increased Flooding of the
          Upper Amazon. Science 210:1354-1356.

Golley, F. B., R. Clements, G. Child, and M. Duever
  1975   Mineral Cycling in a Tropical Forest Ecosystem.
          Univ. of Georgia, Athens. Mimeo.

Goodland, Robert J. A.
  1980   Environmental Ranking of Development Projects
          in Brazil. Environmental Conservation (7)1:
          9-25.

Hébette, J. and R. Acevedo Marin
  1979   Colonização Para Quem? NAEA Serie Pesquisa
          1(1). Belém: Núcleo de Altos Estudos Amazônicos
          (NAEA).

Hecht, Susanna B.
1979   Spontaneous Legumes of Developed Pastures in
        Amazonia and Their Forage Potential. In P. A.
        Sanchez and L. Tergas, eds., _Pasture Production
        in Acid Soils of the Tropics_. Cali: Centro
        Internacional de Agricultura Tropical (CIAT).

1981   Agroforestry in the Amazon. In S. B. Hecht and
        G. A. Nores, eds., _Land Use and Agricultural
        Research in the Amazon Basin_. Cali: Centro
        Internacional de Agricultura Tropical (CIAT).

1982a   Cattle Ranching in the Brazilian Amazon:
        Evaluation of a Development Strategy. Ph.D.
        dissertation, Univ. of California, Berkeley.

1982b   Environmental and Social Implications of
        Converting Forest to Pasture in Eastern
        Amazonia. Paper presented at Conference on
        Frontier Expansion in Amazonia, Univ. of
        Florida, Feb. 8-11.

Herrera, R., C. F. Jordan, H. Klinge, and E. Medina
1978   Amazon Ecosystems: Their Structure and Function-
        ing With Particular Emphasis on Nutrients.
        Interciencia 3(4):223-231.

Kang, B. T.
1977   The Effect of some Biological Factors on Soil
        Variability in the Tropics. _Plant and Soil_
        47:451-462.

Klinge, H.
1973   Root Biomass Estimation in Lowland Tropical
        Rain Forests of Central Amazonia, Brazil.
        Tropical Ecology 14:29-38.

Koster, H., E. J. Kahn, and R. Bossert
1976   Programa e Resultados Preliminare dos
        Estudos de Pastagens na Região de Paragominas
        Pará, e o Nordeste de Mato Grosso. Belém:
        Superintendência do Desenvolvimento da Amazônia/
        International Rice Research Institute.

Lovejoy, T. and H.O.R. Schubart
1980   The Ecology of Amazonian Development. In
        F. Barbira-Scazzocchio, ed., _Land, People, and
        Planning in Contemporary Amazônia_. Cambridge,
        UK: Cambridge Univ. Center for Latin American
        Studies, Occasional Publ. 3.

Lugo, A. and S. Brown
in   Are Tropical Forests Endangered Ecosystems?
press   _Unasylva_. In press.

184

Mc Gregor, D.
   1980   Investigation of the Soil Erosion in the Co-
           lombian rainforest zone. Catena, 1980: 267-273.

Mahar, Dennis J.
   1979   Frontier Development in Brazil: A Study of
           Amazonia. New York: Praeger.

Martins, E. S.
   1963   Carne, Produção e Mercado. Porto Alegre:
           Univ. de Rio Grande do Sul.

Mueller, Charles
   1980   Frontier-Based Agricultural Expansion: The
           Case of Rondônia. In F. Barbira-Scazzocchio,
           ed., Land, People, and Planning in Contemporary
           Amazônia. Cambridge, UK: Cambridge Univ.
           Center for Latin American Studies, Occasional
           Publ. 3.

Myers, Norman
   1979   The Sinking Ark: A New Look at the Problem of
           Disappearing Species. Oxford: Pergamon.

   1980   Conversion of Moist Tropical Forests. Washing-
           ton, D.C.: National Academy of Sciences.

Nye, P. and D. Greenland
   1960   The Soil Under Shifting Cultivation.
           Harpenden, England, Commonwealth Agricultural
           Bureaux.

Pardi, M. C. and R. B. Caldas
   1968   Grandes Deslocamentos de Gado Bovino de Corte
           no Brasil. Anais do XI Congresso Brasileiro
           de Veterinaria. Campinas, São Paulo: Sociedade
           Brasileira de Veterinária e Zootecnia.

Pereira, F. and J. Salinas
   1981   General Evaluation of the Agricultural
           Potential of the Bolivian Amazon. In S. B.
           Hecht and G. A. Nores, eds., Land Use and
           Agricultural Research in the Amazon Basin.
           Cali: Centro Internacional de Agricultura
           Tropical (CIAT).

Pires, J. M. and Ghillean T. Prance
   1977   The Amazon Forest: A Natural Heritage to be
           Preserved. In G. T. Prance and T. Elias, eds.,
           Extinction is Forever. New York: New York
           Botanical Garden.

Pompermayer, Malorí José
   1979   The State and the Frontier in Brazil: A Case

Study of the Amazon. Ph.D. dissertation,
Dept. of Political Science, Stanford Univ.

RADAM
  1973- Levantamento de Recursos Naturais. Vols. 1-7.
  1975   Rio de Janeiro: Ministerio de Minas e Energia.

Salas, G. de la
  1978   El Sistema Forestal de Carare-Upon. CONIF
        Série Técnica #8. Bogotá: Consejo Nacional
        de Investigaciones Forestales (CONIF).

Salati, E., A. Dall'Olio, E. Matsui, and S. R. Gat
  1979   Recycling of Water in the Amazon Basin: An
        Isotope Study. Water Resources Research
        15(5):1250-1258.

Sanchez, Pedro A.
  1976   Properties and Management of Tropical Soils.
        New York: Wiley-Interscience.

  1979   Soil Fertility and Conservation Considerations
        for Agroforestry Systems in the Humid Tropics
        of Latin America. In H. Mongi and P. Huxley,
        eds., Soils Research in Agroforestry. Nairobi:
        International Council for Research on Agro-
        Forestry. (ICRAF).

Sanchez, Pedro A. and T. T. Cochrane
  1980   Soil Constraints in Relation to Major Farming
        Systems in Tropical America. In Priorities
        for Alleviating Soil-Related Constraints to
        Food Production in the Tropics. Los Baños,
        the Philippines: International Rice Research
        Institute (IRRI).

Santiago, P. A.
  1970   Pecuária de Corte no Brasil Central. São
        Paulo: Secretaria de Agricultura de São Paulo.

Santos, R.
  1979   Sistema de Propriedade e Relações de Trabalho
        no Meio Rural Paraense. In J. M. Monteiro de
        Costa, ed., Amazônia: Desenvolvimento e
        Occupação. Rio de Janeiro: Instituto de
        Planejamento Econômico e Social/Instituto de
        Pesquisas.

Sawyer, D.
  1979   Peasants and Capitalism on the Amazonian
        Frontier. Ph.D. dissertation, Harvard Univ.

Schubart, H.O.R.
  1976   Sumario de Ecologia Amazônica. Ciencia e
        Cultura 28(5):513-519.

186

Schuurman, F. J.
1979   Colonization Policy and Peasant Economy in the
        Amazon Basin. Boletín de Estudios Latino-
        Americanos y del Caribe 1(27):29-41.

Scott, G.
1978   Grassland Development in the Grand Pajonal.
        Honolulu: Univ. of Hawaii.

SERETE
1972   Setôres Econômicos e Elementos da Politica
        Setorial: Pecuária Bovina. Belém: Superinten-
        dência de Desenvolvimento da Amazônia (SUDAM).

Serrão, A. and M. Simão-Neto
1975   The Adaptation of Tropical Forages in the
        Amazon Region. In E. C. Doll and G. O. Mott,
        eds., Tropical Forages in Tropical Livestock
        Production Systems. Madison, Wis.: American
        Society of Agronomy Special Publication.

Serrão, A., I. Falesi, J. B. Vega, and J. F. Teixeira
1979   Productivity of Cultivated Pastures on Low
        Fertility Soils of the Brazilian Amazon. In
        P. A. Sanchez and L. E. Tergas, eds., Pasture
        Production in Acid Soils of the Tropics.
        Cali: Centro Internacional de Agricultura
        Tropical (CIAT).

Seubert, C. E., P. A. Sanchez, and C. Valverde
1977   Effects of Land Clearing Methods on Soil
        Properties of an Ultisol and Crop Performance
        in the Amazon Jungle of Peru. Tropical
        Agriculture (Trinidad) 54(4):307-321.

Silva, L. F.
1978   Influencia do Manejo de un Ecosistema nas
        Propriedades Edaficas dos Oxisols de Tabuleiro.
        Itabuna: Centro de Pesquisa do Cacau (CEPLAC).

Simão-Neto, M., A. Serrão, C. Gonçalves, and
David Pimentel
1973   Comportamento de Gramíneas Forrageiras na
        Região de Belém. Communição Técnica 48.
        Belém: Instituto de Pesquisa Agropecuária do
        Norte (IPEAN).

Souza-Martins, J.
1980   Fighting for Land: Indians and Posseiros in
        Legal Amazonia. In F. Barbira-Scazzocchio, ed.,
        Land, People, and Planning in Contemporary
        Amazônia. Cambridge, UK: Cambridge Univ.
        Center for Latin American Studies, Occasional
        Publ. 3.

Stark, N. and C. Jordan
1978   Nutrient Retention by the Root Mat of an
        Amazonian Forest. Ecology 59:434-437.

Tardin, A. T. et al. (10 coauthors)
1979   Levantamento de Areas de Desmatamento na
        Amazônia Legal Atraves de Imagens do Satelite
        LANDSAT. Instituto Nacional de Pesquisas
        Espaciais (INPE) report #411-NTE/142. São José
        dos Campos: Instituto Nacional de Pesquisas
        Espaciais.

Tardin, A. T., A. dos Santos, E. M. Morães-Novo,
and F. L. Toledo
1977   Relatorio das Atividades do Projeto
        Superintendência de Desenvolvimento da
        Amazônia (SUDAM)/Instituto Nacional de
        Pesquisas Espaciais (INPE) #1034 NTE. São
        José dos Campos: Instituto Nacional de Pesquisas
        Espaciais.

Tietzel, J. and R. Bruce
1972   Fertility of Pasture Soils in the Wet Tropical
        Coast of Queensland. Australian Journal of
        Experimental Agriculture and Animal Husbandry
        12:49-54.

Toledo, J. and A. Serrão
1981   Pasture and Animal Production in Amazonia.
        In S. B. Hecht and G. A. Nores, eds., Land Use
        and Agricultural Research in the Amazon Basin.
        Cali: Centro Internacional de Agricultura
        Tropical (CIAT).

Torre, R. de la
1981   Development Policies and Plans for Ecuador's
        Amazon Region. In S. B. Hecht and G. A. Nores,
        eds., Land Use and Agricultural Research in the
        Amazon Basin. Cali: Centro Internacional de
        Agricultura Tropical (CIAT).

Turrenne, J. F.
1977   Cultûre Itinerante et Jachere Forestiére:
        Evolution de la Matiére Organique. IV: Simposio
        Internacional de Ecologia Tropical. Port de
        France: Office de la Recherche Scientifique et
        Technique de Outre-Mer (ORSTOM).

UNESCO
1978   Tropical Rainforests: A State of the Art Report.
        Paris, France: United Nations Educational,
        Scientific, and Cultural Organization (UNESCO).

Vincente-Chandler, J., E. Rivera, R. Boneta et al.
    1973   The Management and Utilization of Forage
            Crops in Puerto Rico. Agric. Exper. Station
            Bulletin #116. San Juan: Univ. de Puerto Rico.

Wood, Charles H. and Marianne Schminck
    1979   Blaming the Victim: Small Farmer Production
            in an Amazon Colonization Project. Studies in
            Third World Societies 7:77-93.

Zinke, P. J.
    1976   Soils of the Amazon Data Base. Univ. of
            California Agricultural Experiment Station,
            Amazon Project. Unpublished data.

Zinke, P. J., S. Sabhasri, and P. Kundstater
    1978   Soil Fertility Aspects of the Lua Fallow
            System. In P. Kundstater, R. Chapman, and
            S. Sabhasri, eds., Farmers in the Forest.
            Honolulu: Univ. of Hawaii Press.

7
Amazonian Fisheries

Michael Goulding

HISTORY OF AMAZONIAN FISHERIES

The first European chroniclers to make note of Amerindian livelihood in the Amazon made it clear in their reports that fish was an important item in the diets of the native populations scattered along the rivers (Acuña 1891; Fritz 1922; Medina 1934). Whether fish was the most important animal protein source is an academic question that can never be fully settled, as the early chroniclers also mentioned manatee, turtle, and terrestrial game as being common in the villages that they saw. I doubt that riparian Amerindian groups in the central part of the Amazon Basin ever suffered for lack of animal protein, and it is highly unlikely that native groups were capable of overexploiting the fisheries in and along the larger rivers. It is highly possible, however, that Amerindian groups were capable of overexploiting other stream fisheries because of the wide use of fish poisons in the Amazon Basin. In the upper Rio Negro basin, for example, I have observed Amerindian groups fishing in small streams with plants containing rotenone and other toxic plant compounds, and informants there told me that in extremely low water years the fish faunas are largely decimated by piscicide fishing and require several years to recover their stocks.

A detailed discussion of native fishing techniques is beyond the purview of the present discussion, and here I would only like to point out that during their long tenure in the Amazon Basin, Amerindian groups developed detailed oral natural histories of the plants and animals that were a part of their livelihood. Even today, the largely acculturated Amerindians living along the upper Rio Negro possess a more complete natural history knowledge than do caboclos, or miscegenated Amazonians, who are now the major cultural group along Amazonian rivers (see Moran 1974 for discussions of caboclo culture and environmental adaptation). The illustrious Brazilian historian and naturalist, José Veríssimo, noted almost a

189

century ago that fish was the principal animal protein source in the European and caboclo conquest of the Amazon region (Veríssimo 1895). The Amerindians knew their environment and how to fish well, and the conquistadores learned from them. Bow-and-arrow, harpoon, rotenone, weirs, and nets were all used in Amerindian fishing, and these methods were adopted by caboclo culture and are still widely used today.

The first commercial fishery of any scale in the Amazon region was based on the large bony-tongued pirarucú (Arapaima gigas; Osteoglossidae). Veríssimo (1895) searched the archives for mention of the exploitation of pirarucú, but turned up nothing of importance earlier than the nineteenth century. It is strange that this large fish is so infrequently mentioned in early accounts, as it is an air-breathing species that surfaces every few minutes and is easily observed and heard. Veríssimo thought that pirarucú began to be substituted for the large river manatee in the salting industry in nineteenth-century Amazônia when the large sirenian began to get rarer because of heavy exploitation. Though not mentioned by Veríssimo, a taboo against eating pirarucú flesh may have been widespread among Amerindian groups and caboclo culture. Even today there are many forbidden fish species in caboclo culture, especially in times of illness and recovery, and pirarucú is often mentioned as one of them (Smith 1979, 1981; I have also noted this taboo on the Rio Negro and Rio Madeira). By the mid-nineteenth century, pirarucú fisheries were well established and nearly all of the naturalists of the period mention them or the presence of the salted product in the regional human diet (Bates 1865; Agassiz 1879; Wallace 1889; Spruce 1908). By 1892, at least one million kilograms of salted pirarucú were being exported from the state of Amazonas to neighboring Pará (Veríssimo 1895), and the fish had already assumed the role of bacalhão, or cod, in the traditional Portuguese diet adapted to Amazonian conditions.

Though the Portuguese had a long history of fishing, for the first 400 years of their, or their descendants', occupation of the Amazon, the only widely adopted devices that they introduced were metal hooks and iron points for arrows and gigs. As early as 1768 the Portuguese explorer and chronicler Alexandre Rodrigues Ferreira was saying that seines would help improve Amazon fishing, though he could find none being used in the Capitania do Rio Negro, or what is now mostly the state of Amazonas (Ferreira 1972). By the 1850s, crude seines were evidently being used near Barra (now Manaus), as Alfred Russel Wallace reported while accompanying an excursion to the Rio Solimões, where a seine was used to catch fishes on beaches (Wallace 1889).

Local fishermen state that the Portuguese took control of the Manaus fisheries sometime in the early part

of the twentieth century and controlled them until the
end of World War II, at which time many of the Luso-
Brazilians in the fishing business emigrated from Brazil.
The Portuguese apparently took control of the fisheries
because they were the first to make significant commercial
use of seines in the Amazon region. In the 1920s or 1930s,
bombs made from dynamite or nitroglycerin were added to
the fishing arsenal of the Manaus fleet, especially for
taking migratory species in the river channels. By the
1950s the Manaus fleet could brag of their ice boats,
though the longest fishing trips appear to have been no
farther than the mouth of the Rio Madeira going east, or
to the lower reaches of the Rio Purus traveling west.
Perhaps the principal fishing area in the 1950s was the
island of Careiro in the Rio Amazonas near the confluence
of the Rio Solimões and Rio Negro, and bombs may have been
the main gear used as they were heard daily in Manaus
(Bitencourt 1951).

The creation of the Zona Franca, or Free Trade Zone,
in Manaus in 1967, and subsequently, the construction of
the Amazon highway network in the 1970s, set the stage
for large-scale urbanization in the Brazilian part of the
Amazon Basin. The demand for locally caught fish increased
astronomically as the towns and cities boomed in population. During the 1970s, the fishing technology of the
Amazon region improved considerably with the introduction
of better seines, gill nets, and the use of styrofoam for
insulating ice boxes. Smaller towns such as Itacoatiara,
Manacapuru, Coari, and Tefé began to support small
commercial fishing fleets, though Manaus still has many
more fishermen and boats than all of the other inland
cities and towns put together. The Manaus fleet increased its catches both by intensification of the local
fisheries--which led to 'fish wars' and deaths in at least
one case (Menezes 1972)--and by expansion into the far-
flung tributaries of the Rio Solimões principally, and
to a lesser extent, those of the Rio Amazonas. Low population densities in the large affluent systems meant that
the Manaus flotilla confronted almost no competition for
the fish stocks. By 1980, however, Manaus fishermen had
reached the end of the Amazon fisheries frontier centering on the Rio Solimões. Manaus fishing boats were
appearing in the headwaters of the Rio Purus, Rio Juruá,
Rio Japurá, and Rio Negro. On the southern axis, Porto
Velho fishermen moved above the rapids in the upper course
of the Rio Madeira and into the Rio Mamoré and Rio Guaporé,
a region that was barely fished commercially before 1978.
Despite the intensification and expansion of Amazonian
fisheries, all of the major towns and cities of the region
were reporting serious fish shortages in their markets in
1981. It may be stated safely that the fisheries
frontier of inland Amazônia is now history.

Belém is situated at the southeastern corner of the
Amazon estuary, and thus is in close proximity to

freshwater, brackish water, and saltwater fishing habitats. The city's geographical situation, however, was taken little advantage of in the development of the local fisheries. As early as the late 1800s, Veríssimo (1895) reported that Belém was importing large quantities of salted pirarucú from the state of Amazonas, implying that the city's local fisheries were little developed. By the mid-1950s the situation was no better, if not worse, and Pinto (1956) stated that, of the fish consumed in the city, fourteen times more was imported (even from as far away as Rio Grande do Sul) than was caught locally. For at least a century Belém fishermen have probably known about the large quantities of catfishes that reside in the brackish and marine waters east of Marajó. Until the 1960s, however, only ariid catfishes (family Ariidae) were exploited on any scale, and these were mostly used for their gas bladders, from which glue was made. In the Belém area, as in much of the Amazon Basin (see below), there are taboos against eating catfish flesh, and this largely explains why the resource, historically, was little exploited until foreign markets were found for it. The principal freshwater fisheries of the Belém area have been at Lago Arari on the island of Marajó, but there is little information on them other than some general comments by Pinto (1956). In any case the Marajó freshwater fisheries account for only a small part of the total catch consumed in or exported from Belém. There is no information indicating the importance of fish in the animal protein supply of Belém, but it appears to be much less than that for Manaus, mainly because of the local disdain for catfish and the availability of beef and water buffalo raised along the lower Rio Amazonas and on Marajó.

In the late 1960s Brazilian business interests recognized the potential export market for the largely unexploited catfishes found near the Amazon estuary. By 1970 trawls had replaced more traditional gear, such as trotlines and seines, in the catfish operations, and large quantities of piramutaba (Brachyplatystoma vaillantii) began to be caught and exported to the United States. By 1980 these export fisheries appeared to account for about 90% of the total catch of the Belém fleet (Cacex/ Banco do Brasil 1980 and SUDEPE 1980). In short, the Belém fisheries developed to feed North Americans, not Brazilians (Penner 1980). It is still questionable whether large quantities of catfish could be sold in Belém, but there is no question that it would find a ready market in Northeastern, Southeastern, and Southern Brazil, but perhaps at a lower price than it brings in the export market.

ESTIMATE OF TOTAL CATCHES

The only year when reasonably accurate data on

Amazonian fisheries were collected over a large area was 1977 (Bayley 1981; Goulding 1979, 1981; Smith 1979, 1981). Bayley (1981) estimated that the 1977 total fishery yield, including both commercial and subsistence operations, of the middle and upper Amazon area in Brazil was about 85,000 tons, of which 20%--consisting mostly of large catfishes and pirarucú--was exported from the region. Though little data are available, reports of Belém fishermen, fishmongers, and exporters indicate that somewhere between 20,000 and 30,000 tons of piramutaba were captured annually in the Amazon estuary in the late 1970s; in 1980 authorities monitored at least 7,000 tons of catfish that were exported abroad from Belém (Cacex/ Banco do Brasil 1980), but the real total is certainly much higher according to local reports. The total annual catch, as of 1980, of Amazonian fisheries--including the estuarine area--appears to be somewhere between 100,000 and 130,000 tons, though not much more can be said because of insufficient data.

The only system for which reliable annual data have been collected over a series of years is the Rio Madeira (Figure 7.1). How representative this system is of larger Amazônia is difficult to say, as it accounts for only 2 to 3% of the total catch. It may be pointed out, however, that the important food fish species of the Rio Madeira are the same as those arriving in the large Manaus market from many river systems, and that seasonal fishing patterns in the respective areas are very similar (Goulding 1981). The Rio Madeira data show that total catches peaked in 1974, and that annual catches have fallen by about 40 to 50 % since then. The conclusion is that not much more, if anything, is to be expected from the Rio Madeira fisheries, and the same is probably true of the Rio Solimões-Amazonas region.

A further discussion of the fisheries can be subdivided into the migratory characin fisheries, river channel catfish fisheries, floodplain fisheries, and estuarine fisheries.

MIGRATORY CHARACIN FISHERIES

There are about 10 genera (Colossoma, Mylossoma, Triportheus, Brycon, Leporinus, Schizodon, Rhytiodus, Prochilodus, Semaprochilodus, and Curimata) and at least 30 species of characins in the Amazon Basin that are known to form large schools and migrate in the rivers at some time of the year. As a group, the migratory characins are the most important food fishes in inland Amazônia. With the exception of large fishes of the genus Colossoma, most catches of migratory characins are made with seines when the fishes are migrating in large schools in the rivers. Most of the Colossoma catch is taken with gill nets (Petrere 1978), though in the Rio Madeira region these large fishes are still principally

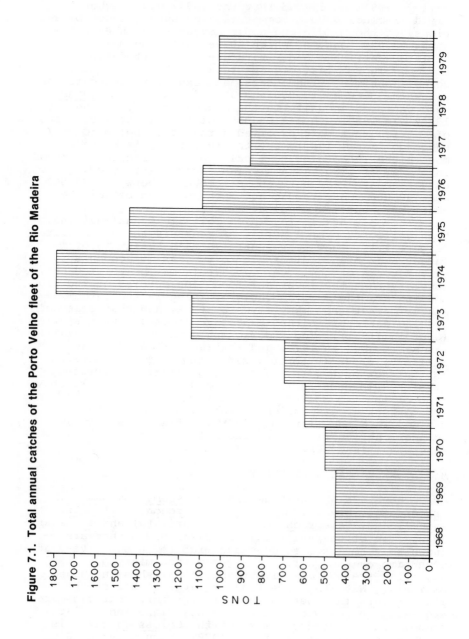

Figure 7.1. Total annual catches of the Porto Velho fleet of the Rio Madeira

captured with seines (Goulding 1979, 1981).

In the central part of the Amazon Basin (centering on the relatively nutrient-rich whitewater rivers, i.e., the Rio Solimões-Amazonas, Rio Madeira, Rio Purus, and Rio Juruá; Figure 7.2) two distinct characin migrations are observed and exploited by commercial fishermen annually. From about the beginning to the middle of the annual floods, the migratory characins descend the nutrient-poor blackwater and clearwater tributaries to spawn in the nutrient-rich whitewater rivers. At this time of year fishermen anchor in the mouth areas of the blackwater and clearwater affluents and wait for the descending schools, though in some cases, such as the large Rio Negro, the migrating spawners are attacked farther upstream where the fishes can be followed for some distance downstream and exploited. Most captures are made before the schools reach the whitewater rivers, for once in the turbid rivers they can no longer be found in concentrations or tight formation. Subsequent to spawning, the migratory characins move back into the blackwater and clearwater tributaries, though some may also enter the floodplain areas of the turbid river waters where they spawned (they can disperse in the flooded forests and feed heavily for several months). It should be pointed out that nearly all of the migratory characins also inhabit the floodplains of the whitewater rivers, but catches here of most species are minimal compared to those taken in the mouths of the blackwater and clearwater rivers. At the beginning of the floods the whitewater river floodplains are invaded by turbid water, and it appears that the migratory characins residing in these areas do not move out into the flowing river to spawn. Instead they spawn in the turbid waters of the floodplain itself, and these schools are reported by fishermen to be much smaller than those encountered in the blackwater and clearwater affluents, and also much more difficult to catch.

The other annual migrations begin at or just after the peak of the floods when fishes of the genus Semaprochilodus move out of the flooded forests, form large schools, and once again descend the blackwater and clearwater tributaries to enter the whitewater rivers. The gonads of these fishes are small at this time of year (having spawned only a few months earlier) and, once entering a whitewater river, in contrast to the spawning migrations, they move upstream in it. These migrations are easily observed by fishermen and the largest catches of Semaprochilodus are made at this time of year. The same basic pattern is repeated with the other migratory characins, and these movements last until the end of the low-water season. The migratory characins that descend the blackwater and clearwater rivers subsequent to the floods are referred to as peixe gordo, or fat fish, as is the commercial fishery name. This is an allusion to the large stores of body fat that these fishes have built

196

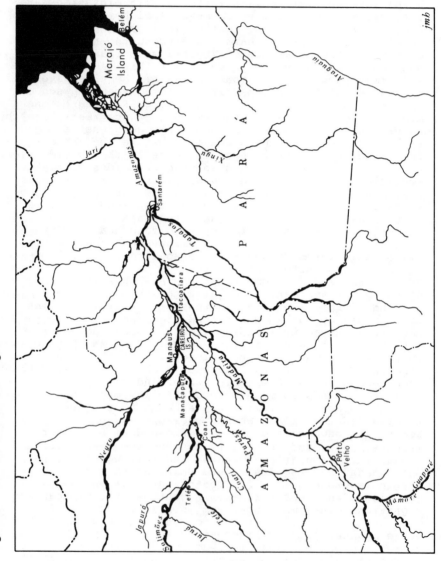

Figure 7.2. The central Amazon region

up while feeding in the flooded forests. During the lowest
water period, most, but not all, of the migratory characin
species are encountered migrating upstream in the whitewater rivers, and these fish migrating upstream (and such
upstream migrations in general) are called the piracema.
This is the time of year when the largest catches of most
species are made because the channels are shallower and
narrower, and large schools can often be captured in
beach areas where seines of 200 to 300 m length can be
employed.

The fry and young of the migratory characins are
raised on the floodplains of the whitewater rivers--
apparently because of the higher primary production per
given area, and hence better food supply in the form of
phytoplankton, zooplankton, and other small plant and
animal life on which they feed--and there is some evidence
that the recruitment of young into the piracema migrations
takes place mostly during the low-water period. These
pre-adults then move into the blackwater and clearwater
affluents to assume the feeding and migratory behavior of
adults of their same species. The ages of these young
fish appear to vary, depending on the species, from about
six months to three or four years. Traditionally these
fishes were little molested by fishermen because of their
small size, but with recent shortages in the markets they
have become more attractive.

In summary, it may be pointed out that the life
histories of the migratory characins embrace large areas
of the whitewater rivers and their blackwater and clearwater affluents. The adult fishes of this group (with
perhaps a couple of exceptions) are highly adapted to
life in the flooded forests during the annual inundations,
where they procure most of their food. The fry and young
fishes of these species, however, require the nutrient-
rich broth of the whitewater river floodplains to support
their feeding requirements. Many if not most populations
of the migratory characins are thought to be born in the
flowing river channels of the whitewater rivers, where
there is a general downstream displacement of them,
probably due mostly to drift; at this time they live off
the energy and nutrients stored in their vitelline sacs.
Only adults and pre-adults are observed to migrate upstream in the whitewater rivers, and it is reasonable
to believe that this counteracts, geographically, the
downstream displacement of their young.

RIVER CHANNEL CATFISH FISHERIES

Amazonian river channels have about 10 species of
large, for the most part predatory, catfishes of the
family Pimelodidae. Brachyplatystoma and Pseudoplatystoma
are the most important food-fish genera of the large catfishes. Traditionally, large catfishes have been held in
very low esteem in caboclo culture, as is true for most

other scaleless fishes as well. In caboclo folklore,
catfish flesh when eaten is said to aggravate inflammation,
encourage miscarriages, swell hemorrhoids, discolor skin,
and aggravate a large number of other illnesses. The
origins of the catfish taboo in caboclo culture are unclear, though the disdain of scaleless fishes may have been
introduced through Christian interpretations of taboos
found in the Old Testament.

The construction of Amazonian highways, and the
introduction of new fishing technologies in the early
1970s, set the stage for the large-scale exploitation and
exportation of river channel catfishes. Brazilian
refrigeration companies recognized that catfish filets
would fetch handsome prices in states such as Paraná and
São Paulo where there were no taboos against eating
siluroid flesh. When the highways opened up, frozen catfish could be shipped economically via Manaus/Porto
Velho/Cuiabá and Santarém/Brasília to Southeastern and
Southern Brazil. On return trips the same trucks brought
back dairy products and poultry. Another main destina-
tion of catfishes in the mid and late 1970s was Bogotá,
Colombia, for which most of the catfishes were captured in
Brazilian waters and shipped from Leticia (in Colombia
at the Brazilian border) by air. Between 1974 and 1979
between 400 and 700 tons of catfishes were shipped
annually from the upper Rio Madeira to Southern and Southeastern Brazil, while Bayley (1981) estimated that at
least 9,000 tons, mostly from the Rio Solimões region,
were exported to Bogotá. The amount that moved through
Manaus, Santarém and Belém has never been recorded by data
collectors, but was probably over 3,000 tons annually in
the late 1970s. The only data available for siluroid
fisheries are those that I collected in the Rio Madeira
basin. Rio Madeira catfish fisheries peaked in 1974, but
since then there has been a general decline, and many of
the region's siluroid fishermen have moved above the
rapids and into the Rio Mamoré and Rio Guaporé (Goulding
1979, 1981).

The caçoeira, or drifting deepwater gill net,
accounts for most of the catfish catch in the river
channels of inland Amazônia. The gear was first introduced by São Paulo fishermen exploiting the Rio Madeira,
and from there it spread to the rest of western Amazônia.
Drifting deepwater gill nets are usually 100 to 300 m
in length, 3 to 10 m high, and their mesh sizes vary from
16 to 24 cm when stretched. The bottom line of a gill
net is heavily weighted with lead to assure that the
caçoeira will sink to the bottom of the river; enough
floats are attached to the top line to maintain the gill
net vertically but not pull it to the surface. To the two
ends of the net at the top are attached long ropes, one
of which is tied to a large float, while the other is
handled by a fisherman in a canoe. The caçoeira is
allowed to drift downstream with the current, while the

fishermen in the canoe above keep the net taut between themselves and the float. When the large catfishes are encountered by the drifting deepwater gill net, they are entangled and can be brought aboard and removed. Trotlines strung to the middle of the river channels, and often supporting as many as 25 hooks suspended on short lines, are also extensively employed in catfish operations, but they account for only a small part of the total catch.

The most unique fishery for catfishes is found at the Teotônio cataract in the upper Rio Madeira above Porto Velho. The most important species captured is the dourada (Brachyplatystoma flavicans), as it migrates upstream during both the low and beginning of the high-water period. The catfishes have a difficult time negotiating the turbulent waters of the Teotônio rapids, and fishermen are able to gaff them at the beginning of the floods or take them with cast nets during the low-water season. In 1977, about 190 tons of catfishes were captured at Teotônio with drifting deepwater gill nets, gaffs, cast nets, and seines.

FLOODPLAIN FISHERIES

The low-lying nature of the Amazonian lowlands, coupled with marked seasonal differences in heavy rainfall, has led to the development of floodplains along all of the larger rivers and most of the smaller ones as well. The floodplains are the main zones of primary production because of the presence of inundation forests (associated with all water types), phytoplankton communities, and "floating meadows" of herbaceous plants (Junk 1970, 1973). Only floodplains associated with whitewater rivers have high enough fish biomasses to support large-scale, annual fisheries in small areas. The highest yielding floodplain fisheries are those of the lower Rio Solimões and the middle Rio Amazonas near the city of Itacoatiara and the mouth of the Rio Madeira. This large floodplain area is intensively exploited because of its proximity to Manaus and Itacoatiara. Petrere (1978) monitored the total catches in 1976 from Lago de Janauacá, a sprawling floodplain area of the Rio Solimões about 40 km from Manaus, and Lago do Rei, a lake on the island of Careiro in the Rio Amazonas near the Rio Negro; the first yielded 1,275 tons in that year, and the latter 700 tons. Smith (1979, 1981) estimated that about 2,000 tons of fish were captured in 1977 in a 60 km radius of Itacoatiara, and most of this appears to have come from the floodplains of the Rio Amazonas. In striking contrast is the Rio Madeira, a relatively channelized river, where only about 40 tons are taken annually on the floodplains in the 700 km stretch above the Rio Aripuaña (Goulding 1979).

For the Rio Madeira fisheries I have shown that about 10 percent of the total catch is taken on floodplains (Goulding 1979). Though no data are yet available, my

general impression is that about 15 to 25 percent of the
total catches centering on the Rio Solimões-Amazonas comes
from the floodplains. Though most food fishes are "produced" on the floodplains, they are much more difficult to
catch here than when migrating in large schools in the
rivers. (Some important food fishes, however, such as
the cichlids, are largely restricted to the floodplains
and do not migrate in the rivers.)

With fish shortages in the local markets and intense
fishing competition near urban centers, commercial fishermen in the last several years have begun to invade the
floodplain lakes of the clearwater (e.g., the rightbank
tributaries of the Rio Madeira) and blackwater (e.g., Rio
Negro) rivers. Most of these nutrient-poor bodies of
water can only be fished once, at the most twice, a year,
as productivity is low and catches are largely made up of
fishes that become entrapped after the floods. The
catches from these lakes represent only a very small
percentage of the total tonnage delivered to the Manaus
and Porto Velho markets.

A wide variety of gear is used in Amazonian floodplain fisheries. In terms of total catches the most
important are gill nets, seines, and gigs, and secondarily,
cast nets, harpoons, bows and arrows, handlines, and trotlines. The widespread use of gill nets in Amazonian waters
dates to about 1969 when relatively cheap monofilament
and nylon line became available in the region. The
diffusion of gillnet technology has been very rapid in
the Amazon, and in the late 1970s the gear gradually came
to dominate floodplain fishing. Initially most gill
nets were designed to catch large characoid fishes of the
genus Colossoma, and especially the tambaqui (C.
macropomum). Small meshes were shunned because of the
higher market price of larger fishes and the constant
and expensive nuisance of piranhas that mutilate gill
nets. Petrere (1978) estimated that the tambaqui represented about 44 percent of the total catch arriving in
the main market in Manaus in 1976, and most of these
fishes were taken with gill nets. Because of over-fishing
in the last several years, tambaqui catches appear to be
declining and fishermen have begun to experiment more
with smaller-meshed gill nets, though their contribution
to the present catches is unknown. Smith's (1979, 1981)
data, however, seem to indicate that smaller meshes are
contributing significantly to floodplain catches in the
middle Rio Amazonas area, and the same is probably true
of the Rio Solimões. Small-meshed gill nets are of
minimal importance in the Rio Madeira fisheries, but this
is mostly a reflection of the relatively small floodplain
areas available where they could be employed economically.

Seines are used in floodplain areas mostly for
schools migrating to and from the river channels. With
declining catches, however, fishermen are beginning to
practice what might be termed blind seining. In this

case the seines are payed out without knowing exactly what
will be caught (in every other type of seine fishery,
Amazonian fishermen know what species they are exploiting
before it is caught), and this seining activity usually
takes place near floating meadows or in the small lakes
of the clearwater and blackwater affluents described
above. In terms of total catches, this type of fishing
is not very productive.

The gig is a pronged spear that is employed to stab
fishes, especially the cichlids, that remain near the
surface at night. The zagáia, as the gig is called in the
Amazon, is used with a light source, usually a flashlight.
When a fish is spotted, the light beam is kept in its
eyes and the fisherman moves in for the gigging. The
tucunaré (Cichla ocellaris, Cichlidae), a favorite food
fish, is captured mostly with this gear.

The only other gear that will be discussed here is
the harpoon, which is used to kill pirarucú. When the
large air-breathing fish surfaces every few minutes it is
vulnerable to the harpoon fisherman. Most of the large
pirarucú, or those over about 50 kg, are taken by harpoon,
while smaller individuals are captured with gill nets.

The most productive period of floodplain fishing is
during the low-water season when fishes become concentrated in the small bodies of water (Goulding 1979).
During the floods the fishes are spread out and much, if
not most, of the biomass is found in the inundation
forests. In the Rio Madeira region, flooded forests
represent only about 2% of the total catch, indicating
how difficult it is to fish at this time of year.

ESTUARINE FISHERIES

The large-scale fisheries of the Amazon estuary and
its adjacent coastal, brackish water zone are based
mostly on the piramutaba (Brachyplatystoma vaillantii)
and, to a much lesser extent, on the dourada (Brachyplatystoma flavicans), both taxa belonging to the freshwater
family Pimelodidae. Little is known about the biology
of the Amazon estuary, but the presence of large biomasses of predatory catfishes strongly suggests that
primary production is relatively high and based on
phytoplankton. Schools of piramutaba and dourada are
known to migrate from the estuarine area and move upstream in the Rio Amazonas and perhaps even go as far as
Peru (via the Rio Solimões) or Bolivia (via the Rio
Madeira). These migrations may be related to reproduction,
but neither the spawning grounds nor large numbers of ripe
fishes have been located in either the estuarine region
or in the inland rivers.

The main zone of piramutuba and dourada fishing in
the estuarine area is in the brackish waters bathing the
coasts of Pará, Amapá and northern Maranhão. Only a very
small part of the total catfish catch is taken in the

complex network of channels to the north and west of the
large island of Marajó. The catfishes are captured mostly
with trawls, at depths of 10 to 12 m, and these catches
are usually accompanied by a wide variety of other taxa,
though in much lesser quantity according to local fishermen. Unfortunately not much more can be said here about
these important fisheries as they have never been studied
in detail.

MANAGEMENT PROBLEMS AND PROSPECTS

Amazon fisheries in their present form loom in the
economic shadows of extractivism that were cast with the
coming of the Europeans in the sixteenth and seventeenth
centuries. Historically, mismanagement of the fisheries--
such as the decimation of the pirarucú in certain areas--
was condoned or ignored because of the belief in super-
abundance. Tem demais ("there's more than plenty") is
still the main chant of Amazonian fishermen and fish
sellers (not fish officials, I am happy to report), but
recent shortages in markets are throwing a dim light on the
cliché. The explosive growth of commercial fisheries
in the past two decades, largely in response to booming
populations and rapid urbanization of the region, has
magnified many times what were once only ecological mis-
demeanors and now made them, collectively, serious
infractions against the proper management of this
important biological resource.

Ichthyologically, the Amazon Basin is the least known
freshwater system on Earth, and in terms of the basic
description of the fauna and annual data collecting on the
fisheries, the region is at least a century behind North
America and Europe. The prospects are not bright,
especially considering the fact that the region's population will at least double by the year 2000, and most of
these people will be living in cities. The forecast by
this writer is for severe animal protein shortages in
Manaus and smaller Amazonian cities, principally along the
Rio Solimões, if the fisheries are not properly managed
and fishes are as central to the diet as they are now.
In view of this I would like to consider, before discussing the management of the fisheries, some of the
alternative animal protein sources that may be substituted, to some degree, for locally caught fish.

Alternative Animal Protein Sources

Of late, aquaculture (including fishes, crustaceans,
and other aquatic animals) has been the opiate of
aspiring animal-protein producers in the humid tropics.
As early as the late 1940s, Sioli (1947), during his
pioneering limnological studies of the Amazon Basin, began
to suggest that the region held much in store for the
future development of fish culture and, in fact, that

aquaculture would eventually be necessary to establish a new equilibrium between fish production and consumption as human populations increased. Among Latin American countries, Brazil has been by far the most active in experimental aquaculture (Bardach, Ryther, and McLarney 1972), but these efforts, concentrated mostly in the Northeast and more recently in the Amazon near Manaus, have yet to provide convincing evidence that the enterprise will be able to supply significant amounts of animal protein to needy regions with large populations. It would be premature and naive to assume that fish culture is just around the corner, technologically speaking, to replace the natural fisheries if they are mismanaged and destroyed. Even if fish culture does prove successful, production on any scale would be, at the minimum, several decades from now. The suggested farming of other aquatic animals, such as turtles (Smith 1974) and manatees (Meggers 1971), is fraught with many biological uncertainties (e.g., failure of the animals to reproduce readily in captivity, slow growth rates, etc.) that appear to have no solutions in the near future. In short, other animal-protein sources must be turned to.

The two major candidates are beef and chicken. The city of Porto Velho, on the Rio Madeira, for example, has already become largely dependent on imported beef (mainly from eastern Bolivia), with the local fisheries supplying only about 15 percent of the total animal protein consumed annually (Goulding 1981). The situation is thought to be similar in Rio Branco, Acre, whose access to productive fishing areas is even less favorable than that of Porto Velho. No studies are yet available, but it is clear from observation in the local markets that Manaus is greatly increasing its imports of beef and chicken in response to fish shortages. The price of imported chicken, in fact, is beginning to compete favorably with that of locally caught fish, especially the first class species that are becoming more expensive. This is not to suggest, however, that imported beef and chicken are substituting, on a per-capita animal-protein consumption basis, for the locally caught fish that was plentiful just a few years ago. In the 1973-1974 period, a detailed study of diet in Manaus revealed that the per capita consumption of fish among the lower classes was as high as 150 g per day (Giugliano et al. 1978). With recent shortages and the price increase of local fish in the Manaus market, it is highly unlikely that per capita consumption of this protein item will remain at the mid-1970s level. With higher priced fish, beef, and chicken, overall animal-protein consumption levels have probably declined, but probably not yet reached a deficiency level.

Management of the Fisheries

The scientific management of fisheries implies, first,

that the taxonomy, ecology, and distribution of fish populations are known, at least in general terms; second, that reliable catch data are being recorded annually; third, that there is a realistic expectation of what role fish are supposed to play in the economy and diet of the region; and fourth, that there is a bureaucratic infrastructure capable of enforcing desired legislation. The management of Amazonian fisheries faces serious problems in fulfilling these requirements, and there is little hope for improvement in the near future.

The direct management of fisheries usually involves closed seasons, closed areas, gear restrictions, species prohibitions, and quotas or other measures to reduce catches and fishing effort. All of these cannot be discussed here, but I would like to consider three strategies that have been attempted by Amazonian authorities and point out the problems involved with each.

The idea of the closed spawning season was borrowed from North American and European concepts of how to protect temperate latitude fisheries in fresh waters. Anadromous fishes, such as salmon and steelhead, migrate but once each year, and this is at the time of spawning when they move up the rivers. It is also the time of year when they are most vulnerable to over-exploitation, and thus it makes sense to prohibit fishing for them during the reproductive period. As discussed earlier, the migratory characins, in great contrast to the northern hemisphere salmonids mentioned above, migrate twice each year in the central part of the Amazon. Only one of these migrations is for spawning, while the other, during lower-water periods, appears to be for dispersal. The migratory characins, then, are vulnerable to heavy exploitation twice each year. Influenced by temperate latitude fisheries concepts, Amazonian authorities have assumed that the greatest damage is done to migratory fish populations during the spawning period, but this is probably not true. During the low-water migrations, in fact, the schools appear to be much larger and are more easily captured because the rivers are down and restricted to their channels. The point here is that even with closed spawning seasons, the migratory characins could still be easily over-exploited by fisheries restricted to non-reproductive periods. It probably makes little difference whether potential reproducers in fish populations are captured a few days or hours before spawning or months before or after. The net result is the same: the removal of potential reproducers from the populations. Moreover, the Amazon system has a built-in closed season-- the period of the floods when the fishes spread out in a greatly expanded environment. For all practical purposes, Nature closes the central Amazonian fisheries for about four to five months each year, and to add even more months to this by legislative decree would raise serious questions of how the fisheries could operate economically.

Amazon food fishes are netted, seined, gigged, gaffed, hooked, bombed, and poisoned, and each of these methods can touch the individual psyches of authorities in different ways. In general, however, seines and gill nets are usually reputed to be the most "humane" methods, but in fact they are far more destructive of fish communities than all the other types of gear used in Amazonian fisheries put together. A gaffed fish can be a bloody sight--hence the method is sometimes considered predatory and inhumane--while characins flopping about in a seine look like they are harmlessly performing piscine acrobatics. The point here is that often too much time is spent worrying about the gore of fishing, instead of concentrating on the methods as a whole and their potential effects on fish communities. In the 1970s little attention was paid to gill nets, even though their use was spreading rapidly, and now it is probably too late to control this type of fishing in any significant way. The deep-bodied fishes of the genus Colossoma will probably be commercially extinct within a few years, and this will be due mostly to the intensive and widespread use of gill nets. In all fairness, however, it must be said that there is no ideal mesh size for multi-species fisheries because of the wide range of sizes and shapes of fishes that make up the commercial taxa. When mesh sizes are increased (which Amazonian authorities usually favor), that theoretically means that fishing effort will be deflected away from young fish and concentrated on adults. If the adults of all the species were about the same size and of the same general morphology, the use of only large mesh sizes would indeed have this effect. As it is, the large-meshed gill nets are responsible for destroying the young of tambaqui (Colossoma macropomum) and pirarucú (Arapaima gigas), the two most endangered species.

In the Amazon the unenforced prohibition of the exploitation of potentially endangered species can actually do more harm than good. When favorite food animals, such as the large river turtle (Podocnemis expansa) and the pirarucú, are designated as protected species and prohibited from sale in the main markets, their prestige and price soars in a brisk illegal trade carried on by poachers and clandestine middlemen. Unless strong enforcement programs can be developed in the near future, it is highly unlikely that species prohibitions will be of much use in the management of Amazonian fisheries.

Fishing efforts in the Amazon are already great enough that many fish species are threatened with commercial extinction within the next decade, and authorities do not have enough time, money, and trained personnel to do much about this. Whether commercial and subsistence fishermen would be able to exploit a given species to the point of biological extinction is difficult to ascertain

at the present time. Of more importance to commercial
and biological extinction, at least in the long run, is
environmental quality. Amazonian floodplains are now being eyed as potential rice paddies and cattle pastures
for increasing food production (e.g., Giugliano et al.
1978). Floodplain agriculture means deforestation and
pollution, and these two aspects need to be weighed
against their effects on the fisheries.

Deforestation of whitewater river floodplains
usually leads to an invasion of aquatic herbaceous plants,
or "the floating meadows", and thus it is difficult to say
whether total primary production is reduced when the tree
and shrub communities are removed from these areas. In
areas that have been heavily modified along the Rio
Solimões, the fruit- and seed-eating fishes have become
rarer, but this is also in part a reflection of fishing
effort. Assuming that deforestation of whitewaver river
floodplains would not damage the commercial fisheries,
but only change their species composition, floodplain
agriculture still presents serious problems because of
the implied use of insecticides and herbicides. During
the low-water period, the lakes and lagoons of the floodplains shrink to only a fraction of their high-water
sizes, and the fishes become densely packed into them.
The young of the migratory characins and cichlids, two
of the three most important commercial fish groups in the
Amazon, depend on these bodies of water for their
survival during the low-water period (the young of
commercial catfishes have not yet been located in either
the rivers or their floodplains). Because of their reduced sizes, floodplain bodies of water would be highly
vulnerable to pollution during the low-water period when
runoff from the surrounding agricultural fields (treated
with insecticides and herbicides) would drain into them.
If the young of the migratory characins were destroyed
because of this pollution, or because of eutrophication
or any other type of environmental damage, that would
also mean eliminating a large (or in some cases, the
largest) part of the future biomass of fishes in the
blackwater and clearwater tributaries, for it is from the
whitewater river floodplains that these fishes would have
to be recruited.

A large part of the commercial catch of fishes from
Amazonian waters is represented by taxa that, as adults,
are sustained on fruits, seeds, insects, and detritus
derived from flooded forests of the clearwater and blackwater rivers. In the nutrient-poor rivers there does not
appear to be an alternative food chain to the flooded
forests. If these flooded forests are destroyed, I believe that the fisheries will be seriously damaged, not
to mention a large number of other species that are of
less commercial importance.

The most important step that could be taken to
protect the fisheries, and the fish fauna in general, is

the establishment of protected areas. This strategy has
the advantage of preserving communities of plants and
animals together, and theoretically assures that sufficient
gene pools will be available in the future when it may be
necessary and desirable to repopulate areas that have been
biologically damaged because of mismanagement. The minimum sizes of protected areas must take into consideration
as many of the plants and animals as possible. Amazon
fish ecology and distribution suggest that these areas
must be relatively large. Of primary concern are the
migratory characins, the most important food fishes, whose
life histories embrace large areas. As discussed earlier,
the young of the migratory characins are nourished in the
relatively nutrient-rich waters of the whitewater river
floodplains, but as these fishes grow up to become pre-
adults and adults, many if not most of them migrate to
the clearwater and blackwater affluents where they are
largely sustained on foods originating in the flooded
forests. Even if we assume that there are three or four
largely distinct population centers of the migratory
characins in the central part of the Amazon Basin involving the Rio Solimões-Amazonas--and that it is desirable
to protect at least one of these from heavy fishing and
environmental destruction--then that would mean a reserved area embracing 300 to 400 km of the main trunk and
all of the tributaries that enter this stretch.

ACKNOWLEDGMENTS

Many of the ideas in this paper were developed in
discussions and debates with Peter Bayley. I also wish
to thank Tom Lovejoy, Stanley Weitzman, Marilyn Weitzman,
Richard Vari, Nigel Smith, and Emilio Moran for criticisms
of the manuscript. George Nakamura is thanked for typing
the manuscript. The research was supported by the
Instituto Nacional de Pesquisas da Amazônia (INPA) and
the World Wildlife Fund.

REFERENCES

Acuña, Fr. Cristóval de
    1891   Nuevo Descubrimiento del Gran Rio de las
            Amazonas por el Padre Cristoval de Acuña
            (1641). Madrid: J. C. Garcia.

Agassiz, Louis
    1879   A Journey in Brazil. Boston: Houghton, Osgood
            & Co.

Bardach, J. E., J. H. Ryther, and W. O. McLarney
    1972   Aquaculture. New York: Wiley-Interscience.

Bates, H. W.
1865   The Naturalist on the Rivers Amazon. London:
       John Murray.

Bayley, P. B.
1981   Fish Yield from the Amazon in Brazil: Compari-
       son with African River Yields and Management
       Possibilities. Trans. Amer. Fish. Soc. 110:
       351-359.

Bitencourt, A.
1951   Aspectos da Pesca na Amazônia. Bol. Soc. Bras.
       Geog. 1(5):135-144.

Cacex/Banco do Brasil
1980   Principais Produtos Exportados pelo Estado
       do Pará, ano - 1980. Belém: Cacex/Banco do
       Brasil.

Ferreira, A. R.
1972   Viagem Filosófica pelas Capitanias do Grão-Pará,
       Rio Negro, Mato Grosso e Cuiabá. Rio de
       Janeiro: Conselho Federal de Cultura.

Fritz, S.
1922   Journal of the Travels and Labours of Father
       Samuel Fritz in the River of the Amazons
       Between 1686 and 1723. London: The Hakluyt
       Society, No. 51.

Giugliano, R., R. Shrimpton, D. B. Arkcoll, L. G.
Giugliano, and M. Petrere
1978   Diagnóstico da Realidade Alimentar e
       Nutricional do Estado do Amazonas. Acta
       Amazônica 8(2):1-54.

Goulding, Michael
1979   Ecologia da Pesca do Rio Madeira. Manaus:
       Conselho Nacional de Desenvolvimento Científico
       e Tecnológico, Instituto Nacional de Pesquisas
       da Amazônia (INPA).

1980   The Fishes and the Forest. Berkeley: Univ. of
       California Press.

1981   Man and Fisheries on an Amazon Frontier. The
       Hague: Junk.

Junk, W. J.
1970   Investigations on the Ecology and Production-
       Biology of the "Floating Meadows" (Paspalo
       echinochloetum) on the Middle Amazon. Part I:
       The Floating Vegetation and Its Ecology.
       Amazoniana 2(4):449-495.

1973   Investigations. . . . Part II: The Aquatic Fauna
        in the Root Zone of Floating Vegetation.
        Amazoniana 4(1):9-102.

Medina, J. T.
1934   The Discovery of the Amazon According to the
        Account of the Friar Gaspar de Carvajal and
        Other Documents. New York: American Geographical
        Society, Special Publication No. 17.

Meggers, Betty J.
1971   Amazônia: Man and Culture in a Counterfeit
        Paradise. Chicago: Aldine.

Menezes, R. S.
1972   Potencial de Pesca e Piscultura na Amazônia.
        In A Amazônia Brasileira em Foco 7:34-61.

Moran, Emilio F.
1974   The adaptive System of the Amazonian Caboclo.
        In C. Wagley, ed., Man in the Amazon. Gaines-
        ville: Univ. of Florida Press.

Penner, M.E.S.
1980   A Pesca no Nordeste Amazônico. Raízes (Belém)
        1(1):47-56.

Petrere, M.
1978   Pesca e Esforço de Pesca no Estado do Amazonas.
        II. Locais, Aparelhos de Captura e Estatísticas
        de Desembarque. Acta Amazônica 8(3):1-54.

Pinto, M.M.V.
1956   Contribuicão ao Estudo da Pesca na Região do
        Rio Arari (Ilha de Marajó). Rev. Bras. Geog.
        18(3):89-123.

Sioli, H.
1947   Possibilidades de Criação de Peixes em Lagos
        Amazônicos. Folha do Norte (Belém, Pará,
        Brazil).

Smith, Nigel J. H.
1974   Destructive Exploitation of the South American
        River Turtle. Ass. Pac. Coast. Geog. 36(c):
        85-102.

1979   Pesca no Rio Amazonas. Manaus: Conselho
        Nacional de Desenvolvimento Científico e
        Tecnológico (INPA).

1981   Man, Fishes and the Amazon. New York:
        Columbia Univ. Press.

Spruce, R.
   1908   Notes of a Botanist on the Amazon and Andes.
           A. R. Wallace, ed. London: Macmillan.

SUDEPE
   1980   Relatórios Trimestrais de Atividades sobre a
           Piramutaba. Belém: Superintendência do
           Desenvolvimento da Pesca (SUDEPE).

Veríssimo, J.
   1895   A Pesca na Amazônia. Rio de Janeiro: Livraria
           Clássica de Alves.

Wallace, Alfred Russel
   1889   A Narrative of Travels on the Amazon and Rio
           Negro. London: Ward, Lock & Co.

8
Precipitating Change in Amazonia

Thomas E. Lovejoy
Eneas Salati

How much of the Amazonian forest has been cleared or destroyed? Not surprisingly, estimates vary considerably. In 1979, the Brazilian Ministry of Agriculture estimate of deforestation was about 1.55% (Carvalho 1981). The denominator for that calculation, however, was "legal Amazonia," essentially double the naturally forested area. Therefore, 3% is closer to representing the extent of forest clearing. That figure reflects only those areas clearly discernible by satellite imagery as deforested and does not include partly degraded areas, areas in secondary succession, or areas that have been selectively logged (cf. Fearnside 1982). The actual figure is probably closer to 10%. Whether it is as high as the 25% estimated by New York Botanical Garden's Amazon forest expert, Ghillean T. Prance, is hard to determine, but there can be little dispute that the areal extent is increasing.

Indeed, if one looks at the official figures in another fashion, deforestation over the three-year period 1976-1978 for legal Amazonia was 129% of that which had occurred up to 1975 (Carvalho 1981). Further, even if one uses the official figure of 1.55% destruction over that three-year period for legal Amazonia, the continuation of that rate of loss would mean complete forest destruction in 200 years.

EXTINCTION

One of the logical concerns about deforestation in Amazonia is the possibility of extinction of species. The 10% of all species on Earth that occur in Amazonia are not uniformly distributed across the entire basin. Many are limited in distribution and often clustered within particular vegetation types, as in white sand campina vegetation, or in particular geographical areas. As a result, forest destruction has the potential to completely extinguish some or many Amazon forest species. This is not a certainty, in that every square meter of Amazonia is not occupied by a particular species that occurs nowhere else, but it does mean that care must be taken to avoid diminishment of Amazonia's important share of the world's biological heritage.

Have there been any extinctions from the deforestation that has occurred so far? No one knows, but the more such destruction is concentrated in one area of the basin, the more likely some extinctions will occur for species restricted in some fashion to that region. In part this is why there is reason for concern about the concentration of deforestation in the southeastern quadrant of Amazonia as a result of ranching and other enterprises.

This kind of problem is accentuated by the presence of smaller geographical areas where there are foci of species ("endemics") with limited distributions. These areas with clusters of endemic species are thought to represent parts of the basin where tropical rain forest was able to persist during the cold dry periods of the Pleistocene when conditions were not favorable for forest throughout the basin. They are, consequently, known as Pleistocene Refugia (Haffer 1969; Prance 1982).

In any event, the more deforestation is prevented in refugia, the less likely it will be to cause extinctions. This is why the main plan for conservation areas agreed upon by the Amazon nations (Wetterberg et al. 1976) is based on refugia. Unfortunately, the biological data base for defining refugia is far from adequate, so ultimately this plan will need review. In addition, one refugium not yet represented by a conservation area is the Belém refugium (south of the capital of Pará, Brazil). This refugium is a matter for major concern because it is located in the southeastern quadrant where so much forest destruction has already taken place. Conversely, it is not likely that the Jari project, despite its vast areal extent, has generated any large numbers of extinctions, since most of that region remains largely intact.

The relationship between the percentage of Amazonia deforested and the percentage of Amazonian biota threatened with extinction depends, therefore, on the extent to which deforestation is aimed toward or away from refugia (Lovejoy 1980b). So far no known refugium has been obliterated. So while it is possible and perhaps even likely that some extinctions have already occurred, the number is probably not very large.

To the extent that protected areas based on refugia as currently defined can protect the Amazonian biota, major progress has been made in recent years. This is particularly so in the Brazilian Amazon where 8 million hectares have been set aside since 1979 in various conservation units, most of which coincide with refugia areas (Wetterberg et al. 1981). More are planned for 1982. To protect the biota properly a conservation system should not only include refugia, but also vegetation types not necessarily covered thereby, as well as freshwater systems (which are largely the responsibility of other agencies).

FORESTS AND FISHES

The fresh waters of Amazonia constitute a massive system of perhaps one-fifth of all the world's river waters; they support fisheries of considerable local importance (Smith 1981). The relative importance of fish for animal protein in the local diet may decline with overfishing and with further human population growth, if Goulding's assessments (Chapter 7 in this volume) hold, but fish will always be an important resource and one deserving proper management. At the moment, the fresh waters of Amazonia do not have a conservation plan, and both research and policy development are required.

Already, development initiatives are likely to affect the fresh waters and the biota. Floodplains are eyed as ideal lands for agriculture because of the annual soil enrichment brought by alluvium deposition. Recent research (Goulding 1979, 1980, 1981) has illuminated a remarkable relationship between the floodplain forests and the food chains supporting the fisheries. Floodplain development will have to be designed very carefully to increase the capacity for direct harvest from these lands without jeopardizing the productivity of the Amazon fisheries. So very little is known of the ecology of the Amazon rivers that the consequences of the major hydroelectric projects such as Tucuruí are virtually unassessable. For example, although fish migrations are known to occur in the Amazon, little is known of the actual patterns and to what extent these barriers will interfere.

Nor is it known how big terrestrial reserves should be. The topic of size and design of reserves has been receiving increasing attention and is not only an Amazon problem but global in scope (Lovejoy 1980a, 1982; Lovejoy and Oren 1981; Simberloff 1982; Terborgh 1974, 1975). It is apparent that the dynamics of natural areas once they are isolated are very different from those of the same areas as former parts of continuous wilderness, but the details are barely known. The understanding of the ecosystem decay (species shedding) that occurs in isolated patches of natural habitat is rudimentary at best. A joint World Wildlife Fund (WWF) and Instituto Nacional de Pesquisas da Amazônia (INPA) project to study this problem is currently underway at Manaus. Most of the results will not be available for many years, so current plans must be sufficiently flexible to allow modification once more knowledge is available. This need for flexibility and a cautious approach to development derives not only from the question of the size of a reserve but from a multitude of topics relevant to Amazon development. The Amazon Basin is one of the least known biological complexes on the planet, and certainly the least known on land. The potential for error is large unless caution is observed.

HYDROLOGIC CYCLE

There probably is no more dramatic example of how much is to be learned about the Amazon than the picture that has been emerging in recent years about the relationship between forests and rainfall. A possible relationship between forests and rainfall has been suggested for centuries in various parts of the world: that the forest attracts rain, that it creates rain, that deforestation reduces rain. Yet the evidence has been largely circumstantial or anecdotal.

Interestingly, it may be that only in Amazonia, with the world's largest forest and fairly predictable weather patterns, that the possible relationship could be properly studied. Air flow is, as best as can be determined from current knowledge, generally unidirectional, from the Atlantic to the Andes. While there may be lines of instability ("squall lines") associated with winds from the Atlantic (Molion and Kousky 1981), and occasional intrusions such as a cold front from the south penetrating as far north as Manaus (an event that does not even happen every year), generally speaking there are no major fronts mixing air masses. As a result, it has been possible to study the movement of air and moisture across the Amazon Basin. Salati (1978), Salati et al. (1978), and Villa Nova et al. (1976) sampled air moistures along an east-west transect across the basin, measuring the changing composition in terms of oxygen isotopes. Water with the heavier (oceanic origin) isotope drops out across the basin, as a consequence of which Salati and his co-workers were able to demonstrate that the remaining rainfall--about half--that falls on the basin is not of oceanic origin.

It is the thesis of a recent workshop at CENA (Centro de Energia Nuclear para Agricultura) at the University of São Paulo, with its proceedings to be published as an issue of Acta Amazônica, that much of this rainfall is produced by the forest itself. Simple measurements of runoff and infiltration rates (Schubart 1977) indicate that runoff is greatly increased without the heavy mass of vegetation to break the fall of rain and that, in addition, infiltration rates are considerably lower in pasture soils compacted by the hooves of cattle. The combined effects of the two mean that most of the water from precipitation does not remain in situ under non-forest conditions, and hence simply is not available for return to the atmosphere.

The effects of deforestation are likely to vary with

the scale of the cleared area. Within a small area, on the order of a few hectares, there is likely to be no measurable effect on air moisture or rainfall due to swamping by moist air from surrounding forest. The recycling of water in the basin will nonetheless have been reduced by an increment, so the effect of small clearings can in the aggregate be a matter of real concern.

Deforestation of larger areas (greater than 1 km and less than 100 km in diameter) is known to present different problems for secondary succession (Gómez-Pompa et al. 1972) and also is likely to result in a detectable reduction in water returned to the atmosphere. One possible consequence would be reduced rainfall immediately downwind. If the drier air were precisely focused, and not rapidly mixed with other air, the forest downwind would be subject to desiccation and eventual degradation; the process would slowly eat away at the forest downwind from major cleared areas.

If, as is more likely, the effects of reduced water vapor are more diffuse, small numbers of such clearings would produce local deviations but not affect the overall hydrology. Yet there is a limit (as yet unknown) to the number of such clearings before cumulative reduction in moisture would affect the climate of the basin.

The climatic effects would not be limited only to rainfall in the Amazon Basin and in the central Plateau of Brazil, which also derives some of its rainfall from the Amazon. There would also be possible global implications deriving from reduced cloud formation. Smaller amounts of water vapor must be lifted higher before a cloud will form, and cloud formation provides a major form of heat transfer, thereby playing a significant role in global heat balance.

The general outline of the relationship is clear, as is the grave significance for human welfare. The possibility of a drying trend in Amazonian climate is a threat to any biologically based undertaking in the basin, whether it be a system of conservation units or a more production-oriented enterprise, such as Jari.

It is clearly of great importance to take the understanding of the relationship from its largely qualitative present state (of knowing that there is recycled Amazonian moisture on the order of 50% in Amazonian rainfall) to a more detailed and quantitative one. Then it should be possible to make some reasonably confident statements about which land uses in which combinations of frequency will maintain the integrity of this relationship. Among the needed lines of research are the following.

1. More detailed study of precipitation patterns within the basin, including isotopic analysis; the Piracicaba workshop recommended 20 stations doing weekly monitoring.
2. Studies, using isotopes where appropriate,

of surface runoff and hydrology (including chemistry and sediment load of runoff, and micrometeorology) under the full variety of possible land uses. These studies should measure the contribution to atmospheric moisture from evaporation and evapotranspiration under various land-use conditions. The work of INPA on a model watershed near Manaus is a pioneering effort of this sort. Similar studies should be made for the full array of Amazonian landscapes and climates.

3. Paleoclimatic studies to give some indication of the sensitivity of tropical forest to climatic change.

4. Remote sensing to help establish general weather patterns in fuller detail.

All the lines of research should ultimately contribute to a model of the Amazon hydrological system so that the consequences of a variety of land-use conditions can be explored to reveal the limits to change, if disruption of the system is to be avoided.

It is important to note that the forest/rainfall relationship described for Amazonia is likely to be--to at least some degree--specific to Amazonia. In the most general terms, the relative contributions of oceanic moisture and recycled Amazonian moisture are likely to vary considerably from region to region and depend to some degree on local weather patterns.

It is interesting, and probably meaningful, that the forms of land use likely to help maintain the integrity of the hydrological cycle are the very ones which have been suggested as preferable from other points of view (Goodland 1980). The Amazon forest depends on the Amazon climate, but the forest is responsible in part for maintaining (and perhaps even developing) the climate. Vegetation also is adapted to the forest and the climate-- not only each plant species individually, but also the sum of the species in their interactions. The problems with agriculture are great, stemming from the usually nutrient-poor soils, from the disruption of the impressively efficient nutrient recycling capacity of the rain forest, the erosion and leaching problems of exposed soils, and the difficulties and expense of using fertilizer under conditions of sharp bursts of heavy rainfall. All these problems are reduced the more the type of land use approaches the natural vegetation, so that pasture is the least desirable form of land use from this point of view, and forest, or at least tree cover, is the most preferable.

RESEARCH AND POLICY CHANGES

It is encouraging that in Brazil the Figueiredo administration has exhibited every intent of establishing

an economic and ecological zoning for Amazonia. Political
considerations aside, it is virtually certain that any
such zoning will be imperfect, simply on the basis of our
inadequate knowledge. Yet zoning would set an enormously
important precedent, and it can only be hoped that the
zoning will be structured in such a fashion as to permit
change as scientific understanding of the basin's ecology
grows--as opposed to permitting economic or political
pressures for increased development to mount.   On March
30, 1982, at a ceremony to bestow the J. Paul Getty Wildlife Conservation Prize on two Brazilians (Dra. Maria
Teresa Jorge Padua, Director of National Parks and Dr.
Paulo Nogueira Neto, Special Secretary of the Environment),
President Figueiredo announced that zoning would begin in
1982.

CONCLUSIONS

    The forest/rainfall and the floodplain forest/
fishery relationships in the Amazon Basin have only become apparent very recently. Other important discoveries
about these forests will continue to be made. It has now
been realized for several years from the work of Daniel
Janzen et al. that the struggle between insect and plant
life in New World tropical forests is an important
generator of biologically active secondary compounds in
leaves with important value in medicine (e.g., curare).
Only last year was this recognized as important from
another practical point of view. The discovery involved
the leaf-cutting ant (Atta), of interest to scientists
because of its habit of defoliating trees and using the
leaves as mulch for the underground fungus farms the
ants tend for food. From the view of a somewhat practical
person, and most certainly any gardener or farmer, these
ants could only be considered pests because of their
ability to defoliate a tree overnight.
    Scientists had been puzzled because in forest
environments the ants defoliated some kinds of trees and
not others. Stephen Hubbell of the University of Iowa,
thinking of the classic neotropical insect-plant tussle,
theorized that the plants eschewed were ones with
secondary compounds noxious or toxic to the leaf-cutting
ants. When he teamed up with a biochemist the answer came
out differently: the ants were avoiding tree species with
natural fungicides in their leaves--which makes a lot of
sense if the leaves are to be used as mulch for a fungus
farm.
    This discovery means that Atta provide a handy key to
identifying those species of tropical forest plants with
natural fungicides, of which there must be plenty to
counter the effects of the multitude of fungi in the forests. Such compounds are useful not only in medicine
(which spends a fair amount of time battling certain kinds
of fungi although the majority of fungi are probably of

benefit to us), but also in agriculture. It is possible
that one or more of the fungicides may prove as important
to people as the Amazon's great contribution of the rubber
tree.

Yet all of this emerging knowledge depends on pro-
tecting the ecology of the basin and the great forest,
known as the hylea, by encouraging only the most considered kinds of development. Indeed, as Professor
Emilio F. Moran points out (personal communication), the
fact that this great forest makes some of its own rain is
reason in itself to protect it. The understanding that
can be gained from studying the hydrologic cycle in
Amazonia may be critical in deciding how to protect rain
forests and precipitation elsewhere, and perhaps even in
restoring precipitation to degraded areas of the world.

REFERENCES

Carvalho, J. C. de M.
    1981   The Conservation of Nature and Natural Resources
            in the Brazilian Amazonia. Revista Companhia
            Vale do Rio Doce (CVRD) 2:1-48.

Fearnside, Philip M.
    1982   Deforestation in the Brazilian Amazon: How
            Fast Is It Occurring? Interciencia 7(2):82-88.

Gómez-Pompa, A., C. Vázquez-Yañes, and S. Guevara
    1972   The Tropical Rain Forest: A Nonrenewable
            Resource? Science 177:762-765.

Goodland, Robert J.A.
    1980   Environmental Ranking of Amazonian Development.
            In F. Barbira-Scazzocchio, ed., Land, People,
            and Planning in Contemporary Amazônia.
            Cambridge, UK: Cambridge University Centre of
            Latin American Studies, Occasional Publ. 3.

Goulding, Michael
    1979   Ecologia da Pesca do Rio Madeira. Manaus:
            Instituto Nacional de Pesquisas da Amazônia
            (INPA).

    1980   The Fishes and the Forest. Berkeley: Univ.
            of California Press.

    1981   Man and Fisheries on an Amazon Frontier. The
            Hague: Junk.

Haffer, J.
    1969   Speciation in Amazonian Forest Birds. Science
            165:131-137.

Lovejoy, Thomas E.
   1980a   Discontinuous Wilderness: Minimum Areas for
           Conservation. Parks 6(2):5-10.

   1980b   A Projection of Species Extinctions. In The
           Global 2000 Report to the President's Council
           on Environmental Quality, Washington, D.C.,
           pp. 328-329.

   1982   Designing Refugia for Tomorrow. In G. T.
           Prance, ed., Biological Diversification in the
           Tropics. New York: Columbia Univ. Press.

Lovejoy, Thomas E. and D. C. Oren
   1981   Minimum Critical Size of Ecosystems. In R. L.
           Burgess and D. M. Sharpe, eds., Forest Island
           Dynamics in Man-Dominated Landscapes. New
           York: Springer-Verlag.

Molion, L.C.B. and V. E. Kousky
   1981   Uma Contribuição à Climatologia da Dinámica da
           Troposfera sobre a Amazônia. Paper presented
           to International Workshop on Precipitation and
           Water Recycling in Tropical Forests. Centro
           de Energia Nuclear para Agricultura (CENA),
           Nov. 11-13. Proceedings to be published as
           special issue of Acta Amazônica.

Prance, Ghillean T., ed.
   1982   Biological Diversification in the Tropics.
           New York: Columbia Univ. Press.

Salati, E., A. Dall'Olio, E. Matsui, and J. R. Gat
   1979   Recycling of Water in the Amazon Basin: An Iso-
           topic Study. Water Resources Research 15(5):
           1250-1258.

Salati, E. et al.
   1978   Origem e Distribuição das Chuvas na Amazônia.
           Interciencia 3(4):200-205.

Schubart, H.O.R.
   1977   Ecological Criteria for the Agricultural Develop-
           ment of the Dry Lands in Amazonia: Forest
           Ecology, Natural Resources Including Wood
           Alcohol, Reclamation. Acta Amazônica 7(4):
           559-567.

Simberloff, D.
   1982   Big Advantages of Small Refuges. Natural
           History 91(4):6-14.

Smith, Nigel J.H.
1979   A Pesca no Rio Amazonas. Manaus: Instituto
        Nacional de Pesquisas do Amazônia (INPA).

1981   Man, Fishes and the Amazon. New York: Columbia
        Univ. Press.

Terborgh, J.
1974   Preservation of Natural Diversity: The Problem
        of Extinction-Prone Species. Bioscience 24:
        715-722.

1975   Faunal Equilibria and the Design of Wildlife
        Preserves. In F. B. Golley and E. Medina, eds.,
        Tropical Ecological Systems: Trends in
        Terrestrial and Aquatic Research. New York:
        Springer-Verlag.

Villa Nova, N. A., E. Salati, and E. Matsui
1976   Estimativa da Evapotranspiração na Bacia
        Amazônica. Acta Amazônica 6:215-228.

Wetterberg, G. B., M.T.J. Padua, C. S. de Castro,
and J.M.C. de Vasconcellos
1976   Uma Análise de Prioridades em Conservacão da
        Natureza na Amazônia. Brasília: Programa do
        Desenvolvimento da Pesquisa Florestal
        (PRODEPEF Série Técnica No. 8).

Wetterberg, G. B., Ghillean T. Prance, and Thomas
E. Lovejoy
1981   Conservation Progress in Amazonia: A Structural
        Review. Parks 6(2):5-10.

Part 3

Methodological Issues and Future Research Directions

Introduction to Part 3

The papers in the third section of this volume are contributions toward refining existing methods and priorities in research on Amazonian development issues. The papers explore the role of indigenous practices, how to study the interrelations between peasant and capitalist production, how modeling can assist development planners predict impacts, how government-directed projects were implemented in the 1970s, and how international financial institutions are becoming increasingly sensitive to the equity dimensions of economic development.

The paper by Posey demonstrates the exquisitely detailed knowledge of resources possessed by the Kayapó Indians and how such expertise can be used to improve the economic uses of resources. He extends the anthropological analysis to the area of policy by suggesting how to formulate a research strategy based upon indigenous knowledge. Indeed, this is not only good economic sense but also reduces environmental costs resulting from the application of inappropriate technologies in given habitats.

Wood, in a very different light, suggests that we need a theory of frontier expansion. Such a theory must be guided by a systems viewpoint that permits the simultaneous study of pre-capitalist and capitalist production, in that they are inextricably intertwined and the development of one need not necessarily lead to the transformation of the other. This position is a departure from common neo-Marxist positions that assume that capitalist expansion always leads to the proletarization of the peasantry. Wood makes a provocative suggestion when he says that at given historical periods in this confrontation the capitalist sector may actually benefit from the expansion of the peasant economy--although such benefit may only be temporary.

Fearnside has become well known in Amazonian research circles for his advocacy of stochastic modeling of carrying capacity. In this paper he attempts to show how such modeling can serve not only as a research tool, but also as a planning and evaluation tool. Given the technocratic bias of Amazonian development agencies, this approach to improving the quality of planning and evaluation of alternative strategies could very well have significant impacts upon the choices made by these institutions. In fact, there is no reason why the alternatives modeled could not include native systems of production (see Chapter 9 by Posey), in addition to the results of experimental research such as that discussed by Nicholaides et al. (Chapter 5 in this volume).

The paper by Moran evaluates the performance of government-directed colonization along the Transamazon Highway. Observers foresaw this project as the acid test of the potential of the Amazonian lowlands for intensive agriculture, and the Brazilian government invested considerable attention, funds, and personnel in this integrated scheme. Moran provides an assessment of the environmental, social, and managerial interactions in what was, then, the largest state intervention seeking to bring about Amazonian development. Moran notes that it was less the environmental constraints than institutional incapacity and lack of flexibility that constrained the flow of inputs into productive activities. In addition, he notes that the policy shift in 1974 toward large-scale development schemes was a response less to the failure of the farmers than to more familiar strategies of development practiced before and since.

The final paper presents a very different view from most of the ones that precede it. Mahar, a senior economist at the World Bank and, earlier, an economist in the Brazilian Institute of Planning (IPEA), brings "the view from above," and he shows uncommon awareness of the relevance of external forces upon the internal processes of Amazonian development. Although he speaks as an individual, rather than for the World Bank, he shares an economist's appreciation for economic growth and for the values espoused by decision makers in high places. This is a valuable counterpoint to the view from the farm or the fishing boat that characterizes many of the other papers in this volume. His perspective is also more positive: Planning is now more realistic than it once was, the pace of development has slowed down from the hectic pace of the 1970s, and such a slowdown provides the needed time to carry out the resource surveys, development of land capability maps, and delineation of forest reserves needed to protect the environment and the rights of native Amazonians. Mahar, however, notes the persistence of lack of detail on how goals are to be achieved in the latest National Development Plan, and the tenuousness of administrative capacity in the 1980s to deal with the chaotic land tenure system. He notes that international donors are now beginning to require certain protections to be extended to native peoples, and to

require detailed resource surveys, before they are ready
to finance Amazonian development projects. The involvement of people throughout the world in pressuring governments and international financial institutions into agree-
ing to these changes is a positive sign. The authors
of these papers hope that their work contributes to the
solution of the dilemma posed by Amazonian development.

E.F.M.

9
Indigenous Ecological Knowledge and Development of the Amazon

Darrell A. Posey

INTRODUCTION

It seems every book and article about Amazonia begins by extolling the grandeur and enormity of the region
while lamenting the fanatical destruction of one of
Earth's last terrestrial frontiers. Some authors seem to
want to freeze Amazonia in its pristine, natural state,
while others are more realistic and seek solutions to
development without total destruction--planning with
conservation. This chapter seeks answers to this
"dilemma" of Amazonia by proposing that systematic study
and understanding of the ecological knowledge systems of
the Amazon Basin's most ancient inhabitants, the
Amerindians, can help us resolve the dilemma.

In this paper I suggest that indigenous cultures
are a valuable human resource that offers a rich and un-
tapped source of information about the natural resources
of the Amazon Basin. If the knowledge of indigenous
peoples can be integrated with modern technological know-
how, then a new path for ecologically sound development
of the Amazon will have been found. Also, if technological civilization begins to realize the practical value
of indigenous societies, then Indians can be viewed as
intelligent, valuable people, rather than just exotic
footnotes to history.

The Amazon forest is one of the most species-diverse
regions in the world (Goodland and Irwin 1977; Sioli
1980:264-265). Yet extinction due to deforestation is
occurring at an alarming rate. Gottleib (1981:23)
estimates that 90% of the natural inventory of organisms
will vanish into extinction before even basic taxonomic
descriptions can be made.

Extinction is only one of the devastating ecological
effects of deforestation. Erosion starts the vicious
cycles of soil compaction, destruction of the nutrient
cycle, and flooding (Moran 1980:4; Sioli 1973:323).
Water pollution soon results with associated changes in
water turbidity and pH that reduce or destroy aquatic

life (Schubart 1977; Lovejoy and Schubart 1980:21).
Widespread deforestation may also significantly alter
rainfall patterns (Sioli 1980:233-262) and threaten the
delicate carbon dioxide balance of the atmosphere
(Pimentel 1979; Sioli 1980:262). Tropical forest ecosystems have been shown to be very fragile and prone to
collapse if disturbed (Farnsworth and Golley 1974). This
collapse is often irreversible (Goodland 1980) and may
contribute to the growing global threat posed by
desertification (Eckholm and Brown 1977; Sioli 1980:264).

The greatest Amazonian "dilemma," however, is a
human one. Peasants with few exceptions (cf. Parker
1982; Smith 1981; Ross 1978b; Moran 1974 for exceptions)
are ignored in Amazonian studies as though they were
cultureless creatures of an economic illusion. Yet they
have borne the brunt of development, being pushed from
their lands as "squatters" and forced into dependency in
favelas or towns (Barbira-Scazzocchio 1980:ix; Wood and
Schmink 1979). American Indians, too, reflect most
vividly the tragic human cost of Amazonian development.
The Indian population in Brazil has dropped from millions
at the time of contact to less than 150,000 today (i.e.,
0.1% of the population in 1492) (Ramos 1980:222;
Denevan 1976); in this century alone at least 87 Indian
groups have become extinct solely in Brazil (Ribeiro
1970:238). One has only to read Davis' (1977) poignant
account in Victims of the Miracle to grasp the impact of
development on native peoples.

With the extinction of each indigenous group, the
world loses millennia of accumulated knowledge about life
in, and adaptation to, tropical ecosystems. This price-
less information is forfeited with hardly a blink of the
eye: The march of development cannot wait long enough
even to find out what it is destroying.

What has this destruction accomplished? To date the
two main solutions to developing the Amazon have been
forestry and cattle ranching. Forest schemes, like the
immense Projeto Jari, have not proven financially
profitable to date (see Chapter 13 in this volume) and,
as was discovered in the famed Fordlandia project of
1926, monocultures of whatever type are highly susceptible
to devastating epizootic pest outbreaks (Sioli 1973:331).
Cattle ranching has been even less successful. Thousands
of hectares of forest have been leveled to make way for
cattle pasture. Yet 80% of recently established cattle
ranches in the Brazilian State of Pará are now unproductive
(Hecht 1982). As Goodland notes (1980:40): "Without
government funding, 70 percent of livestock projects'
costs, almost half the [Brazilian] government's total
Amazonian funding in the last decade, livestock would
have been insignificant."

This obvious lack of economic success, combined with
blatant, irreversible ecological damage and high human
costs, clearly points to the necessity for alternative

models of development in Amazonia. Yet planners and developers are more than reluctant to abandon their "temperate zone mentalities." The only "new" models seem to emerge from old cultural paradigms. But the record of failure speaks clearly: There is little choice but to look for new strategies for development that do not require ecological destruction.

The obvious source of new ideas and information lies in the knowledge systems of indigenous peoples. For many millennia Indians have survived in Amazonia. Their understanding of ecological zones, plant-human-animal relationships, and natural resource management has evolved through countless generations of trial and experimentation. Incredibly little is known about indigenous perceptions of ecology and utilization of natural resources, but Western science should now be sophisticated enough to approach this problem with much-needed success.

LESSONS FROM THE KAYAPÓ

This essay on folk ecological knowledge is based primarily upon data collected during field work with the Northern Kayapó Indians between 1977 and 1978. The Northern Kayapó occupy a 2-million hectare Indian reserve in the Brazilian state of Pará. There are nine villages scattered over the reserve with a current population of 2,500 Indians (see Figure 9.1).

Ethnocentrism and Western belief that indigenous populations were sparse have combined to belittle indigenous ecological knowledge. Recent estimates, however, suggest that aboriginal populations have been vastly underestimated (cf. Dobyns 1966; Denevan 1976). Archaeological and geographical data (Lathrap 1968, 1970; Myers 1974; Smith 1980) seem to confirm historical accounts (e.g., Acuña 1859; Carvajal 1934) of large population centers in the fertile várzea of Amazonia. There is also evidence of sizable villages in the higher savanna regions of the Amazon Basin (Posey 1979b).

European diseases swept with unimaginable speed through aboriginal populations with devastating effects. Dobyns (1966:414) proposes a 20-to-1 depopulation ratio from initial contact with Europeans. Records of death rates as high as 70 to 80% are common from a single viral epidemic (cf. Myers 1973, 1974, 1981a,b). Initial contact with the Kayapó was effected principally because the Indians were too weak from disease to resist Europeans (Banner, unpublished journals).[1] The first Kayapó band shrank from 350 to 85 during the first six months after initial contact with Europeans (Banner, unpublished journals). European diseases continue today to take a large toll despite preventive inoculation; it is not uncommon for an inoculated indigenous group to lose 30 to 40% of its members due to an epidemic (ARC 1981).

Figure 9.1. General geographic orientation of the Kayapó Indian villages of central Brazil

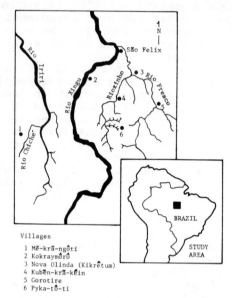

Villages

1 Mẽ-krã-ngôti
2 Kokraymôrô
3 Nova Olinda (Kikrêtum)
4 Kubẽn-krã-kẽin
5 Gorotire
6 Pyka-tô-ti

Kayapó Indian knowledge is an integrated system of belief and practice. There is much shared knowledge in a Kayapó village, although there are many specialists as well (Posey 1979a, 1982e). There are experts on soils, plants, animals, crops, medicines, and rituals. But each Kayapó believes that he or she has the ability to survive alone in the forest indefinitely. This belief offers great personal security and permeates the fabric of everyday life. It is difficult to represent a complete Kayapó ecological view, for this operates within such an intricate network of cultural assumptions. This chapter is meant to be practical and to deal with easily de-lineated categories of indigenous knowledge that suggest fields of research for Western science.

ETHNOECOLOGY

Ethnoecology can be defined as indigenous perceptions of "natural" divisions in the biological world and plant-animal-human relationships within each division. These cognitively defined ecological categories do not exist in isolation; thus ethnoecology must also deal with the perceptions of interrelatedness between "natural" divisions.

a. Recognition of "Ecological Zones"

A great obstacle to understanding Amazonia has been

the tendency to generalize about its ecology and to ignore its highly variable "ecological zones" (Moran 1981). Scientists still suffer from lack of data about the complexities of ecosystems in this enormous region. The Amazon is too often viewed as just one homogenous "counterfeit paradise" or "green hell" (Meggers 1971; Goodland and Irwin 1975).

The Kayapó Indians, however, see their environment in an expanded series of "ecological zones" and "subzones" (see Table 9.1). The three principal divisions are: kapôt (grasslands)[2], krãi (mountains), and bà (forest). There are, however, major subdivisions within each zone and further differentiations too complicated to deal with in this chapter (see Posey and Hecht, in preparation).

One illustrative set of sub-categories of forest types (bà-kamrek, bà-êpti, and bà-kati) are represented graphically in Figure 9.2. Bà-kamrek is subdivided based on vegetative response to flood levels of the Rio Fresco. Suitable farmland is selected from terra firme lands that do not flood (bà-kati), although some fields are carved from bà-êpti, which floods every seven to ten years. The richer alluvial soils of bà-êpti (including much black soil called pyka-tyk) provide sufficient yield increases to chance the periodic, but unpredictable, crop destruction due to flooding. The Kayapó chiefs' communal fields, as well as the women's collective fields (see Posey 1979b), are usually planted in bà-êpti to minimize total crop loss for any one family group.

The Kayapó folk taxonomic system reflects a high propensity for "transitional" ecological categories that grade between two or more semantic (named) divisions or ecological zones[3] (cf. Posey 1981b:168-175). Kayapó village sites are, in fact, purposefully selected to rest in these transitional zones and, therefore, close to a variety of ecological zones. The distinct advantage to such sites is that the Kayapó are in the midst of maximum species diversity, with each zone providing natural products and attracting different game species at different times of the year (Bamberger 1967). Location of the Kayapó village of Gorotire is represented in Figure 9.3 and is surrounded by a variety of ecological zones.

Each ecological zone has associated with it specific plants and animals. The Kayapó have a well-developed knowledge of animal behavior and know which plants are associated with particular animals. In turn, plant types are associated with soil types. Each ecological zone, therefore, is an integrated system of interactions between plants, animals, the earth--and, of course, the Kayapó. Table 9.2 summarizes selected systemic relationships in bà-ràràra, which is forest with intermittent openings and penetration of sunlight. These same relationships hold for abandoned fields (pyru-tym), which

Table 9.1. Major ecological zones recognized by the Kayapó Indians*

---

1. Kapôt (grassland, savanna)

   a. Kapôt-kên - short grass lands

   b. Kapôt-kemẽpti - savanna with tree stands

   c. Kapôt-kam-bôiprek - high grass lands

   d. Pykati'ô'krãi - savanna with intermittent trees

2. Krãi (mountains)

3. Bà (forest)

   a. bà-kamrek - gallery (riverine) forest

   b. bà-êpti - dense jungle (selva)

   c. bà-kati (pi'y-kô) - high forest

   d. bà-ràràra - forest with intermittent openings

---

*This is only a partial typology of ecological zones; there are various subtypes not enumerated. In folk taxonomy, the Kayapó also use "transitional categories" that are interzonal.

the Kayapó see as replicating the natural openings in the bà-ràràra forest. Knowledge of such systemic relationships allows the Kayapó to select agricultural lands from vegetative types as well as to formulate hunting and gathering strategies based on ripening of fruits that attract game animals.

b. Folk ethology

Recent studies (Parker 1982; Smith 1981; Posey 1981a, 1982b; Moran 1981) have emphasized the considerable knowledge about animal behavior that exists in folk and indigenous cultures of Amazonia. The Kayapó have an intricate knowledge of animal behavior, even of animals as small as wasps and ants (Posey 1979a, 1981a, 1982f). There is much to be learned about animal behavior, for example, from hunting strategies. As Carneiro noted for the Amahuaca, "every significant detail of the life habits of animals is part of an Amahuaca hunter's knowledge, including the sound of its cry, its preferred foods, its excrement, its scents, the teeth marks it makes on fruit, etc." (1974:126).

Plant-animal-human relationships can be symbolically represented in rituals and ceremonies (cf. Reichel-Dolmatoff 1971, 1976, 1978). Turner (1966) described various ceremonies that utilize specific plants during Kayapó rituals; however, he does not explain the symbolic

Figure 9.2. Idealized cross section of Kayapó forest ecological zones and subzones near Gorotire

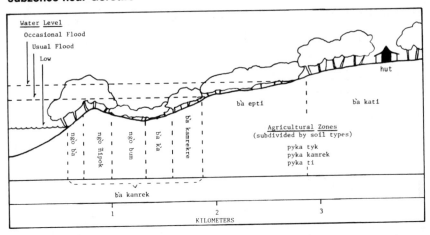

Figure 9.3. Ecological zones surrounding the village of Gorotire as perceived by the Kayapó

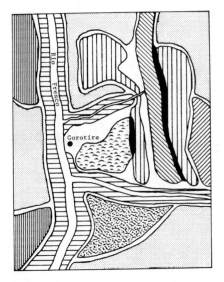

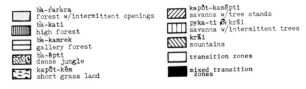

Table 9.2. Selected soil-plant-animal relationships in the selected ecozone (Bà-ràràra)*

Preferred Soil#	Particular** Animal Assn.	Plants Associated With Zone	Use of Plant — Man	Use of Plant — Animal	Kayapó name
1,2	A,B,C,D,E	Humiria balsamifera	eat fruit	eat fruit	bà-rerek
1,2	F	Psidium guineense	eat fruit	eat fruit + leaves	kamokãtytx
3	F	Zingiberaceae	use root for tea; smoke leaves	eat leaves	madn-tu
3		Genus unknown	use for paint		pita-teka
2,3		Catasetum sp.	medicinal		pitu
2,3	C,F	Bignoniaceae	medicinal	eat leaves	ngra-kanê
1,2,3	C,D	Cisampelos sp.	fish bait	eat fruit	tep-kanê
1	A,B,C,D	Piperaceae	fish bait	eat fruit	màkrê-kanê
3		Amasonia sp.	prophylaxis		pidjô-rã
1	A,B,C,D	Oenocarpus distichus	eat fruit	eat fruit	kamêrê (bacaba)
1,2,3	H	Macrostaychia sp.	use wood	?	kukrytmyka
1,3	F	Monotagma sp.	grind leaves eat roots	eat leaves eat roots	küryre
1,2	A,C,D,F	Myrsia sp.	eat fruit	eat fruit + leaves	kônôkô
1,3	H,F	Cecropia leucocoma		eat fruit + leaves	atwỳra'ô'
2		Polypodiaceae	medicinal		tôn-kanê
2	F	Clarisia ilicifolia	medicinal	eat leaves	pidjô-nirê
2,3		Centrosema carajaense	fish poison		akrô
2,3	C,D,F	Cassia hoffmanseggii	medicinal	eat fruit + leaves	pidjô-kakrit

* Identifications made by Dr. Susanna Hecht, Department of Geography, UCLA

Animals:

A = white-lipped peccary (porção)
B = white paca (paca branca)
C = agouti (cutia branca)
D = tortoise (jaboti)
E = red paca (paca vermelha)
F = red agouti (cutia vermelha)
G = deer (veado)
H = tapir (anta)

#Soil Types:

1 = black (pyka-tyk)
2 = red (pyka-kamrek)
3 = yellow (pyka-ti)

§ Note: Identifications made by Dr. Susanna Hecht, Department of Geography, UCLA.

functions or significance of these objects. Research into the relationships between natural objects and ceremonial importance would undoubtedly be fruitful in understanding indigenous perceptions of ecological relatedness and symbolic annual cycles.

Another significant current field of investigation is that of "co-evolutionary complexes," i.e., plant and animal communities that have evolved simultaneously through changing environmental conditions in biological evolutionary history (cf. Gilbert and Raven 1975; Pimentel, Levin, and Olsen 1978). Such complexes are generally complicated and difficult to discover. The Kayapó recognize certain co-evolutionary complexes that are encoded for cultural transmission through myths. Myths often seem nonsense to the casual outside observer. Myths may serve, however, as valuable sources of highly symbolic information about important social and environmental relationships. Take, for example, the following Kayapó myth:

> Why Women Paint Their Faces with Ant Parts
> The trails of the fire ant (mrum-kamrek-ti)
> are long. They are ferocious (akrê) like men.
> But the little red ant of our fields (mrumre)
> is gentle like women; they are not aggressive
> (wajobôre). Their trails meander like the
> bean vines on the maize. The little red ant
> is the relative/friend of the manioc. This
> is why women use the little red ant to mix
> with urucú to paint their faces in the maize
> festival. The little red ant is the guardian
> of our fields and is our relative/friend.[4]

The principal theme of this myth is that a certain ant (mrum-re) is the friend of the fields and the women, who are the cultivators in Kayapó culture. The myth begins to make sense when we understand the co-evolutionary complex of maize, beans, manioc, and this ant (Pogomyrmex sp.).

Manioc produces an extra-floral nectar that attracts the ants to the young manioc plant.[5] The ants use their mandibles to make their way to the nectar, cutting away any bean vines that would prevent the new, fragile manioc stems from growing. The twining bean vines are, therefore, kept from climbing on the manioc and are left with the maize plants as their natural trellis. The maize can shoot up undamaged by the bean vines, while the bean plant itself furnishes valuable nitrogen needed by the maize. The ants are the natural manipulators of nature and facilitate the horticultural activities of the women.

Myth has not seriously been studied as a transmitter of encoded ecological knowledge. This example, however, provides evidence of the need for a serious approach to myth analyses for biological information and ecosystemic relationships.

PERCEPTION OF RESOURCES

Within specific ecological zones the Kayapó have an extensive and varied inventory of utilizable natural resources. Based on indigenous environmental perceptions, the following categories are discernible.

a. Wild Plants

Although the array of wild plants collected by Amazonian Indians is known to be extensive, taxonomic and chemical-nutritional data remain scanty. The Instituto Nacional de Pesquisas da Amazônia (INPA) in Manaus and the Centro de Pesquisas Antropológicas e Folclóricas (CEPAF) in Maranhão have projects underway to systematically gather data on wild plants utilized by indigenous groups of Amazonia. Wild food resources are somewhat better known (cf. Cavalcante 1972, 1974) than medicinal plants, which are regrettably overlooked due to the difficulty and expense of evaluating medicinal properties and a general disregard by Western science for folk medicine. Chemical and nutritional analyses exist for less than 1% of the plants collected by Indians of Amazonia (W. E. Kerr, personal communication).

An estimated 250 plants are utilized by the Kayapó for their fruits alone, plus hundreds of others for their nuts, tubers, and drupes. The list of plants with medicinal value is vast. A partial list of plants gathered by the Kayapó for food can be found in Table 9.3.[6]

b. Domesticated Plants

The Kayapó have a large inventory of aboriginal cultigens. A list of major cultivated plants is found in Table 9.4. Of these, only one, cupá (Cissus gongylodes), is unknown to Brazilian cultivators. There are, however, numerous varieties of major cultigens that the Indians claim to be aboriginal (see Tables 9.5a-9.5g) and which are little known outside the Kayapó region. The Kayapó cultigens alone offer much information about plant genetic variation and a significant genetic pool for botanic research and experimentation.

One domesticate of great interest is cupá (C. gongylodes). It is a fast-growing plant that has considerable vitamin, mineral, and nutritional value (Kerr, Posey, and Filho 1978). Chemical analyses of cupá are summarized in Table 9.6. There are wild and semi-domesticated varieties of cupá. The Kayapó gather wild varieties and replant these in "forest fields" along trek routes. This knowledge suggests that the complete continuum of domestication can be studied for Cissus.

The Kayapó also have several domesticated medicinal

Table 9.3. Partial list of gathered food plants of the Kayapó Indians*

Kayapó	Portuguese	Scientific	Seasonality	Part(s) Eaten
pidjo-rã	açaí	Euterpe oleracea	June-November	Fruit; heart
norã	bacaba	Oenocarpus distichus	September-December	Fruit; leaves[1]
kubenkrã	cacau braba	Theobroma speciosum	December-January	Fruit
pidjóko	cajá	Spondias lutea	March-May	Drupe
pidjó-ti	Castanha do Pará	Bertholletia excelsa	December-March	Nut
ñejaka	cupuaçú	Theobroma grandiflorum	December-March	Fruit
ronkà	babaçú	Orbygnia speciosa	All year	Nut; leaves[1]
pidjo-bà	frutão	Pouteria pariry	December-March	Fruit
pidjo-tyk	genipapo	Genipa americana	All year	Fruit;[2] leaves[3]
rõtu	nájá	Maximilliana regia	August-February	Fruit
pidjo-bàti	piquí	Caryocar villosum	December-February	Drupe
pidjo-kamrek	uxi	Endopleura uchi	November-March	Drupe
Idjy-kryre	fruta de campo	Psidium guineense	January-February	Flower
pitú	orchidia de campo	Catasetum sp.	January-March	False bulb
kryry-re	biro	Monotagma sp.	All year	Tuber
konoko	ingá	Myrsia sp.	August-October	Fruit
mõyt	jatoba		July	Fruit
pidjó kakut		Cassia hoffmanseggii	January-April	Fruit
bàdjum		Psidium sp.	July-August	Fruit

*Note: Identifications based on Cavalcante (1972, 1974).

[1] Leaves used for making salt. [2] Fruit eaten and used as base for body paint.
[3] Leaves dried and smoked.

Table 9.4. Major cultivated plants of the Kayapó Indians

Portuguese	English	Kayapó	Scientific	Use	Number of Folk Varieties[1]
Abacaxí*	Pineapple	akrañitu	Ananas comosus	Food	3
Abóbora	Squash	katere	Cucurbita sp.	Food	8
Algodão	Cotton	kadjatkà	Gossypium arboreum	Cloth	4
Araia	Arrowroot	môp-jabi'ê	Maranta arundinacea	Food	6
Arroz*	Rice	baỳ-gogo	Oryza sativa	Food	6
Banana	Banana	tyryti	Musa sp.	Food	13
Batata doce	Sweet Potato	yàt	Ipomoea batatas	Food	16
Cana*	Sugar Cane	kadjwati	Saccharum offici-narum	Food	4
Cará	?	môp-kaàk	Maranta sp.	Food	6
Cupá babão	Kupa	kupá	Cissus gongylodes	Food	4
Fava*	Broadbean	màt krwàt'ỳ	Vicia faba	Food	2
Feijão	Bean	màt-kwat	Phaseolus vulgaris	Food	4
Feijão andú	Bush bean	màt-kwat'ỳ	Cajanus indicus	Food	2
Inhame	Yam	môp	Dioscorea sp.	Food	17
Macaxeira	Cassava	kwyrà-djài	Manihot esculenta	Food	6**
Mandioca	Manioc	kwyry	Manihot esculenta	Food, medicine	11**
Melancia*	Melon	katekaàk	Citrullus vulgaris	Food	4
Milho	Corn	baỳ	Zea mays	Food	8
Tobaco	Tobacco	cariño	Nicotiana sp.	Smoke	3
urucú	Urucu	pỳ	Bixa orellana	Body paint	6
?	?	màdutú	Zingiber sp.	Medicine	?
Mamão*	Papaya	kàtembaré	Carica papaya	Food, medicine	4

*Recent introduction; the Kayapó say other cultigens are aboriginal.
**The unique gradation of speciation in Manioc makes the determination of exact taxonomy difficult for our own science and causes variation in folk taxonomy as well (see Kerr and Clement 1980).

[1]See Table 9.5.

Table 9.5(a-g). Folk varieties of major Kayapó cultigens

Table 9.5a. Banana (Musa sp.): Tyryti

Kayapó	Portuguese	Utilization[1]	Maturation Time
1. tek ày diagôt[2]	branquinho	A	7 months
2. djô kakô-kukrê ti[2]	peruwara	A	9 months
3. tekà kamrek tú	rocha	C,D	9 months
4. tekà ngra ngra ti	rocha-branca	B,C,D	9 months
5. ô' taben prôre	rangídeira	C,D	9 months
6. teka-pyuhti	comprida	C,D	6-7 months
7. noipoti	papo	A,D	9 months
8. tykre[2]	São Tomé	A,B	9 months
9. rike[2]	nasazinho	A,B	9 months
10. teka ngàite	anôa	A,B,D	5 months
11. takre keti[2]	naja	A,B,D	9 months
12. prĩkamdjô	bahia	A	9 months
13. noi poti kaàk re[2]	-	A	9 months

[1]Utilization code:

A = eaten raw
B = cooked
C = dried and made into flour
D = roasted

[2]Post-contact introduction.

Table 9.5b. Manioc (Manihot esculenta): Kwyry

Kayapó	Portuguese	Preferred Use
1. kwyrà-djà	gerio	sun-dried flour
2. kwyrà-djà-ô-kryre		toasted flour (farinha)
3. kwyrà-ngra-ngra*	mandioca amarela	toasted flour (farinha)
4. kwyrà-pa*		toasted flour (farinha)
5. kwyrà-prĩtu		toasted flour (farinha)
6. kwyrà-djà-ô'-pôti		tapioca
7. kwyrà-ñi-mok-tyk	mandioca preta	sun-dried flour
8. kwyrà-pa-kamrek	mandioca vermelha	toasted flour
9. kwyrà-djà-ô-jabire		toasted flour
10. kwyrà-nô'ô'poti		tapioca
11. my-myt-kàre		sun-dried flour

*Recently imported varieties; others are pre-contact varieties.

Table 9.5c.   Sweet potato (Ipomoea sp.): Yàt

Kayapó	Portuguese
1. yàt-ngra-ngra	batata amarela
2. yàt-jaka-ti	batata branca
3. yàt-kawrek-ti*	batata incarnada
4. yàt-ngrô-ti*	
5. yàt-ñere	
6. yàt-'ôk-re	
7. yàt-kà-tyk-ti*	
8. yàt-jakure*	
9. yàt-'ôk-ti	
10. yàt-kangàrà	
11. yàt-tykre	
12. yàt-krê-jaka	
13. yàt-apàri	
14. yàt-krê-rã	
15. yàt-krê-ngra	
16. yàt-tu-kà*	

*Post-contact introduction.

Table 9.5d.   Yam (Dioscorea sp.): Môp

Kayapó	Portuguese
1. môp-pi-rô-ti[1]	sucurú
2. môp-rô-tu[1]	sucurú
3. môp-jábire	
4. môp-u'i-tôre	
5. môp-punuti[1]	osso
6. môp-jaka[1]	osso branco
7. môp-krê-jaka[1]	branco
8. môp-djà-ni[1]	espinha
9. môp-jà-môp	braba[2]
10. môp-màri	
11. môp-djà-djô	
12. môp-tykre	
13. môp-djô-re	
14. môp-ka-prorô	
15. môp-kà-kamrô[3]	
16. môp-ñere	ossinha
17. pàt-parikàre	

Notes:
   [1]Introduced varieties; others are said to be aboriginal.

   [2]Semi-domesticated variety.

   [3]Bears from 10 to 40 years.

Table 9.5e. Corn (<u>Zea</u> <u>mays</u>): B̀ày

Kayapó	Portuguese	Preparation[1]
1. bày-ka-re		A,B,C
2. bày-ngra-ngra	milho amarelo	A,B,C
3. bày-kamrek-tu	milho vermelha	A,B,C
4. bày-no-tykti		A,B,C
5. bày-ka-ràràre[2]	pipoca	A
6. bày-ngrwa-kà-tire		A,B,C
7. bày-karê		A,B,C
8. bày-noi-bê-tire		A,B,C

Note:
[1]Preparation Code: A = roasted; B = boiled; C = flour

[2]Recently introduced; other varieties very ancient.

Table 9.5f. Urucú (<u>Bixa</u> <u>orellana</u>): P̀ỳ

Kayapó	Portuguese	Comments
1. krã-mêre	urucú	All varieties
2. krã-ô-re	urucú	aboriginal
3. krã-jaka	urucú	
4. krã-kamrek	urucú	
5. krã-kamrek-ti	urucú	
6. krã-kamrekre	urucú	

Table 9.5g. Macaxeira, Sweet Manioc (<u>Manihot</u> <u>esculenta</u>):
          Kroyrà-djài

Kayapó	Portuguese	Preparation[1]
1. mĩ-mut-kàre	macaxeira	B,C
2. no'ô-poiti	macaxeira	B,C
3. krê-kamrek[2]	macaxeira	B,C
4. kwyrà-kamrek[2]	macaxeira	B,C
5. tàp-kyre[2]	macaxeira	A,B,C
6. krê-jaka-pũ-re[2]	macaxeira	B,C

Note:
[1]Preparation Code: A = raw; B = roasted; C = flour

[2]Post-contact introductions.

Table 9.6. Chemical analysis of cupá stems (Cissus gongylodes)*

Per 100 gram sample (65% of the plant is edible):

     77.56% water
      1.2% protein
      1.0% fat
      1.4% ash
     18.84% carbohydrates
     (89.2 calories)

Vitamin content (based on gas chromatograph):

     A, B_1, B_2, B_6, C, D_2, D_3, E

*Taken from Kerr, Posey, and Filho 1978:704.

plants, but only one (madn-tu, Zingiber)[7] is of modern importance. Madn-tu is believed to be an effective medicine against intestinal parasites, one of the principal health problems of the Kayapó (Posey 1979c) and tropical peoples in general.

     Another important domesticate is urucú (Bixa orellana). The red seeds of urucú are used to color and flavor foods and are the principal ingredient of Kayapó body paint. Red body paint is an indispensable part of indigenous body adornment throughout Amazonia, but body paint also has a practical value. I found urucú to be an effective natural insect repellant that effects a significant reduction (as much as 84%) in insect bites when painted on the body (Posey 1979d).

     One can only guess at the vastness of the domesticated plant inventories of Amazonian Indians. As has been recognized by some scientists (Williams 1960; National Academy of Sciences 1975), many of these plants have promising economic value and can be exploited on a large-scale basis.

c. "Nomadic Agriculture"

     As previously stated, Kayapó taxonomic patterns show a propensity for not classifying the natural world into neatly defined categories, but rather rely heavily on "graded" categories of transition. The distinction between domesticated and wild plants is an excellent example of how categories blend into each other.

     During hunting treks,[8] the men may be away from the village two to four weeks. They carry little food with them, relying instead on natural "islands of resources" along the established forest trails. The Kayapó have a vast network (thousands of kilometers) of trails interlacing villages, hunting grounds, gardens, old fields, and natural resource islands. Food supplies, therefore, are hardly left to chance. To further insure food sources, however, the Kayapó also create "forest fields" of semi-domesticated plants. These plants are collected during the day's travels along trails and hunting reconnoiters into the forest. The plants are then replanted near established forest campsites.

There are at least 54 species of plants used by the Kayapó in these forest fields.[9] Most are tuberous plants similar to those described by Maybury-Lewis (1974:334) for the Shavante. All grow naturally in bà-ràràra (forest with intermittent openings and penetration of sunlight), which the Kayapó see as a natural counterpart of their humanmade fields. Replanting is done adjacent to camp-sites--which are always in transitional ecological zones--usually before or after defecation.

Figure 9.4 indicates the route of a trek I made in 1978 to the ancient Kayapó village of Pyka-tô-ti (cf. Posey 1979b). This figure (based on a drawing by a Kayapó informant) shows natural "resource islands" as well as "forest fields" created by the Kayapó.

Elsewhere (Posey 1982a) I have described this system of ecological exploitation as "nomadic agriculture" to emphasize the special adaptation of forest fields to the semi-nomadic system of the Kayapó. The tendency of Western science to analyze only those data that fit into Western categories often leads to underestimating or missing entirely the importance of different categories of ecological exploitation. This transitional system probably is much more widespread in Amazonia than expected and underlines the inadequacies of existing subsistence typologies and carrying-capacity theories.

d. Manipulated Animal Species

Another area of "transitional" knowledge for the Kayapó is semi-domesticated animals. These are perhaps best called "manipulated species" to emphasize the Indians' intentional manipulation of animal behavior.

The larvae of some beetles (Scarabaeidae and Buprestidae), for example, are utilized by various tribes in the lowland tropics (Chagnon 1968; Posey 1978, 1980). The adult beetle lays eggs in the refuse of dead banana plants and old palm trees. The Indians intentionally stack the remains of banana and palm plants near villages, fields, and campsites to attract the adult beetles. After some months (depending on species and region, as well as season of the year), the eggs develop into grubs that are tasty and nutritious. Indians know the life cycle of the beetle and can predict when to collect the mature grubs.

The Kayapó recognize 54 folk species of stingless bees (Meliponidae) and two kinds of stinging bees (both are subspecies of Apis mellifera). All these species are classified by distinctive honeys and waxes (Posey 1982b, 1982f). Honey is a prized food, while the waxes are used as treatments for burns, cures for diseases, disinfectants

Figure 9.4. Trek from Kubĕn-krã-kêin village to abandoned village site (Pyka-tô-ti) showing resource islands and campsites associated with forest fields

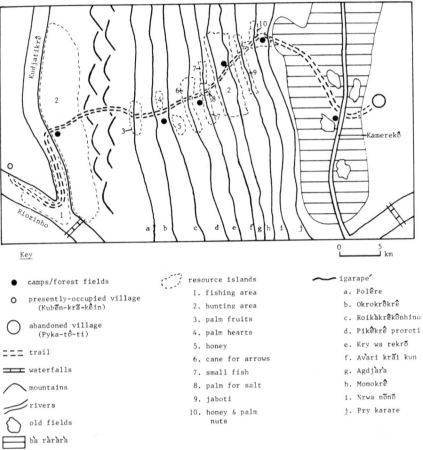

Key

- ● camps/forest fields
- ○ presently-occupied village (Kubĕn-krã-kêin)
- ◯ abandoned village (Pyka-tô-ti)
- = = = trail
- ⬚⬚⬚ waterfalls
- ⌒⌒ mountains
- ≋ rivers
- ⬠ old fields
- ▱ bà ràràra

⌁ resource islands
1. fishing area
2. hunting area
3. palm fruits
4. palm hearts
5. honey
6. cane for arrows
7. small fish
8. palm for salt
9. jaboti
10. honey & palm nuts

⌒ igarapeʹ
a. Polêre
b. Okrokrôkrê
c. Roikàkrêkônhino
d. Pikêkrê proroti
e. Kry wa rekrô
f. Avari krãi kun
g. Agdjàra
h. Momokrê
i. Nrwa nônô
j. Pry karare

for wounds, and adhesives for artifacts.

Six species of stingless bees are "kept" by the Kayapó (see Table 9.7). The Indians know that if a portion of the brood comb with the queen bee is returned to the tree after the honey is taken, certain species of bees will return to re-establish the colony. Thus hives of these six species can be systematically raided seasonally. Utilization by the Kayapó of major stingless bee species is summarized in Table 9.8.

The Kayapó also manipulate the movement of game animals by intentionally dispersing agricultural fields at variable distances from the village. Vegetation of the natural reforestation cycle in abandoned fields attracts and supports hunted species. The use of

Table 9.7. Semi-domesticated (manipulated) species of Apidae (bees)
utilized by the Kayapó Indians

Kayapó Name	Scientific Name
*Ngài-pêrê-ỳ	Apis mellifera
*§Ngài-ñy-tyk-ti	Melipona seminigra cf. pernigra (Moure and Kerr)
*§Ngài-kumrenx (mehn-krak-krak-ti)	Melipona rufiventris flavolieata (Friese)
*Ngài-re	Melipona compressipes cf. fasciculata (sm.) or afinis Moure Ms.
*mykrwàt	Frieseomelitta sp.
*§udjỳ	Trigona amalthea (Olivier)
*§kukraire	Trigona dallatorreana Friese
+mehnôrã-kamrek	Trigona cilipes pellucida (Ckll.)
+mehnôrã-tyk	Scaura longula (Lep.)

*These species are systematically raided in subsequent seasons.

§Those species whose nests are taken to the village.[11]

+Those species that are encouraged to build nests in dry posts in
the houses.

abandoned fields, therefore, helps to insure an easily
available source of game.

MANAGEMENT OF "ABANDONED FIELDS"

A great misconception about traditional indigenous
agriculture is that fields are totally abandoned after
cultivation for a few years.[10] In this slash-and-burn
system, new fields are created each year in forested
areas and the principal production from domesticated
plants ends in two to three years. However, fields are
not totally abandoned after this period as commonly
believed.
Kayapó "abandoned fields," for example, continue to
produce harvests of yams and taro for five to six years,
bananas for 12 to 15, urucú for 20 or more, and cupá for
at least 30 years. Of great importance is the Kayapós'
use of "abandoned fields" (capoeira) to gather plants
and plant products produced in the natural reforestation
sequence. A representative inventory of these plants can
be found in Table 9.2. Research is currently underway to
determine a more complete botanical inventory in
"abandoned field" sites in Amazonia.[11]
Old fields also produce a variety of foods that
attract wildlife such as porco do mato, coati, deer,
paca, agouti, and others (see Table 9.2). Many birds,
particularly sparrows, macaws, and parrots, are also
attracted to old fields and are hunted in the relatively
open capoeira areas. Young Kayapó boys are nearly self-

Table 9.8. Principal species of Apidae utilized by the Kayapó Indians

Kayapó Name	Scientific Name	Wax Use Util.	Cer.	Med.	Honey Seasonal	Amount	Larvae Eaten	Pupae Eaten	Pollen Eaten	Resin Used	Aggressive*	Distinctive Traits
ngài-pêrê-ỳ	Apis mellifera	✓	✓		all year	very much			✓		++++	Honey taken during New Moon
ngài-ñy-tỳk-ti	Melipona seminigra	✓	✓	✓	dry seas.	average					++	Bee parts used for hunting magic
ngài-kumrenx	M. rufiventris	✓	✓		all year	average						Wax used for mẽ-kutôm
ngài-re	M. compressipes	✓	✓		all year	much						Has markings like the "anta"
ngài-kàk-ñy	Partamona sp.	✓										Wax used in magic to make enemy weak
mykrwàt	Frieseomelitta sp.	✓			all year	average	✓	✓	✓			
udjỳ	Trigona amalthea	✓			dry seas.	average				✓		Bee parts mixed with urucú for hunting magic
kukraire	Trigona dallatorreana				all year	much		✓	✓		+	Break off limb with nest and run to expel bees
mehnôrà-kamrek	Trigona cilipes		✓		all year	little				✓		Has skinny eyes like jaguar
mehnôrà-tỳk	Scaura longula		✓		all year	little				✓		Used for jaguar hunting magic
kagnarà-krã-kamrek	Oxytrigona tataira	✓	✓		all year	average	✓	✓	✓		+++	Cut entire tree to take honey
kangàrà-krã-tyk	Oxytrigona sp.	✓	✓		all year	average	✓	✓			++	Bee causes blisters on skin
kangàrà-udja-ti	Oxytrigona sp.	✓	✓		all year	average	✓	✓			+++	Bees used in hunting magic
kangàrà-ti	Oxytrigona sp.	✓	✓		all year	average	✓				+++	Wax used for mẽ-kutôm
mỳre	Trigona pallida	✓	✓		all year	average	✓		✓		+	Sometimes fell tree
ngôi-tênk	Trigona sp.	✓			all year	little						Live in termite nests
djô	Trigona fuscipennis	✓	✓		all year	little	✓		✓			Live in termite hills
imrê-ti-re	Trigona chanchamayoensis	✓										Live in ant nests
kukoire-kà	Partamona sp.	✓	✓		all year	average					+	Nests in termite nests
ô'i	Tetragona sp.	✓			dry seas.	little						Very acidic honey; fell entire tree
tôn-mỳ	Tetragona sp.	✓	✓		dry seas.	average				✓		Fell tree to take honey
rĩ	Tetragona sp.	✓			all year	much						Bee thought to be "stupid" and weak
mehr-xi-we'i	Tetragona goettei	✓	✓		all year	average	✓					Found only in the Xingú
mênire-udgà	Tetragona quadrangula	✓	✓		all year	average	✓			✓		Opening of nest like a vagina
mehnôdjành	F. varia	✓			dry seas.	little					+	Smoke from wax used for curing
mehñykamrek	Trigona spinipes	✓			dry seas.	little	✓		✓			Wax burned; smoke causes dizziness
mehñy-tyk	Trigona banneri	✓			dry seas.	little					++	
pyka-kam	Trigona fulviventris	✓	✓		dry seas.	little					+	Bee deposits drops of resin on skin

*Nests of Aggressive (+++ - very aggressive; ++ - moderately aggressive; + - slightly aggressive) bees are raided using smoke and fire to expel bees first. #Wax use: Utilitarian; Ceremonial; Medicinal.

sufficient in protein intake, and small birds are a major
dietary source (Posey 1979a, 1979d). The Kayapó are aware
of the attractiveness of old fields to wildlife and
purposefully disperse their fields great distances from
their villages. Thus game is attracted in artificially
high densities, improving yields from hunting efforts.
The Kayapó men hunt while the women tend the gardens,
making longer hunting treks less necessary to acquire meat.
    The Kayapó thus do not have a clearcut demarcation
between fields and forest nor between wild and domesticated species. Rather they have a more general system for
classification of ecological resources that forms a continuum between wild species and domestic ones, all of
which figure into integrated management strategies.

ADAPTATIONS OF INDIGENOUS AGRICULTURE

    Slash-and-burn agriculture has too often been con-
sidered primitive and inefficient. Scientists now recognize that indigenous agriculture is more complicated and
better adapted to tropical conditions than previously
assumed (Lovejoy and Schubart 1980; Moran 1981). Indian
fields, for example, minimize the time that soils are left
exposed to the destructive heat of direct sunlight and
compounding force of tropical rains (Vickers 1976).
Vegetative cover is maintained at various heights to insure the protection of soils from rapid erosion and
leaching (Schubart 1977).
    Indigenous agriculture also depends heavily on native
plants that have been shown to be adapted to localized
climatic conditions (Alvim 1980). Native plants have also
been shown to be more efficient in their utilization of
micro-nutrients and less dependent on nutrients considered essential for good soil fertility for the temperate
zones (Posey and Hecht, in preparation).
    Although some large fields have been reported
(Frechione 1981), indigenous agriculture generally relies
on small dispersed fields. The geographic dispersal mini-
mizes the epizootic growth of insect pests as well as
plant diseases (Pimentel and Goodman 1978; Posey 1979a).
Thus expensive and ecologically dangerous pesticides are
unnecessary for productive slash-and-burn agriculture.
Field dispersal, as previously indicated, also stimulates
wildlife populations. Perhaps most importantly, indigenous agricultural systems always include "natural
corridors" between field sites. These natural corridors
form valuable ecological refuges for plant and animal
species (Gómez-Pompa et al. 1972; Moran 1982; Lovejoy
and Schubart 1980). Thus species are not only protected
from extinction, but are reserved close at hand for re-
establishment in "abandoned fields."
    Indian agriculture must, therefore, be viewed as a
system developed to minimize problems of crop pests, while
preserving soil potential and productivity. Most

importantly, the system allows for natural refuges for plants and animals that insure success in long-term ecological planning.

NATURAL HARMONY AND TRIBAL RITUALS

Each indigenous culture has a "belief system" that establishes a relationship between humans and the environment. Cycles of rituals and ceremonies have been shown to regulate natural resources (Rappaport 1967, 1971). It is still difficult, however, to demonstrate direct relationships between social systems and ecological resource management. Attempts have been made to relate food taboos to resource protection (e.g., McDonald 1977; Ross 1978a) and to correlate ritual cycles with natural seasonality (Reichel-Dolmatoff 1976).

The Kayapó belief system is based upon a ubiquitous belief in energy balance (Posey 1982d) similar to that described for the Desana Indians (Reichel-Dolmatoff 1978). All living objects are endowed with this universal energy and, therefore, all life is to be revered and protected.

Energy is encapsulated in living forms, but leaves the physical form (whether plant, animal, or human) at death and is reconstituted into new life.[12] The whole energy transformation process takes a conceptually long period of time that cannot be precisely measured or expressed by the Kayapó; nonetheless, there is a sense of "natural" rate of plant and animal exploitation that, if exceeded, will upset the energy transformation process and thereby upset the natural energy balance.

The Kayapó have specific rituals before and after each trek to hunt or collect plants in order to placate those spirits that will be dispossessed from their physical forms through death. The annual ecological cycles are likewise ritually punctuated to mark the maize and manioc seasons. Other festivals celebrate the hunting "seasons" for land turtle, tapir, anteater, and other game animals. The onset of the rainy season is marked by the appearance in the gallery forests of troops of monkeys, which is symbolically commemorated by a festival with dancers in monkey masks.

Each Kayapó ceremony requires a specific array of natural objects for the completion of the associated ritual (a particular type of feather, plant, or beeswax, for example). This requires an organized trek to procure the needed materials, which leads the Kayapó to different "resource islands" over a vast area. Because needed materials vary with each ritual, the ritual cycle causes the Kayapó to systematically exploit different ecological zones associated with diverse "resource islands."

Without the natural ritual cycle, life would cease to perpetuate itself for the Kayapó. All ceremonies and rituals that are essential for the transformation of life-giving energy are controlled by tribal elders, chiefs,

248

and shamans. Thus ecological management is entrusted to
the highest level of Kayapó leadership and given utmost
priority.

CONCLUSIONS

     The above outline suggests various fields of research
based on indigenous models of ecology in the Amazon
Basin. Although most Indian societies are already extinct,
and those remaining face imminent destruction, there is
still time to salvage knowledge about the Amazon from
surviving indigenous systems. Research must proceed,
however, with the utmost urgency and commitment, for with
the disappearance of each indigenous group the world loses
an accumulated wealth of millennia of human experience
and adaptation.
     Based on what has already been learned from the
Kayapó Indians, the following recommendations can be made
for a more ecologically sound research program for
development in Amazonia:
     1. Recognition of specific ecological zones and
variations in associated biotic communities and soil
types;
     2. Greater use of native plants that are better
adapted to climate and soil conditions of Amazonia;
     3. Maximum use of vegetative cover to protect
fragile tropical soils, and diversified plantings to
utilize naturally co-evolved biological communities;
     4. Use of long-term strategies to utilize
"abandoned fields" left to fallow. This would include
use of semi-domesticated plants and manipulated animal
species, as well as wild species, in an overall management scheme including crop rotation;
     5. Limiting the size of fields to prevent
epizootic surges of insect and disease pests, thereby
reducing the dependency on costly and ecologically
dangerous chemical products;
     6. Use of "natural corridors" between fields to
serve as natural refuges for animal and plant life. This
would not only preserve biological diversity but also
insure rapid reforestation and preservation of ecological
systems;
     7. Study of ecological and evolutionary inter-
relationships as expressed in myth, ritual, and ceremony;
     8. Study of the range of variation in systems of
swidden agriculture in Amazonia including the role of
"resource islands," "forest fields," and "nomadic
agriculture."
     Following the Kayapó model, we might begin to select
as our most important leaders those who will be responsible
for the long-term management of natural resources to
prevent ecological destruction. At the same time, science
must relate its environmental theories in such a way as
to show the relevance of ecological balance to each and

every individual. Then, and only then, can development
proceed with sustainable benefits for the world population
as a whole without exploitive resource destruction for the
short-term benefit of only a few.

ACKNOWLEDGMENTS

Field research was sponsored through two grants from
the Wenner-Gren Foundation for Anthropological Research.
Ethno-historical research was funded by the Newberry
Library and the American Philosophical Society. I thank
the staff of the Museu Paraense "Emilio Goeldi," INPA, and
FUNAI for their generous assistance. I also thank Carol
Jones and Emilio Moran, who assisted in the editing and
preparation of this manuscript. Special appreciation goes
to Dr. John Frechione, Department of Anthropology, University of Pittsburgh, who prepared all the maps, figures,
and artwork in this article.

NOTES

1. The complete writings of Horace Banner include
journals, letters, and manuscripts that cover his 40 years
of life with the Kayapó. These are kept by his widow,
"Dona Eva," in Cheshire, England. Further information can
be obtained by writing to Eva Banner, 351 Thelwall New
Road, Grappenhall (Warrington), England. I spent five
months inspecting these materials and am very thankful to
Dona Eva for her generous assistance as well as to the
American Philosophical Society for financial support.
2. Linguistic symbols conform to the orthographic
form approved by FUNAI. See Stout and Thompson (1974).
3. Grading is a term used to define the cognitive
placement of any given object or concept in relation to
other relative fixed categories. These relationships are
best analyzed as "fuzzy sets" (see Kempton 1978 and Posey
1982c).
4. The mrum-kamrek-ti (fire ant, Atta sp.) has a
vicious sting and is used for the men's hunting magic to
make men and dogs strong and aggressive in the chase.
The mrumre (small red ant, probably Pogomyrmex sp.) does
not sting and is, therefore, considered weak (wajobôre),
but is admired by the women for its industrious and organized activity. It is common for the Kayapó to mix bits
of insects into their body paint (mainly with urucú, Bixa
orellana) in order to acquire the perceived qualities of
the insect utilized in the mixture. This story was related by a female head of household to her granddaughter
(tab djwa) in the village Gorotire, July 1978.
5. The attractiveness of extra-floral nectars to
ants is summarized by Bentley (1977).
6. Unfortunately the bulk of the plant collection was
lost in transit from the field site to the Museu Goeldi in
Belém and identifications were not made. Plans are to

250

duplicate the collection in 1982-1983 so that complete botanical information will be available for future research.

7. The species is undetermined. Madn-tu is not, however, the same wild ginger commonly grown by Brazilians (Zingiber officinalis).

8. The Kayapó have relatively stationary villages, but are nonetheless semi-nomadic, spending four to five months per year away from the main village. Kayapó families often spend weeks at a time in their gardens; women go on frequent gathering trips that may last several days; lineage groups spend one to two months in river camps where the primary activity is gathering Brazil nuts (Bertholletia excelsa). Men are the most fond of trekking, spending two to four months hunting prior to the major festivals in the ecological cycle (Posey 1979b).

9. Identification of plants is currently underway with plans to carry out further research and collecting in the Kayapó area.

10. Usual figures are two to five years for the productive life of slash-and-burn fields (cf. Alvim 1972, 1980).

11. A return to the Kayapó area is planned in conjunction with the Centro de Pesquisas Antropológicas e Folclóricas (a/c D. Posey, Universidade Federal de Maranhão, São Luiz, Maranhão) to make a complete inventory of plants utilized in Kayapó "abandoned fields." Dr. William Denevan is currently engaged in a study of the utilization of old swiddens among the Bora Indians of lowland Peru.

12. The complicated subject of universal energy in the Kayapó belief system is treated in greater detail in Posey (1982b).

REFERENCES

Acuña, Fr. Cristóval de
    1859   New Discovery of the Great River of the Amazons.
            Translated from the Spanish Edition (1641) by
            Clements R. Markham.   In Expeditions into the
            Valley of the Amazonas, 1539, 1540, 1639.
            London: Hakluyt Society.

Alvim, P. de T.
    1972   Potencial Agrícola de Amazônia.   Ciencia e
            Cultura 24:437-443.

    1980   Agricultural Production Potential of the Amazon
            Region.   In F. Barbira-Scazzocchio, ed., Land,
            People, and Planning in Contemporary Amazônia.
            Cambridge, UK: Cambridge Univ. Centre for Latin
            American Studies, Occasional Publ. 3.

ARC (Anthropology Resource Center)
1981   Brazil: A Decade of Disposition. Anthropology
        Resource Center Newsletter 5(3):2-3.

Bamberger, Joan
1967   Environmental and Cultural Classification: A
        Study of the Northern Cayapó. Ph.D. disserta-
        tion, Dept. of Social Relations, Harvard Univ.

Barbira-Scazzocchio, Françoise, ed.
1980   Land, People, and Planning in Contemporary
        Amazônia. Cambridge, UK: Cambridge Univ.
        Centre for Latin American Studies, Occasional
        Publ. 3.

Bentley, B. L.
1977   Extrafloral Nectaries and Protection of
        Pugnacious Body Bodyguards. Annual Review of
        Ecology and Systematics 8:407-427.

Carneiro, Robert
1974   Slash and Burn Cultivation among the Kwikuru
        and its Implications for Cultural Development
        in the Amazon Basin. In P. Lyon, ed., Native
        South Americans. Boston: Little, Brown.

Carvajal, Fr. Gaspar de
1934   The Discovery of the Amazon According to the
        Account of Friar Gaspar de Carvajal and Other
        Documents. H. C. Heaton, ed. New York:
        American Geographic Society, Special Publica-
        tion No. 17.

Cavalcante, Paulo
1972   Frutas Comestíveis de Amazônia, Vol. 1. Belém:
        Publicações Avulsas do Museu Goeldi.

1974   Frutas Comestíveis da Amazônia, Vol. 2. Belém:
        Publicações Avulsas do Museu Goeldi.

Chagnon, Napoleon
1968   Yanomamö: The Fierce People. New York: Holt,
        Rinehart and Winston.

Davis, Shelton H.
1977   Victims of the Miracle: Development and the
        Indians of Brazil. New York: Cambridge Univ.
        Press.

Denevan, William M., ed.
1976   The Native Population of the Americas in 1492.
        Madison: Univ. of Wisconsin Press.

Dobyns, Henry F.
1966   Estimating Aboriginal American Population.
        Current Anthropology 7:395-416.

Eckholm, Erik and L. R. Brown
1977   Spreading Deserts: The Hand of Man. World
        Watch Paper No. 13. Washington, D.C.: World
        Watch Institute.

Farnsworth, Edward and Frank Golley, eds.
1974   Fragile Ecosystems: Evaluation of Research and
        Application in the Neotropics. New York:
        Springer-Verlag.

Frechione, John
1981   Economic Self-Development by Yekuana Amerinds
        in Southern Venezuela. Ph.D. dissertation,
        Dept. of Anthropology, Univ. of Pittsburgh.

Gilbert, L. E. and Peter H. Raven, eds.
1975   Coevolution of Animals and Plants. Austin:
        Univ. of Texas Press.

Gómez-Pompa, A., C. Vásquez-Yañes, and S. Guevara
1972   The Tropical Rain Forest: A Nonrenewable
        Resource? Science 177:762-765.

Goodland, Robert J.A.
1975   The Cerrado Ecosystem of Brazil. Paris:
        United Nations Educational, Scientific, and
        Cultural Organization (UNESCO).

1980   Environmental Ranking of Amazonian Development
        Projects in Brazil. Environmental Conservation
        7(1):9-26.

Goodland, Robert J.A. and H. S. Irwin
1977   Amazonian Forest and Cerrado: Development and
        Environmental Conservation. In G. T. Prance and
        T. Elias, eds., Extinction is Forever. New York:
        New York Botanical Garden.

1975   Amazon Jungle: Green Hell to Red Desert?
        Amsterdam: Elsevier.

Gottleib, Otto R.
1981   New and Underutilized Plants in the Americas:
        Solution to Problems of Inventory through
        Systematics. Interciencia 6(1):22-29.

Hecht, Susanna B.
1982   Cattle Ranching in the Amazon: Analysis of a
        Development Strategy. Ph.D. dissertation, Dept.
        of Geography, Univ. of California, Berkeley.

Kempton, Willett
1978   Category Grading and Taxonomic Relations: A Mug
        is a Sort of a Cup. American Ethnologist 5:
        44-65.

Kerr, W. E. and C. R. Clement
1980   Práticas Agrícolas de Conseqüências Genéticas
        que Possibilitaram aos Índios de Amazônia uma
        Melhor Adaptação às Condições Ecológicas da
        Região. Acta Amazônica 10(2):251-261.

Kerr, W. E., Darrell A. Posey, and W. Wolter Filho,
1978   Cupá, ou Cipó Babão, Alimento de Alguns Índios
        Amazônicos. Acta Amazônica 8(4):702-705.

Lathrap, Donald
1968   Aboriginal Occupation and Changes in River
        Channel on the Central Ucayali, Peru.
        American Antiquity 33:62-79.

1970   The Upper Amazon. London: Thames and Hudson.

Lovejoy, Thomas E. and H.O.R. Schubart
1980   The Ecology of Amazonian Development.   In F.
        Barbira-Scazzocchio, ed., Land, People, and
        Planning in Contemporary Amazônia. Cambridge,
        UK: Cambridge University Centre for Latin
        American Studies, Occasional Publ. 3.

McDonald, D. R.
1977   Food Taboos: A Primitive Environmental Pro-
        tection Agency (South America). Antropos
        2:734-747.

Maybury-Lewis, David
1974   Akwě-Shavante Society. New York: Oxford Univ.
        Press.

Meggers, Betty J.
1971   Amazônia: Man and Culture in a Counterfeit
        Paradise. Chicago: Aldine.

Moran, Emilio F.
1974   The Adaptive System of the Amazonian Caboclo.
        In C. Wagley, ed., Man in the Amazon.
        Gainesville: Univ. of Florida Press.

1980   Mobility and Resource Use in Amazônia.   In F.
        Barbira-Scazzocchio, ed., Land, People, and
        Planning in Contemporary Amazônia. Cambridge,
        UK: Cambridge University Centre for Latin
        American Studies, Occasional Publ. 3.

1981   Developing the Amazon. Bloomington: Indiana

254

Univ. Press.

1982   Human Adaptability. Boulder, Colo.: Westview
        Press. Originally published in 1979.

Myers, Thomas
   1973   Toward Reconstruction of Prehistoric Community
           Patterns in the Amazonian Basin. In D. Lathrap
           and J. Douglas, eds., Variation in Anthropology.
           Urbana: Illinois Archaeological Survey.

   1974   Spanish Contacts and Social Change on the
           Ucayali River, Perú. Ethnohistory 21(2):135-157.

   1981a   Aboriginal Trade Networks in Amazônia. In
           P. D. Francis, F. J. Kense, and P. G. Duke, eds.,
           Networks of the Past: Regional Interaction in
           Archaeology. Calgary: Chacmool.

   1981b   Ethnic Composition and Settlement Patterns on
           the Amazon at the Time of Contact. Paper
           presented at the Annual Meeting, American
           Society for Ethnohistory, Colorado Springs,
           Colorado.

National Academy of Sciences
   1975   Underexploited Tropical Plants with Promising
           Economic Value. Washington, D.C.: National
           Academy of Sciences.

Parker, Eugene
   1982   Cultural Ecology and Change: A Caboclo Várzea
           Community in the Brazilian Amazon. Ph.D.
           dissertation, Dept. of Geography, Univ. of
           Colorado, Boulder.

Pimentel, David
   1979   Increased CO_2 Effects on the Environment and in
           Turn on Agriculture and Forestry. AAAS-DOE
           Workshop on Environmental and Societal Con-
           sequences of a Possible CO_2-Induced Climate
           Change, Annapolis, Maryland.

Pimentel, David and N. Goodman
   1978   Ecological Basis for the Management of Insect
           Populations. OIKOS 30:422-437.

Pimentel, David, S. A. Levin, and D. Olson
   1978   Coevolution and the Stability of Exploiter-
           Victim. The American Naturalist 112(983):
           119-125.

Posey, Darrell A.
1978   Ethnoentomological Survey of Amerind Groups in
        Lowland Latin America. The Florida Entomologist
        61(4):225-229.

1979a   Kayapó Controla Inseto com Uso Adequado do
        Ambiente. Revista de Atualidade Indígena
        3(14):47-58.

1979b   Kayapó Mostra Aldeia de Origem. Revista de
        Atualidade Indígena 3(15):50-57.

1979c   Cisão dos Kayapó, Revista de Atualidade
        Indígena 3(16):52-58.

1979d   Ethnoentomology of the Gorotire Kayapó of
        Central Brazil. Ph.D. dissertation, Dept. of
        Anthropology, Univ. of Georgia.

1980   Algunas Observaciones Etnoentomológicas sobre
        Grupos Amerindos en la América Latina.
        América Indígena 15(1):105-120.

1981a   Apicultura Popular dos Kayapó. Revista de
        Atualidade Indígena 20(1):36-41.

1981b   Ethnoentomology of the Kayapó Indians of Central
        Brazil. Journal of Ethnobiology 1(1):165-174.

(1982a) Nomadic Agriculture of the Amazon. Garden
        (New York Botanical Garden). 6(1):18-24.

(1982b) Folk Apiculture of the Kayapó Indians of Brazil.
        Biotropica. In press.

(1982c) Ethnomethodology as an Emic Guide to Cultural
        Systems: The Case of the Insects and the Kayapó
        Indians of Amazônia. Antropológica (Univ. de
        Brasília). In press.

(1982d) A Non-Lineal Universe and the Struggle for
        Survival. Revista Brasileira de Antropologia.
        In press.

(1982e) The Journey of a Kayapó Shaman. Journal of
        Latin American Indian Literature. In Press.

(1982f) Keeping of Stingless Bees (Meliponidae) by the
        Kayapó Indians of Brazil. Journal of
        Ethnobiology. In press.

Posey, Darrell A. and Susanna B. Hecht
   in   Kayapó Indian Agriculture and its Effect on
prepara- Nutrients in Amazonian Soils.
tion

Ramos, Alcida
   1980   Development, Integration and the Ethnic
           Integrity of Brazilian Indians. In F. Barbira-
           Scazzocchio, ed., Land, People, and Planning in
           Contemporary Amazônia. Cambridge, UK: Cambridge
           University Centre for Latin American Studies,
           Occasional Publ. 3.

Rappaport, R. A.
   1967   Pigs for the Ancestors: Ritual in the Ecology
           of a New Guinea People. New Haven: Yale Univ.
           Press.

   1971   The Flow of Energy in an Agricultural Society.
           Scientific American 224(3):116-132.

Reichel-Dolmatoff, Gerardo
   1971   Amazonian Cosmos. Chicago: Univ. of Chicago
           Press.

   1976   Cosmology as Ecological Analysis: A View from
           the Rain Forest. Man 11(3):307-318.

   1978   Desana Animal Categories, Food Restrictions,
           and the Concept of Color Energies. Journal of
           Latin American Lore 4(2):243-291.

Ribeiro, Darcy
   1970   Os Índios e a Civilização. Editôra Civilização
           Brasileira.

Ross, Eric B.
   1978a   Food Taboos, Diet, and Hunting Strategy: The
           Adaptation to Animals in Amazon Cultural
           Ecology. Current Anthropology 19(1):1-16.

   1978b   The Evolution of the Amazon Peasantry. Journal
           of Latin American Studies 10(2):193-218.

Schubart, H.O.R.
   1977   Ecological Criteria for the Agricultural
           Development of the Drylands in Amazônia.
           Acta Amazônica 7(4):559-567.

Sioli, Harold
   1973   Recent Human Activities in the Brazilian Amazon
           Region and their Ecological Effects. In B.
           Meggers et al., eds., Tropical Forest Ecosystems
           in Africa and South America. Washington, D.C.:

Smithsonian Institution.

1980   Foreseeable Consequences of Actual Development
        Schemes and Alternative Ideas. In F. Barbira-
        Scazzocchio, ed., Land, People, and Planning in
        Contemporary Amazônia. Cambridge, UK: Cambridge
        University Centre for Latin American Studies,
        Occasional Publ. 3.

Smith, Nigel J.H.
    1980   Anthrosols and Human Carrying Capacity in
            Amazônia. Annals of the Association of American
            Geographers 70(4):553-566.

    1981   Man, Fishes, and the Amazon. New York:
            Columbia Univ. Press.

Stout, Mickey and Ruth Thomson
    1974   Fonémica Txukuhamei (Kayapó). Série Lingüistica
            3:153-176.

Turner, Terrence
    1966   Social Structure and Political Organization
            among the Northern Cayapó. Ph.D. dissertation,
            Dept. of Social Relations, Harvard Univ.

Vickers, William T.
    1976   Cultural Adaptation to Amazonian Habitats.
            Ph.D. dissertation, Dept. of Anthropology,
            Univ. of Florida.

Williams, Llewelyn
    1960   Little-Known Wealth of Tropical Forests.
            Proceedings, Fifth World Congress, Seattle
            (Vol. 3), pp. 2003-2007.

Wood, Charles H. and Marianne Schmink
    1979   Blaming the Victim. Studies in Third World
            Societies 7:77-93.

10
Peasant and Capitalist Production in the Brazilian Amazon: A Conceptual Framework for the Study of Frontier Expansion

Charles H. Wood

INTRODUCTION

A central feature of the contemporary settlement of the Brazilian Amazon is the simultaneous expansion into the region of capitalist enterprises and peasant farmers. The dual character of the frontier is, to a large extent, a consequence of the development policies adopted by the state. The Program for National Integration (PIN), launched with much fanfare in 1970, explicitly envisioned the creation of a class of prosperous small farmers. The construction of the Transamazon Highway and the creation of publicly financed colonization projects were among the key programs undertaken by the federal government (Camargo 1973). By providing land to the landless the PIN was designed to relieve population pressure in the Northeast and to elevate the standard of living in rural areas. These measures, highly publicized throughout Brazil, stimulated the immigration of small farmers in search of agricultural plots (Moran 1981; Smith 1981).

The public colonization scheme, coordinated by the newly created National Institute for Colonization and Agrarian Reform (INCRA), was the cornerstone of the overall development strategy that included numerous other initiatives. In conjunction with the effort to settle small farmers, government agencies, notably the Superintendency for the Development of the Amazon (SUDAM), offered an array of incentives to attract private capital to the region (Kleinpenning 1975). By the late 1970s, however, priorities shifted away from federally funded colonization projects, and the preference for large-scale investments in Amazonia became the dominant theme in development planning (Cardoso and Muller 1977; Wood and Schmink 1979). This policy trend has been interpreted as the institutional "closing of the frontier" to poor migrants who nonetheless continue to stream into the Amazon (Schmink 1982; Silva 1979).

The relative dominance in the regional economy of large capitalist venture and small farmer production will

profoundly influence the character of the development
process underway in Amazonia. The range of possible outcomes is defined by the questions raised by concerned
analysts: Will the socioeconomic transformations taking
place lead to the formation of a viable small farming
system and, hence, to a more equitable distribution of
income and land ownership (as the PIN anticipated)? Or,
does the frontier expansion in Amazonia embody the reproduction of the highly polarized class structure typical
of the rest of the country (as the current development
priorities would appear to suggest)?

The very size and diversity of the Amazon makes any
generalization about the region precarious. Moreover, the
difficulties involved in carrying out social science research are compounded by the speed of the changes underway. But, quite apart from these essentially logistical
problems are other issues that, from the standpoint of
the theory and the method of research, are equally
important. Of special concern are two aspects of the
existing body of Amazon-related research that undermine
our ability to address the question posed above.

One is the incomplete and selective nature of the
available findings. While small farmers have been a
principal target of social science study (perhaps because
they are relatively powerless and hence accessible to the
investigator), scant attention has been given to corporate entities and to other powerful investors (for an
exception, see Pompermayer 1979). The record, as a consequence, is weak with regard to precisely those groups
whose actions have the most far-reaching and decisive
impact on the evolving pattern of land use in Amazonia.

A second issue is the need to abandon the standard
approach that implicitly treats capitalist and noncapitalist forms of production as discrete entities.
It is necessary to construct, in its place, a framework
that conceptualizes the various social actors on the
frontier as interrelated parts of a single system. A
brief overview of pertinent research findings presented
in the following section provides the basis for elaborating
such an alternative perspective.

PERSPECTIVES ON THE FRONTIER

Much of the existing literature on the Brazilian
frontier focuses exclusively on small farmers. Although
limited in its scope to the level of the farm, the findings generated from this research tradition contribute to
an assessment of the feasibility of agricultural production in Amazonia. Moran's (1981) study of an official
colonization project along the Transamazon Highway, for
example, looks at ecological, institutional, and individual
processes of change. His results indicate that, given
appropriate environmental and institutional knowledge,
a substantial proportion of the colonists could achieve

relatively high levels of income and productivity (see also Smith 1978). As a group, the farmers and their families successfully established a stable community life, despite the initial hardships endured (Moran 1981: Chapter 9). Even in Rondônia, where the investment in basic infrastructure was far less than in Altamira, colonists were able to overcome massive obstacles. "What is amazing," Mueller (1980:151) concludes, "is not that the colonization projects did not become the model cases dreamt by INCRA in 1970, when the PIN was conceived, but that, in spite of enormous difficulties they face, so many of the migrants were able to survive and continue to struggle."

By confirming the possibility of establishing small farms, these findings contradict the widely held negative view of the region's agricultural potential (see also Chapter 5 by Nicholaides et al. in this volume). This pessimistic conclusion, drawn primarily from aggregate data on Amazonian soils, overlooks the marked variability in soil types revealed by site-specific sampling techniques (Moran 1975; Fearnside 1978). If development planning is sensitive to this micro-environmental heterogeneity (Moran 1981) and if the necessary infrastructure is provided (Mueller 1980), colonists can be expected to prosper. Because these findings counter arguments that would, on purely "technical" or "ecological" grounds, eliminate the small farmer from consideration (see, for example, SUDAM 1976), they play an important role in the current debate over the style of development appropriate to Amazonia.

Participants in planned communities, however, are a special group of small farmers. Other things being equal, the 100-hectare lots provided by INCRA constitute a sufficiently large resource base to permit year-round employment of the head of the household and the working-age members of the unit. Moreover, within the boundaries of the project, the colonist's claim to his land is relatively secure. Not all farmers have definitive title to the lot that they work. But, as members of an official settlement scheme, they are nonetheless afforded a degree of protection from direct expropriation.

Neither of these conditions applies to the vast majority of migrants to Amazonia. Those who attempt to stake out a lot beyond the limits of a government-sponsored project are extremely vulnerable. Speculators, cattle ranchers, and other interest groups that compete for land on the frontier pose a constant threat to the small farmer. As a result, the migrant is often relegated to agricultural plots that are too small to meet subsistence requirements, and he has no guarantee that he will be able to hang on to what little land he may have cleared.

It is generally understood that the relationship between small farmers and capitalist entrepreneurs changes with the expansion and consolidation of the agricultural frontier. Attempts to conceptualize this process typically seek to identify the various stages by which a region is settled and then incorporated into the national economy. Katzman (1976) refers to the change from a "subsistence" to a "market-oriented" frontier. Similarly, Martins (1975) distinguishes between the "expansion" and the "pioneer" front, while Foweraker (1981: Chapter 2), adding a third category to the process of occupation of land, identifies the "non-capitalist," the "pre-capitalist," and the "capitalist" stages. Each of the proposed typologies stress somewhat different factors (see also Velho 1972; Reboratti 1979), yet all of them share, to a greater or lesser degree, the same essential elements.

In the initial stage, the frontier is isolated from the national system of production and distribution. Traditional extractive activities exist, but there is no market for land or for labor. Peasant migrants (posseiros) informally appropriate state property for the production of subsistence crops, plus a small marketable surplus. Labor exchange, clientage, debt relations, and forced work are common forms of labor control. In the subsequent stage (or stages, depending on the scheme adopted), agriculture is capitalized, and the newly settled region is progressively linked to the national economy. Concurrently, there is heavy in-migration, an increase in the price of land, and the emergence of a wage labor market. Although the petty commodity sector persists, and may even expand, capitalist social relations of production become dominant.

The reorganization of the structure of production and accumulation, which defines the stages of the moving frontier noted above, does not occur without social conflict. The penetration of capitalism implies the private appropriation of the means of production and the creation of a "free" labor force. The imposition of these conditions is resisted by those engaged in the non-capitalist sector. This fundamental antagonism is concretely expressed in the struggle for land, a form of class conflict peculiar to the frontier. Disputed claims are resolved through violence, or through face-to-face negotiation between the various parties. In other instances, the state is more directly involved via the intervention of bureaucratic or legal institutions. But, with or without the mediation of the state, there is a systematic tendency for the outcome of land conflicts to lead to the concentration of land ownership and to the creation of a semi-proletarianized labor force compelled to work on a seasonal basis in clearing and logging operations (Schmink 1982).

The appeal of stage theories of development lies in the identification of critical moments in the transition from one system of production to another. Although the categories singled out by the various frameworks are

neither discrete nor mutually exclusive, they serve to
order the discussion and the analysis of the process
whereby the rural economy is transformed. But an approach
that divides social change into consecutive stages is
premised on a dualist conception of social structure, a
factor that ultimately renders the perspective insensitive
to some of the principal mechanisms by which change occurs.
      According to the dualist model the frontier is
comprised of two radically different economies: the
traditional, noncapitalist sector, which is subsistence-
oriented and has minimal ties to the marketplace; and the
modern, capitalist sector, which is market-oriented and
which follows the logic of profit maximization.   As in
the case of earlier dualist frameworks (e.g., Lewis 1954)
the two forms of production are treated, for the most
part, as largely independent of one another (Foweraker
1981 is an exception).   To the extent that they are viewed
as related at all, the emphasis is generally on the
antagonisms between the two sectors.   Thus, the underlying
cause of the high incidence of violence on the frontier
is attributed, as noted earlier, to the conflict of
interest between the capitalist and the noncapitalist
economies.
      The opposition between capitalist and small farmer
agriculture, however, is only one aspect of the interaction between the two forms of production.   In addition
to the direct and unequal competition between them,
functional relationships also exist that link the
capitalist and the noncapitalist sectors.   Thus, the
presence of a subsistence economy may, through various
mechanisms, enhance the profitability of capitalist
production.   Similarly, the penetration of capitalist
social relations on the frontier may bolster rather than
destroy the small farm sector.   From this standpoint
the capitalist and the noncapitalist economies are neither
separate nor autonomous, as the dualist model would have
it, but are viewed instead as integral parts of the same
regional system.
      A more systematic elaboration of this approach is
presented in the following section.   Of special concern
is the definition of the basic concepts and relationships
that serve to identify the capitalist and the noncapitalist modes of production.   On the basis of this
distinction, the framework is then used to illustrate the
various mechanisms by which the two modes are interrelated.   Subsequent sections of this study specify the
way in which the social relations of production that
emerge on the frontier, and the manner in which different
forms of production are (or are not) articulated, are
conditioned by such factors as the role of the state,
the degree of social conflict, and the relative supply
of labor.

THE ARTICULATION OF MODES OF PRODUCTION

The first task to confront in a conceptual framework that purports to analyze modes of production is an unambiguous definition of capitalism. Despite its currency, the meaning of the concept is much debated.[1] For the purpose of this discussion, a capitalist system is one where the laborer neither owns nor controls the means of production (in this case land). In return for a wage, the worker sells his labor power to the landowning class. The wage received, however, reflects only a portion of the value the worker creates, the balance being appropriated by the employer as unpaid labor (surplus value). Thus, the capitalist mode is characterized by the particular form of surplus extraction that occurs through the social relations that unite landowner and laborer in the profit-oriented production of marketable commodities. Thus defined, capitalism is a distinct phenomenon that can be identified historically, and the structure of which can be distinguished from noncapitalist forms, of which there are many variants.[2]

Capitalist and noncapitalist social relations co-exist, not in isolation of one another, but rather as interrelated aspects of the frontier economy. To explore the implications of this interaction, researchers have amended the classic Marxist view of the Manifesto--i.e., that noncapitalistic economic formations are destroyed everywhere that capitalism expands. They argue that various modes of production exist simultaneously within a given social formation, and that these modes are "articulated" with one another. The precise meaning of this term is much debated, and its usage has undergone many transformations (see Bartra 1975; Bradby 1975; Coello 1975; Olmeda 1976). The term as Foster-Carter (1978:214) put it, is not "simply a long-winded synonym for (say) 'link,' and thus a typically sociological instance of never using words of one syllable when five will do." Rather, it refers to capitalism's paradoxical relationship to other modes of production: on the one hand capitalism undermines noncapitalist formations; on the other it serves to preserve, and in some instances even extend, the noncapitalist economy (Bettelheim 1972: 297).

To say that modes of production are articulated implies, specifically, that a transfer of value takes place from one mode to another. The mechanisms whereby this occurs vary from direct and forcible appropriation to methods that are complex and indirect. In order to identify the various ways in which a transfer of surplus is achieved we can, for the sake of clarity, confine attention to peasant producers. Three issues are of specific concern: primitive accumulation, the migration of labor, and the labor-intensive production of commodities. The discussion that follows is presented primarily

to outline the principal lines of reasoning that follow
from a conceptual framework based on modes of production
and their articulation. The examples do not constitute
an empirical analysis of a particular case. They serve
only to illustrate the central elements of a perspective
that provides a theoretical alternative to the dualist
approach.

Primitive Accumulation

Legal rights to land in newly settled areas are
notoriously confused, especially in the initial stages of
an expanding frontier. As a consequence of the overlapping authority of state and federal institutions, the
intricacies of legal procedures in Brazil, and, in some
instances, because of outright fraud, land on the frontier
is often titled many times over. As a result, there is
little security of land ownership, even for those who
hold documents that lay claim to clearly bounded areas.
For the posseiro (squatter) who bypasses government
institutions and merely occupies land, the insecurity is
greater. Although special circumstances entitle the
posseiro to certain rights, in practice he can rarely
muster the legal or economic resources to defend himself
(see Schmink 1982).
As the frontier is linked to wider markets, property
values rise, the competition for land intensifies, and
the posseiro becomes increasingly vulnerable to expropriation. Where legal rights to private property are in
dispute, it is a common occurrence for land speculators
and cattle ranches to expand into areas of peasant production. The small farmer is forcibly dispossessed without compensation for the value of the labor he has
expended, or for the other investments that he may have
made to clear and cultivate his plot. In this instance
the transfer of value from the noncapitalist to the
capitalist mode of production is achieved through non-
economic coercion, or plunder.
Insofar as the peasant farmer is divorced from the
means of production, the appropriation that takes place
is primitive accumulation. In its original formulation
the concept implied the conversion of peasants to
proletarians, a transformation that provided the historical
conditions for the emergence of capitalism. But such a
total transformation, as Foweraker (1981: Chapter 8)
notes, cannot occur on the frontier where there is more
land to take into production. While some of those who have
lost their land may work for wages in new capitalist
enterprises in the countryside, others move further on to
repeat the process of "spontaneous" occupation of land in
more distant places. From this standpoint the primitive
accumulation that occurs on the frontier is a hybrid
form: it may impel the transition to capitalist social
relations, yet, at the same time, it may also expand the

noncapitalist economic environment (Foweraker 1981:176).

Labor Migration

In contrast to primitive accumulation, which represents a direct and often violent transfer of value, there
are indirect and less-coercive forms of articulation.
One example is the seasonal circulation of labor between
the peasant and the capitalist economy. The theoretical
implications of this movement can be explored through a
discussion of the expansion of cattle ranches in the
Amazon frontier. In the case of Brazil, the process
whereby pastures are created occurs in different ways
depending on the size of capital involved. An examination
of each method illustrates the various forms of articulation associated with the migration of labor.

Large-scale capitalist ventures employ a combination
of archaic and advanced technologies at different stages
in the formation of cattle ranches. In some instances
thoroughly mechanized procedures are used to clear the
tree cover and to plant pasture grass. A more common
method is to use rudimentary technology and traditional
forms of worker recruitment, at least during the most
labor-intensive phase. Crew leaders (gatos) are contracted to hire and supervise work gangs who use machetes,
axes, and occasionally chain saws to fell the vegetation.
The employment is seasonal because the demand for such
labor exists only during the dry months (June to
September-October). It is also transitory because the
large unskilled labor force is no longer needed after the
land is prepared for pasture. Once the cattle ranch is
in operation, it employs only a small number of skilled
workers.

Small capital relies on mechanisms that differ substantially from those described above. Unable to muster
the resources to employ equipment or large work crews,
the small rancher must turn to clearing strategies that
take longer, and that expose him to greater risk. The
practice goes by the name troca pela forma, or (roughly)
"exchange for the formation (of pasture)." As the term
implies, the arrangement entails an exchange agreement
between the landholder and the worker (and his family).
The landholder turns over to the latter a portion of the
property to be cleared and planted. Following the first
harvest of food crops, the farmer agrees to plant grass
where rice and beans once grew. The rancher thus gains
an additional plot of pasture and the farmer, if he is
lucky, produces sufficient food staples to tide him and
his family over another season. The agreement is sometimes further extended in favor of the landholder to
include a share of the farmer's crop. The "exchange for
the formation" contract is repeated year after year until
the pasture is completely established, whereupon the
farmer and his family must search elsewhere for the means

of their survival.[3]

The formation of pastures through the seasonal and transitory employment of work gangs represents an articulation of modes of production via the movement of labor from the noncapitalist to the capitalist economy. In the Marxist framework the value of labor power is determined, like that of any commodity, by the labor time necessary for the reproduction and the maintenance of the worker. In a fully capitalist system the cost of the reproduction of labor is primarily covered by the direct wages paid to the worker during employment. The rest is accounted for by the indirect wages he receives in the form of social security benefits, unemployment compensation, and health care services institutionalized by the welfare state. However, in a rural area characterized by the simultaneous existence of more than one mode of production, labor power physically reproduced in a noncapitalist economy can enter into the circuit of capitalist production at a level of remuneration that covers only a small part of the total cost of the maintenance and the reproduction of the worker.

According to this argument, the preservation of semi-autonomous households, that are compelled to send some members into the market in search of part-time wage employment, facilitates the expansion of capitalist enterprises by serving as a source of "cheap" labor during periods of peak demand. Labor power produced in a non-capitalist economy need only be remunerated at a level that covers the immediate sustenance of the worker while on the job. Easily laid off at the end of the season, the worker returns to the subsistence plot that is managed by other household members during the period of absence. In effect, this implies that the remainder of the maintenance and reproduction cost of labor is shifted back to the subsistence economy until the next season, when the cycle is repeated (Long 1977:101; Meillasoux 1974; Portes 1978; Wolpe 1975). The availability of low-cost labor, which bolsters the viability of capitalist production, thus stems partly from the patterns of seasonal migration that constitute the sustenance strategies formulated by households in the noncapitalist mode of production (see Wood 1981).

The combined troca pela forma and sharecropping arrangement employed by small capital represents a more extreme form of exploitation, which operates in three different ways. Some portion of the surplus product generated by the small farmer is appropriated directly by the rancher as a form of rent. Second, the value of the farmer's labor expended to clear an agricultural plot to reproduce his own existence is subsequently transferred to the rancher in the form of an area of finished pasture. The arrangement further operates in favor of capital in that, once the whole pasture is completed, the worker and his family are divorced from the means of production, and are forced to enter a similar agreement with another

landholder. _Troca_ _pela_ _forma_ can thus be viewed as a
kind of institutionalized primitive accumulation whereby
small capital is guaranteed a supply of labor however
pernicious the terms of exchange may be for the farmer.

The Production of Commodities

As in the case of the production of low-cost labor
in the noncapitalist sector, the peasant economy also
serves as a source of cheap commodities. The intensive
application of the peasant's own labor power, together
with that of members of his household, implies that
staple goods and raw materials can enter the market at a
cost lower than that which would obtain if they were
produced in a system based on capitalist social relations.
As a consequence, the presence of a peasant economy can,
in some instances, retard the expansion of capitalism.
Unlike the remarkable resilience of peasant producers
(Chayanov 1966), agriculturalists who are dependent on
wage laborers and who compete with peasants are unable to
survive low crop prices during periods of depression.
Brading's (1977) work on Mexico, for example, documents
historical instances in which the expansion of capitalist
production was forestalled by the prevalence of a peasant
economy in the region studied.

On the Brazilian frontier, capitalist enterprises
rarely compete with peasants in the production of rice,
beans, and other staples. Under these circumstances, it
is argued that the availability of low-cost commodities
operates in favor of capital (Foweraker 1981; Velho 1972),
a conclusion derived from the analysis of the labor
process in the capitalist mode. Within the firm, the
ratio between surplus labor and necessary labor (which
accrues to the worker in the form of wages), is, in Marx's
terms, the rate of surplus value. Other things being
equal, the rate of surplus value, and consequently the
rate of profit, varies inversely with the proportion of
time devoted to necessary labor (Wolpe 1975). It follows
that the availability of low-cost commodities reduces the
proportion of necessary labor time, and increases the rate
of surplus value. In other words, the capitalist enterprise can pay lower wages and hence reap higher profits
as a result of the production of low-cost commodities in
the highly labor-intensive peasant economy.

LAND SCARCITY, VIOLENCE, AND THE STATE

The discussion in the previous section of the
principal mechanisms by which a transfer of value can
occur between modes of production provides the basis for
an analysis of the way these relationships are modified
by the constellation of socioeconomic, political, and
demographic events that characterize different stages in
the process of frontier expansion. A brief study of

selected aspects of the Brazilian Amazon serves to illustrate this point. Of special interest is the concentration of landholdings, the level of social conflict, and
the initiatives undertaken by the state. Specifically,
the objective is to examine how these factors influence
the type of social relations that emerge, and how they
affect the manner in which capitalist and noncapitalist
forms of production are articulated.

To demonstrate these interrelationships, examples
are drawn from field work carried out in 1976 and in 1978
in the southern region of the state of Pará, Brazil. As
in the earlier sections of this paper, the discussion
that follows does not strive to present a thorough
empirical analysis of the moving frontier. The principal
objective, rather, is only to illustrate how the evolution of capitalist and peasant production is contingent
on the interplay of forces that comprise particular
historic moments in the process of frontier expansion.
To explore this issue I will begin with a discussion of
the implications of the most central aspect of the
economy in this region of Brazil: the concentration of
land ownership.

Land Scarcity

Despite the expanse of unoccupied territory in
Amazonia, the largest proportion of accessible land is
monopolized by a relatively small number of landholders.
While the expansion of the frontier has brought vast new
areas into use, analysis of the recent agricultural
censuses indicate that the distribution of landownership,
as reflected by changes in the Gini coefficient between
1970 and 1975, has become increasingly concentrated
(Hoffman 1979).

In an agricultural region the monopoly of land is
among the principal conditions that permit the emergence
of capitalist social relations. As numerous observers
note, there is an incompatibility between the existence
of a free peasantry, an open agricultural frontier, and
a class of nonworking landholders. If peasants have free
access to land, they can hardly be induced to work for
others, or to migrate in search of jobs (Balán 1979;
Domar 1970). In Marx's (1967 Vol. I:767) words: "So
long ... as the laborer can accumulate for himself--and
this he can do so long as he remains possessor of the
means of production--capitalist accumulation and the
capitalist mode of production are impossible."

The concentration of landholdings on the frontier
permits capitalist accumulation in several ways. What
land is available to the smallholder, at least in areas
outside the official colonization projects, results in
the reproduction of the minifundio-latifundio complex.
The creation of semi-autonomous households in need of
sources of supplemental income makes available to capital

a ready supply of temporary labor. The presence of a
peasant economy, which absorbs the maintenance and reproduction costs of the work force during periods of unemployment, also serves to lower the cost of labor.
Large cattle ranches that rely heavily on seasonal workers
for land clearing are thus guaranteed a supply of workers
that can be recruited at low wages.

In areas of heavy in-migration the concentration of
landholdings creates intense population pressure. This
factor, in turn, is the sine qua non for the existence of
such institutions as troca pela forma. This can be
posited on the reasonable assumption that a migrant,
rather than subject himself to the extreme exploitation
entailed in this arrangement, would opt, if the opportunity were available, for even a small plot of his own
land. Indeed, it can be hypothesized that, ceteris
paribus, the prevalence of this institution is directly
proportional to the degree of surplus population. By
making troca pela forma possible, we can conclude that
land scarcity contributes to the viability of small
capital on the frontier.

Violence

The intensity of social conflict in an area (which
itself is related to the scarcity of land) can also
modify the character of the social relations of production
that emerge. During periods of calm, small ranchers can
engage in troca pela forma with the assurance that the
contract can be enforced. However, when claims to private
property are disputed and when land conflict is prevalent,
the small rancher may run a considerable risk in adopting
this method to establish a pasture. If he permits a
group of families onto his land he may find it difficult
to drive them off at the end of the harvest. The practice
of troca pela forma has thus fallen into disuse in those
areas in southern Pará where violent land conflicts have
become widespread.

In contrast to the small rancher, the threat of land
invasions at times forces large landholders to take
actions designed to foster a stable small farming sector.
One of the biggest cattle enterprises in the Conceição do
Araguaia area, for example, encourages the settlement of
migrants around the perimeter of the ranch. A patronage
relationship is established with them through the purchase
of rice, even when it is not needed, and by providing
part-time employment to those in economic straits. The
maintenance of a well-disposed and strategically located
group of small farmers creates a borderline communications
network that would otherwise require constant patrol to
establish. In an area of intense conflict over land,
small farmers, in effect, provide the large capitalist
firm a buffer against land invasions.

The State

The relationships discussed above place in clearer relief the fundamental contradictions that characterize the process of capitalist expansion in Amazonia. From the standpoint of the logic of capital accumulation, certain conditions are required. Because of the need for manpower it is necessary to attract population to the area. But a ready supply of cheap labor is not created if migrants are able to appropriate land and to become successful small farmers. To insure the availability of workers compelled to seek wage labor employment, access to the means of production must be curtailed. However, in places of heavy immigration the monopoly of land also creates the structural conditions for social conflict. In the later stages of frontier expansion an unstable pattern of land tenure, and the presence of widespread violence, jeopardizes further capital investment. Under these circumstances the state can be viewed as having two sometimes-contradictory functions: to preserve the conditions that permit the continued expansion of capitalist production, and, simultaneously, to prevent the degree of conflict from "getting out of hand."

An example of this form of government intervention is provided by the newly formed Grupo Executivo de Terras do Araguaia-Tocantins (GETAT), a committee of high-level civilians who report directly to the National Security Council. Armed with the power to cut through bureaucratic red tape, GETAT was created specifically to deal with the increasing prevalence of violent conflicts in southern Pará. Granted the authority to hand out land titles (which formerly had to be approved in Brasília), GETAT's objective is to carry out what Schmink (1982:24) calls a "crisis colonization" program. In areas of intense conflict, titles are given to migrants involved in a volatile dispute. These actions explicitly aim to reduce the level of social tension, to create a potential support group for government action in the region, and to undermine, through localized reform, the grounds for opposition to the government.

Such action is neither unique nor unprecedented. Indeed, the formation of GETAT represents the institutionalized recognition of practices that have long been carried out on an ad hoc basis in the region. On numerous occasions the federal government intervened directly in local matters on behalf of small farmers when the magnitude of the potential conflict posed a "problema social." In several cases in southern Pará the authorities acted in favor of large groups of small farmers who militantly opposed the efforts of cattle interests to remove them from the place they had settled.

Direct intervention by the state thus takes place sporadically, on a case-by-case basis, depending on the extent to which a confrontation between contending groups threatens to erupt into a major conflagration. State initiatives can therefore be seen to operate, in isolated instances, in the interest of small farmers, thereby perpetuating the existence of the noncapitalist economy. But these very actions, by defusing social conflict and by bolstering the legitimacy of public authority, foster the conditions that lead, in the later stages of the consolidation of the frontier, to the concentration of land ownership, to the implantation of a regime of private property, and to the dominance of capitalist social relations in the region.

CONCLUSIONS

The central objective of this paper has been to outline a conceptual framework for the study of frontier expansion. Of particular concern, as noted in the first section, is the need to move beyond the assumptions of duality that often underlie the analysis of social change and rural development. As the discussion of cattle ranching and peasant farming indicates, capitalist and noncapitalist modes of production should not be treated as discrete economies that exist and evolve in isolation from one another. The challenge, both conceptual and empirical, is to capture the interrelationships between them, and to specify the mechanisms by which the existence of one mode enhances or retards the expansion of the other. Approached in this way, the perspective outlined here recognizes the often-contradictory nature of the process of social change: Whereas in some instances the viability of the peasant economy may be bolstered, in other cases, the same forces may lead to its dissolution. These tendencies and countertendencies, however, do not imply that changes in the structure of the regional economy are idiosyncratic, hence unknowable. On the contrary, as the last section attempts to illustrate, the social relations of production that emerge on the frontier, and the manner in which different forms of production are interrelated, are conditioned by a limited number of factors subject to empirical investigation. Moreover, the discussion underscores the need to pay greater attention to capitalist production, and to abandon the tendency to treat it as homogeneous. The distinct investment strategies pursued by large and small ranchers, and the different implications of each course of action for small farmers, provide examples of the importance of accounting for different capitalist formations. Finally, the analysis presented, as I have sought to emphasize throughout, is suggestive and far from definitive. I hope the ideas put forth, as incomplete as they are, may contribute to our ability to make sense of the complexities that characterize the process of frontier expansion.

ACKNOWLEDGMENTS

This analysis is the result of field work carried out in 1976 and again in 1978. On both occasions a number of other people participated in the data collection. I am therefore indebted to the CEDEPLAR staff, and others affiliated with the study of migration in the area of Marabá in 1976: Carminha, Fernando, José Alberto, Marianne, Morvan, Malorí, Teresa, Tostão, and Totonho. The second stage of fieldwork included Marianne, Raquel, and Fernando. The data collection and the ongoing discussions with members of both teams provided many useful insights. Comments on an earlier draft of this paper were generously provided by Emilio Moran, Pamela Richards, Marianne Schmink, and Glaucio Soares. I am, however, solely responsible for the analysis presented here and for any errors of fact or theory that are contained in this paper.

NOTES

1. Capitalism, for example, is sometimes considered to be any commercial system of exchange that is based on profit rationality (see Frank 1969). But, as critics have noted (e.g., Laclau 1971), such a definition is historically imprecise since commerce and money exchange have existed since antiquity. For the term to retain any analytical utility capitalism must therefore be identified, not in the realm of exchange, but in the space of production and appropriation.

2. "Noncapitalist" is used rather than the more common term "pre-capitalist" to avoid unwarranted assumptions potentially implied by the latter. To speak of a pre-capitalist formation can mean one that is historically prior to capitalism, or one that is logically prior to capitalism. The first is empirically inaccurate; the second precludes the whole problem of articulations, which envisages the expansion of capitalism as a process that not only conserves ambiguous entities but even, in defiance of diachrony, actively creates them.

3. There are many variants of the _troca pela forma_ agreement. In some cases the landholder provides seeds and tools, and may establish with the farmer and his family a patron-client relationship that entails other forms of exchanges. The extent of exploitation in _troca pela forma_ is therefore of varying degrees. Depending on the terms of exchange and on other factors (e.g., the fact that the labor process is controlled by the farmer) it is possible that the _troca pela forma_ may not in all instances, as implied in the discussion here, be the worst of all options.

274

REFERENCES

Balán,J.
1979   Agrarian Structures and Internal Migration in
        a Historical Perspective: Latin American Case
        Studies. Mimeo.

Bartra, R.
1975   Sobre la Articulación de Modos de Producción en
        América Latina: Algunos Problemas Teóricos.
        Historia y Sociedad 5:5-19.

Bettelheim, C.
1972   Appendix I: Theoretical Comments. In A.
        Emmanuel, Unequal Exchange. London: New Left
        Books.

Bradby, B.
1975   The Destruction of Natural Economy. Economy
        and Society IV:127-161.

Brading, D.
1977   Hacienda Profits and Tenant Farming in the
        Mexican Bajio, 1700-1860. In P. Duncan and I.
        Rutledge, eds., Land and Labour in Latin
        America. Cambridge, UK: Cambridge Univ. Press.

Camargo, José G. de Cunha
1973   Urbanismo Rural. Brasília, D.F.: Instituto
        Nacional de Colonização e Reforma Agrária
        (INCRA).

Cardoso, Fernando H. and Geraldo Muller
1977   Amazônia: Expansão do Capitalismo. São Paulo:
        Editôra Brasiliense.

Chayanov, A. V.
1966   The Theory of Peasant Economy. Homewood, Ill.:
        American Economic Association.

Coello, M.
1975   Caracterización de la Pequeña Producción
        Mercantil Campesina. Historia y Sociedad 8:
        3-19.

Domar, E. D.
1970   The Causes of Slavery or Serfdom: A Hypothesis.
        Journal of Economic History XXX:18-32.

Fearnside, Philip M.
1978   Estimation of Carrying Capacity for Human Popu-
        lations in a Part of the Transamazon Coloniza-
        tion Area of Brazil. Ph.D. dissertation, Dept.
        of Biological Sciences, Univ. of Michigan.

Foster-Carter, A.
    1978   Can We Articulate 'Articulation'? In J. Clammer,
            ed., The New Economic Anthropology. New York:
            St. Martin's.

Foweraker, Joe
    1981   The Struggle for Land: A Political Economy of
            the Pioneer Frontier in Brazil, 1930 to the
            Present. London: Cambridge Univ. Press.

Frank, A. G.
    1969   Capitalism and Underdevelopment in Latin America:
            Historical Studies of Chile and Brazil. New
            York: The Free Press.

Hoffman, Rudolfo
    1979   A Concentracão da Posse da Terra no Brasil.
            Encontros com a Civilização Brasileira
            7:207-221.

Katzman, M. T.
    1976   Paradoxes of Amazonian Development in a
            'Resource-Starved' World. Journal of Developing
            Areas 10(4):445-460.

Kleinpenning, J.M.G.
    1975   The Integration and Colonization of the
            Brazilian Portion of the Amazon Basin.
            Nijmegen: Institute of Geography and Planning.

Laclau, E.
    1971   Feudalism and Capitalism in Latin America.
            New Left Review 67:19-38.

Lewis, W. A.
    1954   Economic Development with Unlimited Supplies of
            Labour. Manchester School of Economics and
            Social Sciences 22:139-191.

Long, N.
    1977   An Introduction to the Sociology of Rural
            Development. London: Tavistock.

Martins, José de Souza
    1975   Capitalismo e Tradicionalismo: Estudos sobre as
            Contradições da Sociedade Agrária no Brasil.
            São Paulo: Pioneira.

Marx, Karl
    1967   Das Capital. Volume I. New York: International
            Publishers.

Meillasoux, C.
    1974   Imperialism as a Mode of Reproduction of Labour

Power. Mimeo.

Moran, Emilio F.
1981   Developing the Amazon. Bloomington: Indiana
        Univ. Press.

1975   Pioneer Farmers of the Transamazon Highway.
        Ph.D. dissertation, Dept. of Anthropology,
        Univ. of Florida.

Mueller, Charles
1980   Frontier-Based Agricultural Expansion: The
        Case of Rondônia. In F. Barbira-Scazzocchio,
        ed., Land, People, and Planning in Contemporary
        Amazônia. Cambridge, UK: Cambridge University
        Centre for Latin American Studies Occasional
        Publ. 3.

Olmeda, Raúl
1976   Sobre la Articulación de Modos de Producción.
        Historia y Sociedad 10:5-16.

Pompermayer, Malorí José
1979   The State and the Frontier in Brazil: A Case
        Study of the Amazon. Ph.D. dissertation, Dept.
        of Political Science, Stanford Univ.

Portes, Alejandro
1978   Migration and Underdevelopment. Politics and
        Society 8(1):1-48.

Reboratti, Carlos E.
1979   Phases of the Colonization Cycle in the
        Misiones-Paraná. Paper presented at the
        Conference on the Development of Amazonia in
        Seven Countries, Cambridge, September 23-26.

Schmink, Marianne
1982   Land Conflicts in Amazonia. American
        Ethnologist 9(2):341-357.

Silva, José Graziano da
1979   A Porteira ja Esta Fechando? Revista Ensaios
        de Opinião, March.

Smith, Nigel J.H.
1978   Agricultural Productivity Along Brazil's
        Transamazon Highway. Agro-ecosystems 4:415-432.

1981   Colonization Lessons from a Tropical Forest.
        Science 214:755-761.

SUDAM
 1976   II Plano de Desenvolvimento de Amazônia:
         Detalhamento do II Plano Nacional de
         Desenvolvimento (1975-1979). Belém: Superin-
         tendency for Development of the Amazon (SUDAM).

Velho, Otávio G.
 1972   Frentes de Expansão e Estrutura Agrária.
         Rio de Janeiro: Zahar.

Wolpe, H.
 1975   The Theory of Internal Colonialism: The South
         African Case. In I. Oxaal, T. Barnett, and D.
         Booth, eds., Beyond the Sociology of Development:
         Economy and Society in Latin America and Africa.
         London: Routledge and Kegan Paul.

Wood, Charles H.
 1981   Structural Change and Household Strategies: A
         Conceptual Framework for the Study of Rural
         Migration. Human Organization 40:338-344.

Wood, Charles H. and Marianne Schmink
 1979   Blaming the Victim: Small Farmer Production in
         an Amazon Colonization Project. Studies in
         Third World Societies 7:77-93.

11
Stochastic Modeling in Human Carrying-Capacity Estimation: A Tool for Development Planning in Amazonia

Philip M. Fearnside

CARRYING CAPACITY IN AMAZONIAN DEVELOPMENT PLANNING

Human carrying capacity refers to the maximum human population size that can be supported indefinitely by a given area at an acceptable standard of living, without environmental degradation, and given certain assumptions regarding resource exploitation technology, consumption patterns, and the defining criteria for an acceptable living standard and levels of environmental degradation. The assumptions associated with carrying-capacity estimates have been a major limitation on attempts to make meaningful estimates. Relaxing the most restrictive assumptions is an important step in arriving at useful estimates. Along with the need for progress in theory, there is special urgency given the many humans who now live or soon will live with environmental degradation resulting from exceeding carrying capacity.

Carrying capacity provides an ideal framework for examining and organizing development goals. The focus of carrying-capacity estimation on sustainability is highly appropriate, and unfortunately often lacking, in development considerations (Fearnside 1979b). The question of adequate living standards must be addressed in estimating carrying capacity, as well as the question of to whom these standards apply. Distribution of income has a close link with carrying capacity and cannot be left out of development planning. Standards for permissible environmental degradation must also be addressed in assessing carrying capacity, as they should be in all development plans. The landscape can be viewed as a patchwork of areas to which different environmental quality standards apply (Margalef 1968; Odum 1969). Defining these standards, and the limits of different zones, as in demarcating the various classes of parks and reserves set aside by the Brazilian government, is an urgent priority following naturally from consideration of human carrying capacity. Consequences of ignoring carrying capacity in planning can be expected to be severe in terms of the

279

suffering and the sacrifice of other goals, such as areas designated for preservation of natural habitats, Amerindian tribes, and so forth.

Development planning is usually perceived as a process of optimization, often based on a measure such as gross national product (GNP), being maximized in the objective function of the optimization problem.[1] Standards are needed that better reflect public well-being than does GNP. GNP includes pollution, armaments, and many other "bads" among the "goods and services" measured, in addition to ignoring the distribution of the product within the population. Similarity exists between the per-capita consumption measures used in carrying-capacity estimation and appropriate measures of well-being for any index to be maximized in an objective function.[2] Carrying capacity must be included as one of the constraints within which any optimization is done.[3] Carrying capacity is one of several necessary constraints on sustainable development.

I view sustainable development as requiring at least five conditions, after first designating reserves from which such developments are excluded. First, human population must be maintained below sustainable carrying capacity. Second, agroecosystems employed must be agronomically sustainable at adequate levels of return. This includes a minimal demand on nonrenewable resources, restricted demand on renewable resources to allow regeneration, and an acceptable risk of failure from insect or disease attack, technological breakdown, or market fluctuations. Third, agroecosystems must be socially sustainable, not containing the seeds of their own destruction in the form of social injustice, reliance on unenforceable regulations, and the like. Fourth, a limit to concentration of land holdings must apply to prevent unacceptably high probabilities of failure at meeting minimal living standards. Fifth, there must be a limit to total consumption. Such a "limit to greed" presumably might be attained in part by restraining maximum consumption.

Carrying capacity estimation should be encouraged as a part of the planning process for all new colonization projects. Survey information would be needed for each area, together with information on expected population composition and agricultural technology levels to be applied. Improved chances of avoiding unacceptable colonist failure levels and environmental degradation justifies the added effort. Carrying-capacity information would lead to wiser choices of project types to be promoted. Such studies would encourage examination of underlying motives for colonization programs, as well as their long-term consequences. Ultimately, recognition of the limits implicit in carrying capacity would lead to a greater realization that colonization alone cannot solve social and economic problems often declared as primary goals of the programs. The roots of these problems--i.e., inequitable land distribution and exponential population growth--must be faced.

The most basic tenet of the concept of carrying capacity, namely that resources are finite, has not yet been accepted by many in Brazil and elsewhere, although recognition of these limits is slowly increasing. Amazonia is the region where the illusion of infinite resources is strongest, due to the vastness of the remaining forests relative to the perspective of any individual observer and the still-powerful myth of hidden "El Dorados." That the agricultural potential of each hectare in Amazonia is limited becomes quite clear in studying carrying capacity. Regardless of the level at which agricultural production becomes limited, the region's finite size immediately implies the limited capacity of Amazonia as a panacea for exponentially growing national problems. Purely as an illustration, if one were to make the highly improbable assumption that the entire 5 million square kilometer area of Brazil's Legal Amazon were divided equally into 100 hectare (1 km^2) lots, as was done in the Transamazon Highway colonization areas, only 5 million families, or about 25 million persons at 5 persons/family, would fill the entire region. This represents slightly less than eight years of growth for Brazil's 1980 population of 119 million, increasing at the current rate of 2.4% per year. Fine-tuning of lot sizes to fit carrying capacity would alter such a calculation somewhat and would bring the benefits of such estimates mentioned earlier, but population policy implications of finite land resources are evident even without such studies. Relationships of population size, land distribution, and production limitations of sustainable agroecosystems form an interlocking system with implications for any appropriate long-term development goal. Carrying-capacity estimation through stochastic simulation modeling is a valuable tool for achieving these goals.

A PROBABILISTIC APPROACH TO HUMAN CARRYING CAPACITY

Any plans to avoid exceeding carrying capacity cannot be made, and are unlikely to succeed, without reliable estimates of sustainable carrying capacity. Carrying capacity studies are thus closely linked with the fate of those who must live with future consequences of the current race to convert remaining areas of natural ecosystems into poorly understood, and even more poorly controlled, agroecosystems.

One major limitation of carrying-capacity estimation efforts in the past has been the assumption that relevant processes are deterministic--i.e., having fixed outcomes given initial conditions. Usually, mean values for relevant parameters are used: for example, to calculate population sustainable by a system of shifting cultivation given specified farmed and fallow times, average yields, consumption, and nutritional requirements.[4] Variability in these parameters, and in many ecological and social factors underlying them, is itself an important factor in restricting carrying capacity.

Tropical agriculture is generally characterized by widely fluctuating yields from one year to the next and among individual farms in any given year. Even when mean yields are reasonably high, many individuals will fail to meet minimum consumption standards. The probability that a farmer will fail to meet these standards can be expected to increase with population density, in some range of density values within which agricultural production fails to accompany the rise in population, and effects of population are felt in environmental degradation, including that of the agricultural resource base. At very low densities the opposite outcome for failure probabilities would result from a kind of "Allee effect": the pattern common to many species of organisms whereby fitness is reduced at densities below a minimum critical level. As population density increases, probability of failure would fall from a value near one (indicating certain failure) to some much lower level, and eventually rise again to approach a probability of one at high density. Carrying capacity is best defined operationally in terms of such a gradient of individual failure probability or "colonist failure" for the family-level failures used in models developed for Brazil's Transamazon Highway (Fearnside, n.d.a). Failure probabilities represent proportions of colonists falling below specified consumption levels, or lots in which environmental quality criteria are not met, when a simulated population inhabits an area over a long period of years.

The purpose of a carrying-capacity estimate is to be the primary factor shaping the approach used in estimating and selecting component parts to be included in a development study. The importance of variability to tropical agricultural systems, and the human perspective of living standards in terms of individual food needs rather than aggregate statistics, both point to stochastic modeling as an appropriate approach for human carrying-capacity studies, both normative and explanatory. Stochastic models allow for the possibility of more than one outcome, changes in states being described by probabilities less than one. Model behavior takes, therefore, probabilistic form.

STOCHASTIC MODELING OF HUMAN ECOSYSTEMS

A model is "a formulation that mimics a real-world phenomenon, and by means of which predictions can be made" (Odum 1971:6). In other words, it is an analog of a real system used to investigate the real system under different circumstances. Models may be of several types, from "mental models" used daily by everyone to judge the probable outcome of social and other interactions, to physical models to represent a system in concrete form that can be manipulated and visualized on a human scale, to mathematical or analytical models representing a system by a set of equations. Analytical models, such as the exponential and logistic equations for describing population growth, have the advantage of giving quantitative results, but present-day mathematics is only capable of summarizing the most rudimentary of ecological processes in this way, often only after leaving out many relevant aspects of the systems under study, due to the difficulty of representing them. This is particularly true of the stochastic aspects.

Models never mimic entire systems, but only approximate behavior of certain aspects of them. Massive simplification in constructing any model limits the range of outcomes tremendously. Simplification facilitates interpretation of results for a lower cost, but there is a loss of realism from the parts omitted. Choosing elements and relationships to be included in a model should be guided by the importance of different elements to the "system behavior" under study. Modeling goals and roles of the component parts should be paramount--rather than ease of data collection or facility of inclusion in a particular type of pre-existing model. Distortion of system relationships to fit a convenient available model is known as a "procrustean bed," after the mythical giant of Attica who stretched and chopped travelers at his inn to fit an iron bedstead. One of the most frequent simplifications made in modeling is to ignore stochastic effects--i.e., assuming that deterministic mathematical relationships adequately represent a real-world system's behavior. Since it is characteristic of systems generally that, if subdivided enough, the elements of interest eventually become stochastic (Innis 1979:300), the level of examination is a key factor in judging whether this type of simplification is justified. Stochastic and deterministic models are not mutually exclusive. Each is appropriate for a given problem (Poole 1979).

Simulation is now common in both deterministic and stochastic ecosystem models.[5] Simulations lack the elegance of analytical solutions but have great advantage in ease of construction and flexibility in representing more complex phenomena. A simulation is a use of a model to provide empirical solutions to equations included, to obtain information about model response to specific sets of input parameters. Experiments can be performed by manipulating the simulation model rather than the real-world system itself. Computers have made this approach a cheap and practical solution for researchers in many fields.

Simulation models have distinct advantages for use by researchers and planners. Simulations are quantitative and fast. They are also repeatable, increasing the chances that errors in model structure or input parameters will be discovered and rectified, either by the researcher or by the scientific community at large. Simulations have the additional advantage of imposing a certain discipline on the researcher in forcing consideration of all components and functional relationships included in the model. Simulation can yield information on hypothetical scenarios that, if investigated through experimentation on real-world systems, would be impractical due to excessive requirements for time or other resources, or for ethical or other reasons. Studies involving human societies are particularly poorly suited to traditional manipulative experimentation, making simulation a highly advantageous solution to an experimental dilemma.

Simulation models also have great utility as a framework for interpreting new information. Models can be altered and expanded to reflect changes, such as government policy decisions, or inclusion of new components and better measurements of model parameters and functional relationships.

Finally, building simulation models forces close examination of modeling motives, as the ultimate objective of any modeling effort is, or should be, criteria for the many choices researchers must make in winnowing information for inclusion and allocating data acquisition and modeling efforts. Although this ideal is frequently not realized by individual practitioners, the need to have clear research goals in the course of a modeling project can help focus attention on the validity of these goals, as well as on the methodology used to attain them.

Use of simulation modeling has particular advantages in development planning. It forces planners to confront the implications of development strategies advocated, since simulation outputs characteristically contain projections of future trends of state variables, given conditions specified. Projections of this type help to lengthen the planner's time horizon, discouraging the prevalent tendency to consider only the balance of short-term costs and benefits in planning decisions.

Simulation modeling states the planning recommendations in a form in which any rebuttal must be carefully considered. Recommendations are not as subject to casual dismissal as are opinions backed by verbal arguments alone--and for two reasons. First, model construction transforms opinions into testable statements--if someone disagrees, the model can be altered and consequences of the alternative formulation obtained. Second, modeling must be based on a logical sequence of arguments. Each individual result represents a chain of deductive reasoning to which the rules applying to classical syllogisms obtain: if the model structure is logically valid,[6] and

the information embodied in the model and its input
parameters also correspond to reality, then the conclusion
must be accepted as true. The argument cannot be dismissed
by saying "I accept your model and your data, but not your
conclusion." If the conclusion is to be rejected, then
some flaw in either the logic of the argument or the
truth of its premises must be found (W. W. Fearnside 1980:
102). It is important to note that the use of simulation
results to draw conclusions is an inductive process,
which, although lacking the rigor of the deductive portions
of the process, can be done to the same standards that
normally apply in drawing conclusions in science. Input
parameter estimates and decisions regarding model structure
are also generally based on induction.

Much development planning is done in an atmosphere
of conflicting goals and differing beliefs regarding the
functioning of systems affected by the planners' decisions. Internal inconsistencies in the planner or
decision maker's mind can often lead to ineffective, or
worse, counterproductive decisions. In Brazil, a long
tradition of maintaining overlapping and conflicting
mandates among different institutions (Bunker 1979) makes
inconsistency an especially acute problem. The process
of model building requires an examination of the implied
vision of system structure to make the model internally
consistent. Clear demonstration of what consequences
result from each possible set of initial precepts is an
important step in encouraging more coherent development
strategies, with greater likelihood of attaining development goals. Conflicting views of what may result from
different actions can be resolved by identifying those
actions following as logical consequences from agreed-
upon goals and "facts." Further, unanticipated results
may sometimes be discovered. Forrester (1971) stresses
the value of simulations in uncovering potential counter-
intuitive behavior in systems, consequences of which
would otherwise be classified as unthinkable and hence
not faced seriously. At the same time, simulation has
often been criticized as a waste of effort since it
frequently produces results confirming intuition. Even
in cases where intuition is confirmed, modeling has
utility in allowing examination of the worth of the
differing intuitions advocated by different people. My
own, perhaps faulty, intuition has not always foreseen
the results obtained through my simulations.

Computer simulations have been criticized as means
of hiding simple arguments behind a mask of needless
ornamentation and complexity: "a Stalinist mass of
tightly bunched capital letters," as Berlinski (1976:55)
describes the world models of Forrester (1971) and
Meadows et al. (1972). Use of complexity to conceal
should be condemned in modeling, as in any field. Intent
to conceal, however, need not be assumed to lie behind
model complexity. In my opinion, the need for explicit

mention of every step in a calculation procedure mandated by computer programming reduces, rather than increases, the chance of concealment. Computer programs represent an aid rather than a hindrance to understanding complex problems.

The speed and flexibility of simulation models make them potentially the most effective tool for dealing with frequent switches in official development policies. In the Brazilian Amazon, constantly changing government recommendations mean that almost any policy has already been rejected officially before it can be criticized based on data, although often it has not been rejected before bringing about significant environmental and social impacts (see Chapter 12 in this volume). For example, colonization programs for small farmers based on upland rice cultivation were de-emphasized in 1974 in favor of large ranching operations based on unfertilized guinea grass (Panicum maximum) pasture, after only three years of the Transamazon Highway colonization initiative (Moran 1976, 1981). The recommendation of unfertilized guinea grass, introduced as a "sustainable" land use mistakenly believed to improve soil quality for pasture growth (Falesi 1974, 1976; see Fearnside 1979a, 1980b), was dropped in 1977 in favor of fertilized guinea grass pastures. Two years later official favor switched to creeping signal grass or "Quicuiu da Amazônia" (Brachiaria humidicola), and in the same year new fiscal incentives were discontinued for pastures in the part of the Amazon officially classed as high forest. Simulation allows quick evaluations of consequences of proposed policy recommendations, and evaluations of discrepancies between results based on assumptions of prompt applica- tion of all recommended changes and more likely scenarios with imperfect application. Ideally, inadvisable courses of action could be avoided before massive development plans are mounted.

THE KPROG2 MODEL FOR THE TRANSAMAZON HIGHWAY

A stochastic simulation model, KPROG2, has been written for estimating carrying capacity in a part of Brazil's Transamazon Highway colonization area (Fearnside 1978, 1979c, n.d.a). The model is intended to allow evaluation of factors affecting carrying capacity in tropical farming areas. Specifically, KPROG2 is designed for investigating the effect of variability on carrying capacity, especially variability in crop yields and in factors affecting yields. As a supplementary benefit of the modeling effort, it is hoped that information ob- tained will prove useful in developing human carrying- capacity estimation methods which can serve as tools for development planning in tropical areas. To this end, features have been incorporated to relax a number of the restrictive assumptions limiting usefulness of past techniques. The model and its inputs are based on field research, a fact considered more important than the program's complexity and capabilities.

The KPROG2 model calculates probabilities of colonist failure needed for estimating carrying capacity (the operational definition of carrying capacity is expressed in terms of a gradient of probability of colonist failure with increasing population density in the appropriate density range). "Failures" are judged relative to a set of consumption and environmental criteria, rather than by a single limiting factor. The model's population sector may be frozen to test effects of different fixed-population densities by varying the size of simulated colonist lots. Alternatively, a dynamic population sector option permits simulated population changes to occur in accord with either observed or assumed patterns.

Technological changes are included in the form of crop yield increases expected from agronomic programs improving seed stock, and in the form of changes in proportions of colonists adopting different land-use strategies reflecting the observed pattern of change with colonist turnover (Fearnside 1980a). Simulated colonists can also "learn" to adjust subsistence crop allocations to the mean and variance of yields experienced in the simulated area.

Soil quality is modeled to reflect the patchiness characterizing the Transamazon Highway and many other tropical areas (cf. Moran 1981). Both initial soil quality information, and soil quality as changed by the many possible agricultural and fallowing treatments, are stored separately for small "patches" of land. Fallow times are variable, in accord with observed patterns rather than being assumed adequate to regenerate soil quality degraded during periods of cultivation--although such an assumption can be specified if desired. Variable burn quality in farmers' fields, an important feature of agriculture in the area, is linked with weather and clearing behavior (Fearnside 1981). Erosion is also predicted from weather, soil, topography, and land use (Fearnside 1980c). Simulated colonists use fertilizer and lime on the two crops for which real colonists use these inputs, black pepper and cacao (Fearnside 1978, 1980d).

Agricultural yields are affected by colonist behavior in interplanting, seed variety, and planting density, as well as by effects of crop diseases, rats, insects, and other problems depending on the particular crop. Crops included are upland rice, maize, Phaseolus beans, Vigna (cowpeas), sweet manioc, cacao, black pepper, and pasture.

Simulated colonist economic behavior reflects strategies of land use and labor allocation associated with distinct colonist types, patterned after a typology of colonist backgrounds devised by Moran for Transamazon colonists (1976). Labor and capital--with supplies of each subdivided by type and season (Fearnside 1980a)-- limit the use of land available to the simulated colonist. Health problems affect family labor supply, as has some- times been the case on the Transamazon Highway (cf. Moran 1981: Chapter 10). Financing, as well as nonagricultural income sources, supplements cash income from selling agricultural production, and can be used to hire labor or purchase goods for consumption and investment. A number of buffers shield the colonist from failure should harvests be insufficient to meet all subsistence needs. When buffers are insufficient to compensate for production shortfalls, colonists fail to meet specified consumption standards, resulting in simulated colonist failures that are used to compute failure probabilities for estimating carrying capacity.

FUTURE DIRECTIONS OF CARRYING-CAPACITY ESTIMATION METHODOLOGY

The KPROG2 program represents a starting point for many possible improvements in the theoretical basis of carrying-capacity estimation. Much can be done to elaborate the impacts of social effects. More detailed behavioral information on decisions related to lot sales and abandonment, and reproductive decisions, would im- prove realism. The vital role of land values and land speculation in motivating colonist actions needs to be modeled. A finer breakdown of the component processes of social change would strengthen the model.[7] More inclusive models should elaborate the agricultural area's links with the urban sector, as well as land tenure conflicts and political forces affecting institutional policy decisions (see Wood, Chapter 10 in this volume).

Better modeling of decision making would include a balance of risk aversion with opportunity costs in sub- sistence and cash crop allocation decisions. The present program includes cushions in subsistence allocations to reduce risk of shortfalls, but extreme yield variability for some crops has sometimes meant that actual colonists prefer to count on purchases, for example of beans, to supply subsistence needs for these crops. Opportunity cost in terms of what could be earned on a given piece of land by planting a cash crop can become sufficient to induce the colonist to abandon the goal of complete subsistence self-sufficiency. Variable perceptions of risks and appropriate responses can also be important.

More information is needed on effects of soil on crop yields, and on soil changes, especially during fallowing. Better linkage is needed of simulated land- use decisions with soil quality and site history, especially as these affect the area's transition from annual crops to pasture and, to a lesser extent, perennial crops.

A series of simulation models needs to be constructed, at different levels of detail, for answering other questions about carrying capacity. More highly aggregated models should be included for regional simulations. The problem of aggregation and complexity in models must be faced by modelers working in any field. Models at either end of the continuum of possible levels of aggregation, whether the extreme of highly aggregated global models or of detailed case studies in small areas, have limited usefulness for aiding practical planning decisions. Greater progress must be made in filling gaps in this continuum with models addressing the different levels of analysis at which decision makers must act without confusing these levels (Moran 1981: Chapter 11).

Much remains to be done before carrying-capacity estimation becomes a practical tool for development planners. KPROG2 is only a beginning. A major reduction in data requirements for making estimates is a high priority, to allow sufficiently fast and cheap applications to other areas. To a certain extent this could be accomplished by using available data from other than field sources, or by assuming that information collected in one locality can be retained for use in other, similar areas. Savings from such steps must be balanced against loss of reliability. A second approach to reducing data needs is to use simplifying models so that fewer input parameters need to be specified. Complex models commonly serve a role as reference models against which relevant behavior of their simpler counterparts can be compared. Care is needed in such a process, as robustness is lost with removal of a model's latent structure, or those parts coming into play when variables are outside of their normal ranges. To give an example from a widely known deterministic modeling effort, the WORLD3 model of the Limits to Growth study (Meadows et al. 1972; Meadows et al. 1973) produces results in standard runs with little difference from those obtained from a greatly simplified version of the same model with most of its agriculture sector removed (Thissen 1977). However, goals of the WORLD3 modeling effort centered around comparing runs outside these standard ranges, for which the simplifications would be inappropriate (Meadows 1977:273). Simplifications that involve changing a model's level of aggregation, if not changing output behavior modes outright, can change how results come about. This is evident from differences between results of WORLD3 and the less-aggregated Mesarovic-Pestle world models (Mesarovic and Pestle 1974a, 1974b).

For estimates in wider areas of the Brazilian Amazon, adaptations need to be made to permit better use of information from available survey data sources, such as that collected by the RADAM (Radar da Amazônia) project (Brasil, Ministério de Minas e Energia,

Departamento de Produção Mineral, Projeto RADAMBRASIL, 1973-1979), the LANDSAT satellite image interpretation project (Brazil, National Institute for Space Research [INPE--Hammond 1977]), and Brazil's regular census of agriculture and ranching (Brasil, Presidência da República, IBGE, 1981). Appropriate data banks with information retrieval capabilities are needed. Data collection and processing procedures must be streamlined to supply parameter estimates from field research (Fearnside n.d.b).

Progress toward these goals must be made with an appropriate balance between data collection and modeling effort. INPA's Carrying-Capacity Estimation in Amazonian Agroecosystems project is currently working to improve both the theoretical and practical basis for human carrying-capacity estimation on the Transamazon Highway in Pará, and on the Cuiabá-Porto Velho highway in Rondônia.

ACKNOWLEDGMENTS

The carrying-capacity project in the Brazilian Amazon, on which most statements made in this paper are based, has enjoyed financial support from many sources over the past eight years, including Resources for the Future, National Science Foundation (GS-42869), Institute for Environmental Quality, Programa do Trópico Úmido do Conselho Nacional de Desenvolvimento Científico e Tecnológico, Interamerican Development Bank, and Instituto Nacional de Pesquisas da Amazônia (INPA). None of the views expressed are the responsibility of organizations that have supported the project nor of the many individuals who have generously contributed comments and suggestions. All errors are my own responsibility.

NOTES

1. Particularly true in Brazil, where the much-publicized economic "miracle" of the late 1960s and early 1970s was based solely on dramatic increases in GNP. The well-being of poor Northeasterners (Kutcher and Scandizzo 1980) and indigenous groups (Davis 1977) was not much improved.

2. Or conversely, to minimize indices reflecting the lack of items considered.

3. The differing goals and assumptions of optimization and social system models generally make application of optimization techniques inappropriate. See Naill's (1976) criticisms of efforts to optimize Forrester's (1971) WORLD2 model.

4. E.g., the algebraically interchangeable shifting cultivation carrying-capacity formulas devised by Allan (1949), Conklin (1959), Carneiro (1960), Gourou (1966), and Fearnside (1972). See discussion of the evolution

and critiques of the concept in Fearnside (n.d.a).

5. See the following discussions of the evolution and intellectual background of modeling: Watt (1966), Patten (1971), D. L. Meadows et al. (1973:3-26), Innis (1979), and editors' remarks in Shugart and O'Neill (1979).

6. The term "valid" has a different sense to logicians and modelers. In logic an argument is valid if the reasoning is sound, regardless of the "truth" (correspondence to reality) of the premises. Modelers speak of "validating" a model (Caswell 1976) meaning checking agreement of relevant aspects of the model with the real world.

7. Only two of the four "distinctive features" of colonists' backgrounds developed by Moran (1976, 1981) were used in my simulations. Collection of field data on the two other factors (i.e. past rate of residential mobility and ownership of durable goods on arrival) could improve the accuracy of these socioeconomic predictors of behavioral performance.

REFERENCES

Allan, W.
1949   Studies in African Land Usage in Northern Rhodesia. Rhodes Livingstone Papers, No. 15: 1-24.

Berlinski, D.
1976   On Systems Analysis: An Essay Concerning the Limitations of Some Mathematical Models in the Social, Political, and Biological Sciences. Cambridge, Mass.: M.I.T. Press.

Brasil, Ministério de Minas e Energia, Departamento de Produção Mineral, Projeto RADAMBRASIL
1973-   Levantamento de Recursos Naturais. Vols. 1-18.
1979   Rio de Janeiro: Departamento de Produção Mineral.

Brasil, Presidência da República, Instituto Brasileiro de Geografía e Estatística (IBGE)
1981   Censo Agropecuário. Rio de Janeiro: IBGE.

Bunker, Stephen G.
1979   Power Structures and Exchange Between Government Agencies in the Expansion of the Agricultural Sector in Pará. Studies in Comparative International Development 14(1):56-76.

Carneiro, R. L.
1960   Slash-and-Burn Agriculture: A Closer Look at Its Implications for Settlement Patterns. In A.F.C. Wallace, ed., Men and Cultures: Selected Papers of the Fifth International

Congress of Anthropological and Ethnological Sciences. Philadelphia: Univ. of Pennsylvania Press.

Caswell, H.
1976   The Validation Problem. In B. C. Patten, ed., Systems Analysis and Simulation in Ecology. Vol. IV. New York: Academic Press.

Conklin, H. C.
1959   Population-Land Balance Under Systems of Tropical Forest Agriculture. Proceedings of the Ninth Pacific Science Congress 7:63.

Davis, Shelton H.
1977   Victims of the Miracle: Development and the Indians of Brazil. New York: Cambridge Univ. Press.

Falesi, Ítalo Claudio
1974   O Solo na Amazônia e sua Relação com a Definição de Sistemas de Produção Agrícola. In Vol. 1, Reunião do Grupo Interdisciplinar de Trabalho sobre Diretrizes de Pesquisa Agrícola para a Amazônia (Trópico Úmido), Brasília, Maio 6-10, 1974. Brasília: Emprêsa Brasileira de Pesquisa Agropecuária (EMBRAPA).

1976   Ecosistema de Pastagem Cultivada na Amazônia Brasileira. Belém: Centro de Pesquisa Agropecuária do Trópico Úmido (CPATU), Boletim Técnico No. 1.

Fearnside, Philip M.
1972   An Estimate of Carrying Capacity of the Osa Peninsula for Human Populations Supported on a Shifting Agriculture Technology. In Organization for Tropical Studies (OTS), Report of Research Activities Undertaken During the Summer of 1972. San José, Costa Rica: OTS.

1978   Estimation of Carrying Capacity for Human Populations in a Part of the Transamazon Highway Colonization Area of Brazil. Ph.D. dissertation, Division of Biological Sciences, Univ. of Michigan.

1979a Cattle Yield Prediction for the Transamazon Highway of Brazil. Interciencia 4(4):220-225.

1979b The Development of the Amazon Rain Forest: Priority Problems for the Formulation of Guidelines. Interciencia 4(6):338-343.

1979c   The Simulation of Carrying Capacity for Human
        Agricultural Populations in the Humid Tropics:
        Program and Documentation. Manaus: Instituto
        Nacional de Pesquisas da Amazônia (INPA).

1980a   Land Use Allocation of the Transamazon Highway
        Colonists of Brazil and Its Relation to Human
        Carrying Capacity. In F. Barbira-Scazzocchio,
        ed., Land, People, and Planning in Contemporary
        Amazônia. Cambridge, UK: Cambridge Univ. Centre
        of Latin American Studies, Occasional Publ. 3.

1980b   The Effects of Cattle Pastures on Soil Fertility
        in the Brazilian Amazon: Consequences of Beef
        Production Sustainability. Tropical Ecology
        21(1):125-137.

1980c   The Prediction of Soil Erosion Losses Under
        Various Land Uses in the Transamazon Highway
        Colonization Area of Brazil. In J. I. Furtado,
        ed., Tropical Ecology and Development: Pro-
        ceedings of the 5th International Symposium of
        Tropical Ecology, 16-21 April 1979, Kuala
        Lumpur, Malaysia. Kuala Lumpur: International
        Society for Tropical Ecology (ISTE).

1980d   Black Pepper Yield Prediction for the Trans-
        amazon Highway of Brazil. Turrialba 30(1):
        35-42.

1981   Burn Quality Prediction for Simulation of the
        Agricultural System of Brazil's Transamazon
        Highway Colonists for Estimating Human Carrying
        Capacity. Paper presented at the Symposium on
        Ecology and Resource Management in the Tropics,
        Bhopal, India, October 5-10. International
        Society for Tropical Ecology (ISTE), Varanasi,
        India.

n.d.a   Carrying Capacity for Human Populations: the
        Colonization of the Brazilian Rainforest.
        Forthcoming.

n.d.b   Data Management Package for Carrying Capacity
        Estimation in the Humid Tropics. In preparation.

Fearnside, W. W.
    1980   About Thinking. Englewood Cliffs, N.J.:
            Prentice-Hall.

Forrester, J. W.
    1971   World Dynamics. Cambridge, Mass.: Wright-Allen
            Press.

294

Gourou, P.
1966   The Tropical World: Its Social and Economic
        Conditions and Its Future Status. 4th ed.
        New York: Longman.

Hammond, A. L.
1977   Remote Sensing (I); LANDSAT takes hold in South
        America. Science 196:511-512.

Innis, G. S.
1979   A Spiral Approach to Ecosystem Simulation, I.
        In G. S. Innis and R. V. O'Neill, eds., Systems
        Analysis of Ecosystems. Statistical Ecology
        Series. Vol. 9. Fairland, Maryland: Inter-
        national Co-operative Publishing House.

Kutcher, G. P. and P. L. Scandizzo
1980   The Agricultural Economy of Northeast Brazil.
        Washington, D.C.: The World Bank.

Margalef, R.
1968   Perspectives in Ecological Theory. Chicago:
        Univ. of Chicago Press.

Meadows, D. H.
1977   Discussion. In G. Bruchmann, ed., MOIRA:
        Food and Agriculture Model: Proceedings of
        the Third IIASA Symposium on Global Modelling.
        Laxenburg, Austria: International Institute for
        Applied Systems Analysis (IIASA).

Meadows, D. H., D. L. Meadows, J. Randers, and
W. W. Behrens III
1972   The Limits to Growth. New York: New American
        Library.

Meadows, D. L., W. W. Behrens III, D. H. Meadows,
R. F. Naile, J. Randers, and E.K.O. Zahn
1973   The Dynamics of Growth in a Finite World.
        Cambridge, Mass.: Wright-Allen Press.

Mesarovic, M. and E. Pestle
1974a   Mankind at the Turning Point: The Second Report
        to the Club of Rome. New York: Dutton and
        Reader's Digest Press.

Mesarovic, M. and E. Pestle, eds.

1974b   Multilevel Computer Model of World Development
        System. Laxenburg, Austria: International
        Institute for Applied Systems Analysis (IIASA).

Moran, Emilio F.
1976   Agricultural Development in the Transamazon
        Highway. Bloomington: Latin American Studies
        Program Working Papers, Indiana Univ.

1981   Developing the Amazon. Bloomington: Indiana
        Univ. Press.

Naill, R. F.
1976   Optimizing Models of Social Systems. Institute
        of Electrical and Electronics Engineers (IEEE)
        Transactions on Systems, Man and Cybernetics.
        (IEEE Annals No. 603SM007).

Odum, Eugene P.
1969   The Strategy of Ecosystem Development. Science
        164:262-270.

1971   Fundamentals of Ecology. 3rd ed. Philadelphia:
        Saunders.

Patten, B. C.
1971   A Primer for Ecological Modeling and Simulation
        with Analog and Digital Computers. In B. C.
        Patten, ed., Systems Analysis and Simulation in
        Ecology. Vol. I. New York: Academic Press.

Poole, R. W.
1979   Ecological Models and the Stochastic-
        Deterministic Question. In G. P. Patil and
        M. L. Rosenzweig, eds., Contemporary Quantitative
        Ecology and Related Econometrics. Statistical
        Ecology Series. Vol. 12. Fairland, Maryland:
        International Co-operative Publishing House.

Shugart, H. H. and R. V. O'Neill, eds.
1979   Systems Ecology. Benchmark Papers in Ecology.
        Vol. 9. Stroudsburg, Pa.: Dowden, Hutchinson
        and Ross.

Thissen, W.
1977   An Analysis of the WORLD3 Agricultural Submodel.
        In G. Bruchmann, ed., MOIRA: Food and Agricul-
        ture Model: Proceedings of the Third IIASA
        Symposium on Global Modelling. Laxenburg,
        Austria: International Institute for Applied
        Systems Analysis (IIASA).

Watt, K.E.F.
1966   The Nature of Systems Analysis. In K.E.F.
        Watt, ed., Systems Analysis in Ecology.
        New York: Academic Press.

12
Government-Directed Settlement in the 1970s: An Assessment of Transamazon Highway Colonization

Emilio F. Moran

INTRODUCTION

The construction of the Transamazon Highway initiated a process of colonization in the Brazilian Amazon that has begun to change the appearance of that once tranquil rain forest (see Figure 12.1). Road construction and directed settlement were but the pioneer fronts for a larger-scale process of resource development and geopolitical integration guided by direct government intervention. In this paper my aim is to synthesize what we have learned from the process of colonization in the Transamazon Highway. The paper begins by examining the motives and aims for Amazonian colonization, proceeds with an examination of the determinants of farmer success, and then with an examination of the Altamira Project in the Transamazon Highway. The final section of the paper evaluates the viability of current trends in development policy oriented at promoting small farmer settlement.

MOTIVES FOR COLONIZATION

Among the motives that have been cited for occupying the Amazon, the major ones appear to be geopolitical, social/demographic, economic, and political (cf. Wagley 1974). The geopolitical motives were articulated several decades before the construction of the highway. The Amazon River was seen as a major system of communications within South America, the occupation of which guaranteed control and/or influence over the major resource areas of the continent (cf. Couto e Silva 1957; Tambs 1974; Katzman 1977). The social and demographic motives were given the most attention during 1971 when the Transamazon Highway and the Program of National Integration (PIN) were announced. The highway and its attendant colonization were hailed as solutions to underemployment and drought in Northeast Brazil, to inequities in access to land in the Northeast and elsewhere in Brazil. In short, as a solution to the overpopulation of the Northeast and

297

the underpopulation of Amazonia (Kleinpenning 1975; Ministério da Agricultura 1972).

Perhaps more important than the motives mentioned so far may have been the hopes, later to be confirmed by aerial surveys, of significant natural resources that could help solve the severe negative balance of payments and foreign indebtedness of Brazil. Hopes were pinned not only on the production of staple commodities by small farmers, but also on livestock production, forestry, silviculture, and minerals. What the surveys of RADAM identified (1974) by means of sideways-looking radar were riches beyond the expectation of most government planners, together with the realization of the difficulty of exploiting these resources given the undeveloped state of basic infrastructure in the region.

Finally, the Brazilian government appears to have had an interest in focusing national attention on a major challenge that might serve to enhance nationalism and lend legitimacy to what had been until then a regime more noted for its repression than for its social conscience (Pompermayer 1979). By the time the PIN and colonization began, the regime had brought inflation under control but needed a focus that would divert attention from opposition goals that wished to return the government to civilian control.

TYPES OF COLONIZATION PROJECTS

The literature on colonization makes three distinctions based upon the degree of government participation in discussing projects: directed, semi-directed, and spontaneous colonization. Spontaneous colonization is characterized by minimal government involvement in the process once it is initiated. The forces that start it, however, may very well be government actions such as the construction of a road into a pioneer zone. The occupation of the lands along the Belém-Brasília highway is a classic case of spontaneous settlement in the Brazilian Amazon (Valverde and Vergolino Dias 1967; Hébette and Acevedo 1979). Nelson (1973) in his evaluation of tropical land development considered spontaneous colonization as the most successful type because of its low cost to government and the self-selection of colonists with a high degree of initiative and risk-taking potential. Over 2 million people in less than one decade moved to the margin of the Belém-Brasília highway and produced numerous urban and rural settlements.

Directed colonization, on the other hand, involves a high degree of government intervention not only in the initial stages but throughout the process of occupation. There have been relatively few of these projects in Latin America or the Amazon due to the high cost implied and the mixed results from the few attempts undertaken (Nelson 1973). Directed colonization projects are characterized

Figure 12.1. Roads and colonization in the Brazilian Amazon

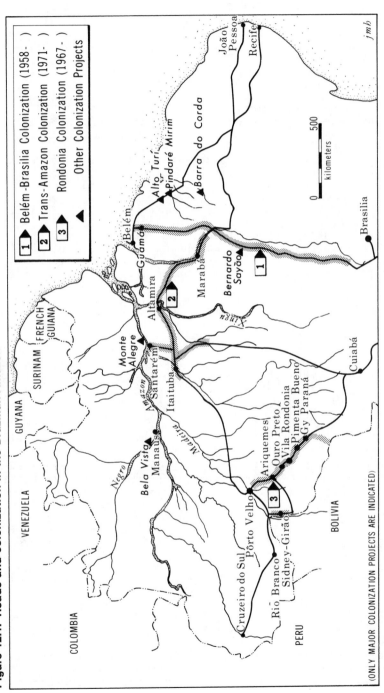

(ONLY MAJOR COLONIZATION PROJECTS ARE INDICATED)

by "total design" based on a high degree of planning that includes not only major and feeder roads, but also design of communities, provision of inputs, selection of colonists, and promotion of specific priorities. The Integrated Colonization Project (PIC) at Altamira was the main show-case for such a type of settlement along the Transamazon Highway (Ministério da Agricultura 1972; Moran 1981). The PICs were designed to address the recurring problems that had plagued settlements in tropical areas: lack of year-round all-weather roads; lack of credit; poor health care and educational facilities; unclear titles to land; and isolation of settlers from markets.

Semi-directed colonization projects are harder to define. They imply a lesser degree of government involve-ment than directed projects but considerably more than spontaneous settlement. In semi-directed projects the effort is to regularize the spontaneous flow of migrants and to reduce the potential for land conflicts arising over litigation over titles. In these projects the government not only builds the access roads but also may demarcate the landholdings, play a role in issuing titles to land, and put in place banking facilities, schools, and public health services. Unlike its role in directed projects, the government is unlikely to get involved in colonist selection and direct provision of inputs such as tools and seeds. In some cases, the government itself will not be involved in land demarcation and provision of services but may allow private colonization firms to carry out those tasks--using the successful experience of the Companhia Melhoramentos Norte do Paraná as a model (Margolis 1973; Nicholls 1969). The currently dominant form of government-directed colonization in the Brazilian Amazon seems to be semi-directed with Rondônia as the center of attention (see Figure 12.1). Spontaneous colonization continues unabated since by its very nature it cannot be controlled once the means of access have been put in place. In fact, there are numerous cases through-out the Amazon wherein spontaneous migrants have <u>preceded</u> penetration roads into an unoccupied zone (Casagrande, Thompson, and Young 1964; Bromley 1980).

The rest of the paper focuses on the Altamira Integrated Colonization Project in the Brazilian state of Pará, which was the focus of fieldwork by the author in 1972, 1973-1974, and 1976-1977, and by other fieldworkers (cf. Moran 1981 and other references in the bibliography; Smith 1982, 1981, 1976; Fearnside 1978, 1980; Contini 1976). Of central concern in this discussion will be the determinants of colonist success in farm management and what these determinants might tell us about the potential of colonization as a development strategy.

DETERMINANTS OF COLONIST SUCCESS

If one of the goals of colonization is to bring into

production land that remains unused and in this manner
increase the income of the farming population and the output of food and fiber, then it becomes of great significance to examine what the determinants and/or constraints
to colonist success have been. One must begin by saying
that there is no single determinant for success. W.
Arthur Lewis summarized what we knew in 1954 about the
subject by saying that site selection, colonist selection,
site preparation, capital, organization of services, land
area, and land tenure were important in determining the
success of colonization projects. It appears that in the
nearly 20 years since then, countries throughout the
world have acted as if nothing were known about the
limiting factors to colonization.

Clearly, all colonization projects would have a
higher incidence of success if they were preceded by
feasibility studies and, especially, by agricultural
sector assessments. However, it is unlikely that such
studies will be normally funded. An excellent example is
provided by the Huallaga Central Project study that
covered an area only 33,600 km^2 at a cost of over $4
million and took six years to complete (Nelson 1973).
The colonization polygon along the Transamazon was twice
as large and Rondônia's colonization will probably surpass
it. On the other hand, proceeding without feasibility
studies can lead to costs at least as high. The Bolivian
Alto Beni, Chimoré, and Yapacani projects were undertaken
without such pre-studies--only to discover that 60% of
the areas occupied proved to be unsuitable for settlement
due to periodic flooding (Nelson 1973). Abandonment of
a colonization area means the loss of forest cover,
infrastructure, land improvements, loans, and other
structures. Given current ways in which national budgets
are formulated, it appears that governments prefer to
accept the latter costs to the former.

Given the inability to preselect settlement areas
through field studies, it becomes all the more important
to select colonists with experience in commodity production. The colonization literature suggests that there
are two major ways in which governments appear to proceed with colonist selection: (1) requiring agricultural
experience of some sort as a qualification, or (2) giving
preference to specific geographical areas, ethnic groups,
or income groups. The latter is the most common pattern
used since it is politically more attractive to administrators (Nelson 1973).

Scholars have long pointed out the constraint posed
by the lack of all-weather roads (cf. Crist and Nissly
1973). The isolation associated with the lack of feeder
roads has led, in project after project, to farmer
isolation, lack of access to health care facilities,
lowered working capacity, loss of harvested produce, and
lack of access to credit and other facilities. In sum,
the decision to build main highways while neglecting

feeder roads results in the replication of all the classic constraints to the success of small farmer colonization in projects lacking the provision of inputs.

From the colonist point of view, health stands as the single most limiting factor to his agricultural production (cf. Moran 1981; Weil 1981). In the aggregate, the health problems of the population are rarely a major constraint to production unless particularly low and unsanitary areas are chosen for settlement. Settlers in communities away from the main highway tend to suffer most severely due to the lack of medical services and difficulties of access in or out (Tcheyan 1980; Moran 1981). If the transportation problem is properly dealt with, health is rarely a serious constraint to colonist success.

Most studies view security of title as a relevant variable in farmer satisfaction and in choices of production strategies (Wood and Schmink 1979; Tcheyan 1980; Moran 1981). For the Amazon, the problems faced by farmers in obtaining secure title to land seem particularly severe: there is a longstanding lack of cadastral surveys; conflicting and unresolved land titles and deeds; personnel in cadastral offices are notoriously poorly paid and easily bribed; and laws that protect squatters' rights encourage land invasion. Despite the well-known difficulties of obtaining clear title to land and the numerous documents required to process titles, the colonization of Amazonia applied these laws and thereby limited access to credit to persons with definitive title only. Most colonists receive at arrival only an "authorization of occupation" which gives them access only to short-term loans. The inefficient issuing of titles to land, even in an area wherein past claims had been nulled by the national security law, suggests that there is both a structural and an interactional resistance to responding to the needs of agricultural development by means of a small farm sector.

THE ALTAMIRA PROJECT IN THE TRANSAMAZÔNICA

In this paper I will not attempt to fully summarize the design and implementation of this complex project due to space limitations. I have made a more complete assessment of the social and ecological consequences of this project in a recent book, Developing the Amazon (Moran 1981). What is of interest here is the gap between planning and the realities of implementation and what this gap implies for future directed and semi-directed projects.

The PIC Altamira was selected as the showcase for the execution of Transamazon Highway colonization because of the terra roxa soils (Alfisols), which had been noticed in a soil survey of the lands immediately west of the city of Altamira (IPEAN 1967). Planners proceeded with the design of the project despite the conspicuous absence of a solid data base.

A national campaign, made a part of the Program of National Integration announced in 1971, was undertaken to attract colonists. The opportunities offered to potential colonists were irresistible: 100 hectares of virgin forest; minimum salary for the initial 6 months; credit for food production at 7% annual rate; provision of inputs such as seeds and fertilizers; a ready-built house; roads linking farms to markets, schools, and health services; guarantee that the government would purchase production if the market did not provide a price above production costs; and soils hailed to be as fertile as those of Paraná (Kleinpenning 1975; Moran 1976). Indeed, the government mobilized an impressive array of government institutions to serve this small farm sector being created in Altamira, Maraba, and Itaituba--the three designated Integrated Colonization Projects (see Figure 12.1).

Land conflict was virtually eliminated by repossessing all land alongside the highway (100 km on each side) and declaring the zone as being of interest to national security. In turn, the Institute of Colonization and Agrarian Reform (INCRA) was given the charge to regularize colonists' claims to land and issuing of land titles. The old problems of poor health and education and social isolation were attacked by promoting what was dubbed "rural urbanism." A complex set of planned communities, with differing scales of complexity and services, was designed and spaced to facilitate provision of services and bring urban conveniences to the countryside.

INCRA offices throughout Brazil were overrun with applicants during the first year. The seriousness with which the government began the mobilization of its resources to carry out the project reminded everyone of the construction of Brasília, and the Transamazon became the center of media attention. The growth of population on Altamira's rural and urban sector is indicative of the changes brought by the road and its attendant colonization (see Figure 12.2). However, despite the rapid population growth, the colonization projects had been given a government goal of 100,000 families in the first three years. The Maraba Integrated Colonization Project was severely curtailed by the high incidence of malaria and the Itaituba Project by poor soils encountered in the vicinity of the city--problems that led to the abandonment of the rural urbanism model (IPEAN 1974). In all, about 7,000 families had taken residence along the Transamazon Highway by 1975.

The Altamira Project was spared such drastic changes in colonization policy. Nevertheless, settlement of the Altamira lands proved to be far more complex than planners had expected. The soils of the Altamira region were not homogeneously <u>terra roxa</u>. They proved to be composed of a varied array of soils which gave differential results

Figure 12.2. Altamira population (source: IBGE, Altamira office)

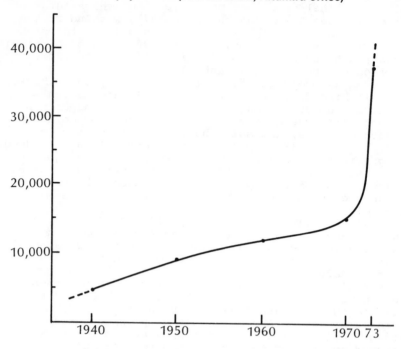

to cultivators. Social differentiation was also present
and contradicted the social design of the project.
   Over 30% of the population in PIC Altamira were
Amazonian <u>caboclos</u> (cf. Wagley 1953; Moran 1974) who had
occupied lands in the county since the early 1950s or
earlier. During this period preceding the Transamazon
they had explored, hunted, and cultivated areas near
Altamira. The colonization plans failed to mention the
presence of this population in the area, as well as their
possible contribution to the process of settlement and
food production. It is not surprising, therefore, that
for the first years of settlement, the immigrants from
Northeast (30%), Southern (23%), and Center-West (13%)
Brazil interacted little and learned little from these
Amazonians. It became clear to me during field research
that the <u>caboclos</u> in Altamira appeared to recognize
accurate plant indicators of poor and good agricultural
soils. Soil sampling confirmed their environmental perceptions to have been very accurate. (See Figure 12.3.)
Immigrants, on the other hand, could not recognize plant
species, nor did the criteria relevant in their places
of origin apply in their new environment (Moran 1977,
1981). As research progressed, it became increasingly
evident that some immigrants had superior results from

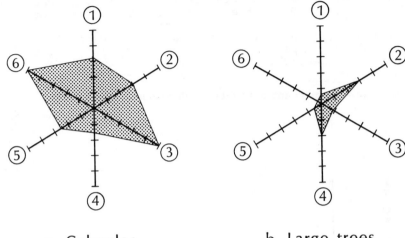

Figure 12.3. Criteria for soil selection by local and nonlocal homesteaders

a. Caboclos　　b. Large trees

Key to fertility diagrams

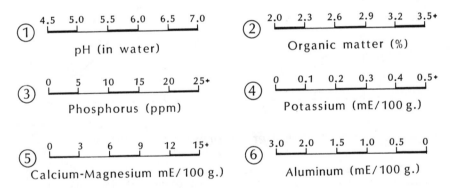

their farm management efforts, whereas others were going into even greater debt in their effort to bring their land into production.

The Altamira Project mixed the two classic systems of colonist selection. Allegedly, it gave preference to poor Northeasterners (projected to be 75% of the total) who had no land of their own, but it also gave a selective advantage to persons with agricultural experience and a 2.5 minimum labor force (Ministério da Agricultura 1972; Kleinpenning 1975). The criteria for selection were neither implemented effectively nor proved to be, when field tested, accurate predictors of farming success. Scarcely over 30% of the migrants came from the Northeast. Size of family did not predict for the amount of family labor actually used in farm production. Generalized agricultural experience was insufficient in predicting farm management skills (Moran 1979).

Figure 12.4. Mobility and agricultural yields (source: Moran 1975)

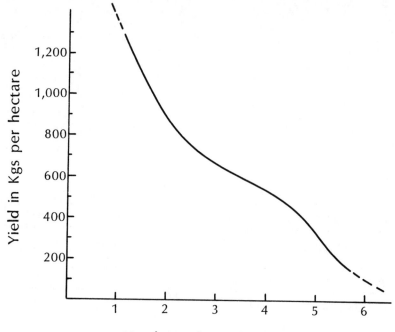

Number of previous migrations

    The four criteria that predicted the results achieved by the colonists were, in order of importance: previous management experience, residential stability, previous credit experience, and initial capital or liquid assets (see Figure 12.4). The accuracy of these indicators was confirmed by Fearnside in another colonization area of Altamira (1980), even though he used only two of the four criteria in selecting his sample. The more experienced managers sought out the caboclos and followed their advice in managing their farms from the start. The results were impressive: accurate soil selection with areas with a pH in excess of 6.0; twice the yield per hectare; diversified cropping practices bringing in a higher income than cropping dominated by rice farming; greater use of family labor in farm production processes;

greater use of technology available; lower expenditures in consumption items; less dependence on salaries to meet food needs--to name but the most important results (Moran 1979).

The Altamira Project was hailed by Nelson (1973) as the acid test of the potential of tropical lands for settlement. Unfortunately, what it proved was that there is a serious problem in the linkage between functional performance and the structural organization of development institutions. The numerous institutions that were placed in the Altamira colonization areas were unable to make adjustments to the differences between what the plans had indicated and the empirical realities that they faced. It remains to be studied why the organizations' personnel could not inform central decision-makers that the population projection of 100,000 was both unrealistic and undesirable given the lack of knowledge of the area in question; that credit incentives should not have been tied to specific cereals, given the spotty performance of cereal production in the humid tropics and the lack of agronomic research on Altamira soils in 1971; that roads could not be kept open during the long rainy season and that reassessment of road specifications should be implemented to avoid further losses as construction continued; that farm produce was rotting in the fields due to lack of feeder roads and storage facilities throughout the region; that the planned communities along feeder roads were unable to attract and keep educational and health personnel; and that farmers were moving to their lots suggesting that the construction of such communities was unjustified. What emerges from a close examination of the colonization process in Altamira is that whereas local personnel were aware of many of these problems, the information did not flow to decision-nodes in the Brazilian planning institutions so that changes might be made, nor were local adjustments made to meet the problems encountered (Moran 1981, 1982). It strikes me that this is the subject of a much-needed study (Moran n.d.).

OBJECTIONS TO AMAZONIAN DEVELOPMENT THROUGH COLONIZATION

Critics of the efforts to colonize the Amazon in the past decade point out that land is available elsewhere; that the environment of Amazonia is imperiled by these activities; that the soils of Amazonia cannot sustain sedentary agriculture; that the environment is unhealthful; that the government has a poor record of support for colonization; that local markets are inadequate to absorb production; and that colonists lack managerial skills.

There can be little doubt that there is a high degree of maldistribution of land in Northeast Brazil as in much of Southern Brazil. The latifundium/minifundium problem that plagues Latin America as a whole has not exempted Brazil. Despite some localized increases in the

number and size of small farm holdings (Dias 1973), much
of the land continues to be held by a small proportion of
owners. What many fear, and the evidence is on their
side, is that this same system will be reproduced in the
Amazon and, in due time, generate the same underdevelopment
and social differentiation which is, in part, responsible
for the poverty of great masses of the population (Forman
1975).

A more international concern with Amazonian colonization arises over fear of environmental degradation.
Ecologists have cited loss of species diversity, fragility
of the ecosystems, destruction of native people's ways
of life, and global changes in climate as only a few of
the potential dangers associated with the process of
deforestation and development (Goodland and Irwin 1975;
Lovejoy and Schubart 1980). The evidence accumulated up
to now suggests that some Amazonian habitats are more
fragile than others and special care should be taken to
keep developments from affecting fragile areas (Farnsworth
and Golley 1974; Goodland 1980). The loss of species is
a real and grave danger that is being addressed by the
creation of forest reserves--although we are only now
beginning to understand the appropriate size of reserves
to protect given Amazonian species (Lovejoy and Schubart
1980). Increasing concern is being expressed for the
decimation of native Amazonians as a result of exposure
to Western diseases to which they have no immunities.
Policies have been inconsistent and reflect a long-held
view that the native peoples are an obstacle to progress
(Davis 1977; Barbira-Scazzocchio 1980:210-255).

An underlying objection to the occupation of the
Amazon is based on the assumption that the soils are
acidic, leached, low in soluble nutrients, and lateritic
(turning to hardpan after minimal erosion). Popular
wisdom has it that soils have to be abandoned after a
couple of years because they cannot sustain further
cultivation. If cultivated too long, they might even
develop into deserts (cf. Goodland and Irwin 1975).
Recent research has balanced our views of the soils
of the Amazon (cf. Sanchez 1976). They are now recognized by a growing number of persons as highly variable
in quality and with a broad range of potential. Some
indeed live up to the stereotype mentioned, whereas
others can be highly productive over many years. The
problem is one of developing proper management systems
for each of the soils (Sanchez 1976; Furley 1980).

The disease hazards of the Amazon have long acted
as a brake on the colonization of the area (Weil 1981).
The problems of the Amazon are not very different from
those of any other environment where there is a lack of
accessible medical care. Malaria, Chagas disease, and
helminth and pathogenic protozoans leading to gastro-
intestinal problems are among the more serious problems
but they can be managed with proper personal care and

accessible public health facilities (Navarro 1974).

The poor record of government support for past colonization projects was ably documented by Anderson (1976) in her study of colonization in Pará from 1758 to 1930 (cf. also Crist and Nissly 1973; Nelson 1973). Indeed, inflated expectations of benefits to lure colonists, lack of delivery of promised services, shifts in priorities, and inadequate support for productive activities have been constraints in the past. Efforts to correct these deficiencies have commonly taken the form of pouring limited funds into more government agencies rather than improved management to assure delivery of services (Mahar 1979; Moran 1981).

Studies of colonization have long pointed out that successful projects are characterized by ready access to markets (Tavares et al. 1972; Nelson 1973). This is accomplished by locating them near population centers, assuring producers of good roads, low transportation cost, and production of goods that the market desires and is willing to pay attractive prices for. Many colonization projects appear to be planned with opposite goals in mind and high rates of failure have become expectable.

Government planners have tended to view colonization projects as welfare rather than economic projects. It is assumed that colonists have poor managerial skills, have low capital to invest in modernizing operations, have low levels of education, low levels of technology applied to production, and unfamiliarity with formal credit (Ministério da Agricultura 1972). This leads to extreme solutions: either to select colonists on the basis of need (i.e., no land) or on the basis of productive potential. Many studies have pointed out that selection of colonists could well influence the successful development of projects, but governments have been reluctant to apply effective criteria (Nelson 1973; Moran 1979). Of the objectives to Amazon colonization the ones that seem to underlie many of the problems center on institutional and/or structural constraints. These constraints seem to function by reducing the flexibility of response of service delivery, thereby leaving colonists attracted to an area to fend for themselves.

CONCLUSIONS

What is most needed in the process of Amazonian development through small farmer colonization is an incrementalist approach that allows for the need for initial testing and for constant adjustment of strategies to make the sector operate at a desirable level. See Figure 12.5 for a proposed incrementalist model. Clearly the lack of personnel and capital is a constraint, but a clear focus on the major needs of the population in the pioneer stages could permit better service delivery and encouragement of new solutions. For example, from the

310

Figure 12.5. Colonization: an incremental approach

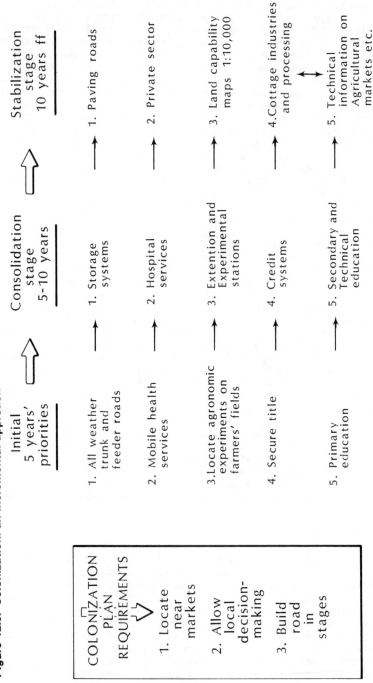

farmers' point of view, their major need is adequate
health services. From the government's point of view the
major need is surplus production and marketing (Moran
1981). Both of these goals can best be accomplished by
assuring that all-weather roads are in place to the farms
and that adequate storage and public health facilities
are available. It is inefficient use of scarce capital to
provide a great deal of credit to farmers while they are
trying to experiment with crop choices and production
mixes. Bank credit simply leads to large areas being
improperly cleared during the initial stages. Major
provision of seeds and fertilizers may also be improper
since in the pioneering stages it is unlikely that the
varieties that yield well under local climatic and soil
conditions have been developed. Public expenditures in
extension, credit, social work, and other services are
appropriate during what Nelson (1973) calls the "consolidation stage" of colonization. During the early or
pioneering stages the main determinants of success are
good roads, good health care, secure title, and
accessibility to markets.

In short, the central problem to Amazonian development through colonization appears to be the same as that
faced by development planning in general: a tendency to
attempt to solve all problems at once--rather than
approaching the basin as a complex region that must be
gradually and carefully studied and managed if it is to
yield the benefits expected. In policy terms this would
mean building smaller stretches of highway and providing
services in a gradual and incremental form so that they
can be most effectively utilized without distorting the
human response to the incentives provided.

Colonization of the Brazilian Amazon has been costly
in environmental, economic, and social terms. Many areas
of forest along the Transamazon were cut down--only to
find out that the soils could not support farming. The
plans failed to incorporate feedback loops that would
permit adjustments in implementation in response to
environmental and social variation. This inflexibility
in institutional response harmed the project as a whole,
despite considerable success by individuals in the
projects.

There is nothing in the design of the Rondônia
colonization projects currently underway that would
suggest that the fundamental constraints to the success
of colonization have been addressed (Gall 1978; Mueller
1980). Resource maps at a scale of 1:10,000 are not the
basis for farm management decisions. The population has
not been selected for its experience in making farm
management decisions (IBRD 1981). There is considerable
interference in farm management decisions by government
through promotion of perennial export crops. These crops
do not seem appropriate to the optimum use of family labor
and the size of the family farms. Location of the

Rondônia project is not likely to promote the development of the small farm sector but rather the development
of a middle to large sector geared at export crops rather
than staple commodity production. Priority is not being
given to the fundamental needs of the small farmer:
health, security of tenure, good roads, and education.
These four priorities continue to be neglected in service
delivery systems. The concerns of policy still focus on
aggregate yields and on institutional processes relevant
at later stages in the development of colonization:
provision of credit, export crop production, quality of
administration, and maximum output from the sector.
There is very little in current development policy that
would suggest that an answer has been generated to the
question of the potential of the humid tropics for intensive agriculture or the role of colonization in the
resolution of the agrarian crisis in Latin America.
Latin American institutions and their allied lending
agencies continue to treat the Amazonian frontier in ways
that fail to respond to the special characteristics and
goals of the small farm, that fail to recognize small
farmers' important role in staple commodity production,
and that fail to recognize the experimental nature of all
Amazonian agricultural and conservational activity. The
caution and adjustment to variable responses that should
characterize any experimental approach are rarely
observable in Amazonian development and colonization.
Unfortunately, the experiment continues, this time in
Rondônia and Carajás, at a scale that makes careful
monitoring difficult, and the results more costly in both
environmental and human terms than they need be.

ACKNOWLEDGMENTS

Portions of this paper were presented at the
Conference on Frontier Expansion in Amazonia held at the
Center for Latin American Studies, University of Florida,
Gainesville, Feb. 8-11, 1982. I appreciate the useful
comments provided by W. Vickers, G. Velho, D. Mahar,
A. Stearman, C. Wood, and others.

REFERENCES

Anderson, Robin
    1976   Following Curupira: Colonization and Migration
            in Pará (1758-1930). Ph.D. dissertation, Dept.
            of History, Univ. of California, Davis.

Barbira-Scazzocchio, François, ed.
    1980   Land, People, and Planning in Contemporary
            Amazônia. Cambridge, UK: Cambridge Univ.
            Centre of Latin American Studies, Occasional
            Publ. 3.

Bourne, Richard
    1978   Assault on the Amazon.   London: Gollancz.

Bromley, Ray
    1980   The Role of Tropical Colonization in the
            Twentieth Century Economic Development of
            Ecuador.   In F. Barbira-Scazzocchio, ed.,
            Land, People, and Planning in Contemporary
            Amazônia.   Cambridge, UK: Cambridge Univ. Centre
            of Latin American Studies, Occasional Publ. 3.

Casagrande, J., S. Thompson, and P. Young
    1964   Colonization as a Research Frontier: The
            Ecuadorian Case.   In R. Manners, ed., Process
            and Pattern in Culture.   Chicago: Aldine.

Contini, E.
    1976   A Colonização na Transamazônica.   M.A. thesis,
            Fundação Getúlio Vargas, Rio de Janeiro, Brazil.

Couto e Silva, Goldberry do
    1957   Aspectos Geopolíticos do Brasil.   Rio de
            Janeiro: Bibliotêca do Exército.

Crist, R. and C. Nissly
    1973   East from the Andes.   Gainesville: Univ. of
            Florida Press.

Davis, Shelton H.
    1977   Victims of the Miracle: Development and the
            Indians of Brazil.   New York: Cambridge Univ.
            Press.

Dias, Gentil Martins
    1973   Roçeiros and Townsmen in Brazil.   Ph.D.
            dissertation, Univ. of Sussex, England.

Farnsworth, E. and F. Golley, eds.
    1974   Fragile Ecosystems.   New York: Springer-Verlag.

Fearnside, Philip M.
    1978   Estimation of Carrying Capacity for Human
            Populations in a Part of the Transamazon High-
            way Colonization Area of Brazil.   Ph.D.
            dissertation, Division of Biological Sciences,
            Univ. of Michigan.

    1980   Land Use Allocation of the Transamazonian High-
            way Colonists of Brazil and Its Relation to
            Human Carrying Capacity.   In F. Barbira-
            Scazzocchio, eds., Land, People, and Planning
            in Contemporary Amazônia.   Cambridge, UK:
            Cambridge Univ. Centre of Latin American Studies,
            Occasional Publ. 3.

Forman, S.
1975   The Brazilian Peasantry. New York: Columbia
         Univ. Press.

Furley, Peter
1980   Development Planning in Rondonia Based on
         Naturally Renewable Resource Surveys. In F.
         Barbira-Scazzocchio, ed., Land, People, and
         Planning in Contemporary Amazônia. Cambridge,
         UK: Cambridge Univ. Center of Latin American
         Studies, Occasional Publ. 3.

Gall, Norman
1978   Letter from Rondonia. American Universities
         Field Staff Reports No. 9-13/South America.

Goodland, Robert J.A.
1980   Environmental Ranking of Amazonian Development
         Projects in Brazil. Environmental Conservation
         7(1):9-26.

Goodland, Robert J.A. and H. S. Irwin
1975   Amazon Jungle: Green Hell to Red Desert?
         Amsterdam: Elsevier.

Hébette, J. and R. Acevedo
1979   Colonização para quem? Belém: Univ. Federal do
         Pará, Núcleo de Altos Estudos Amazónicos/Série
         Pesquisa.

IBRD
1981   Brazil: Integrated Development of the Northwest
         Frontier. Washington, D.C.: World Bank.

IPEAN
1967   Contribuição ao Estudo dos Solos de Altamira.
         Belém: Instituto de Pesquisa Agropecuária do Norte
         (IPEAN). Circular No. 10.

1974   Solos da Rodovia Transamazônica: Trecho
         Itaituba-Rio Branco. Belém: Instituto de
         Pesquisa Agropecuária do Norte (IPEAN).

Katzman, M.
1977   Cities and Frontiers in Brazil. Cambridge, Ma.:
         Harvard Univ. Press.

Kleinpenning, J.M.G.
1975   The Integration and Colonization of the
         Brazilian Portion of the Amazon Basin. Nijmegen:
         Inst. of Geography and Planning.

Lewis, W. Arthur
    1954   Thoughts on Land Settlement. Journal of
            Agricultural Economics 11(1):3-11.

Lovejoy, Thomas E. and H.O.R. Schubart
    1980   The Ecology of Amazonian Development. In F.
            Barbira-Scazzocchio, ed., Land, People, and
            Planning in Contemporary Amazônia. Cambridge,
            UK: Cambridge Univ. Centre of Latin American
            Studies, Occasional Publ. 3.

Mahar, Dennis J.
    1979   Frontier Development Policy in Brazil: A Study
            of Amazonia. New York: Praeger.

Margolis, Maxine
    1973   The Moving Frontier. Gainesville: Univ. of
            Florida Press.

Ministério da Agricultura
    1972   Altamira 1. Brasília: Instituto Nacional de
            Colonização e Reforma Agrária/Ministério da
            Agricultura.

Moran, Emilio F.
    1974   The Adaptive System of the Amazonian Caboclo.
            In C. Wagley, ed., Man in the Amazon.
            Gainesville: Univ. of Florida Press.

    1975   Pioneer Farmers of the Transamazon Highway.
            Ph.D. dissertation, Dept. of Anthropology,
            Univ. of Florida.

    1976   Agricultural Development in the Transamazon
            Highway. Bloomington: Latin American Studies
            Program Working Papers, Indiana Univ.

    1977   Estrategias de Sobrevivencia: O Uso de Recursos
            ao Longo da Rodovia Transamazônica. Acta
            Amazônica 7(3):363-379.

    1979   Criteria for Choosing Homesteaders in Brazil.
            Research in Economic Anthropology 2:339-359.

    1981   Developing the Amazon. Bloomington: Indiana
            Univ. Press.

    1982   Ecological, Anthropological, and Agronomic
            Research in the Amazon Basin. Latin American
            Research Review 17(1):3-41.

    n.d.   Amazonian Development: Structural and Inter-
            actional Constraints. In preparation.

316

Mueller, Charles
  1980   Frontier-Based Agricultural Expansion: The
         Case of Rondônia.   In F. Barbira-Scazzocchio,
         ed., Land, People, and Planning in Contemporary
         Amazônia.   Cambridge, UK: Cambridge Univ. Centre
         of Latin American Studies, Occasional Publ. 3.

Navarro, V.
  1974   The Underdevelopment of Health or the Health of
         Underdevelopment: An Analysis of the Distri-
         bution of Human Health Resources in Latin
         America.   Internat. Journal of Health Services
         4:5-27.

Nelson, M.
  1973   The Development of Tropical Lands.   Baltimore:
         Johns Hopkins Univ. Press.

Nicholls, William
  1969   The Agricultural Frontier in Modern Brazilian
         History: The State of Parana, 1920-65.   In
         MALAS, Cultural Change in Brazil.   Muncie:
         Ball State Univ.

Pompermayer, Malorí José
  1979   The State and the Frontier in Brazil: A Case
         Study of the Amazon.   Ph.D. dissertation, Dept.
         of Political Science, Stanford Univ.

RADAM
  1974   Levantamento de Recursos Naturais.   Vol. 5.
         Rio de Janeiro: Ministério de Minas e Energia.

Sanchez, Pedro A.
  1976   Properties and Management of Soils in the
         Tropics.   New York: Wiley-Interscience.

Smith, Nigel J.H.
  1976   Transamazon Highway: A Cultural Ecological
         Analysis of Settlement in the Lowland Tropics.
         Ph.D. dissertation, Dept. of Geography, Univ.
         of California, Berkeley.

  1981   Colonization Lessons from a Rainforest.
         Science 214:755-761.

  1982   Rainforest Corridors.   Berkeley: Univ. of
         California Press.

Tambs, Lewis
  1974   Geopolitics of the Amazon.   In C. Wagley, ed.,
         Man in the Amazon.   Gainesville: Univ. of
         Florida Press.

Tavares, V. P. et al.
1972   Colonização Dirigida no Brasil. Rio de
        Janeiro: Instituto de Planejamento Econômico
        e Social (IPEA) No. 8.

Tcheyan, Nils
1980   A Comparative Study of the Administration of
        Two Amazon Colonization Projects: Alto Turi
        and Ouro Preto. Washington, D.C.: Center of
        Brazilian Studies, Johns Hopkins Univ. School
        for Advanced Internat. Studies. Occasional
        Paper Series No. 10.

Valverde, Orlando et al.
1979   A Organização do Espaco na Faixa da
        Transamazônica. Vol. 1: Rondônia. Rio de
        Janeiro: Instituto Brasileiro de Geografia
        e Estatística (IBGE).

Valverde, Orlando and C. Vergolino Dias
1967   A Rodovia Belém-Brasília. Rio de Janeiro: IBGE.

Wagley, Charles
1953   Amazon Town. New York: Macmillan.

Wagley, Charles, ed.
1974   Man in the Amazon. Gainesville: Univ. of
        Florida Press.

Weil, Connie
1981   Health Problems Associated with Agricultural
        Colonization in Latin America. Unpublished
        manuscript.

Wood, Charles H. and Marianne Schmink
1979   Blaming the Victim: Small Farmer Production in
        an Amazonian Colonization Project. Studies in
        Third World Societies 7:77-93.

13
Development of the Brazilian Amazon: Prospects for the 1980s

Dennis J. Mahar

INTRODUCTION[1]

Despite the intense developmental efforts of the past two decades, the Brazilian Amazon remains, to a large degree, an undeveloped frontier region. Islands of development may be observed in the region's main population centers and around occurrences of better soils, minerals, and other natural resources, but an integrated, self-sustaining regional economy has not yet emerged. Intraregional economic linkages may be expected to become more prevalent over the decade of the 1980s as population grows, and as transportation and communications networks improve. But it is likely that, as in the past, the medium-term trajectory of Amazonian development will be determined primarily by exogenous factors. To the extent that the nature and influence of these factors is unpredictable, there is considerable uncertainty over what the future might hold for the region.

Keeping in mind the dangers of futurology, especially with regard to a frontier region, the present essay attempts to explore in general terms the likely course of Amazonian development over the rest of the 1980s. Certain basic policy decisions have already been taken and these offer some clues. The greatest area of uncertainty at this point refers to the future strength of the domestic and international economies. This factor, by essentially determining the demand for Amazonian products and the availability of investment resources, will exert a powerful influence on the rate of implementation, and the ultimate viability, of the policies proposed.

RECENT POLICY DIRECTIONS

In principle, the guidelines for Amazon policy in the first half of the 1980s are contained in the Third National Development Plan (III PND). In practice, however, this document provides little more than a vague statement of national intentions in the region (Brasil 1980:86). It calls for the "gradual occupation and integration" of the region based on the "non-predatory exploitation" of its natural resources, and respect for the natural environment and indigenous Amerindian population. The III PND also refers to the need to "diversify, expand and strengthen the regional economy" and to "absorb migratory flows." It is difficult to fault these objectives, although no details are given as to how they would be achieved. In the past such details were included in regional development plans, but no Amazon-specific plan has been produced (or at least published) as a supplement to the III PND.[2] Thus, one must look elsewhere for enlightenment.

THE JARI AFFAIR

The recent experience of Jari provides some insights into the government's views on appropriate development models for the region. Situated on some three million hectares straddling the state of Pará and the territory of Amapá, Jari was established in 1967 by the North American entrepreneur Daniel K. Ludwig. Between 1967 and 1982 Ludwig reportedly sunk three-quarters of a billion dollars in the project, establishing a 750 ton per day vertically-integrated bleached Kraft pulp complex, a sophisticated floodplain (várzea) rice development scheme, and a high-grade kaolin mine. The project directly employed some 10,000 workers in 1982.

Almost from its inception Jari has been the object of considerable controversy. On the one hand, serious questions have been raised about the ecological and economic viability of plantation forestry in Amazonia, as well as about the cost-effectiveness of energy-intensive rice development. On the other hand, nationalist factions have characterized Jari as a "foreign enclave," condemning the veil of secrecy maintained by Ludwig and the alleged maltreatment of his Brazilian workers. In the face of these criticisms, however, Jari enjoyed the tacit support of the government for more than a decade.

During the late 1970s and early 1980s, Jari's fortunes took a decided turn for the worse. The problems it encountered were closely related to a downturn in the world economy combined with an apparent decline of official support for the project. If the former created some financial difficulties for the project, the latter made it untenable. The ebb of government support was manifested in many ways. Among other things, Ludwig was able to establish legal title to only about one-fifth of the original project area, and encountered silence in response to his request that the government assume financial responsibility for the social services provided to Jari workers.

As economic and political pressures mounted, and

with his health failing, Ludwig seemingly lost interest in the further development of Jari. As a consequence, a deal was struck in early 1982 whereby he transferred ownership of the project to a consortium of 27 Brazilian corporations for a sum of $280 million. Of this total, $100 million is to be contributed by private corporations over a three-year period. The remaining $180 million would be accounted for by the Bank of Brazil's assumption of an outstanding foreign loan previously contracted by Jari with the guarantee of the National Development Bank (BNDE). As part of the deal, it is reported that the government agreed to assume responsibility for the project's social infrastructure. The clear message to potential foreign investors was that Jari had become a political liability to the government, and that projects of this type were not to be replicated in the future.

THE CARAJÁS PROGRAM

It should not be assumed that the fate of Jari portends a decline of foreign involvement in the Brazilian Amazon during the 1980s. On the contrary, the future development of the Carajás sub-region of eastern Amazonia counts heavily on the mobilization of external resources. In order to assure Brazilian control over this initiative, however, a Greater Carajás Executive Secretariat, linked to the Federal Planning Secretariat, was recently created to serve as the principal coordinating agency.

The Carajás program is by far the largest undertaking ever attempted in the region, and will surely dominate the economy of eastern Amazonia for many decades to come. At its core is the exploration of the sub-region's rich iron ore deposits, estimated at 18 billion tons.[3] This component, already initiated, involves the development not only of mining infrastructure per se, but also the construction of a 890-kilometer railroad and deep-water port facilities near São Luis, Maranhão. The total costs of the iron ore project, including the railroad and port, are estimated at $5 billion, to be financed by a Brazilian state enterprise (Companhia Vale do Rio Doce-- CVRD), BNDE, and a consortium of foreign lenders. Exports from the project, which are projected to eventually reach 35 million tons per year in 1987, are expected to start in 1985.

The iron ore project is just one component of a much larger development scheme. The master plan for developing the Greater Carajás sub-region has not yet been fully detailed, but preliminary indications are that the government intends to promote the development of an integrated mining-metallurgical complex, based on the extraction and processing of bauxite, copper, cassiterite, nickel, and other minerals found in the area, and associated forestry, livestock, and agricultural projects. In order to realize this objective, it is estimated that $40 to $60

billion of investment funds will be needed over the 1980s.
These funds are expected to come mainly from the private
sector, both domestic and foreign. The attractiveness
of this plan to the private sector (aside from the extensive mineral deposits in the program area) lies in the
availability of abundant energy from the 4,000 megawatt
(MW) Tucuruí hydroelectric project, scheduled to come on
line in 1983, and special fiscal incentives.

POLONOROESTE

A development model of a quite different sort is
envisaged for the so-called Northwest of Brazil, actually
a sub-region of southwestern Amazonia comprising Rondônia
and parts of Mato Grosso. Whereas the Carajás program
emphasizes a capital-intensive, export-oriented approach,
POLONOROESTE (as the integrated development program for
the Northwest is known) is primarily concerned with the
promotion of small-scale agriculture. Funded at $1.5
billion for the 1981-1985 period, POLONOROESTE would
pursue its basic objective through measures to improve
the physical and social infrastructure and services
available to farmers already settled in the 410,000 square
kilometer zone of influence of the Cuiabá-Porto Velho
highway (which would itself be paved as part of the
program) and to establish new settlement projects in
presently unpopulated areas (IBRD 1981; Mahar 1979).
At first glance, POLONOROESTE would appear to be a
repeat of the government's ill-fated attempts to settle
migrants along the Transamazon Highway in the early
1970s (Moran 1981; Smith 1981). There are some similari-
ties. The rate of migration to Rondônia, which reached
some 4,000 persons per month in 1980, has severely
strained the region's administrative capacities. Consequently, delays have been experienced in providing
titles and other forms of support (rural credit, roads,
social services, etc.) to prospective settlers, and unsound ecological practices (e.g., predatory uses of the
forest and cultivation of inappropriate crops) have proven
difficult to monitor and control (Moran 1982). However,
the differences between POLONOROESTE and Transamazon
colonization are important.
First, in contrast to the Transamazon experience,
migration to the Northwest has been spontaneous. This
implies that the beneficiaries of POLONOROESTE would have
a greater commitment to developing their holdings.
Second, the agricultural exploitation of the Northwest
is based overwhelmingly on the cultivation of tree crops
such as cocoa, coffee, and rubber. These crops are
ecologically preferable to annuals (see Lovejoy and
Salati, Chapter 8 in this volume), and their relatively
high value-to-volume ratios help offset the high costs of
transport from remote frontier areas to the major
consumption and/or export centers. Finally, and perhaps

most importantly, the planning for POLONOROESTE has benefited from the lessons of the past. This is most clearly revealed in the environmental component of the program, which calls for expanded ecological research, for the strengthening of IBDF's (National Forestry Development Institute) capacity for monitoring and controlling deforestation, and for detailed land-use surveys to be carried out prior to the selection of new settlement sites (all of which were noted in Chapter 1 as requirements to sustainable development). There is also an "Indian component," which provides for measures (e.g., the demarcation of reserves, improved medical services) to protect the Northwest's highly vulnerable Amerindian population.

CONCLUSIONS

In many ways, the prospects for Amazonian development are brighter than they have ever been. Much more is now known about the region's potential and diversity, and this has helped inject a much-needed dose of realism into development planning. Quite rightly, less is expected of Amazonia than in the past. The previously held notion that Amazonia could act, in a major way, as a "safety-valve" for population pressures and social tensions in the Northeast and elsewhere in Brazil has generally fallen into disrepute. Also, the region is no longer viewed as the world's future "breadbasket" except by a few diehards, and the development of annual crops and cattle ranching in densely forested upland areas (terra firme) is not officially encouraged. What is encouraged are integrated development models that exploit Amazonia's comparative advantages in mining, forestry, tree crops, and hydroelectric power.

Though the prognosis for the 1980s is generally good, one must not forget that Amazonia is still a frontier region. Administrative control over its occupation and development is thus likely to remain tenuous for the foreseeable future. This might imply delays in achieving important policy objectives, like straightening out the region's chaotic land-tenure system and preventing unnecessary deforestation and other ecologically unsound practices. One must also keep in mind that domestic economic growth is expected to be lower in the 1980s than in the previous decade, and that the world markets for some major Amazonian products such as cocoa and coffee are likely to be soft. The combined effect of these economic factors could be to reduce the volume of resources available for Amazonian development, and to lower the rates of return of undertakings emphasizing certain products. But if these factors act to slow down the pace of migration and development, this should not necessarily be interpreted in a negative light. With some of the pressures for rapid development removed, more time will be made available for further resource surveys and zoning, agricultural research, demarcation of Indian lands, and for absorbing prospective settlers already in the region.

NOTES

1.   The views expressed in this paper are the author's and do not necessarily represent those of the World Bank.
2.   The earlier Amazon development plans are reviewed in D. J. Mahar (1979: Chapter 1).
3.   For greater details see Companhia Vale do Rio Doce (1981).

REFERENCES

Brasil, República Federativa do
    1980   III Plano Nacional de Desenvolvimento, 1980-85.
            Brasília: República Federativa do Brasil.

Companhia Vale do Rio Doce (CVRD)
    1981   Projeto Ferro Carajás.   Rio de Janeiro: CVRD.

IBRD
    1981   Integrated Development of the Northwest
            Frontier.   Washington, D.C.: World Bank.

Mahar, Dennis J.
    1979   Frontier Development in Brazil: A Study of
            Amazonia.   New York: Praeger.

    1982   Public International Lending Institutions and
            the Development of the Brazilian Amazon.
            Paper presented at the Conference on Frontier
            Expansion in Amazonia, Center for Latin
            American Studies, Univ. of Florida, Feb. 8-11.

Moran, Emilio F.
    1981   Developing the Amazon.   Bloomington: Indiana
            Univ. Press.

    1982   Colonization in the Transamazon and Rondônia.
            Paper presented at the Conference on Frontier
            Expansion in Amazonia, Center for Latin American
            Studies, Univ. of Florida, Feb. 8-11.

Smith, Nigel J.H.
    1981   Colonization Lessons from a Tropical Forest.
            Science 214:755-761.

About the Contributors

Emilio F. Moran is chairman and associate professor of anthropology at Indiana University. He is also on the faculty of the School for Public and Environmental Affairs at Indiana University. He is the author of Human Adaptability (Westview, 1982) and Developing the Amazon (1981) and has contributed articles to journals both in the United States and in Latin America. His research has taken him to the Brazilian and Venezuelan Amazon several times.

William T. Vickers is associate professor of anthropology at Florida International University, Miami. He is the author of numerous articles on the indigenous peoples of Ecuador and is currently working on a monograph on the Siona-Secoya and has coedited two volumes, one on applied anthropology, the other entitled Adaptive Strategies of Native Amazonians (with R. Hames). He has traveled to the Ecuadorian Amazon several times both as a researcher and in helping to demarcate Indian lands.

Allyn MacLean Stearman is associate professor of anthropology at Central Florida University, Orlando. She is the author of a monograph on colonization in the region of Santa Cruz and of several articles in the journal Human Organization. She has shared her knowledge of apiculture with Bolivian farmers.

Darrel Miller is visiting assistant professor at the College of William and Mary. He has carried out studies of Amazonian urban places for both his master's and doctoral degrees. He is currently working on a monograph on entrepreneurship in Amazonian cities.

John Nicholaides III is engaged in a cooperative research program between the North Carolina State Univ. Tropical Soils Research Program, the Agency for International Development, and the Peruvian Ministry of Agriculture. The Program is now in its tenth year and is the most significant research effort aimed at developing econom-

325

ically-sound management systems for tropical rain forests. Numerous publications have resulted and are cited in Chapter 5. He is associate professor of soil science at North Carolina State University.

P. A. Sanchez is coordinator, with J. Nicholaides, of the Tropical Soils Research Program and professor of soil science at North Carolina State University. He is the author of the most comprehensive book on tropical soils published to date, Properties and Management of Soils in the Tropics (1976).

D. E. Bandy is the on-site leader of the Yurimaguas Project and visiting assistant professor of soil science at North Carolina State University.

J. H. Villachica is director of the Jungle Research Institute and professor of soil science, National Agrarian University, Peru.

A. J. Coutu is professor of economics and business at North Carolina State University.

C. S. Valverde is director of planning and international collaboration, National Institute for Agricultural Research and Promotion, Ministry of Agriculture, Peru.

Susanna Hecht is an assistant professor in the Department of Architecture and Urban Planning at the University of California at Los Angeles. She has carried out extensive research on cattle ranches in the Brazilian Amazon and has cooperated with agronomic institutions in assessing this system of production. She recently edited Amazonia: Agriculture and Land Use Research for the Centro Internacional de Agricultura Tropical at Cali, Colombia (1982).

Michael Goulding is a research scientist at the Instituto Nacional de Pesquisas da Amazônia, Manaus, Brazil. He is the author of two books on Amazonian fisheries: The Fishes and the Forest (1980) and Man and Fisheries on an Amazon Frontier (1981). He is currently designing an effective system of conservation for fisheries with the cooperation of the World Wildlife Fund.

Thomas Lovejoy is vice-president for science at World Wildlife Fund-U.S. He has extensive experience in conservation research and is the author of numerous articles on forest and wildlife ecology. He will be a traveling lecturer in 1982 for Sigma Xi, the scientific research honor society.

Eneas Salati is currently director of the Centro De Energia Nuclear para Agricultura (CENA) at Piracicaba, and was previously director of the National Institute for Amazonian Research at Manaus. A specialist in hydrology and biogeochemistry, he is co-investigator of a joint Brazilian-U.S. study of carbon in the Amazon River system. Using isotope techniques he has done pioneering work on recycling of water in the Amazon Basin.

Darrell Posey is Mellon Visiting Professor at the Center for Latin American Studies, University of Pittsburgh. He is also founder and director of the Centro de Pesquisas Antropológicas e Folclóricas at the Universidade Federal do Maranhão. He serves on the editorial board of the Journal of Ethnobiology and is active in the preservation of indigenous ecological knowledge.

Charles Wood is associate professor of sociology and Latin American studies at the University of Florida. He has written numerous articles on demography and Amazonian topics for publication in journals such as Human Organization and the Population and Development Review. He worked for three years at CEDEPLAR, in the Universidade Federal de Minas Gerais--at which time he worked on a SUDAM-funded study of internal migration in the Amazon region.

Philip Fearnside is a research scientist at the Instituto Nacional de Pesquisas da Amazônia, Manaus, Brazil. He is the author of numerous articles in Interciencia, Tropical Ecology, Turrialba, Acta Amazônica, and other journals. He is the leader of an INPA-based project on the study of carrying capacity.

Dennis Mahar is senior economist at the World Bank, Washington, D.C. He previously served with the Ford Foundation and the Institute of Social and Economic Planning in Rio de Janeiro, Brazil (IPEA). He is the author of Frontier Development Policy in Brazil (1979) and numerous articles analyzing efforts at Amazonian urban and regional development. He was actively involved in the feasibility study and protections built into the POLONOROESTE project discussed in his paper.

Abbreviations

AID	Agency for International Development (United States)
BASA	Banco da Amazônia (Bank of the Amazon, Brazil)
BB	Banco do Brasil (Bank of Brazil)
BIS	Batalhão de Infanteria da Selva (Jungle Infantry Battalion)
BNDE	Banco Nacional de Desenvolvimento Econômico (National Development Bank)
CEDEPLAR	Centro de Desenvolvimento e Planejamento Regional (Center for Development and Regional Planning, Minas Gerais, Brazil)
CENA	Centro de Energía Nuclear para Agricultura (Center for Nuclear Power Applied to Agriculture, São Paulo, Brazil)
CEPAF	Centro de Pesquisas Antrópologicas e Folclóricas (Center for Anthropological and Folkloric Research, Maranhão, Brazil)
CEPCO	Consortium of Cities Investing and the Corporacion Estatal Petrolera Ecuatoriana, Ecuador
CEPLAC	Centro de Pesquisas do Cacau (Cacao Research Center, Itabuna, Bahia, Brazil)
CIAT	Centro Internacional de Agricultura Tropical (International Center for Tropical Agriculture, Cali, Colombia)
CONDEPE	Conselho de Desenvolvimento da Pecuária (Commission for the Development of Cattle Raising, Brazil)
CPATU	Centro de Pesquisa Agropecuária do Trópico Úmido (Agricultural Research Center for the Humid Tropics, Belém, Brazil)
CVRD	Companhia Vale do Rio Doce (Company of the Rio Doce Valley, Brazil)
DNER	Departamento Nacional de Estradas de Rodagem (National Roads Department, Brazil)

Additional abbreviations and acronyms used in Chapter 4 appear as footnotes to Table 4.3.

EMATER	Emprêsa de Assistência Técnica e Extensão Rural (Agricultural Extension Service, Brazil)
EMBRAPA	Emprêsa Brasileira de Pesquisa Agropecuária (Brazilian Enterprise of Agricultural Research)
FAO	Food and Agriculture Organization (United Nations)
FCC	Fertility Capability Classification
FUNAI	Fundação Nacional do Indio (National Indian Foundation, Brazil)
GETAT	Grupo Executivo de Terras do Araguaia-Tocantins (Executive Group Overseeing the Land of the Araguaia-Tocantins)
IBDF	Instituto Brasileiro de Desenvolvimento Florestal (Forestry Development Institute, Brazil)
IBGE	Instituto Brasileiro de Geografía e Estatística (Brazilian Institute of Geography and Statistics)
IBRD	International Bank for Reconstruction and Development (World Bank)
ICA	Instituto Colombiano Agropecuário (Colombian Agrarian Institute)
ICRAF	International Council for Research on Agro-Forestry (Nairobi, Kenya)
IDB	Interamerican Development Bank
IERAC	Instituto Ecuatoriano de Reforma Agraria y Colonización (Institute of Agrarian Reform and Colonization, Ecuador)
IFDC	International Fertilizer Development Center, Muscle Shoals, Alabama
IIASA	International Institute for Applied Systems Analysis
IICA	Instituto Interamericano de Ciencias Agrícolas (Interamerican Institute of Agricultural Sciences, Costa Rica)
INCRA	Instituto Nacional de Colonização e Reforma Agrária (Institute of Colonization and Agrarian Reform, Brazil)
INCRAE	Instituto Nacional de Colonización de la Región Amazónica Ecuatoriana (Institute of Colonization for the Amazon Region, Ecuador)
INIPA	Instituto Nacional de Investigación y Promoción Agraria (Institute of Agrarian Research and Development, Peru)
INPA	Instituto Nacional de Pesquisas da Amazônia (Amazon National Research Institute, Manaus, Brazil)
INPE	Instituto Nacional de Pesquisas Espaciais (National Institute of Space Research, Brazil)
INPES	Instituto de Pesquisas (Planning Ministry's Research Institute, Rio de Janeiro, Brazil)
IPEA	Instituto de Planejamento Econômico e Social (Institute of Social and Economic Planning, Rio de Janeiro, Brazil)

IPEAN	Instituto de Pesquisa Agropecuária do Norte (North Region Institute of Agricultural Research, Belém, Brazil)
IRRI	International Rice Research Institute, Los Baños, Philippines
ISTE	International Society for Tropical Ecology
LANDSAT	Land-Imaging Satellite (United States)
MEC	Ministério de Educação e Cultura (Ministry of Education, Brazil)
NAEA	Núcleo de Altos Estudos Amazônicos (Center of Higher Amazonian Studies, Federal University of Pará, Brazil)
ORSTOM	Office de la Recherche Scientifique et Technique de Outre-Mer (Agricultural Research Center, France)
PIC	Projeto Integrado de Colonização (Integrated Colonization Project, Brazil)
PIN	Projeto de Integração Nacional (Project of National Integration, Brazil)
PND	Projeto Nacional de Desenvolvimento (National Development Project, Brazil)
POLO-NOROESTE	Development Pole of the Northwest Amazon, Brazil
RADAM	Radar da Amazônia (Radar of the Amazon, Brazil)
SEDUC	Secretaria de Educaçao e Cultura (State-Level Secretariat of Education, Brazil)
SIDA	Swiss International Development Agency
SIL	Summer Institute of Linguistics (United States)
S.P.I.	Serviço de Proteção aos Indios (Indian Protection Service, Brazil)
SPVEA	Superintendência do Plano de Valorizacão Econômica da Amazônia (Superintendency for the Economic Valuing of the Amazon, Manaus, Brazil)
SUDAM	Superintendência do Desenvolvimento da Amazônia (Superintendency for Development of the Amazon, Brazil)
SUDEPE	Superintendência do Desenvolvimento da Pesca (Superintendency for Development of Fisheries, Brazil)
SUFRAMA	Superintendência da Zona Franca de Manaus (Superintendency of the Manaus Free Trade Zone, Brazil)
UEPAE	Unidade de Execução de Pesquisa de Ambito Estadual (State-Level Research Unit, Brazil)
UFMG	Universidade Federal de Minas Gerais (Federal University of Minas Gerais, Brazil)
UNESCO	United Nations Educational, Scientific, and Cultural Organization
WWF	World Wildlife Fund

Index

APR